THE CINEMA OF STEPHANIE ROTHMAN

THE CINEMA OF STEPHANIE ROTHMAN

Radical Acts in Filmmaking

Alicia Kozma

UNIVERSITY PRESS OF MISSISSIPPI / JACKSON

The University Press of Mississippi is the scholarly publishing agency of
the Mississippi Institutions of Higher Learning: Alcorn State University,
Delta State University, Jackson State University, Mississippi State University,
Mississippi University for Women, Mississippi Valley State University,
University of Mississippi, and University of Southern Mississippi.

www.upress.state.ms.us

The University Press of Mississippi is a member of
the Association of University Presses.

Any discriminatory or derogatory language or hate speech regarding race,
ethnicity, religion, sex, gender, class, national origin, age, or disability that
has been retained or appears in elided form is in no way an endorsement of
the use of such language outside a scholarly context.

Copyright © 2022 by University Press of Mississippi
All rights reserved

First printing 2022
∞

Library of Congress Control Number: 2022942045

Hardback ISBN 978-1-4968-4099-8
Trade paperback ISBN 978-1-4968-4100-1
Epub single ISBN 978-1-4968-4101-8
Epub institutional ISBN 978-1-4968-4102-5
PDF single ISBN 978-1-4968-4103-2
PDF institutional ISBN 978-1-4968-4104-9

British Library Cataloging-in-Publication Data available

CONTENTS

Acknowledgments vii

PART I.
INDUSTRIES, THEORIES, AND THE TROUBLE WITH ARCHIVES

1. Radical Acts 3
2. The Limits of Exceptional Women. 18
3. Margin and Center: Locating Second Wave Exploitation
   in US Film History. 42
4. Stephanie Rothman Does Not Exist. 63

PART II.
INTERVENINGS

5. Everyone Starts Somewhere 91
6. Imagining a Post-Patriarchy 108
7. New Worlds. 134
8. Memories of Underemployment. 157

Appendix 174
Notes 221
Bibliography 248
Index 260

ACKNOWLEDGMENTS

All intellectual projects are the result of collaboration. From advisement to feedback to inspiration, the project is the culmination of the intellectual prowess, camaraderie, and mentorship of a wide network of people. Throughout my time at various intuitions, I've somehow been lucky enough to benefit from the tutelage of world-class scholars. As an undergraduate at the University of Vermont, Dr. Frank Manchel first showed me that the academic study of film was possible, exposing to me to my first real understanding of the flows of film histories as social histories. It quickly became my goal to make him proud of my work, something I've been trying to do since 1998. Also, at UVM, Dr. Hilary Neroni exposed me to feminist film studies. It is not an understatement to say her Women in Film seminar dramatically changed how I thought, and think, about film. My gratitude to my partner in cinephilia, Matt Warner, for collaborating with me during that influential process.

I was afforded the great opportunity to complete my master's work at the Graduate Center of the University of New York. I have a very vivid memory of my first class there: the classroom was in the basement, and when I arrived it was locked. I sat down on the floor to wait across from another student with the same idea. She and I began chatting, talk quickly turning to horror and exploitation films. Bekah McKendry and I are still having that conversation to this day. At the Graduate Center, my master's work was significantly influenced by Dr. Stuart Ewan, Dr. Heather Hendershot, Dr. Allison Griffith, and, particularly, Dr. Robert Singer, who pushed me harder than I had been pushed before, and happily accepted my attempts to aggravate him. He has continued to encourage and support me well past our time together; his championing of my work remains unfailing. Thanks, Old Man.

The Institute of Communication Research at the University of Illinois, Urbana-Champaign, provided me the great fortune to learn from, and with, an extraordinary network of people. Dr. Angharad Valdivia has been a tireless advocate for me and my work and has dedicated herself to progressive, justice-based, and critical research while empowering generation after generation of scholars. Her devoted fan base stretched far and wide—me included. The Institute of Communication Research is often called ICR Nation. It is a nation, and Anghy is our fearless leader; we all owe her a great debt. Dr. James Hay is a source of consistent intellectual stimulation and has been critical in my scholarly development. Dr. Hay models the type of intellectual respect all professors should aspire to. James, I am forever grateful for your conversation, friendship, stories, and support, and for being welcomed into the best restaurant in town. Dr. Richard Rodríguez exemplifies compassionate and unflinchingly progressive academic inquiry of which I can only hope to aspire. Ricky, your love for the academically deviant showed me that this book was possible, and the mix of consciousness, compassion, and rigor you infuse into your pedagogy is something I try to emulate every time I step into a classroom. Other irreplaceable scholars within and without UIUC generous with their time and support include Dr. Cameron McCarthy, Dr. Amanda Ciafone, Dr. Rachel Dubrofsky, Dr. Kent Ono, and Dr. Isabel Pinedo.

Fairly early in my time at UIUC Dr. Julie Turnock became my guide and confidant. It was an informal process, and certainly she didn't outright agree to it—I simply would not leave her alone. It is to my eternal benefit that she tolerated me. Dr. Turnock expanded my thinking and theorizing around film in ways I could have never anticipated, and she's made me love movies even more deeply than before. This project would not exist without her measured guidance, incisive feedback and questioning, and unending support. Her passion, good humor, rigor, and voracious appetite for knowledge are inspirational. Julie, your mentorship, generosity, and camaraderie are beyond invaluable. I am so proud to be your student.

I am constantly in awe of my network of brilliant scholar-activists, all remaking the world. The gorgeousness, resilience, and affable genius of Dr. John Musser and Dr. Silas Moon Cassanelli. The tireless advocacy of Dr. Brenda Nyandiko Sanya, Dr. Rico Kleinstein Chenyek, Dr. Karla Palma-Millanao, Dr. Anita Mixon, Dr. Kerry Wilson, and Dr. Stephanie Brown. The critical compassion of Dr. Molly Niesen, Dr. Ben Bascom, Dr. Robert Mejia, Dr. Mandy Tröeger, and my dear Dr. Wendy Truran. Dr. Mel Stanfill's refusal to back down from anything. Dr. Sarah Roberts and Dr. Safiya Umoja Noble, who show me every day how academic work can change the world. The sheer righteousness of Dr. Myra Washington. Read their work. Cite them. Invite them to speak on your campus or to your organization. Your life will be better when you do.

There is a network of adult film history scholars whose work has been inspirational and motivating, including Dr. Whitney Strub, Dr. Peter Allinius, Dr. Finley Freibert, and Dr. Elena Gorfinkel. Peter introduced me to this network, and I am so grateful. I owe a special thanks to Elena, who after receiving a cold email from me, generously offered me her time, expertise, and encouragement in my work.

I must extend a very special thanks to Dr. Michael Shetina. Michael graciously agreed to act as my research assistant for this project. His input, ideas, intimate command of film history, keen eye, and devastating wit have shaped this project immeasurably. Michael is the rare scholar who provides an equal amount of critical challenge and inspiration. Simply put, Michael makes ideas better. I am very lucky he agreed to work with me.

This book would be a much different thing without the generosity and time of Stephanie Rothman. Thank you, Stephanie. Being your interlocuter these years has been so rewarding.

A special thanks to my West Coast family: BD, Luzmilla Baldwin, Mark Brown, Amber Rodgers, and of course, George, for allowing me to invade your lives, homes, and cars on my Los Angeles research trips.

I am obscenely lucky to be surrounded by unendingly supportive people. Matt Cross, Rebecca Greenlee, Brad Cunningham, Dr. Ned Prutzer, Kaitlyn Hale, Shanna Meyer, Courtney Liesener, and Melissa Starr provided that elusive ingredient missing from the lives of most academics: balance between work and life. My gratitude to my parents is never-ending, just as their support has been. Dr. Martina Baldwin, Dr. Arnau Roig-Mora, and Dr. Emily Dworkin are my biggest supporters, fiercest challengers, kindest hearts, and are wholly indispensable to me. Last, but never least, my undying thanks to Max (and Iggy Pop) for their persistent calm, encouragement, support, sacrifice, and excitement. Thank you, Maxy.

Art Lives.

Part I

INDUSTRIES, THEORIES, AND THE TROUBLE WITH ARCHIVES

Chapter 1

RADICAL ACTS

When a woman makes a film, that is a radical act.
—AVA DUVERNAY[1]

Standing in front of a classroom full of undergraduate students, I ask: "Who is your favorite film director?" Shouts of "Tarantino," "Scorsese," "Anderson," "Kubrick," "The Wachowskis," and more volley back at me. The follow-up question, "Who is your favorite woman director?" sits in silence and confusion. The less subjective question, "Can anyone name a woman director?" doesn't fare much better. "The girl who did *The Hurt Locker*?" or "The *Lost in Translation* woman . . . I can't remember her name" are answers when answers are hazarded. More representative, however, is when a student said, befuddled: "I never realized it before, but I can't name a single woman director." This is not a phenomenon relegated to college campuses. Many in the general public would be hard pressed to name a woman film director, and, I would wager, may be equally surprised by their inability to do so. As an exercise, ask yourself: When was the last time you watched a film directed by a woman? How many films by women directors does your local movie theater, mainstream and independent, regularly offer? Film students, how many films by women directors do your professors screen in your classes? Professors, how many do you program? And, perhaps most critically, have you noticed women directors are often missing?

The position of "film director" in the public consciousness is regularly attached to ideas of creativity, control, authorship, and the cult of personality. The disconnect between the concept of "the director" and the embodied subjects that occupy that role often obscures the unhappy truth: the overwhelming majority of film directors embedded in past and present cultural consciousness are male. Public-facing cinephilic rankings reinforce this. For example, the "American Film Institute's 100 Years . . . 100 Movies," which lists the organization's 100 "greatest" US movies of all time, includes only films by male directors. *Sight and Sound*'s "Greatest Films of All Time" has two women directors represented in the list of ninety-three films. In the ninety-plus years of the Academy Awards, only seven women have been nominated for Best Director, and only three have ever won. "Director" is synonymous with a "male" in the public consciousness. Intellectually this is an obvious statement—a fact, not a great revelation. My interest, however, is in how this statement works in practice; the consequences that stem from a lack of industrial, disciplinary, and archival attention paid to women's directorial labor, and interventions that can reinsert women into film histories, archives, and public consciousness. To answer these questions, this book offers a case study of second wave exploitation director Stephanie Rothman. Second wave exploitation films were produced in the United States under the exploitation style from 1960 to 1980; second wave exploitation served as a transitory space that linked alternative and mainstream filmmaking practices and, in many ways, as a template for contemporary Hollywood. Rothman, the first woman to win the Directors Guild of America student fellowship, was a screenwriter, productive executive, story editor, and director; she made seven films between 1966 and 1974, and remained in the industry in minor capacities until 1980.

The Rothman case study is the fulcrum on which turns a set of interrelated argumentative positions and corresponding interventions embedded in this project. First, I contend that traditionally understudied filmic production cycles provide untapped spaces for discovering women's directorial work. In support of this assertion, I historicize and establish the period of second wave exploitation as a discrete filmic cycle that provided a transitory space for the industrial development of contemporary Hollywood while opening up opportunities for women practitioners. I build on this claim by narrating the biographic and cinematic history of Stephanie Rothman. Second, I posit *how* women have been written into film histories and archives deeply affects whether or not women's directorial labor is or is not understood across scholarly and popular frameworks. Here, I use my Rothman case study to examine the strictures of the rhetorical language used to mark women filmmakers and their labor in film histories, tracing the imbrications of the historical archive and current labor practices. Of course, there is a long history of excellent feminist scholarship constructed to highlight—and force recognition of—women's directorial accomplishments. Lastly, I advance how methodological diversity, including alternative archive creation and case studies, opens multiple parallel and intersecting interventional paths to advocate against the problematics, and highlight the successes, of the historicization of women's directorial labor industrially, academically, and publicly.

This tiered examination structure yields my specific interventions. Articulating second wave exploitation as a discrete filmic cycle contextualizes a new historical area of film production that, as transitory industrial space, breaks down the boundaries between mainstream and marginal production, offering a paradigm that accounts for the practical fluidity of flows of labor, artistry, and filmic output in the film industry. Rather than set second wave exploitation in hard opposition to mainstream Hollywood filmmaking, I argue that its production paradigm was influenced by, and influential to, Hollywood filmmaking and the rise of foreign film distribution in the United States between 1960 and 1980. This reciprocal influence accounts for the practical materiality and labor of film production while simultaneously opening up a new historical sphere in which to uncover the contributions of women's cinematic labor.

Following, I contend that the rhetoric used to mark women's directorial labor in film history has led to the continued spectacularization of women as cinematic authors, de-normalizing their participation in film production and reinscribing the hegemonic maleness of film directors. This discourse, what I call the *paradigm of exceptional women*, writes the history of women directors as exceptions to the rule of male authorship rather than as viable and valuable equals. This allows for the continued labeling of a token group of women directors as exceptions to the male authorship rule, maintaining women directors' role as outsiders to the normative creative structure in film production. These historical limitations are underpinned by traditional archival practices. To counter this historical lack, I propose the use of alternative archival methods and curatorial practices when studying women in film production as a specifically feminist intervention into the way women's labor is constructed in industrial and cultural film history. Finally, I offer the first comprehensive biographic, thematic, and analytic investigation into the life, career, and films of Stephanie Rothman as a practical alternative to archival intervention as well as a space to highlight the persistent, systemic, and institutional barriers to women's participatory labor in film production, both historically and contemporaneously.

My inclusion of a case study follows Vicki Mayer's contention that stories of labor can illuminate larger lessons around the relationship between the economics and production of culture.[2] Using the micro history of Rothman's career to articulate the macro-level connections between gender, labor, and Hollywood grounds the positions and interventions contained within this project in practice and possibility. A focus on Rothman provides a critical link between the selective erasure of women's directorial labor in film history and the continuing overwhelming disparity in gendered labor in contemporary film production. Her career and its industrial roadblocks illuminate the deeply entrenched and persistent sexism and discriminatory standards that define gendered employment in the present-day film industry. Exposing this systemic discrimination and its historical threads is crucial given repeated calls for women's increased participation in filmmaking as a panacea to gender disparity, a call that elides the deeply entrenched institutional barriers for gender equality, equitable working conditions, and safe working spaces. A Rothman case study exposes the hostile working conditions for women in the film industry in the 1960s and 1970s as the same ones operating today. This connection necessitates more than just an increased call for women's participation in the industry to solve the problem. Safiya Umoja Noble notes that industries often label women's missing labor as a "pipeline problem,"[3] yet there is no lack of women ready to work in Hollywood. Rather, there must be explicit linkages made between the lack of women laborers and the discriminatory structures modeled as "best" practices in the industry. The solution requires a complete uprooting and reconstruction of hiring, employment, and labor systems within Hollywood.

Accordingly, my Rothman case study serves as a remedy to the tendency of feminist film studies to overlook women filmmakers in favor of examining their films. As Alexandra Juhasz theorizes, the rise of feminist film studies in the 1970s and 1980s and the overall academic turn toward theory in cinema studies was beneficial as it prompted a move toward the feminist.[4] This turn, however, she continues, "also had the effect of separating us from others who matter: those women who practice and engage with media-making outside academe."[5] As products of an industrial artistic system, films should not be separated from the labor and production conditions that form them. The labor of someone like Rothman—a woman working in a primarily masculine profession and creating films in an overwhelmingly masculinized filmic paradigm—provides crucial historical data on the way women have participated in the cultural work of film production.

A Rothman case study also epitomizes the need for alternative archive constructions and methodologies when compiling film history. As is the case with many others, Rothman is a negligible presence in traditional film histories. Therefore, the case study presented in this book is the result of four years of research guided by alternative archival methodologies. The outcome is the most complete primary and secondary chronicle of the director to date, as well as the first analytical consideration of her entire filmic *oeuvre*. The collection of materials I have assembled speaks to the necessity of alternate archival methods and the value in self-curated archival practices. This book offers the biographic, professional, and filmic life of Stephanie Rothman as a practical and political feminist intervention in broadening the historical and cinematic memory of women in film and awareness around their cinematic labor.

PROMISCUOUS METHODS FOR A PARA-INDUSTRY

This project employs a variety of methodological frameworks under the guiding infrastructure of Miriam Hansen's promiscuous methodology, which contends that "cultural configurations that are more complex and dynamic than the most accurate account of their function within any single system may convey and that require more open-ended, promiscuous, and imaginative modes of investigation."[6] This approach guides my investigation as I tackle questions of labor and gender across the para-industry that is Hollywood's flexible media networks, histories, and archives, combining production studies, historiography, and feminist archival and rhetorical interventions. John T. Caldwell's work structures the idea of Hollywood as a para-industry, where the production of film as an industrialized art form exists as:

> an economic and cultural-industrial interface woven together by socio-professional media communities, through trade narratives, ritualized interactions and conventionalized self-representations that viewers and scholars must wade through before they can find a primary text or featured on-screen content.[7]

Hollywood as a para-industry removes its veil of self-mythology, forcing us to understand filmmaking as the production of labor instead of "movie magic" so often invoked by studios and press.[8] Magic doesn't make movies, bodies and labor do. Critical to highlighting the too-often overlooked place of labor in film production is to remove the mythos and public structure of Hollywood as a monolithic industry and understanding it as an amalgam of micro-industries, organizations, actors, and processes that make up an ever-changing whole. Refocusing, then, on the parts as well as the whole, Miranda J. Banks's tactic of oral history as a mode of reinserting the personal into production is foundational to my Rothman case study, which is informed by conversations with the director herself.[9]

With this industrial roadmap of Hollywood's para-industrial structure grounding my Rothman case study, I approach film history as new cinema history, specifically drawing on Rick Altman's crisis historiography combined with Thomas Elsaesser's construction of film studies as media archaeology.

A new cinema history approach provides a historical method that complements traditional film history while integrating its conditions of production, organizational cultures, distribution and exhibition, and the flow and effects of financial networks.[10] This holistic approach is crucial when considering the interwoven factors of industrial production standards, labor, and cinematic output; one cannot be considered separate, or more important than another. Altman's crisis historiography is particularly important for my consideration of second wave exploitation. His method assumes that the definition of an area of study is "*both historically and socially* contingent. That is, the media are not fully self-evidently defined by theory components and configurations. They also depend on the way users develop and understand them."[11] Second wave exploitation cannot be defined historically as it is defined today, nor can it be understood as simply an offshoot of classical exploitation or as a poor imitation of classical Hollywood style.[12] Like all film, it must be informed by laborers within it and the multiple economic, production, distributive and exhibition networks that composed it. The object of study must be understood within its own socially defined existence and through its own crisis of identity, which Altman defines as comprising of "three separate but closely connected processes: multiple identification, jurisdictional conflict, and overdetermined solutions."[13] Considering multiple identification allows for the evaluations of overlapping production and artistic influences; jurisdictional conflict provides an understanding of how these multiple identities coexisted in an industrial and economic sense; and querying overdetermined solutions—where second wave exploitation exists in film history—aids in removing biases and simplistic determinations around the nature of the filmic cycle itself.[14]

Underpinning my historical investigation is Thomas Elsaesser's approach to film history as media archaeology, which draws not from the materiality of media archaeology but from its reconfigurations of historical time. Elsaesser advocates for film history as media archaeology, disrupting standard boundaries between historical divisions,[15] and allowing for the integration of points of view, production models, industrial histories, filmic cycles, and artistic output that would have been siloed from one another under traditional film history. This temporal fluidity is critical when establishing second wave exploitation as transitory industrial space with multidirectional flows of influence. Rethinking time in this way also plays a significant role in this project's feminist archival intervention and in the work of "doing" women's film history. Alternate archival usage and creation is critical in women's film history as scholars engage in what Christine Gledhill and Julia Knight call the "search for new sources of evidence in the absence of traditional archives and utilize a diversity of innovative methods that open up new historiographic perspectives or questions."[16] This requires a tactile and affective engagement with the past as well as a willingness to see the connections between past, present, and future histories as circularly connecting through the annals. Alterative records enable scholars working in women's film history to read the influences of the past in the present and leverage contemporary issues and questions to introduce generative fissures in past accountings. Through this type of engagement, scholars undertaking the work of women's film history

> ask of their work questions they did not think to ask, their works may gesture to future conditions and perspectives different from those that constrained them. Thus, in reimagining their career and recirculating their films, we enable their historical projects to continue in the present through our collaboration with the past.[17]

Feminist archival interventions are theoretically and politically salient here. One cannot ascribe a specific feminist ideology to any given woman working in the film industry, but that does not preclude a feminist interventionist methodology in studying women's labor in the entertainment industry. Instead, I orientate this work through Vivian Sobchak's statement that "feminist concerns are not necessarily (nor obligatorily) *imposed* from the beginning but rather *emerge* and take their particular and various forms and the research—not the dogma—dictate."[18]

Feminist methodologies strive to highlight and address the systemic inequalities of power that are entrenched into our social, cultural, and economic systems.[19] The intersection of feminism and cinema studies, then, provides what Vicki Callahan terms "new ways of seeing and thinking about the world."[20] Understanding and articulating how gender is understood in a popular industrialized art such as film and its correlative labor practices, histories, and archives is a critical move in illuminating and potentially dismantling systemic inequalities. This includes the ways knowledge is built from historical preservation; the political economy that forms these systems under a capitalist paradigm; and the practical functions of industry as the production mechanism that generates the material artifacts of film. This tactic pushes critical questions about how the creativity of women cultural producers and the materials that tell women's stories have been dismissed or undervalued.

The redefinition of textual validity in academic study is pivotal for scholars working in feminist archival practice and theory. Whereas texts produced by women, and the women themselves, have been treated by traditional filmic records and history at best as token examples of exceptionalism and at worst as liminal traces, feminist archival studies push for a reconfiguration of textual validity, drawing objects of study from the historical "scrap heap." As Kate Eichhorn proclaims:

> The scrap heap, then, is not a site of refuse/refusal but a complex site where the past accumulates in the present as a resource to be embraced and rejected, mined and recycled, discarded and redeployed. As such, feminism's scrap heap is both a site of abjection—that which must be expelled but that which we cannot live without—and simultaneously a playground, a refuge, a scene on innovation, humor, hope, and longing. In every respect, feminism's scrap heap is integral rather than superfluous, vital rather than stagnant.[21]

Alternative archives, imagined through feminist, queer, and affective models, provide the methodological rigor necessary for mining the scrap heap and reassessing normative, and restrictive, standards of curation and remembrance.

WHY DIRECTORS, WHAT EXPLOITATION

Stephanie Rothman was a screenwriter, story editor, production executive, and director. My focus on Rothman primarily as a director is not to promote the unchallenged and unquestioned positioning of the director as the embodiment of unchecked agency, nor to elevate the position of director above other facets of production labor. Rather, it's a strategic move in service of three goals. First, I leverage the public's awareness of directorship as a strategic pathway to reengineer it, decoupling directorship from maleness. The public interest in, and knowledge around, film directors is outsized compared to their colleagues and peers. The classroom anecdote that opened this chapter would be a much different, and likely fruitless, endeavor if I had asked students to name their favorite (or any) screenwriter, cinematographer, costume designer, or editor. The concept of the director has a conventional cultural cachet attached to it, bred in large part by a simplistic narrative around who creates a film, the privileged position mythologized as the charismatic leader valiantly leading his troops in the execution of his creation vision. The rise of auteur theory in the United States—the idea that a director is the author of a film and therefore the film and director are necessarily reflections of one another—in the 1960s quickly fell out of academic favor but has held strong in the public consciousness. The singularity of film authorship is bolstered by the continued reliance of public film criticism on auteurism, industry awards that recognize individual creative talent, and the obfuscation of the collaborative nature of filmmaking. To be sure, those who work in or study the film industry know the idea of singular authorship is untrue; filmmaking is a collaborative endeavor carried out by hundreds of workers of which the director is just one. It would be impossible for a director to achieve a cinematic vision if the unit production manager was not ensuring bills were paid or craft services was not feeding cast and crew alike. Even so, the director is broadly familiar and recognizable in the public sphere as a singular author. The director is a useful and recognizable entry point into divorcing naturalized maleness from directorship.

Second, I focus on Rothman as director to expand filmic histories and archives that have disregarded women directors, despite their regularized contributions to cinema over its evolution. Beyond a doubt, film studies is primarily interested in male filmmakers.[22] The inconsistent analysis paid to women filmmakers across the breadth and depth of cinema studies has left a dearth of historical and archival information, impeding scholars working to recirculate them into historical and industrial understanding.[23] This distortion compounds their already precarious position as subjects of study and analysis. The excellent work scholars have done despite these limitations has aided in reversing said precarity. Yet this work is often concentrated in one of two time periods: the early development of the entertainment industries in the United States and the particular history of women in silent film (roughly 1895–1930)[24] or contemporary work (1990s–present) on women working today.[25] Focusing on Rothman as director begins to fill in some historical gaps as a starting point for building a continuum of women's filmmaking across time rather than in discrete moments.

While feminist film theory and criticism has taken up the broad role of women in film, Kaja Silverman observes that is has "manifested only an intermittent and fleeting interest in the status of authorship within the classic text."[26] Judith Mayne also highlights the lack of interest in women's directorial labor in feminist film theory: "even though discussions of the works of women filmmakers have been central to the development of feminist film studies, theoretical discussions of female authorship in the cinema have been surprisingly sparse."[27] The discrepancy Mayne points to here is a critical one: although films made by women have been significant and influential texts in the development of feminist film studies, the authorship position and embodied labor of the women who directed these films, and others, has been notably overlooked. The exemption of women's directorial labor in feminist film study and criticism results from a number of factors including "theoretical frameworks in which any discussions of 'personhood' are suspect [and] the peculiar status of authorship in the cinema."[28] While avoiding discussion of women directorships in feminist film studies has the benefits of sidestepping the essentialism vs. anti-essentialism arguments of the 1970s and 1980s, it unintentionally forecloses wide-ranging discussions of women directors. The impacts of this are critical, and fully addressed in the following chapter. Undeniably, the industrial focus on the director remains a critical factor in the practical everyday of film production and employment dynamics and cannot be overlooked because it is academically outmoded. To do so furthers the divide between industry and academia that production studies works so hard to overcome. Additionally, the idea of personal authorship *was* integral to how Rothman worked and how she understands her own career. Any study of her work must interrogate why and how said authorship functioned as a critical node in the construction of her professional and filmic self. Foregrounding her authorship—or, as Mayne contends, any women's authorship—"is not simply a useful political strategy; it is crucial to the reinvention of the cinema that has been undertaken by women filmmakers and feminist spectators."[29]

A continuum of women's labor does more than intercede into exclusionary histories; it undermines the idea that Hollywood, in its current incarnation, can be a willing and productive home to women directors. Of all directors, writers, producers, executive producers, editors, and cinematographers involved with the 500 highest-grossing US films in 2019, women filled only 23 percent of these roles.[30] Women working in other behind-the-scenes positions were even fewer, particularly in the case of technical positions. For example, 99 percent of these films had no women working as special-effects supervisors.[31] Only 14 percent of said projects were directed by women.[32] This disparity is compounded for women directors of color; the ratio of white women directors versus women directors of color helming films in 2019 is five to one.[33] Rothman's career, while laced with disappointment and unmet goals, is notable for its legacy of perseverance, a trait that defines the history of women's participation in the industrial production of film. This Rothman historiography links her career to the role of women in present day film production, providing necessary connective tissue around the interplay between film history, archives, and women's past, present, and future cinematic labor. Building these bonds also stresses the limits of the film histories that construct women as aberrations in directorial labor, resulting in their continued de-integration into film production. The Rothman case study presented here builds a more robust and comprehensive archive and filmic history around women directors as an "intervention into the system," helping to normalize women's participation as film directors.

Investigations into women's directorial labor through second wave exploitation has its own particular scholarly problem: both are under-examined areas in cinema studies. While I addressed women's directorship previously, I map the same explanatory attention to second wave exploitation films. Exploitation films have a difficult place within cinema studies. They are variously understood as a genre, a production aesthetic motivated by scant economic resources, a calculated response to the growing divergence in audience types in the US begun in the 1950s, and as spaces of independent production. Definitions of exploitation seem to encompass any, all, or sometimes none of these considerations in their employment by various authors. Generally, the term "exploitation film" has come to signify what Linda Williams summarizes as

> low-budget filmmaking that "exploits" particular sensational, shocking and taboo subjects (violence, perversion, drugs, cruelty, abnormality, sex and its perils) in genre feature film or pseudo-documentary format. Because exploitation films often excite the curiosity of the viewer or provoke active physical responses (lust, disgust, terror), these thrill-films (and their makers) have been seen as "exploiting" the desire of audiences to indulge in guilty cultural pleasures.[34]

Many of the traits Williams describes hold across definitions and interpretations while some, including the root of the term "exploitation," are contested. Eric Schaefer's book *Bold! Daring! Shocking! True! A History of Exploitation Films, 1919–1959*, a watershed moment in the study of the exploitation industry and its products, contends that the term "exploitation" derives from the aggressive and nonstandard advertising practices undertaken by producers and distributors, which became key in the films' success.[35]

Part of the difficulty in placing exploitation films within cinematic history and the public imaginary has to do, in large part, with the very label "exploitation." The endemic pejorative power in the word inherently marginalizes exploitation films. When we name *cinema*, we conjure art: experimental, avant-garde, powerful, emotive, and brimming with consciousness. When we think of *movies*, we see the popular: multi-level cineplexes, lavish award ceremonies, and summer blockbusters. When we invoke *exploitation films*, we recall little, a vague memory of a grainy image on late night television or a strain of the iconic theme song from *Shaft* (Gordon Parks, 1971). These are fragmentary remembrances, out of context and out of time, referents to a text that is at best illusive, and at worst, completely missing. Exploitation films are visual artifacts bordering the outer edges of the frame of cinematic history and memory. They are films that have been traditionally defined through and against a strict binary with mainstream film, constructing them through their lack rather than through their industrial, aesthetic, and narrative contributions and components.

Known for their low-budget aesthetics, sensationalist storylines primarily focused on vice and sin, and narratives that alternate between spectacle and monotony, exploitation films allow for an alternative approach to cinematic construction and interpretation.[36] Although they are encumbered with historical and cultural baggage, exploitation films have been a staple of the cinematic industry since the early twentieth century. Often referred to monolithically, they can, and in fact should, be separated into distinct phases. These chronologically bounded phases are fairly stable markers of the formulation and evolution of filmic narrative, content, marketing and advertising practices, target audiences, and cultural relevance of exploitation films. As such, exploitation films can be roughly divided into three phases: classical exploitation (1919–1959), second wave exploitation (1960–1980), and neo-exploitation (1980–present).[37]

This book is concerned with the period of second wave exploitation films that first evolved in the 1950s, as the independent production and distribution markets thrived in an open market. Second wave exploitation films were cheap to make, and their short production time allowed them to capitalize on trends and fads. As films catering to a growing population of suburban teenagers, they monopolized the thriving drive-in market of the 1950s and early 1960s, before moving to urban grindhouses in the late 1960s and 1970s. Working with a stylistic pattern closely inspired by classical Hollywood cinema, second wave exploitation films bound moments of sensational spectacle with predictable narratives, creating films that were simultaneously shocking and rote.

My goal here, however, is not to attempt to construct a single definition for exploitation film and its iterations. It is futile and naïve to segregate any of these definitions from one another; they are all nodes on the definitional chain of exploitation films. Rather than attempting to narrow the understanding of exploitation films into a strict genre-based definition, they should be understood as a cinematic style which encompasses various aesthetic, economic, and narrative conventions and inventions. Akin to the way in which film noir has been contextualized within cinematic history, formulating exploitation films as a *style* allows for a fluidity in construction and analysis that is critical to making sense of the various ways and forms these films have developed. Throughout this project, then, I refer to the "exploitation film paradigm" or "exploitation style" as terminology meant to signal the industrial, artistic, narrative, ideological, labor, distributive, exhibitive, and cultural networks under which films labeled second wave exploitation were produced.

Exploitation, like all film industries, has a history constituted through a variety of actors, institutions, and cultural shifts. However, their industrial history, content, aesthetic, style, and reach are prone to academic marginalization. This makes it difficult to find scholarly work that considers the exploitation industry as a whole. Most scholars have instead chosen a piecemeal focus on either the industrial production and economic logics of the style or on the films themselves, albeit primarily removed from their industrial context. Although there is a small group of scholars who have produced work aimed at a holistic understanding of exploitation as a strain of, rather than foil to, classical film history, most of this work does not center around second wave exploitation nor on women's industrial labor. Eric Schaeffer's germinal work on exploitation constrains itself to the period from the mid-twentieth century until the late 1950s.[38] Elena Gorfinkel's[39] excellent work temporally grounds itself in the second wave exploitation period but narrows its focus to the space and place of urban grindhouse cinemas and sexploitation films. Andrea Juno and V. Vale book's *Incredibly Strange Films* is a key repository of information for films in the second wave exploitation period. Its chronological scope is vast; it primarily concerns itself with filmic texts divorced from their industrial histories. Theorist Pam Cook's[40] brief investigation of Stephanie Rothman is one of the closest examples of an examination of women's filmmaking in second wave exploitation. But like Juno and Vale, Cook focuses on select filmic texts only, leaving questions around women's directorial labor unasked and unanswered. The result of the narrow historical and scholarly record around second wave exploitation and women's directorial labor creates the gap in knowledge this work addresses.

Indebted to these foundations, this manuscript is divided into two sections. Section one addresses the academic and archival conditions that combine to obscure the breadth and depth of women's directorial labor while advocating for exploring alternative spaces like second wave exploitation as a corrective to restrictive conceptions of our collective cinematic past. To establish the problematics around the integration of women's directorial labor into film histories and archives, chapter two explicates the paradigm of exceptional women—the idea that a narrow and repetitive group of women directors are positioned as representative for all women's cinematic labor, existing as exceptions to the rule of the naturalized maleness of directorship—and details how said exceptionalism imparts a series of destructive impacts on the realized potential of a plurality of directorial identities. By privileging homogeneity in personal and artistic identity, and evading the regularized disrespect granted to women's directorial labor, the paradigm of exceptional women advances tokenism cloaked as equity. Alternative archival and queer and feminist interventions, however, offer a reparative, and I demonstrate how these practices work to envision a broader and more diverse spectrum of women in cinematic history. Lastly, I close the chapter with an account of my own alternative curation via the Rothman archive.

With traditional histories and archives closed to most women directors, where does one find them? In chapter three, I argue one rich space is second wave exploitation. To substantiate, I illuminate the historical and theoretical construction of second wave exploitation as an industrial and filmic paradigm while arguing for temporal fluidity in historical configurations to open up critical gaps through which women's filmic labor can materialize. Following a brief review of the extent configuration of the classical exploitation period of 1919–1959, the bulk of the chapter makes the case for understanding 1960–1980 as a discrete period in the exploitation style, and thereby critical to understanding Rothman's industrial milieu. Indeed, this project distinguishes itself from both other studies of exploitation film and women directors by advocating for scholastically untapped spaces like second wave exploitation as fertile ground for uncovering women's cinematic labor. Shifting from the filmic paradigm to a practitioner within it, section one closes with chapter four's personal and professional biography of Rothman. This biographical account is coupled with an evaluation of her directorial personality and major filmic philosophies. In doing so, I inspect Rothman's *oeuvre* holistically, mapping consistent themes, stylistic approaches, and ideological underpinnings across her seven films. This includes a discussion of what I term the "Rothman Rules:" a set of formal and informal guidelines Rothman set to negotiate the tensions between her convictions and beliefs and the content demands of second wave exploitation.

Part two of the book is invested in the praxis of intervention, providing in-depth textual, thematic, and stylistic evaluations of Rothman's films as explicitly political intercessions into film histories. The cinema of Stephanie Rothman documents the complications of contemporary life while simultaneously offering resolutions to its persistent conflicts: patriarchal control, repressed desire, and unfulfilled ambition. Grounding her films in a specific time and place—Los Angeles in the1960s and 1970s—Rothman incorporates the multifaceted energies of the city, its diverse populations, and its shifting social and cultural mores. While Rothman's films cannot be separated from their industrial conditions of production, and her shifts between companies, distributors, and business partners play a key role in the genesis of her filmography, her work is most effectively considered thematically, rather than chronologically. Rothman's seven films—and one unrealized project—offer their most substantive reflection of her directorship and their industrial home in second wave exploitation when considered as thematic couplets, rather than teleological products.

These chapters are deeply indebted to textual and formal analysis, yet they retain an industrial through line. Chapter 5 begins by examining the set of her films that firmly embed Rothman in the industrial milieu that is second wave exploitation: *Blood Bath/Track of the Vampire* (1966) and *It's a Bikini World* (1967). Critically, it is *Blood Bath*, a film she does not consider her own, that is the catalyst for an extended historicization of the director in film histories outside of her own subjectivity, voice, or narrative. Chapter 6 tackles *The Student Nurses* (1970) and *Terminal Island* (1973), perhaps Rothman's only widely known films. Both films highlight women's struggle against patriarchal control, albeit in distinctly different ways. Between the liberal individualism of *The Student Nurses* and the anarcho-communitarianism of *Terminal Island*, Rothman attempts to map pathways into a post-patriarchal future. Chapter 7 draws inspiration from the changes wrought by the sexual revolution of the 1960s and 1970s, uncovering the women's shifting desires and social expectations in *The Velvet Vampire* (1971) and *Group Marriage* (1972). Traversing through polyamory, fetish, collective living, and queer world-making, these films are speculative imaginings of the possibilities of women's realized desires, sexual and otherwise. Finally, chapter 8 closes the volume with Rothman's most personal film, *The Working Girls* (1974), and an unproduced adaption of Philip K. Dick's novel *The Man in the High Castle*, representative of the unfulfilled potential of her career. As a chronicle of un- and underemployment, *The Working Girls* roils with the frustration of talented women forced to abandon their goals; capitalist subsistence, stability, and mobility are always just out of reach. It's a telling insight into the director that narrativizes the limits of optimism. It's fitting, then, that the film would be Rothman's last, as she struggled for years to materialize her take on Dick's uncanny, alternate America onto screens to no avail.

Chapter 2

THE LIMITS OF EXCEPTIONAL WOMEN

> We locate ourselves and orientate our own work toward a future in part determined by the nature and quality of our engagement with the past.
> —BILL NICHOLS[1]

Considerations of women film laborers and their creative output are deeply indebted to feminist film theory and analysis. It is a persistent rupture in the routinized "maleness" of cinema studies, histories, and archives. Feminist film theory's explosive intrusion into cinema studies in the 1970s and 1980s radically transformed what cinema studies' work can be, alongside who gets to do that work. To be sure, my own research and writing would not be possible without the long tradition of feminist scholars who have taught and influenced me. Feminist film scholars are one-part historical detective, one-part theorist, and one-part rabble-rouser. It is this productive formula that empowers my investigation into the often-fraught position of women directors within feminist film theory and analysis.

Discussions of women's authorship in early feminist film theory and analysis are somewhat sparse. Kaja Silverman notes: "Feminist film theory and criticism have manifested only an intermittent and fleeting interest in the status of authorship within the classic text."[2] My interest here is uncovering some key roots of this intermittent interest and how it impacts the breadth and depth of women film directors in academic and popular memory. To do so, I trace the consequences of debates around essentialism and anti-essentialism in feminist theory—exemplified by the study of "women's films" in early feminist film analysis—and the temporal confluence of feminist appraisals of women film workers and the declension of authorship as interpretative and analytic filmic framework. The result of these intersecting circumstances is a narrowed conception of "women directors," or what I term the *paradigm of exceptional women*: tokenized women whose directorial positions are coded as "exceptions to the rule" of the standardized maleness of film directors. An overemphasis on exceptional women first implies a homogeneity of women directors that reinforces inequities in industrial and historical power structures, second, upholds normative notions of filmic and artistic taste, and third, sidesteps the deeply engrained industrial disesteem of women's directorial labor. Thankfully, feminist film scholars provide paths past these ramifications, and the second half of this chapter reviews recent work in feminist and queer theory that provides models for expanding the breadth and depth of women film workers in filmic archives and histories, and thereby in collective cultural memory. I end with a review of my own archival work on Stephanie Rothman, wholly indebted to the models provided by feminist scholars who have come before me. I begin with a brief review of the tenacious specter of essentialism in feminist theory broadly before discussing feminist film theory specifically.

The elision of women's authorship has intertwined theoretical and political roots in the essentialism and anti-essentialism debates of the 1960s and 1970s and the theoretical turn away from auteur theory. Investigations into the essential nature of women, and the push against such notions, were significant during the second wave feminist movement in the United States in the 1970s. The search for women's essential nature is underpinned by the belief that there is a great truth about all women buried by the patriarchy in an attempt to erase the power endemic to womanhood. For example, the Radicalesbians' 1970 manifesto "The Woman-Identified Woman," encouraged women "to develop their 'authentic selves' as well as build their collective power."[3] Author and activist Shulamith Firestone argued for women and men's biological difference as naturalized, yet oppression based on said difference as artificial and initiative of women's domination as a sex class. Her treatise *The Dialectic of Sex* argued that women, as the sex class, have been oppressed by men through the biological family; the only antidote is a complete seizure of reproduction and a focus on childrearing in collective women-only spaces.[4] She declared: "For unless revolution uproots the basic social organization, the biological family—the vinculum through which the psychology of power can always be smuggled—the tapeworm of exploitation will never be annihilated."[5] Firestone cut at the very fabric of a gendered society where women are forced to mitigate their essential selves under patriarchal control. Groups like the Redstockings, the New York Radical Feminists (NYRF), and the Women's International Terrorist Conspiracy from Hell (WITCH) all advanced some version of essentialist feminism that asserted women were fundamentally the same.[6]

Anti-essentialist contemporaries of Firestone et al., refused claims of a single, constitutive womanhood "on the grounds that universal claims about women are invariably false and effectively normalize and privilege specific forms of femininity."[7] Reviewing their disputations, Charlotte Witt classifies anti-essentialist claims across three related but independent argumentative categories: the exclusion argument, the instability argument, and the power argument.[8] The exclusion argument emphasizes essentialist feminism's flattening of identity difference in favor of a "general" womanness that implicitly aligns with middle-class, cisgendered, white women, while the instability argument invalidates any categories as "arbitrary and instable because of the nature of language."[9] Finally, the power argument highlights that gender typologies, as a social process, are constructed through power and hence must be unraveled to understand who that power, and its related groupings, serve. The exclusion argument is forcefully taken up in Elizabeth Spelman's *Inessential Woman*, which argues that essentialism in feminist thought necessarily foregrounds the experiences of racially, sexually, and economically privileged women.[10] The specter of these debates hangs heavy over feminist theory and advocacy of the 1970s,[11] simplistically memorializing, as Kathi Weeks notes, "the time when feminists essentialized the category of woman, neglected race, constructed maniacally totalizing theories, and exposed themselves in public with their intemperate speech, overwrought emotions, and utopian dreams."[12]

THE DOUBLE BIND

Feminist film theory developed in this milieu, grappling with what Annette Kuhn historicizes as "two rather different desires: to understand the nature of film, in particular its metapsychology, in relation to sexual difference; and to understand how gender informs the contents of films and/or how men and women relate to film and/or cinema."[13] These two paths manifest in early feminist film theory's reliance on a psychoanalytic model, imbricating the cinematic production of sexual difference with the representative construction of women on film and spectator interaction. Early feminist film theory, then, tended to take one of two positions, what Kuhn calls either the "psychoanalytic" or the "social":[14] the metapsychological approach or the content/audience approach. For instance, Laura Mulvey's germinal 1975 essay "Visual Pleasure in Narrative Cinema" exemplifies the psychoanalytic, and the early feminist film study of women's films, in texts such as Molly Haskell's *From Reverence to Rape: The Treatment of Women in the Movies*, the social.

Women's films also offer an apt example of the mirrored complications between the political and social feminist movement of the 1970s and growth of early feminist film theory. As Alison Butler notes, the term "women's films" is a broad identifier that

> suggests, without clarity, films that might be made by, addressed to, concerned with women, or all three. It is neither a genre nor a movement in film history, it has no single lineage of its own, no national boundaries, in filmic or aesthetic specificity, but traverses and negotiates cinematic and cultural traditions and critical and political debates.[15]

Despite this expansive and unfixed definition, Kuhn explains how the term was practically applied more narrowly, "referencing a subtype of the film melodrama whose plot is organized around the perspective of a woman (or women) and which addresses women spectators through thematic concerns socially and culturally coded as 'feminine.'"[16] Women's films often focused on sexuality, marriage, family, and domestic spaces.[17] Notwithstanding, they differed from traditional melodrama in their emphasis on women as narrative nucleus and in the care with how women's issues were explored. They do not foster the false implication that women-centered narratives are predictable, stereotypical, or specific to women only. Rather, films like *Mildred Pierce* (Michael Curtiz, 1945), *Stella Dallas* (King Vidor, 1937), *Brief Encounter* (David Lean, 1945), and *Letter from an Unknown Woman* (Max Ophüls, 1948) negotiate the tension between women's stories as specific and universal. That is to say, while thematics in women's films are seemingly essentialist, their development is broadly applicable to modern, capitalistic life both in and outside of gender. Women's films, then, have the burden of representing women and their stories as universal and singular.[18] This two-pronged encumbrance is a mirror of the essentialist and anti-essentialist debate. Regrettably, feminist film theory has often universalized women's lived experiences through whiteness, with some notable exceptions including, but not limited to, the work of Jane Gaines, bell hooks, Celine Parreñas Shimizu, Fatimah Tobing Rony, and Anna Everett.

The friction around flattening intersectional identity in service of an increased visibility and narrative focus constituted what pioneering feminist film theorists Mary Ann Doane, Patricia Mellencamp, and Linda Williams see as a "tendency to deconstruct and disavow all notions of identity, ownership, possession. The demand for the delineation of a female specificity is countered by the refusal to espouse an identity, any identity."[19] The dynamic between a need for specificity and a refusal to essentialize signals the precarious position of the feminist film theoretician as an outside agitator whose provocations are contained within—and shaped by—the very system they are critiquing. This puts theorists in what Doane et al. describe as a double bind, as the feminist film theorist

> can continue to analyze and interpret various instances of the repression of woman, of her radical absence in the discourses of men—a pose which necessitates remaining within that very problematic herself, always risking a recapitalization of patriarchal constructions and a naturalization of 'woman.' The choice appears to be a not very attractive one between a continual repetition of the same gesture of demystification (itself perhaps mystified as to its methodological heritage) and a possible regression to ideas of feminine identity, which threaten to constitute a veritable re-mystification.[20]

This precipitous position was exacerbated, in part, by the films scrutinized in early feminist film theory. The women's films analyzed by early feminist film theorists were products of classical Hollywood, the output of male directors and the patriarchal system under which they flourished.[21] This created a sustained need for constant oppositional or recuperative readings of mainstream filmic texts to generate the critical analysis necessary to engage the viewer in the reciprocal production of meaning, forcing "the spectator to participate in a dialectical process by which consciousness is formed and transformed."[22] While this process of "working within the system" demonstrated the deep patriarchal constructs embedded in mainstream Hollywood films, it also hampered potential paths of moving past the system itself by virtue of its embeddedness within it.

Recognizing this issue, feminist film theory turned toward films directed by women working in counter-cinema in an effort to move outside the system of patriarchal image production.[23] Peter Wollen's 1972 article "Godard and Counter Cinema: Vent d'Est" established a typology of the virtues of counter-cinema in contrast to the seven "deadly sins" of Hollywood filmmaking: narrative transitivity vs. narrative intransitivity; identification vs. estrangement; transparency vs. foregrounding; single diegesis vs. multiple diegesis; closure vs. aperture; pleasure vs. displeasure; and fiction vs. reality.[24] While seemingly offering an avenue out of the feminist theoreticians' double bind, Claire Johnston's "Women's Cinema as Counter-Cinema" cautioned the wholesale adoption of the "revolutionary" nature of counter-cinema as a panacea for the tensions created between gender, the cinematic apparatus, and the ensuring text, noting that "the tools and techniques of cinema themselves, as part of reality, are an expression of the prevailing ideology: they are not neutral, as many 'revolutionary' filmmakers appear to believe."[25]

In acknowledging that the very implements of cinematic creation were connected to a capitalist and patriarchal Hollywood, Johnston argued that an approach to counter-cinema must account for "films as a political tool and film as entertainment,"[26] with ideas of the political and entertaining offering reciprocal influence as an instrument of anti-oppression. In an explicit nod to the double bind, Johnston advocates for examining the films of women directors working within Hollywood—she analyzes Dorothy Arzner's *Dance Girl Dance* (1940) and Ida Lupino's *Not Wanted* (1949)—as potential sites of ideological dislocation while also emphasizing the need for change in the form and function of filmmaking towards a counter-cinematic approach. She declares: "the 'truth' of our oppression cannot be 'captured' on celluloid with the 'innocence' of the camera: it has to be constructed/manufactured."[27] This type of fabrication—what Lucy Fisher calls a *"counter-heritage"*[28]—is embedded in films like Shirley Clarke's *Portrait of Jason* (1967); Yvonne Rainer's *Lives of Performers* (1972); Jackie Raynal's *Twice Upon a Time* (1968), and much of visual artist Carolee Schneemann's cinematic work.

WRONG TIME: WOMEN'S AUTHORSHIP (RE)CONSIDERED

Whether focused on mainstream or counter-cinema, the emphasis on evaluating film directed by women again forced feminist film theoreticians to grapple with the essentialism/anti-essentialism fracas, as feminist film theory became embroiled in the consternation around auteur theory. Despite the fact that in contemporary academic film study "auteurism is rarely invoked, and when it is, it is more as a curiosity, as a historical development surely influential, but even more surely surpassed,"[29] its impact has been wide-ranging, and specifically affected debates around emphasizing women's authorship in early feminist film studies.

The auteur theory emerged from France in the mid-1950s, advanced in part by theorist and critic André Bazin, critic/filmmaker François Truffaut, and influential work of the journal *Cahiers du Cinéma*. Evolving from the *politique des auteurs*, which was foundationally concerned with the director as the author of a film and the film as a text that reflects the director's personal vision, the auteur theory courted advocates and dissenters as it migrated across countries, contexts, and languages. The auteur theory migrated from France to the United Kingdom, where it was taken up "chiefly through the journal *Movie* and writers including Robin Wood, V. F. Perkins, and Ian Cameron."[30] It soon made its way to the United States, where it was translated into a US film context and advocated by one its most vocal proponents, critic Andrew Sarris, whose essay "Notes on the Auteur Theory in 1962" passionately advocated for auteurship as the primary mode for film evaluation.

Auteurism as a broad theoretical conceit was challenged as often as it was invoked. Indeed, privileging directorial authorship was a contentious point well before the formalization of the *politique des auteurs*. In 1921, filmmaker Jean Epstein applied the term to directors such as Griffith and Eisenstein, and by the 1930s, author/theorist Rudolph Arnheim was pushing back against the idea.[31] In the 1940s, literary theory's New Criticism movement chided the focus on authorship and its ambitions as the intentional fallacy, with critics noting that "the design or intention of the author is neither available nor desirable as a standard for judging the success of a work of literary art."[32] While different in approach and aim from the New Critics, Roland Barthes's widely influential 1968 essay "The Death of the Author" argued a similar, if discrete, point noting that highlighting an author forecloses any input of the reader, thereby limiting the text's possibilities and reducing its inherent multiplicities into an authorial singularity. Film critics admonished auteurism for its de-emphasis on the collaborative nature of filmmaking and its overvaluation of the ineffably vague idea of the "genius" director. While many thinkers repeated this assessment, legendary critic Pauline Kael's 1963 essay "Circles and Squares" was perhaps the most public rebuke.[33] Offering a point-by-point dismissal of Sarris's criteria, Kael highlighted how the underlying components of Sarris's exaltation of auteurism—technical competence, repetition, and "interior meaning"—were either antithetical to the development and evolution of great filmmaking or too vague to be of value. Following such a trenchant critique, the focus on authorship continued waning academically as feminist film theory was developing.

The precarious place of auteur theory in film studies in the 1970s and during the development of feminist film theory intertwined issues of essentialism, anti-essentialism, and authorship that significantly shaped how women's directorship was—or was not—incorporated into early feminist film study. Essentialist feminism became a repetitive hurdle, as with the theoreticians' double bind previously discussed, while an anti-essentialist frame allowed for the obfuscation of oppression. This combined the dismissal of auteur theory as a hyperfocus on the "great men" conceit of directing, and as a result, emphasizing women's authorship was often seen as what Christine Gledhill calls a "patriarchal equation," as "construction of our culture-heroines as strong and powerful bring charges of male identification, or substitution."[34]

More often than not, this problematic was sidestepped by avoiding the idea of "women" and authorship in favor of the singular author.[35] A reluctance to negotiate the complexities between the categories of "woman" as a singular entity (read: director) and "women" as broadly constructed social and gendered populations that necessarily force complicated discussions of intersectionality compounded the double bind. It is worth quoting Judith Mayne at length on these interrelated issues:

> The reluctance to speak of a "female tradition" has perhaps been most influenced, however, by the fear of essentialism—the fear, that is, that any discussion of "female texts" presumes the uniqueness and autonomy of female representation, this validating rather than challenging the dualism of patriarchal hierarchy. However, the act of discarding the concept of female authorship and of an attendant female tradition in the cinema as necessarily compromised by essentialist definitions of woman can be equally dualistic, in assuming that the only models of connection and influence are unquestionably essentialist ones.[36] [. . .] Central to a theorizing of female authorship in the cinema is an expanded definition of textuality attentive to the complex network of intersections, distances, and resistances of "woman" to "women." The challenge of female authorship in the cinema for feminist theory is in the demonstration of *how* the divisions, overlaps, and distances between 'woman' and 'women' connect with the contradictory status of cinema as the embodiment of both omnipotent control and individual fantasy.[37]

The conundrum of essentialism, its overdetermination around authorship, and the attending categorical complexities are powerful motivators for circumventing discussions of women's directorial authorship or addressing it mainly through the "woman." Angela Martin explains: "Female or feminist authorship tends to be sought in what can be identifiably-linked to the filmmaker (as woman): a film's autobiographical reference; a filmmaker's actual presence in the film; the evidence of a female voice within the narrative (however located)."[38] This is the difference between saying that all women directors do not *de facto* make films differently than men and declaring that Stephanie Rothman's films are inherently feminist because she is a woman. In other words, one should not consider a woman director essentially different than a male director, but if one does, one must consider a woman director as essentially a feminist director. Hence, a woman director who doesn't foreground her womanhood, her gender identity, or her feminism in the film is passed over in discussions of authorship. Indeed, as Gaines reminds us, *gender is a genre*.[39]

THE LIMITS OF EXCEPTIONAL WOMEN

The de-emphasis of the author, the menace of essentialism, and the focus on women directors as feminist directors combine to decentralize women's authorship in feminist film theory and analysis. To be quite clear, I am not arguing that women's authorship is wholly erased from feminist film theory; it is not. However, its considerations are significantly restricted by the same factors that complicate it. Indeed, when women directors are considered theoretically, historically, and archivally, they are filtered through the paradigm of exceptional women. Exceptional women are those filmmakers whose position as filmmaker is an inherent exception to the rule of the accepted and standardized maleness of directors. The idea of the "exceptional" here does not refer to the talent or skill of the directors, or to the success of their films. Any woman who has overcome the deeply misogynistic film industry to direct a feature film is exceptional in the strongest sense of the word. The exceptionalism I posit here is not one of success, but tokenism disguised as parity. Exceptional women encapsulate how women filmmakers are regularly positioned as sanctioned diversions to the rule of male dominance in directing, conveying aspirational status for present and future women directors while simultaneously de-normalizing their very existence. Exceptional women directors are limited token examples of a long and unexamined history of women as cinematic authors, and the overreliance on exceptional women serves to narrow the breadth and depth of women directors in accumulated filmic histories. This causes three significant problems: an implicit homogeneity of women film laborers that mirrors existing industrial and historical power structures; an exclusionary and hierarchical valuation of cinematic styles; and an elision and reinforcement of the systemic discreditation of women's film labor.

Firstly, the paradigm of exceptional women constructs a narrow and uniform cadre of women as representatives of both the population and idea of "women directors." The assemblage of women plus director is overwhelmingly white, Western, cisgender, and heterosexual. A practical example is the Criterion Collection, a company that produces specialty releases of films for home viewing; it is one of the most well-known public archives of cinema history. In establishing that reputation, Criterion has "developed a legitimizing function that empowers it with an ability to affirm what films should be deemed important."[40] Who is represented in the Criterion Collection matters. Criterion's winter 2020 catalog of purchasable films boasts 1,369 films. Of that total, fifty, or approximately 4 percent, are directed by women. Drilling down more deeply, those fifty films represent only thirty-two different directors,⁴¹ and only two of those thirty-two directors are women of color: Mira Nair and Euzhan Palcy.⁴² The Criterion Collection, which is "dedicated to publishing classic and contemporary films from around the world," has allocated only 4 percent of its collection to women directors and just *one-tenth of 1 percent* to women of color.⁴³ Certainly, male directorial histories are most often white, Western, cisgendered, and heterosexual. Yet, when so few women are considered in the annals of directing histories, and done so as exceptional rather than normative examples, the industrial allowance for women of color directors shrinks precipitously.

Secondly, exceptional women are representative of cinema histories' stylistic exclusion and hierarchical evaluation of artistic taste. Film histories have long been burdened with hyperinflated concerns of legitimacy, in many ways a result of film's liminal place as both art and commerce, its early juridical exclusion from artistic protections, and its tumultuous social standing. Consequently, cinema histories and archives are overly reliant on Pierre Bourdieu's notion of pure taste, which assigns the highest artistic legitimacy to cultural objects associated with "highbrow" culture.⁴⁴ These associations are laden with exclusionary, hegemonic notions of class, race, nationality, sexuality, and gender. To be sure, as Dick Hebdige notes, "where to draw the line between good and bad, high and low, the ugly and the beautiful, the ephemeral and the substantial—emerges at certain points as a quite explicitly political one."⁴⁵ Women directors frequently memorialized in film histories and archives are molded by these politics of taste and art, representing a constricted field of cinematic styles, genres, and movements aligned with "legitimate" cinema: avant-garde or experimental, new wave, documentary, or classic Hollywood. A small selection of hyper-invoked women directors exposes these patterns: Maya Deren and Chantel Akerman's experimental and avant-garde work; Agnès Varda's French New Wave filmmaking and enduring documentary realism; and Lois Weber's and Dorothy Arzner's pioneering careers in early and classic Hollywood. Critically, as Jane Gaines notes in related to the search for women in filmic archives, "it is no wonder that 'no women in film' were found since the search was for ideal women but not for all women."⁴⁶ *Who* is remembered and *how* they are remembered reinforces women's directorial value primarily in filmic styles with high levels of artistic and cultural cachet. Film histories and archives position this as naturalized artistic credibility rather than a specific reinscription of social power relations. To be sure, as Randall Johnson notes,

> the role of culture in the reproduction of social structures, or the way in which unequal power relations, unrecognized as such and thus

accepted as legitimate, are embedded in the systems of classification used to describe and discuss everyday life—as well as cultural practices—and in the ways perceiving reality that are taken for granted by members of society.[47]

The hegemonic naturalization of taste and legitimacy acculturate the paradigm of exceptional women, as ideas of women's indicia to cinema histories filter broadly into scholarly work. Particularly insidious is how these ideas structurally undermined work specifically dedicated to encyclopedic remediation of women's narrow directorial histories past the exceptional. For example, 1983's *Women in Motion*—an encyclopedia of women film workers—caveats processes of inclusion as dependent on representativeness and importance.[48] The question here must be: important and influential to whom? The naturalization of exception must be critically interrogated as systemic exceptionalism in the form of tokenism.[49]

Without challenging those structures, the paradigm of exceptional women continues to enable its third negative impact: the obfuscation of Hollywood's systemic discreditation of women's directorial labor and its naturalized misogynistic structures. Women film directors are rare in Hollywood because the system is designed to bar them from entry. Furthermore, they are subject to sex stereotyping, employment discrimination, hostile working environments, and simply afforded less missteps than male directors.[50] A narrow history filtered through the paradigm of exceptional women forces an emphasis on successes while disguising the industry's oppressive structures and ignoring the legacy of women who have been set up to fail. Exceptional women show others that if they've failed, it is their own fault, simultaneously absolving the prejudicial system itself and falsifying the overall history of women's filmic labor, directorial or not.

Key to overcoming exceptional women is attacking or ignoring restrictive filmic archives and histories. The dearth of regularly accessible archival information is a substantial hurdle in expanding histories of women in film. Additionally, the same tokenism that pervades the paradigm of exceptional women must also be avoided in the archive. Sexploitation director Doris Wishman is an apt example. Between 1960 and 2002, Wishman directed thirty-one films, moving back and forth between sexploitation, horror, and hardcore pornography.[51] And yet, until recently, one could count on a single hand the number of scholarly articles dedicated to her and/or her work.[52] Indeed, the first book-length study of her work was not produced until 2021.[53] Additionally, most of her films are lost to history, and there is anathema when it comes to preserving exploitation films. Yet Wishman is often cited as an example of the democratization and inclusivity of filmic archives—the token exploitation director—despite her minimal presence. The scourge of exceptionalism repeats.

It is critical, then, to discuss strategies for moving to archival interventions and alternative archival practices that offer solutions to this barrier while working to move past the limits of exceptional women. Indeed, as Bourdieu reminds us, "there is no way out of the game of culture; and one's only chance of objectifying the true nature of the game is to objectify as fully as possible the very operations which one is obliged to use in order to achieve that objectification."[54]

ARCHIVAL POLITICS AND POSSIBILITIES

Institutional archiving has long shaped the construction of film histories and the types of scholarly work fostered by available collections. While curation is preservative, it is also exclusionary, endangering cultural work deemed unnecessary for conservation. This neglect is particularly prevalent for second wave exploitation, broadly, and Stephanie Rothman, specifically. The same inattention holds true for many women film laborers, with unethical implications and untenable ramifications. I am particularly interested in unwinding the roadblocks inherent in women's film historiography as archival process and examining generative spaces of alternative archival curation, method, and scholarship to detail how feminist archival interventions can be weaponized to broaden, deepen, and diversify the spectrum of women in cinematic histories.

Expanding archival and historical knowledge in alternative spaces is an intentional process of scholarly disidentification. Disidentification, a tactic developed by José Esteban Muñoz, indicates the "survival strategies the minority subject practices in order to negotiate a phobic majoritarian public sphere that continuously elides or punishes the existence of subjects who do not conform to the phantasm of normative citizenship."[55] Disidentification disrupts the rules and regulations of enforced normalization and restricted access to alternate identities. Scholarly disidentification is not simply a methodological structure for archival intervention, but is instead a political imperative. Embracing this imperative, I look to reparative, interventional work done by feminist film scholars and queer and affective alternate archive curation, all destabilizing projects in the best ways possible.

Feminist archival interventions are generative disruptions that challenge institutional archives as repositories of information while refocusing how knowledge derived from them is created and used. They combine memory, knowledge, and impact rather than standard documentary reiteration, a critical function since

> the archive is not one and the same as forms of remembrance, or as history. Manifesting itself in the form of traces, it contains the potential to fragment and destabilize either remembrance as recorded, or history as written, as sufficient means of providing the last word in the account of what has come to pass.[56]

As explicitly political projects they force us to face, head-on, the authority is still assumed in the institutionality of archives. In choosing what information is deposited and preserved, institutions and their archivists overdetermine what is sanctioned as knowledge, and as knowledge demanding preservation.[57] Archival deposits code knowledge as legitimate through inclusion and delegitimate through exclusion. This codification serves Diana Taylor's "myths of the archive":

> One is that it is unmediated—that objects located there might mean something outside the framing of the archival impetus itself. What makes an object archival is the process whereby it is selected for analysis. Another myth is that the "archive" resists change, corruptibility, and political manipulation.[58]

Exposing archives' subjectivism explicates how hegemonic historical power is maintained by exclusion and erasure. Jacques Derrida notes that those who control knowledge through its preservation, its sanctioning, and its dissemination, are unequivocally in a position of power shaped by social, political, and economic forces. He argues that "there is no political power without control of the archive, if not memory. Effective democratization can always be measured by this essential criterion: the participation in and access to the archive, its constitution, and its interpretation."[59] Foregrounding the implicit structures of power in the archive reconstructs it as a necessarily subjective reformation of history representing limited perspectives and not unmediated access to the past.[60]

Archival interventions benefit from disrupting time as much as institutionality. Fluid constructions of space and time in the vein of Siegfried Zielinksi's deep time of media provide scaffolding reducing temporal linearity and the hierarchies it sustains. Deep time of the media argues that "the notion of continuous progress from lower to higher, from simple to complex, must be abandoned, together with all the images, metaphors, and iconography that have been—and still are—used to describe progress."[61] Investigative histories of the process of media and mediated systems large and small have unwound the notion of graduated progress as a dominant narrative, even if not consciously invoking deep time of the media, then certainly embodying its potential. In *Reclaiming the Archive: Feminism and Film History*, Vicki Callahan explores the potentialities of deep time as a way for feminist film historians to re-vision time, space, and historical narrative toward inclusivity. She understands the value in the deep-time methodology of media archaeology as a way to "open the possibilities for film history and theory by envisioning temporality as a nonlinear, multidirectional flow of information rather than a singular reductive and evolutionary system of apodictic data."[62]

Callahan advocates for variant understandings of historical time as a method for opening fissures in established film history, and how these spaces can be utilized as progressive feminist interventions into the archive and film history to expand the breadth and depth of memory around women in film. A salient example is Erin Hill's *Never Done: A History of Women's Work in Media Production*. Despite the established history of the classical Hollywood studio system as resolutely male, Hill recounts women's labor in under-considered Hollywood studio careers: clerical workers, studio tour leaders, secretaries, readers, researchers, etc.[63] Providing a variant on traditional filmic histories wherein women's labor is either deeply historicized in early cinema or in the hyper-contemporary now, Hill provides comprehensive details about the hidden women workers who made up the everyday functionality of studios.

Hill's work follows Lana Rakow's germinal *recovery and reappraisal* methodology: a formal and theoretical practice that provides a framework for allowing feminist scholars to reconsider materials and authors traditionally deemed unworthy of study and analysis.[64] Although feminist archival interventions are ideologically grounded in the concept of recovery and reappraisal, materially they practice something closer to recovery and *appraisal*—elucidating women's labor and cultural contributions that have yet to appear in significance and depth in film histories and its associated archives. Similar in thought to Rakow, Jane Gaines has more recently termed this process *"restoration as restitution."*[65] In intervening into the archives, "historical telling becomes symbolic *restitution* for acts of exclusion, obliteration, exploitation—*reparation*, really, for what happened in the past."[66] Gaines's Women Film Pioneers Project, a free, online "scholarly resource exploring women's global involvement at all levels of film production during the silent film era"[67] is the manifestation of restoration as restitution and an example of the type of groundbreaking work possible through feminist archival intervention.

Importantly, restoration and restitution allows scholars to push past high-profile histories and elevate what Antoinette Burton calls *small stories*: "fragments of lives and dramas that we have only glimpses of but that serve as testimony to the fugitive work of gender and equally fleeting presence of women as subject across a vast landscape of the past."[68] Feminist archival intervention transforms small stories into broader narratives, moving them from historical fragments into holistic constructions, rebalancing the power differentials endemic to normative historical memory. Helen Warner's "Below-the-(Hem)line" demonstrates how small stories indicate a larger narrative of gendered Hollywood labor. Warner uses *Costume Designer*, the trade publication of the Costume Designers Guild, and its practitioner-generated content to counter production studies' normalized focus on men above-the-line while illustrating how storytelling "plays a crucial role in community building, particularly for the socially marginalized."[69] Vicki Mayer's *Below the Line* mobilizes small stories from below the line film and television workers to shed much needed light onto critically understudied film workers. Editors Tristan Taormino, Celina Parreñas Shimizu, Constance Penley, and Mireille Miller-Young combine small stories from adult film performers, directors, scholars, and advocates in their influential collection *The Feminist Porn Book*. Maya Montañez Smuckler's *Liberating Hollywood* uses a hyper-specific site, the Women's Committee of the Directors Guild of America, to map shifting flows of feminist reform and women's directorial labor in the 1970s. This work is an example of "how feminist labor scholarship coheres around key areas: on the one hand, accounting for women's work that has been ignored or poorly understood, and on the other, examining categories of work as they inform individual or collective identity."[70]

As feminist archival interventions, these projects are scholastic activism. In *The Archival Turn in Feminism: Outrage in Order*, Kate Eichhorn advocates for the appraisal of feminist histories and the beginnings of radical knowledge production in archival spaces. She notes: "The archive is where academic and activist work frequently converge. Indeed, the creation of archives has become integral to how knowledge is produced and legitimated and how feminist activists, artists, and scholars make their voices audible."[71] For this focus on the past should not be understood as a move to escape the present but "rather as an attempt to regain agency in an era when the ability to collectively imagine and enact other ways of being in the world has become deeply eroded."[72]

Part of regaining agency is the flexibility scholars across disciplines have applied to archival curation, understanding archives as both physical spaces and collection of materials, and developing theoretical structures around collecting and preserving in micro, macro, and mutable forms. Scholars in queer and affect theory have been predisposed to this process, and I take theoretical and methodological inspirations from two in particular, Sara Ahmed and Anne Cvetkovich. In *The Cultural Politics of Emotion*, Ahmed theorizes alternative archives through contact rather than materiality:

> a model of the archive not as the conversion of self into textual gathering, but as a "contact zone." An archive is an effect of multiple forms of contact, including institutional forms of contact (with libraries, books, web sites), as well as everyday forms of contact (with friends, families, others.) Some forms of contact are presented and authorized through writing (and listed in the references), whilst other forms of contact will be missing, will be erased, even though they may leave their trace.[73]

Evidentiary hierarchies are flattened in alternate archives-as-contact zones, allowing the curator to interpret contact as material and immaterial, institutional and non-institutional, textual, oral, temporary, etc., centralizing curatorial positionality a factor in the collection. An archive of contact speaks to what we do with objects and what those objects do to us, and how our own passive and active material and immaterial "doing" creates the archive. Ahmed's alternative archive is one where she considers objects, their cultural life, the affective current developed between curator/object and researcher/object, and the emotional resonance of "doing" archival work contributes to the totality of the alternative archive itself.

Similar to Ahmed's archive of contacts is Cvetkovich's alternative archive of emotion. In *An Archive of Feelings*, Cvetkovich creates alternate archives of emotions that construct the everyday. The "archive of feelings" is a mode of understanding cultural texts as a depository of the feelings and emotions both encoded in these texts and generated from their production, use, and reception.[74] She describes:

> The archive of feelings therefore holds many kinds of documents, both ephemeral and material. It has its own forms of unabashed sentimentality [. . .] But it also documents those moments when it is not possible to feel anything and when something other than a familiar or clichéd scene is necessary to conjure sentiment. [. . .] Sometimes the

archive contains tears and anger, and sometimes it includes the dull silence of numbness. Its feelings can belong to one nation or many, and they are both intimate and public. They can make one feel totally alone, but in being made public, they are revealed to be part of a shared experience of the social.[75]

As feelings, emotions, and use evolve across space and time, archives of feelings necessarily evolve along with them. Cvetkovich's conception of an alternative archive is not meant to exist permanently; it directly refutes long-term preservation beyond the materials that are curated at any given time. These materials then, like the text *An Archive of Feelings* itself, serve both as a product of the archive Cvetkovich has created, as well as a type of archive in and of itself. Archives of feeling are archives of survival.

The archive of feelings is tangible, intangible, and personal. The imbrications of feelings and emotions generated as a result of reception and use, the materiality of cultural texts, and their histories of production allow for an archive that will vary with each creator, and even vary within creators. This is a particularly useful idea when thinking through the creation of alternative filmic archives, as it acknowledges that a significant part of the archival life of any given historical artifact is the cultural life it inhabits. Film, once released from the machine of industrial production into the cultural world, develops its own life across space and time. This allows for developments in feeling, emotions, and experiences that evolve the conception of a singular object history into a multiplicity of histories, which aids in accounting for transformations in spectatorship, reception, exhibition, and memory as the film moves through culture.

These scholars provide innovative modes of archival construction and cultural analysis as spaces of scholarly disidentification. If traditional archives and the scholarship they engender normalize protocols of academic inquiry, interventionalists engage scholarly disidentification as a tool for anti-hegemonic knowledge production. "Disidentification is the third mode of dealing with dominant ideology, one that neither opts to assimilate within such a structure nor strictly opposes it; rather, disidentification is a strategy that works on and against dominant ideology."[76] Alternate archives, created to address the gaps and erasures of traditional archives, take up this third way, generating new cultural repositories and fundamentally altering what we understand "archive" to signify at all.[77] Inspired by the examples that wrought this third way into scholarly being, I compiled an institutionally disidentified repository of materials: the Rothman archive.

OF ORPHANS AND ARCHIVES OF OUR OWN

My research into Stephanie Rothman began in earnest in 2011 in a film historiography graduate seminar and quickly morphed into an initial three-year curatorial period and a secondary seven-year period of ad hoc additions. In all honesty, my dedication to curating a Rothman archive was driven by irritation in many ways: I was *annoyed* I didn't have access to more Rothman-related material, and a combination of that exasperation, as well as a sense of excitement, spurred me on. Cari Beauchamp articulates this feeling well when reflecting on her critical work on screenwriter Frances Marion: "I became frustrated, irritated and eventually inspired by the fact that I could find so little on women whose names I recognized from the credits of films I loved. I began what soon became a mission to excavate their stories."[78] While Rothman was occasionally the subject of press and critical writing while working and immediately after, a significant cache of primary and secondary sources that considered her labor and body of work was noticeably absent. Rothman moved "in and out of textual existence,"[79] and I set out to do what I could to stabilize her presence.

While some of this work took place in institutional archives like the library at the University of Illinois, Urbana-Champaign, and the Margaret Herrick Library of the Academy of Motion Picture Arts and Sciences, most of it was a process of historical scavenging. Passing references to Rothman speaking at film festivals motivated emails to festival organizers for transcripts, flyers, programs—copies of anything they retained. Very kind strangers responded sometimes with a repository of information and often with regrets. I followed a newspaper article to a previously undiscovered journal article, and then to a long-archived blog post Rothman wrote on a cult movie fan website. One sentence in a popular press book on fellow exploitation director Jack Hill referenced a defunct movie journal: three months and eight dollars later, I owned a copy of the three-part history the journal wrote about *Blood Bath/Track of the Vampire*. The more I looked outside library walls, the more material I found. Eventually, after the delicate courtship of six months of emails, I was in Stephanie Rothman's home having the first of many conversations—formal and informal—I was to have with the director. Toward this end, I eventually amassed 114 primary and secondary textual sources, two formal interviews, and over 100 email messages. This type of breadcrumb research isn't unusual—indeed, far from it. But it *felt* thrilling.

My guiding principle in curating a Rothman archive was not simply to pull together the information necessary to wedge her into existing film history. Indeed, "merely to introduce women into the dominant notion of film history, yet another series of "facts" to be assimilated into the existing notions of chronology, would quite clearly be sterile and regressive. "History is not some abstract thing which bestows significance on past events in retrospect."[80] Rather, its collation was inspired by Cvetkovich's archives of survival: survival for Rothman's career, her films, for the idea of women filmmakers, and for the potential for women to exist in hegemonically masculinized spaces. The archive became a living, breathing entity, simultaneously offering more proof of women's directorial competency across the long arcs of film histories and exemplifying why that fact must be repetitively validated. Yet, as an archive of survival, the Rothman archive is also an archive of possibility.

Perhaps the trickiest aspect of this process was screening all of Rothman's films. Attempts to screen Rothman's films highlighted the tenacious issues in film preservation broadly, and the perpetuation of marginal films like second wave exploitation more specifically. Filmic preservation wrestles with the same questions of power, control, and subjectivity that haunt all archives while also subject to industrial and material roadblocks. The earliest significant film archives emerged in the 1930s in Western Europe and the United States, established by cultural institutions like the British Film Institute (BFI) and the Museum of Modern Art (MoMA).[81] Hollywood studios and other commercial film production companies were largely uninterested in film preservation after initial distribution and subsequent theatrical runs until the 1950s, primarily because there were no economic imperatives to preservation. This changed with the introduction and mass adoption of television as companies realized they could repurpose their older films as television products, providing secondary economic value.[82] Due to the late start of film preservation, it is estimated that "fewer than half of the feature films made before 1950 have survived, and less than 20% survived from the 1920s."[83]

The Science and Technology Council of the Academy of Motion Picture Arts and Sciences state that celluloid film, properly stored, is far and away the most effective and cost-efficient preservation method.[84] The result is such that the best options for preservation are based in maintaining the materiality of film prints. For researchers, however, material prints present issues of access: the researcher needs the time and financial ability to travel to film archives, often multiple times, across the globe to interact with their object of study. The materiality of filmic archives is the film historian's boon and curse: the stability of new preservation methods has saved hundreds of thousands of films from destruction, but access to them, and by proxy their study, is restricted by physical location and the researcher's ability to access that location.

Technological advances have increased distant access to film archives, but new technologies are not a panacea for issues of preservation and researcher access. Digitization for celluloid prints, what Giovanna Fossanti calls "film born" as they originated on and are preserved through celluloid,[85] is a difficult proposition. Digitizing film born prints requires vast digital storage space. A single "35mm film with a running time of 90 minutes, once digitized, can reach 1.5 to 6 terabytes and more of data, depending on the scanning resolution."[86] Recurring costs for digitizing are high. Data storage, lack of standardization in digital formats, data migration, and new purchases necessitated by rapid hard and software obsolescence, and the requisite training in digital preservation all contribute to the high economic cost of film archive digitization.[87]

Ontological concerns compound the practical and material issues. Fossanti:

> Caught up in everyday practicalities, film archivists rarely have time to reflect on the nature of film and on the consequences deriving from new technologies on the viability of film as a medium. On the other hand, researchers investigating the ontology of the medium theorize future scenarios at a much faster pace than practice can keep up with, often without considering the material and the institutional realities underlying the medium. This situation is leading to an increasing estrangement between theory and practice.[88]

These missing conversations and their associative estrangements often result in theorists and researchers working at cross archival purposes. For example, as the academic study of exploitation and adult film grows, researchers face significant roadblocks from the intersection of archival practice and cultural taste. Eric Schaefer notes that the preservation of adult films is a risky proposition exacerbated by adult films' pejorative cultural reputation as unimportant.[89] While adult film and second wave exploitation films are not reducible to one another, they share similarities around cultural importance. It is not difficult to see how logics of non-preservation for adult films are similar to those that led to the mass loss of exploitation film prints: the assigned cultural cachet of the films did not justify the time, space, and expense required to preserve them.

One example of how creative filmic archival practices can sidestep both archivist/research disunity and narrowed notions of cultural importance is the orphan film movement. Orphan films are "any film whose future is in jeopardy—due to its diminished status in film history and its low priority in the usual operations of the archive."[90] In the early 1990s, the term "orphan" was bound up in legal distinctions of US copyright laws,[91] but soon took on broader implications than loss of copyright (read: parent), as Heidi Solbrig explains:

> The orphan genre as a designator also tends to indicate that these were films that had been deemed, at one time or another, less valuable and disposable—ephemera in the timeline of culture. The orphan cinema movement has encouraged scholars to examine these films as cultural artifacts whose production, distribution, and exhibition—as well as the texts themselves—can tell stories about communities, institutions, governmental initiatives, and educational and social movements.[92]

Operationally, the orphan film movement exists within institutional, alternative, and impermanent archives. Archivist and scholar Rick Prelinger founded one of the first repositories of orphan films in 1982. The Prelinger Archives, a "collection of ephemeral films, including advertising, industrial, educational, amateur, and documentary films that depict everyday U.S. life and culture throughout the 20th century,"[93] amassed over 60,000 films before the physical collection was obtained by the Library of Congress, Motion Picture, Broadcasting and Recorded Sound Division, in 2002.[94] Prelinger has made over 6,500 titles available for download and use on the Internet Archive, a free, online, nonprofit library. Lastly, the biennial Orphan Film Symposium creates spaces for viewing and inquiry, furthering the broader goal of the orphan film movement.

Constructing the archive as an orphanage has the power to transform it from site of sanctioned remembrance to living repository of "forgotten, abandoned images and texts."[95] This expands the range of film history by examining cultural histories of the ordinary or forgotten, rather than focusing solely on master works.[96] The orphanage approaches filmic archives outside strict institutionality by offering new "storytelling techniques that challenge traditional linear narratives by juxtaposing fragments of aural and visual testimony of a time, people, and place."[97] While the orphan film movement doesn't eschew institutional archives, it reminds us that expansive and accessible filmic archives allow for a more dynamic and generative production of film histories.

EMBRACING IMPERMANENCE

Combining the ethos of the orphan film and pathos of Cvetkovich's impermanent archives, I jettisoned my idealistic idea of "original" films and began amassing Rothman's material output as a collection of the available now rather than the static past. This meant welcoming varied multiple filmic and material realities. Rather than a detriment to curation, this process more closely mirrored the life of the films themselves. Second wave exploitation films were, more often than not, exhibited in versions far from their original. Exhibited over a number of years and altered exhibitor to exhibitor through the addition and deletion of footage, the exhibitive structure these films inhabited were often quite different than their original print. If my goal was to understand these films and their influence as cultural products, conceptualizing them as iterative as opposed to fixed texts was crucial.

Rothman never had physical control of the original negatives of her films—they belonged to the production companies she worked for—and most of them have disappeared over time.[98] This means that copies of her films available to purchase are most often made from prints with unknown provenance, which is not uncommon for exploitation films. The Museum of Modern Art and the Academy of Motion Picture Arts and Sciences have both undertaken restorations of some Rothman films from found prints or, in the case of *The Student Nurses*, from negatives donated by producer Roger Corman himself. Despite this, many of her films are publicly available in variable states of deterioration, may have sustained heavy edits, or are not available at all.[99] During my research, the most difficult titles to find were Rothman's early films; *Blood Bath/Track of the Vampire* was virtually unavailable publicly. Eventually, a very kind friend found a copy on a torrent website. The file was very obviously missing several scenes; large chunks of the film hastily edited out resulted in giant leaps in time and narrative. A fan edit found at the same time had sections of pornographic sex, obviously from a different film, spliced into *Blood Bath/Track of the Vampire* but had also clearly been made from the previously discovered torrent; it was missing the same sections of film. Both versions are contemporary representations of the historical exhibitive life of exploitation films: missing scenes, added sensationalism, and dubious distribution methods. They also mirrored the idea of object stickiness embedded in Ahmed's affective archives—the edits, the missing footage, the illegal distribution, and viewing illuminating the stickiness of cultural life these products accumulate as living material objects.

The search for *It's a Bikini World* raised another issue that troubles present-day home video distribution of second wave exploitation films. After finding the title available from various distribution companies, I did as much due diligence as possible to purchase the film from a company with a solid reputation for delivering on the promise of their content. When the DVD arrived, it was a burned disc containing a version of the film that had been played on the cable station Turner Classic Movies (TCM). The film clearly had been edited; about fifteen minutes of the later section of the movie was gone with no thought toward narrative or visual continuity. I don't know if the edits were native to the print TCM showed, were made by the network as a "cut for time," or if the edits were made by the company selling the disc. Alterations like this are common as "the commercial video enterprises will often release a film regardless of condition. In many instances, their offerings are washed-out, splicey dupes that were destined for the dumpster."[100]

The University of Los Angeles (UCLA) Film & Television Archive had copies of several of Rothman's films. However, the process of accessing them speaks to a critical issue in the development of a Rothman archive, and more broadly to the feasibility of conducting scholarly research into marginalized filmmakers, films, or the industrial spheres: the economic cost of scholarship. Often ignored, hushed, or cause for neoliberal embarrassment, the economics of cinema studies research is a salient and pressing issue particularly for junior scholars and any scholars working with marginalia. Digitization is not a curative; the effectiveness of celluloid preservation upholds physical access to archives as routinely necessary for cinema studies research. The economic cost of archival research must be taken into account. This is of the utmost importance when considering the restitution of film laborers of difference. The corporatization of the neoliberal university squeezes funds that support research travel, particularly for graduate students and junior scholars that are not invested in economically derivate scholarship. The American Academy of Arts & Sciences reports that between 2005 and 2015, "spending for humanities research equaled 0.7% of the amount dedicated to science and engineering."[101] The costs of archival research—travel and accommodations, access costs, funds for reproducing materials, and more—can be quite high, with the potential to climb into the thousands of dollars depending on where the archive is located.

These issues impact researchers and archives. For example, UCLA archives held several of Rothman's films on 35mm. In order to view the films, they had to be transferred from celluloid to tape. The cost of the transfer and overall archival management costs blocked the archive from transferring any film publicly available for purchase, regardless of price. This is a critical distinction; at the time I was doing this research, the only available DVD of *The Student Nurses* was $80, adding a necessary but significant cost to my research budget.[102] The only films I was able to have transferred were the two hardest to obtain: *Blood Bath* and *It's a Bikini World*. The transfers were made from prints donated to the archives from MGM, who had obtained them from American International Pictures as TV prints edited for content and time. As for the other Rothman films the collection held, it remains to be seen in what version they exist. I was able to travel to archives halfway across the country in small part from departmental funding, but primarily because I am exceedingly privileged to have a network of friends who let me stay in their homes, drive their cars, and eat their food.[103] This necessarily begs critical questions: at what point is the cost of archival research, especially for junior scholars, too high? And when the cost of archival research continues to rise as the rate of funding decreases, what are the economic impacts of archival work, and how do those impacts foreclose new and generative research?

The archive is not a solvable problem, but it does force us to consider creative and proactive ways to work around the roadblocks it often places in the researcher's path. To that end, I've included as an appendix in this book transcripts of two interviews I conducted with Rothman and selections of our email correspondence; my hope is that other scholars may be able to use these documents in their work around Rothman and her films in the ways they see fit. This book should be the first, not the only, work dedicated to Rothman, and it is my responsibility as feminist interventionist scholar to do what I can to allow others take up that work. It's my hope that this step towards collaboration can aid other scholars and overcome some of the persistent issues archival research engenders. This appendix is far from a totalizing solution, but feminist interventions must be built on collaboration and mutual aid in all forms.

Chapter 3

MARGIN AND CENTER

Locating Second Wave Exploitation in US Film History

> As a film historian, I must be, first of all, not a historian at all. I am a natural and cultural being who has, for irrelevant biographical and psychological reasons, hardly apparent to myself, shaped a life in large part after the representation afforded to me in motion pictures, or rather, certain movies.
> —DUDLEY ANDREW[1]

To lay bare the links between women's directorial labor and its rhetorical constructions, exploitation film, and contemporary labor—and how the career and legacy of Stephanie Rothman exemplifies these connections—I must articulate second wave exploitation as the particular filmic circumstances Rothman worked in. To that end, this chapter establishes second wave exploitation film as a discrete filmic cycle within the historical context of exploitation film and the broader US film industry.

As foundation for the historical time and space of second wave exploitation film I am interested in—the US from 1960 to 1980—I briefly review classical exploitation, a critical progenitor. I move then to the evolution of second wave exploitation, its intersections with classical exploitation as its past, the rise of the foreign film movement in the US as its contemporary, and its overlap with the rise of the Hollywood blockbuster as its future. In tracing this course, I will attend to the various aspects of the production of film as an industrial art, including content, production, economics, distribution, and exhibition practices. Second wave exploitation is often reduced to analysis through these individual elements in siloed understandings; my goal here is to map their intersections, creating a three-dimensional portrait of the cycle.

The outline of my historiographic process is strategically specific. Film historiography is fraught, often overwhelmed by the preoccupation of its own function. Oscillating between the history of film as the history of individualized elements—culture, economics, aesthetics, or technologies—film histories run the risk of privileging a singular focus. This is an unfortunate reality, as the multivariate function of film history limits itself when it places multiple historical factors in opposition rather than conversation. As a result of these tensions, film history as form has produced siloed variations of histories and counter histories, separate but ostensibly equal.

Film historiographies also bear the burden of the emotional investment of their authors. Dudley Andrew's epigraph in the chapter's opening importantly pinpoints the role of the historian in film histories as partly motivated by their affective attachment to film and their own filmic consciousness. Acknowledging the dual composition of the film historian as subjective viewer and objective historian is critical in articulating how film histories are constructed. As Vivian Sobchack explains:

> Indeed, the practice and writing of film history are bound irreducibly to our current consciousness of "history" and its representation in general—and that consciousness has been complicated by our own historically-altered sense of what "being-in-time" in relation to "the past" feels like and what it means in a culture of pervasive massmediation and "present" second-hand experience.[2]

The temporal relationships Sobchack references here are critical to understanding how complicated film historiography can be. Film acts as a preservative for the futurity of visual images, bringing the past into the present, collapsing the distance between the two, and allowing film historians to experience the past within the present as its own type of contemporary moment. This particular feature complicates the very idea of film history as history. If, as Paolo Cherchi Usai posits, "moving images arise out of intent to transform into an object whatever is forgettable and therefore doomed to decay and oblivion,"[3] then each film in and of itself is its own micro-history, encompassing the variables of culture, economics, production, technology, and art in a singularly defined spatial and temporal moment. In this sense, film history is the process that transforms these micro-histories into macro-formations, narrating the overarching ontology of film.

These constructions of the form and function of film histories contextualize my own historiographic compositions, influenced by media archaeology. Media archaeology is critical specifically because of its methodological embeddedness in, as Wolfgang Ernst says, an "epistemologically alternative approach to the supremacy of media-historical narratives."[4] This allows my historical narratives to acknowledge the constant interchange of time, where the past reaches forward to the present, the present speaks back to the past, and where temporalities function as genealogies, not chronologies. Here, then, I take inspiration from Thomas Elsaesser's formulation of film history as media archeology as a compass to conceptualize and narrate the history of second wave exploitation.

Elsaesser advocates for film history as media archaeology, using historiographic and ontological processes to disrupt divisions between historical stages, thereby integrating points of view formerly deemed disparate. It is worth quoting Elsaesser at length here:

> The project of a "film history as media archaeology" is thus intended to liberate from their straight-jackets all those re-positionings of linear chronology that operate with hard binaries between, for instance, early cinema and classical cinema, spectacle versus narrative, linear narrative versus interactivity. Instead, film history would acknowledge its peculiar status, and become a matter of tracing paths or laying tracks leading from the respective "now" to different pasts, in modalities that accommodate continuities as well as ruptures. We would then be mapping media-convergence and self-differentiation not in terms of either a teleology or a search for origins, but in the form of forking paths of possibility, i.e., as a determined plurality and a permanent virtuality.[5]

This plurality—of time, space, potentiality, and directionality—is how I ground second wave exploitation film: a discrete filmic cycle that simultaneously flows from, into, around, and through cycles that existed before, alongside, and after it. Elsaesser identifies the specific challenge of attempting this type of work as being able to locate "a place that is not fixed in respect to either position or direction, one that permits space to coexist and time frames to overlap."[6] As existing neither in the margins nor center of the filmic spectrum, second wave exploitation embodies this possibility. Consequently, this allows second wave exploitation to emerge as a discrete entity rather than simply a remnant of classical exploitation or a poor imitation of classical Hollywood filmmaking, as previously scholarship has classified it.

While my narrative construction involves periodization, it is not used to divide time concretely. Rather, periodization aids in highlighting when in time each of the phases I address were ascendant and descendent, mapping their flows and reciprocal nodes of influence. By incorporating periodization within the spectrum of a past, present, and future of second wave exploitation, time can be used to signpost—rather than divide—phases of development and evolution.

EXPLOITATION FOUNDATIONS

Like any cultural product, exploitation films did not arise in a vacuum. Their piecemeal progenitors include carnivals and burlesque, the prefilmic visuality of World's Fair exhibits, social and political movements, and early fiction and nonfiction film production. Given this eclectic set of influences sitting alongside the numerous tributaries exploitation film flowed through, it is critical to note that the term "exploitation" cannot be fashioned as a monolithic category across space and time. While many of the industrial practices built into early exploitation production remained consistent over the course of its evolution, there have been significant changes in its content, function, style, audience, and role in the industrial landscape as exploitation has shifted from phase to phase.

Precisely because of the term's simultaneous consistencies and inconsistencies, it is best understood in connective phases rather than in totality. The first phase of exploitation was well detailed in Eric Schaefer's watershed *Bold! Daring! Shocking! True! A History of Exploitation Films, 1919–1959*. Whereas previous scholarship on exploitation film was focused on its status as cinematic abnormality,[7] Schaefer worked historiographically, attempting—if not always successfully—to move past the aesthetics and taste judgments that had previously plagued the minimal study of exploitation film and constructed a history that worked to locate the exploitation paradigm in time, space, and industry.

In the late 1910s and 1920s, when the growing Hollywood industry was coalescing into a vertically integrated system, exploitation filmmaking paralleled classical Hollywood, existing outside of the auspices of any major studio.[8] The films were first and foremost identifiable by their focus on socially taboo content, the major areas of which Schaefer notes included "sex, and sex hygiene, prostitution and vice, drug use, nudity, and any other subjects considered at the time to be in bad taste."[9] This focus on spectacle had a direct and disruptive impact on the style and narrative cohesion of exploitation films, positioning them in diametrical contrast to classical Hollywood films and traditional documentaries.[10] While spectacle still existed in Hollywood films like musicals, it existed to advance the film's narrative function within the filmic diegesis. In exploitation, narrative was a pretense for spectacle, and that spectacle would seep past narrative constraints, distorting the mise-en-scène and overall diegesis.

This function of spectacle was a tremendous audience draw and configured exploitation films as drastically different from conventional Hollywood fare. As a result, there was no difficulty differentiating the two filmic and aesthetic styles. Schaefer notes that, for exploitation films, the "reliance on spectacle as organizing principle forged their squalid style and resulted in an experience for the spectator that can best be described as delirium [. . .] exploitation films could be 'bad' because there was no compelling need for them to be 'good.'"[11] Always industrially liminal, exploitation films were a hybrid of attraction and feature, loosely wrapping the narrative function of a feature *around* the spectacle at the core of the cinema of attractions.

The expectation of spectacle was high for audiences, in large part because of the aggressive and hyperbolic ways in which the films were advertised. There were, seemingly, no limits to the advertising tactics of exploitation film, schemes that can trace their influence back to the ballyhoo of carnivals, vaudeville, and burlesque. Among other tactics, scandalous and salacious advertisements, films labeled as "adults only," gimmicks and giveaways, advance men traveling from town to town to hype the films, stressing the "necessary education" the audiences gained from the films, and limited engagements were all used to lure in audiences.[12] Of course, classical exploitation advertisements spotlighted "not necessarily what the films actually showed on screen, but what the audience 'might' see if they paid for a ticket."[13]

As classical exploitation film moved into the 1950s, the industrial landscape began to slowly shift under its feet. The Paramount Decision—the US Supreme Court decision that ended the studio system[14]—threw Hollywood into turmoil. Pioneering exploiters were passing away and censorship regulations became slightly laxer, allowing Hollywood to creep into the content areas formally the province of exploitation. The demographics of audiences were changing, and the rise of television began siphoning off members of the moviegoing public. In this fluctuating environment, the once formulaic world of the classical exploitation industry and its products were changing quickly. By the end of the 1950s, the classical period would be over, giving way to a new generation of exploitation film, one that would move closer to the mainstream and leave an indelible mark on Hollywood for years to come.

RIDING THE SECOND WAVE OF EXPLOITATION (1960-1980)

The 1950s was a decade of overlapping transition for the exploitation paradigm, from which it would emerge transformed by new audiences, new exhibition spaces, and new content areas. Schaeffer has little regard for exploitation films past 1959 and uses them as a straw man of sorts through which he authorizes and legitimizes classical exploitation as "outsider" cinema. Reflecting on film produced under the exploitation paradigm in the 1950s, he notes:

> Though their budgets may have been closer to those of the classical exploitation films, their stories of juvenile delinquency, hot cars, and rock music were generally even tamer than increasingly controversial movies released by the majors. For audiences, critics, and the film industry itself, it was becoming more difficult to make the distinction between exploitation and mainstream product that had been so clear as little as a decade earlier.[15]

Mapping the transformation in exploitation films not as a break but as an evolution fostered by intersecting vectors allows for more generative and expansive work. Therefore, an exploration of the transitions taking place in the 1950s and 1960s understood as a spectrum of change contextualizes how second wave exploitation is implied and explicates the industrial conditions that germinated Rothman's career.

Rock 'n' Roll in the Passion Pits

Popular cultural memory indexes the 1950s as the decade when the teenager was "discovered" in the US. Less easily recalled is that researchers across multiple disciplines had been developing the concept of adolescence as a distinct phase in human physical, social, and cognitive development since the early 1900s.[16] It wasn't, however, until the 1950s when the idea of the teenager as the incarnation of adolescence reached contemporary everyday usage, promoted in large part by the growing counterculture teenagers were participating in, including the "fad" of rock 'n' roll. Thanks to a growing population—in part the product of a strong economy, the suburbanization of the US, and the increasing emphasis on consumable luxury goods such as cars and television—the teenager became the target for retail and entertainment industries.

The teenager was not the only intrusive cultural force. The popularization of the television as a necessary home amenity grew along with the suburbs, and the comfort and accessibility that came with in-home entertainment began to affect the number of people going to the movies in the 1950s and 1960s. As Paul Monaco notes:

> A high point for movie attendance in the United States was reached in 1946 when an average of 90 million admissions to movie theaters were recorded weekly, constituting a record 75 percent of the estimated "potential audience" nationwide. During the next ten years, however, average weekly attendance dropped rapidly: in 1956, figures set weekly movie theater audience numbers at 46 million; four years later, in 1960, that figure was 40 million; attendance plummeted to 20 million by 1970.[17]

The cinema's new teenager demographic consisted of suburban kids with newfound freedoms—facilitated by easy transportation and disposable cash—motivated towards leisure time and entertainment, preferably away from home and the prying eyes of their parents. Second wave exploitation films would come to be built, in no small part, by catering to this audience.

The term "exploitation," always fluid and dynamic, would metamorphose in the 1950s and beyond. Moving past the classical exploitation traits of narrative as the Trojan horse of spectacle, exploitation film in the 1950s became the teenpic, which would morph into second wave exploitation in the 1960s and 1970s. Teenpics in the 1950s were cheaply made genre films with topical or faddist bents meant to appeal to the teenager market. Barbara Brickman contextualizes:

> As it develops from the mid-1950s to the early-1960s, the teenpic, often B-quality fare from independent producers [. . .], exploited a number of topics or sensational issues. Hundreds of films appeared, with topics ranging from juvenile delinquency and rock n' roll to teenage monsters and drag racing, which turned generic cycles of their own. Made for very little money, these films were produced quickly in order to capitalize on current situations and events.[18]

Leading the way in this transformation was the independent production and distribution company American International Pictures (AIP), founded in 1954 by Jim Nicholson and Samuel Arkoff.[19] Over the years, AIP would become a successful independent production and distribution company on the strength of its position in the second wave exploitation film market across the 1950s and 1960s. The company's first distributed film was *The Fast and the Furious* (John Ireland and Edward Sampson, 1954), produced by a man named Roger Corman.[20] The film marked AIP's foray into the market and the company's first deal with Corman, a partnership that would go on to last over the course of fifteen-plus years and thirty-three films.[21] Corman, now known as the "King of the B's," was a graduate of Stanford University's engineering program who began working in the film industry after leaving the navy. Quickly disillusioned with the low-level studio jobs, he began producing and directing his own pictures. His contract with AIP to distribute *The Fast and the Furious* was a three-picture deal and he continued working with Arkoff and Nicholson until 1969 when, irate with cuts made to a film without his approval, he left to develop his own company, New World Pictures.[22] Although Corman was certainly not the only person making second wave exploitation films, he was likely the most successful, and has come to represent this phase of the exploitation industry.

Corman quickly developed a reputation for working cheaply and quickly, producing films that were financed on the profits of previous releases, much like classical exploitation producers. His primary goal when producing films was to make them as economically efficient as possible to reduce waste and maximize profits. Recalling classical exploitation film production, his crews lacked divisions of labor, actors would play multiple roles in films, rehearsals were unheard of, most anyone who could point a camera could direct, nothing was allowed to run over-schedule or -budget, and—above all—Corman retained ultimate control.

Since his low budgets depended in large part on the return on investment he could earn with untested and inexperienced actors and crew, Corman films became an informal training center for a new crop of actors, directors, writers, and more. What has gone on to be known as the "Corman school" produced some of the Hollywood insiders who would radically reshape the industry in the 1970s and beyond.[23]

The films Corman and company produced were a different type of exploitation film from their predecessors in content, style, and certainly in terms of their positionality within the cinematic landscape. Opposed to classical exploitation, second wave exploitation was less concerned with individual moments of complete spectacle than it was with integrating smaller moments of spectacle into a larger, more formal narrative. It worked to move spectacle away from uniqueness and toward a commonplace filmic existence, thus reducing its very nature as pure spectacle. In this way, second wave exploitation films adhered more closely to the standard Hollywood norms of narrative and form—and as Monaco, Neale, and others note—can be understood as prefiguring contemporary high-concept blockbuster films and their emphasis on the totality of spectacle. Other differences between classical and second wave exploitation included larger budgets in the second wave (although nowhere near mainstream Hollywood size), different audience targets (broad vs. niche), and more conventional stories during the second wave. However, these were still films primarily constructed around hastily written scripts, debatably talented actors, first-time directors, and low budgets; these similarities tied them back to the tradition of classical exploitation.

One of the major differences between classical and second wave exploitation was their space of exhibition. While classic exploitation found exhibitive homes in independently owned hardtop theaters, in the 1950s and 1960s second wave exploitation films became heavily associated with the drive-in theater, a phenomenon that originated in the early 1930s and achieved major popularity in the 1950s.[24] Richard Hollingshead, the creator of the drive-in, visualized them as spaces that catered to families and individuals for whom hardtop theater seats posed accessibility issues: for example, the disabled and the elderly and those customers in rural areas who were cinematically underserved.[25] However, in the 1950s and 1960s drive-ins firmly catered to the suburban teenager subculture and market. The popularity of drive-ins shifted the idea of exactly who comprised the moviegoing public, moving away from families and toward the age demographic of fifteen to twenty-five.[26] Drive-ins courted the teenager audience with spaces for dance floors, per car load (rather than per person) admission prices, late-night double features, and plenty of dark spaces that helped to earn drive-ins a reputation as "passion pits."[27] Second wave exploitation films catered their content to this group, evidenced by films such as *Sorority Girl* (Corman, 1957), *Motorcycle Gang* (Edward L. Cahn, 1957), *I Was a Teenage Werewolf* (Gene Fowler Jr., 1957) and *The Diary of a High School Bride* (Burt Topper, 1959).

Drive-ins could be counted on to consistently book exploitation films. Reaching back to the double-bill exhibitive tactic begun in the 1930s, drive-ins provided a package of material for the price of a single admission. Double features were standard, built on the rationale that the longer the customer remained inside the theater park, the more concessions—the primary revenue source for theaters—they would purchase.[28] Teenpics became a valuable and affordable resource for filling screen time. Interestingly, drive-in double features packages did not usually rank films in terms of A and B offerings, as had been the case in the 1930s and onward in hardtop theaters. Rather, drive-ins tended to screen films on equal billing,[29] which served as a micro repositioning of films produced under the exploitation paradigm within the mainstream cinematic landscape.

Although audiences and exhibition spaces evolved in significant ways from the classical to the second wave era, tried and true methods of distribution remained. The states' rights system,[30] leveraged to great success during classical exploitation, continued as the most effective distributive practice. Roadshowing—the classical exploitation exhibition tactic that marketed a film as a limited run "event" rather than as an extended theatrical engagement—became increasingly antiquated in favor of saturation booking. Saturation booking, the practice of booking a film to open simultaneously in as many theaters as possible, became a critical second wave exploitation distribution strategy. It allowed films to quickly recoup their costs, generate profit, and avoid declining audiences for subsequent showings based on negative word of mouth.

The aggressive and lurid sensationalism attached to marketing campaigns would remain consistent across phases and would play an increasingly active role in shaping second wave exploitation content. Progressively, exploitation production companies would concoct film titles and advertisements *before* the movie itself, and then attempt to structure the film to fit into the campaign.[31] More often than not, the finished product and the campaign did not match; occasionally they came close. For producers, the idea was to get people into the theaters; fulfilling audience expectations would be nice, but not necessary. After all, they had already paid their admission.

The push toward the teenager market as the regular and desirable demographic solidified in the 1960s. As movie attendance steadily dropped, particularly in the once solid middle-aged women demographic, the remaining moviegoing public was routinely represented by a constituency that was distinctly younger and progressively male.[32] By catering to this audience, second wave exploitation flourished. Keeping with a faddist and topical bent, the 1960s saw exploitation films in new cycles: beach movies like William Asher's 1965 films *Beach Blanket Bingo* and *How to Stuff a Wild Bikini* and Rothman's *It's a Bikini World* (1967); motorcycle gang movies like *The Wild Angels* (Roger Corman, 1966) and *The Born Losers* (Tom Laughlin, 1967); and psychedelic movies like *The Trip* (Roger Corman, 1967) and *Riot on Sunset Strip* (Arthur Dreifuss, 1967).

As the 1960s wore on and the teenager subculture turned into the hippie counterculture, second wave exploitation films increasingly became a place where the cultural zeitgeist was manifest and beamed out to the masses. Steadily, contentious social issues were creeping into exploitation. After the phenomenon that was *Easy Rider* (Dennis Hopper, 1969), a film born out of the exploitation industry but produced and distributed by Columbia Pictures,

Hollywood could not afford to marginalize the exploitation industry. Here again, the dynamic and flexible understanding of "exploitation" is highlighted. As Paul Monaco describes:

> the low-budget films of Roger Corman, producer/director at American International Pictures, best defines the directions in which feature films were going after the mid 1960s. Adolescents and young adults who had been raised in the American suburbs of the late 1950s and early 1960s favored eclectic and slightly rebellious films, ranging from horror to softcore sex movies to action-adventure films populated with characters whose screen presence invariably expressed some measure of alienation and existential *angst*.[33]

These changes wrought another evolution of the exploitation label, what I call "nichesploitation": films branded through a portmanteau algorithm which affixed a prefix to the word exploitation that served to describe what aspect of culture or identity the film was focused on "exploiting." Teenpics transformed into sexploitation, hippiesploitation, Blaxploitation, nunsploitation, hicksploitation, and many more. The nichesploitation of second wave exploitation films was regularized, so much so that many of Rothman's films were categorized as such—*The Student Nurses* and *The Working Girls* as sexploitation, *Terminal Island* as Blaxploitation, for example—despite the fact the films didn't really meet the criteria of their classification. Regardless, nichesploitation and its implications would come to define second wave exploitation films in the 1970s.

CAPTURING CULTURAL CHANGE

The United States in the 1970s was a decade that bore the positive and negative fallout of the 1960s. As a result, the 1970s brought massive social change: the normalization of birth control pills; the upward growth in size of the antiwar movement and its correlative downward growth in effectiveness; the full-scale escalation of the conflict in Vietnam; the Stonewall riots; governmental suppression of civil rights groups and their leaders; Watergate and Nixon's impeachment; second wave feminism; the 1973 *Roe v. Wade* decision; and much more.[34] These examples define a decade swirling around multiplicities of identities, and a time where "discrete codifications of identity and of cultural energies came to dominate our lives."[35] These codifications of identity became glaringly apparent in the exploitation films of the 1970s, whose narratives became increasingly focused on the commodification of race, sex, and violence, almost to the exclusion of any other narrative organizational device. Exemplifying this are the three types of exploitation film that would come to define the decade: Black action films (or Blaxploitation film), martial arts films, and sexploitation films. Martial arts films were primarily dubbed imports produced by the Shaw Brothers and other Hong Kong producers, which would appear both in theaters and on television. Blaxploitation, however, was reserved primarily for the theatergoing audience.

Stephanie Dunn recounts that Blaxploitation films relied on "historic and contemporary race, gender, and sexual mythologies to affect exhilarating sensationalist racial dramas."[36] They featured primarily, if not exclusively, Black casts; often took place in cities; positioned contemporary clothes, music, and language as part of the necessary cultural life of Black Americans; contained significant amounts of nudity, sex, drugs, and violence; espoused ideas and concerns germane to the Black population; and importantly, allowed Black men and women to be heroes. Independent producers spearheaded Blaxploitation films, and early entries into the cycle include *Sweet Sweetback's Baadasssss Song* (Melvin Van Peebles, 1971), *The Spook Who Sat by the Door* (Ivan Dixon, 1973), and *Black Mama White Mama* (Eddie Romero, 1973). Critically, a significant number of the early independent Blaxploitation films would be directed by Black filmmakers. Blaxploitation films had, and still have, a difficult reputation among Black critics and audiences and the larger moviegoing public. For some, Dunn notes, they are a "hotly contested site over the proliferation of negative black imagery," and for others, they can provide a fantastical space for "the reversal of the racial and/or patriarchal status quo, tapping into the social reality of racial oppression and racial tensions."[37]

Regardless of reception of the politics of Blaxploitation films, they exemplify the significant changes in content of second wave exploitation films in the 1970s and the types of populations they were showcasing. Historically, marginalized groups were beginning to find their voice in exploitation films and changing the types of narratives—and filmmakers—active within the exploitation paradigm. Similarly, the 1970s saw the apex of the sexploitation filmic cycle that helped to transform and complicate the position of gendered and sexualized subjects in second wave exploitation by providing alternate representation of spectacularized female bodies and sexual agency through gradations of difference in representation.

Sexploitation films are heavily invested in the spectacularization of women's lives and bodies and present this spectacle in simultaneously celebratory and uneasy ways. While Elena Gorfinkel's *Lewd Looks* is an exceptional history and analysis of sexploitation films, they are worth briefly exploring here as pivotal objects of second wave exploitation. Produced primarily in New York and Los Angeles, sexploitation films were a short-lived phenomenon appearing primarily in the 1960s and 1970 identifiable by their "crude mise-en-scène, sensationalist narratives of sex and its discontents, and aggressively lurid marketing strategies."[38] While superficially built in explicit service of the male gaze, sexploitation films "imagined the experience of women as they contended with the possibility of erotic and economic autonomy."[39] Narratives often concerned bored or unfulfilled women who ventured into sexual curiosity and experimentation, including sex work, and were then brutalized by men as an extension of patriarchal punishment. While nudity was presented on screen, explicit sex often took place outside of the frame. However, the focus on women's motivations, desires, and bodies squarely positioned the defining factor of sexploitation films to be a "'problem' of female erotic agency and subjectivity."[40]

Sexploitation films were the evolution of prior attempts to integrate visible nudity and sex, rather than just their suggestion, on screen. Early ventures include the nudist camp film and the nudie cutie, both of which were tame exhibitionist fare.[41] As these films grew in popularity, producers and directors yearned to increase their salacious content. Restrained by censorship regulations, more explicit nudity and sex was not a readily accessible option.[42] As a result, the films began progressively adding violence, transforming into "roughies" or "kinkies." Roughies, epitomized by Russ Meyer's *Lorna* (1964), were equal parts sex and sexualized violence. Kinkies increased sensationalism by adding "perversions" into the formula.[43]

Once again, the exhibitive spaces of second wave exploitation films shifted around Blaxploitation and sexploitation films. Although drive-in theaters had boomed in the 1950s, by the 1970s they were in steady decline.[44] By the late 1960s and 1970s, drive-ins as spaces of second wave exploitation exhibition were being replaced by urban grindhouse theaters, that is, formerly mainstream theaters, rapidly declining due to changes in the population and demographics of their locations, that were screening exploitation in a last-ditch effort to keep their doors open.

Sexploitation films' connection with urban space was deeper than just their exhibitive space in grindhouse theaters; city space became integral to their construction. Films were set in anonymous apartment buildings and showcased exteriors easily recognizable as New York City, and the idea of "the city" would come to play a critical role in character definition. The women of sexploitation films were those urbanites who had succumbed to the temptations and degradations of the city, rewarded for bucking traditional gendered roles with violence, debasement, rape, and often, death. The link with New York City, and in particular the seedy and dangerous spatiality of Times Square in the 1960s and 1970s—the literal and mythical center of the grindhouse exhibition circuit—would be endemically connected with sexploitation.

Linking sexploitation to urbanity and the city elucidates how female bodies were positioned in sexploitation films, and how the films themselves attempted to deal with the "problems" of female sexual desire and agency. Gorfinkel contextualizes:

> As a cinema inordinately preoccupied with the dangers posed by the sexual autonomy of women, particularly as they became unbound from domestic and reproductive space in a post-Kinsey era of the birth control pill, Helen Gurley Brown's "single girl," and the stirrings of sexual liberation, sexploitation often capitalized on the trope of the small-town girl in the big metropolis and, in a moralistic, leering register, would entail the degradations that would inevitably befall the naive and the unwitting when caught in the grip of the "naked city."[45]

Superficially, these films may seem aggressively negative toward women as gendered and sexual beings. However, sexploitation was not afraid to promise pleasure in spectacularized female bodies and then forcefully deny that pleasure to the audience, simultaneously indicating their initial desires.[46]

Sexploitation and Blaxploitation films alike signaled new types of cultural narrative in second wave exploitation in the 1970s. Indicators of rapidly changing sociocultural contexts, these shifts were felt across the broader cinematic landscape, reverberating through the mainstream Hollywood industrial complex. It would not be long, then, until Hollywood began to look at second wave exploitation seriously, particularly as an opportunity for content cooption and economic gain.

SECOND WAVE EXPLOITATION AS TRANSITORY INDUSTRIAL SPACE

As earlier established, some scholars have characterized classical exploitation as a necessarily separate industry from classical Hollywood. However, as I gestured to earlier, second wave exploitation had a much more fluid history of integration with the mainstream industry. Thus, I conceptualize second wave exploitation as an open and fluid transitory industrial space, located neither centrally nor completely separate from mainstream Hollywood. This fluidity fostered an evolution of style, content, and distribution strategies that positioned second wave exploitation films as a liminal space between the "outsider" status of classical exploitation and mainstream Hollywood cinema.

Transitory multiplicities existed between the second wave exploitation industry and its mainstream Hollywood counterpart in various ways. Critically, artistic and creative professionals worked across both industries. Exemplified by *Easy Rider* and the rise of the cadre of professionals comprising the "New Hollywood," second wave exploitation served as a "training ground" for up-and-coming Hollywood professionals.[47] Corman began his career in the studio system and, prior to forming New World Pictures, would variously work with Hollywood studios to distribute a selection of his films. Although directors like Coppola and Scorsese came out of established film schools with ties to the mainstream industry, they found initial work in exploitation, an eventual springboard to mainstream success for both.[48] Writer and director Peter Bogdanovich was an established film critic before working behind the camera for Corman. Actor Dennis Hopper made his film debuts in two studio features, *Rebel Without a Cause* (Nicholas Ray, 1955) and *Giant* (George Stevens, 1956), before being ensconced in second wave exploitation. The professional flow was multidirectional and frequent; individuals would move back and forth between second wave exploitation and mainstream Hollywood. This type of movement bolstered Rothman's belief that she would be able to move from second wave exploitation to mainstream Hollywood. Although Rothman was unable to make that jump, many others who trained in the "Corman school" would become the backbone of New Hollywood, while former Hollywood stars whose advance in age or decline in popularity made securing mainstream work almost impossible would end their careers in second wave exploitation. Classic Hollywood stars, including Vincent Price, Boris Karloff, and Joan Crawford, would all find subsequent careers in second wave exploitation.

During classical exploitation, this type of crossover was exceedingly rare. As Maitland McDonagh notes, professionals "might end their careers in exploitation, but exploitation didn't parlay their experience into mainstream Hollywood careers. Once an outsider, always an outcast; to make films beyond the mainstream was to be tainted, slightly disreputable in a culture predicated on the image of respectability."[49] Second wave exploitation upended this stigma, as professionals fluidly crossed, and further blurred, the boundaries between the two industries. It is, however, critical to note that this fluidity was primarily accessible to male professionals; subsequent chapters will detail the difference in opportunity for a woman working in second wave exploitation.

Additionally, second wave exploitation films intersected with Hollywood in their simultaneous emphasis on the figure of the producer. This is an area where all three industries—classical and second wave exploitation, as well as Hollywood—found commonality. Producers in exploitation phases were the main drivers of production, distribution, and exhibition; the "talent" came and went while producers held steadfast. The names most often associated with exploitation in both phases—Esper, Sonny and Friedman, Corman, Arkoff, and Nicholson—were first and foremost producers.

The classical Hollywood studio system was also increasingly producer driven, even as the classical period waned.[50] The director-management system that dominated until early Hollywood would shift significantly to a producer-management system, standardized between 1930–1960;[51] producers like David O. Selznick and Irving Thalberg became household names. The 1970s would see the rise of the mainstream Hollywood "super producer," exemplified by Paramount's Robert Evans, corresponding with the mainstream peak of second wave exploitation and the producer's importance within it.

A companionate of artistic and creative professionals and the emphasis on the figure of the producer were not the only associations between the two industries during this period. Second wave exploitation would go on to provide a pivotal service to the film industry as a whole: replacing B-movies, whose Hollywood studio production decreased with the correlative decline of the drive-in, the double feature, and forced changes in the studio structure. Post-divestiture order, it took time for the studios to reconstruct their operative business models and for studios and the market to feel the full impact of the Paramount decision. In the aftermath of the decree, mandated divestment resulted in studios cutting ancillary production departments as a way to recoup a measure of the staggering profit losses facing them as a result of the elimination of distribution and exhibition from their business models. Tino Balio narrates:

> The majors ceased producing B pictures, shorts, cartoons, and newsreels, and instead concentrated on making fewer and more expensive A pictures. The studio system that had supported the industry since the 1920s went by the boards as companies disposed of their back lots, film libraries, and other assets, and dropped producers, directors, and stars from their payroll.[52]

The phased closures of studio B-picture units slowly opened a product void in the marketplace. Although double features as an exhibition strategy had declined, theaters still needed new product for their screens. As studio production decreased across the board, second wave exploitation producers were poised to dramatically increase their business.

Independent production companies, already on a steady rise, boomed. By 1958, 50 percent of films produced in the US were by independent companies (up from one third in the 1930s and 1940s), and by 1960, there were 165 different independent production entities pumping films into the marketplace.[53] Unsurprisingly, a majority of these specialized in second wave exploitation productions, solidifying them as viable film products shown in non-marginalized theatrical spaces to broader, more mainstream audiences. This positioned second wave exploitation as a critical node in the filmic landscape and served to facilitate the multivariate crossover previously noted.

Critically, second wave exploitation's move toward the mainstream was not just industrially motivated. The style and content of the films themselves were in high demand by audiences who recognized in the films their own complicated and rapidly shifting lives. Stylistically, second wave exploitation—unlike its classical progenitor—did not eschew Hollywood style and aesthetics but worked toward its integration. The familiarity in style sparked recognition in audiences and allowed the films to more easily exist alongside mainstream products in theaters. However, the second wave exploitation style was not a mere imitation of Hollywood. Indeed, there are crucial differences that established the films as simultaneously similar and disparate.

Classic Hollywood's cinematic style and its corresponding components are the organizing principles of narrative logic, cinematic time, and cinematic space.[54] This style allows the audience to assemble a consistent temporal and spatial universe in which narrative and action is presented. Fabricated through repetition, habit, and flexibility, this style depended on logical narrative transmission cultivated through narrative patterns centered on characters, cause-and-effect relationships to actions, and importantly, continuity built through time and space. Temporal and spatial continuity is instituted and maintained through specific editing formulas, rationalized mise-en-scéne, idealized views of action, and consistent spatial orientation for on-screen action.

Classical exploitation's overriding emphasis on spectacle rendered this type of filmmaking unnecessary. However, second wave exploitation's move away from unadulterated spectacle and toward its integration as a normalized function of narrative enabled the integration of the classical Hollywood stylistic and aesthetic guidelines. This is, in part, a repercussion of the blurred boundaries between the two industries. To have worked—or to aspire to work—within a Hollywood studio required familiarity with and the ability to execute or participate in the dominant style of filmmaking. Although economic and experience limitations on second wave production have led scholars like Schaefer to characterize it as an "impoverished imitation of mainstream Hollywood filmmaking,"[55] it should be understood as a hybridized aesthetics and style, not solely an imitative one.

Drawing from the classical techniques and more modern stylistic practices, both self-created and integrated from different non-mainstream film types like foreign, art, and *avant-garde* films, second wave exploitation represented a hybrid cinematic style. Indeed, this type of stylistic experimentation would critically inform the studio-produced work of the members of the New Hollywood who had trained in the second wave. This is not meant to generalize hybridity as the goal of all second wave exploitation films. It is meant, however, to call attention to hybridity as an alternative way of understanding the specific style and aesthetics of a significant number of second wave exploitation films, especially in the late 1960s–1970s.[56] It was, in part, this hybridity in style that allowed for experimentation in narrative, spatial, and temporal continuity that helped delineate second wave exploitation from conventional Hollywood fare.

As second wave exploitation drew stylistic cues from the mainstream, the mainstream reciprocated through content appropriation. Classical Hollywood cinema had been subject to a series of industry and non-industry censorship codes and enforcers, most notably the Production Code Administration (PCA). Classic and second wave exploitation film producers ignored the code to create their spectacle, integrated or not; producing, distributing, and exhibiting outside on the industrial fringes allowed them to ignore mainstream stipulations like the PCA. As the spectacularization of controversial topics of exploitation films became increasingly normalized throughout the 1960s, and as the cultural tenor of the country changed, the code became outdated. The line between Hollywood and exploitation films grew progressively thinner. The year 1967, in particular, would be a turning point for the embrace of exploitation-like content by Hollywood. That year's releases of *Cool Hand Luke* (Stuart Rosenberg), *The Graduate* (Mike Nichols), and *Bonnie and Clyde* (Arthur Penn)—all of which drew on exploitation traits and tropes like sex, nudity, scandal, and gratuitous violence—brought dangerous men behind bars and scantily clad women, a salacious sexual affair, and young murderous lovers on the run, respectively, into the mainstream.[57]

It was, however, the success of Blaxploitation films in the 1970s that convinced studios of the economic merit of second wave exploitation films, and they began their production in earnest. Studio-produced Blaxploitation films did not simply draw from their second wave counterparts; they coopted the film's styles, narratives, and ideologies wholesale. Indeed, many of the films remembered from that phase, such as *Shaft* (Gordon Parks Jr.,

1971), *The Legend of Nigger Charley* (Martin Goldman, 1972), *Cleopatra Jones* (Jack Starrett, 1973), and *Superfly* (Gordon Parks Jr., 1972), were produced by mainstream studios: MGM, Paramount, and Warner Bros., respectively. Critically, Hollywood's incursion did not completely drown out independents: the AIP-produced Pam Grier films of the cycle like *Foxy Brown* (Jack Hill, 1974) and *Coffy* (Jack Hill, 1974) are still endemically connected with the history and legacy of Blaxploitation.

Hollywood's move toward second wave exploitation was not contained to Blaxploitation. Spurred on by the success of independent producers, and the replacement of the PCA by the rating system, major Hollywood studios began moving more and more toward exploitation and their audiences. As David Cook states:

> majors embrace[d] exploitation as a mainstream practice, elevating such previous B genres as science fiction and horror to A-film status, retrofitting "race cinema" as "blaxploitation," competing with the pornography industry for the 'sexploitation' market share. Grindhouse-style gore was injected into seemingly conventional Westerns and gangster films, and four-letter words became obligatory in all but family rated genres (G and GP categories).[58]

These content shifts offer further justification for the flexible boundaries between second wave exploitation and its mainstream counterpart.

Second wave exploitation served as a transitory cinematic space not just in context with Hollywood, but within a larger industrial framework. The foreign film market, especially during its peak in the 1960s and early 1970s, is another useful node for understanding the curated, flexible, and positive liminality of second wave exploitation. Foreign films trickled into US theaters, primarily in urban markets, in a haphazard fashion in the early twentieth century. The stateside debut of Rossellini's *Rome, Open City* in 1946 made a significant impact on wider exhibition and public awareness of foreign films. The film, although associated with the now-canonical Italian neorealist movement, was marketed similarly to exploitation films with the tagline "Sexier than Hollywood ever dared to be."[59] This would begin a trend that established foreign films as distinctly different from Hollywood production primarily based on their foregrounding of issues of sex and sexuality, much like second wave exploitation.

The emphasis on sex and controversial content was a major draw for US audiences. As Andrew Sarris observed, "No one on either side of the Atlantic—or Pacific—wants to admit it today, but the fashion for foreign films depended a great deal on their frankness about sex."[60] Unlike Hollywood, but similar to second wave exploitation, foreign films ignored the PCA. Sex was played up in advertising in techniques freely adopted from the exploitation market, and as such, "the line between art cinema and exploitation was often a thin one."[61] Images of scantily clad women like Brigitte Bardot and Sophia Loren would be the focus of advertising campaigns, emphasizing titillation and scandal much like exploitation films. Sex, obscenity, and foreignness were imbricated, often to the benefit of the US distributors. Sex was critical to foreign and second wave exploitation films alike as a strategy for building and retaining audiences.

Further blurring the boundaries between the two industries was the propensity for independent production and distribution companies to distribute foreign films in the US. Films like Fellini's *La Dolce Vita* (1960) and Bergman's *Cries and Whispers* (1972), among others, would be distributed in the US by companies whose stock-in-trade was second wave exploitation. Additionally, the role foreign films played in helping to dismantle legal film censorship in the United States would help facilitate the production of increasingly outrageous exploitation films.[62]

Although foreign films and second wave exploitation shared a number of traits in common, including nonstandard Hollywood aesthetics and style, foreign films would enjoy an enduring place in the US film market in ways second wave exploitation never would. This was in large part due to the cultural capital that was placed in foreign films that was decidedly missing from exploitation.[63] Foreign films would eventually be considered "high" art while exploitation would remain "low" art in context with both the foreign and Hollywood industries. And as with Blaxploitation film, Hollywood would see the profits to be made in foreign films and quickly move into the market by the late 1950s. By the mid-1960s, mainstream Hollywood dominated foreign film distribution, using superior economic resources to cannibalize the exploitation industry.[64]

Exchange between these industries would eventually spell the end of second wave exploitation film, and more strikingly, the general viability of theatrically released exploitation film. Once New Hollywood gained access to the studio's industrial complex, they were free to take the themes and content that had resonated with audiences to a higher level of production, distribution, and exhibition than the second wave exploitation industry could ever have offered. Historians like Thomas Schatz have suggested this rupture, when fluidity and consistently traversed boundaries transformed from generative to destructive for second wave exploitation coalesced around Steven Spielberg's *Jaws* (1975).

Jaws was the epitome of a second wave exploitation narrative—a group of scantily clad teenagers being hunted by a killer shark, which can only be stopped through massive violence—run through the Hollywood machine. While it certainly was not the only mainstream film to ape second wave exploitation style, it stands as a high-profile example of how the successful narrative, concept, and marketing/distribution of second wave exploitation film was co-opted by Hollywood. The marketing for the film, in particular the image of a teenage girl in a bikini tantalizingly close to being swallowed by the eponymous shark, was a provocative image taken directly from the exploitation play book, and as Thomas Schatz notes, set new standards for film promotion.[65] The success of *Jaws*, standing as the prototypical "high-concept"[66] film, has also been largely attributed to its distributive model of saturation booking. A long-time standard of second wave exploitation, Hollywood studios tested the strategy with Spielberg's film to enormous success. *Jaws* opened simultaneously in more theaters than any previous Hollywood film. Saturation booking quickly became adopted by Hollywood, rebranded as "wide release." Second wave exploitation films made for teenagers featuring killer monsters quickly transitioned from the "trash" of exploitation to the "high concept" or "blockbuster" films of the Hollywood machine.

The repercussions of the success of *Jaws* were widely felt. Second wave exploitation saw its films produced on increasingly larger economic scales by Hollywood. Increasingly unable to compete, the industry was irreparably damaged. Although second wave exploitation was still producing a significant number of films, they were not able to access enough screens to generate adequate profit. For, while independent features were about 75 percent of all US productions in 1976, they only generated ten to 15 percent of box-office rentals, having been pushed off of screens by the new Hollywood blockbusters in wide release.[67] No longer having controversial content to differentiate their films from the mainstream, second wave exploitation films soon moved primarily to television and the burgeoning home video market, and began the slow decline from widespread cultural relevance and memory.

Chapter 4

STEPHANIE ROTHMAN DOES NOT EXIST

> The most bitter irony of Stephanie Rothman's career is that the one woman filmmaker of the Seventies with a consistent and solid body of work—a body of work that expresses the possibilities of American society—seems to have a better future as a cause than as a director.
> —TERRY CURTIS FOX[1]

The quantity of films produced by the second wave exploitation industry ensured one thing: there was always work to be had. Requiring more and more people power to maintain the pace of production, second wave exploitation production companies had a more relaxed hiring process than their mainstream compatriots. The meant employing people who could get the work done, and for whom getting a shot at the movie industry was more important than a livable wage. One outcome of this was that second wave exploitation producers like Corman eschewed some typical hiring falsehoods, including the idea that women could not direct films. If a director could get the film done on time and on budget, they were right for the role. It was this mindset that opened up the industry to Stephanie Rothman.

Unraveling Rothman's career is often a tricky proposition awash in contradiction. Rothman embodies feminist ideas of political and gender equality, yet she was disconnected from the women's movement of the 1960s and 1970s. She made second wave exploitation films and yet constructed a purposeful content framework that steered her films away from the salaciousness stereotypically attached to exploitation. Her films strongly reflect her own ideological positions and ethical compass, but Rothman herself has been largely absent from her own history. Perhaps most critically, her films have been defined by their success in overcoming economic scarcity, but little attention has been paid to how professional scarcity intimately shaped Rothman's filmmaking philosophy.

To navigate these confutations, narrate Rothman's professional biography, and assemble her overarching filmic and directorial philosophies, this chapter delves first into Rothman's personal history and career trajectory and second considers her *oeuvre* in totality, drawing out embedded and persistent themes, techniques, and stylistics across her seven films. In doing so, this chapter highlights how Rothman's filmmaking aesthetic and ideological philosophy, her commitment to films that tackled ethical and political issues, her self-imposed content guidelines, and her relationship to the tumultuous gender politics of the 1960s and 1970s converged into an unusual set of influences for second wave exploration filmmaking.

BIOGRAPHICAL BEGINNINGS

Stephanie Rothman was born on November 9, 1936, in Patterson, New Jersey. In 1945, her family moved to the Los Angeles area, settling first in the San Fernando Valley and later in Brentwood. Rothman's early experiences in California impressed on her the stark socioeconomic class differences in her new home:

> I went to school—grammar school, junior high school, and the first year and a half of high school—with people who were from different backgrounds than my own; they were lower middle class to poor and mostly Mexican American or children of Oklahoma migrants from the dustbowl who had come to California in the 1930s. I learned about the struggles of people who I otherwise would not have met. My parents, who came from poor immigrant backgrounds themselves, thought this was a good education for me.[2]

As a child, Rothman spent a majority of her time with adults, often the artists, intellectuals, and musicians in her parents' social circle. Rothman was regularly encouraged to pursue the arts and was an accomplished ballet dancer by the time she was in high school. As enriching as the emphasis on cultural activities was in the Rothman household, it created a divide between Rothman and her classmates, often leaving her isolated.

> There was a complete disconnect between the cultural activities in my home and the socioeconomic level of my home and the children I went to school with, and it isolated me [...] after school I didn't play games, I went home and I read and I did my homework, you know. That's what I did. [...] I was always an outsider.[3]

Rothman considered the structure of her broader world at an early age, particularly the role of women within it. This was unusual for a girl coming of age in the late 1940s and 1950s, particularly in light of the retrenchment of the nuclear family through rigid and prescriptive gender roles as a reaction to the number of women who had flooded the workforce during World War II. However, Rothman, like her mother, was always career-oriented and independent-minded: "I had never bought into the belief that I was put on this earth to marry and reproduce and keep the home of a man and be socially subservient and financially dependent on him."[4] Rothman did not disavow the institution of marriage itself, merely the social imperative that forced women to choose either a career or a husband. She was determined to have both.

Rothman graduated from high school at sixteen and entered the University of California, Los Angeles (UCLA), where she stayed for two and a half years. In 1955, she became engaged to a young medical school student, and transferred to the University of California, Berkeley. She first considered filmmaking while at Berkeley after becoming enamored with Bergman's *The Seventh Seal* (1957) and Kubrick's *Paths of Glory* (1957). She recalls, "It sort of occurred to me that it would be wonderful to make films at that time, but I did not think of it as a career goal because I had no idea how one could go about doing this."[5] Following graduation in 1958, Rothman entered the UC Berkeley Sociology Graduate Program, studying briefly with famed sociologist Erving Goffman. A consummate pragmatist, Rothman left the program a year later after seeing the almost total lack of opportunity for women in higher education at that time. That same year, she decided she was too young to marry and broke off her engagement.

Rothman returned to Southern California a graduate-school escapee, and in 1959, began working as a technical writer and then editor at Systems Development Corporation, which contracted with the air force on defense systems. Unlikely as it may sound, this job was the first step in her path to a career in film. Planning to have Rothman join their filmmaking division, Systems Development Corporation subsidized evening courses at the University of Southern California (USC) in basic camera, editing, sound, and screenwriting. Rothman saw it as a way to test the filmmaking waters, her own creative ability, and her aptitude behind the camera. In those evening classes she fell in love with filmmaking, and in 1962 she entered the USC graduate program in filmmaking full time.

PRE-INDUSTRY FORESHADOWING

Rothman had doubts about her decision to enroll in film school. She recalls worrying not about her ability to do the work, but her acceptance by male peers: "How am I going to do this? Also: Would I be accepted? Would they make life difficult for me? Would they sabotage my work? What would happen? But I decided to do it anyway."[6] Rothman's fears were initially unfounded. As one of only two female graduate students in the program, she was strongly encouraged by the faculty.

> Aside from me, there were only two other women there. Two graduate students, of which I was one, and one undergraduate. We were very rare indeed, and we were treated very well and taken very seriously. I think that they tried, because we were so unique, to make us feel more welcome.[7]

Although intent on directing, Rothman spent time absorbing film history, theory, and criticism, most notably as a teaching assistant for Arthur Knight.[8] Tenacious, she bore down on absorbing her craft. Her first directorial credit came in 1963 on the student film *We Look and See*.

A collaborative project between Rothman and her classmates—including Charles S. Swartz—she helmed the film that the students described as "satirical view of children's primers in which the seamier side of adult life is seen and described by a child."[9] Using the familiar "See Spot" formula from children's books, the short follows a middle-class family whose emphasis on public appearance and the performance of propriety veils the alcoholism, vanity, empty promiscuity, and vapid consumerism at their core.

Although Rothman remembers her time in film school as one free from bias, a group of documents from the *We Look and See* production book hint at a more complicated experience. *We Look and See* exposed friction between Rothman and two male classmates, Eric Timmerman and Anthony "Chick" Fowles, both editors on the project. Disagreements over editing choices led to an initial scrapping of Fowles's edit of the film, which was followed by a "lengthy shoot-out"[10] between Rothman and Fowles. Both Fowles and Timmerman, in their postproduction assessments of the project, deemed the film and the process a misuse of their time. Timmerman specifically highlighted Rothman as problematic:

> Only one <u>unusual</u> problem presented itself during production [. . .] I refer to a certain shall we say strong willedness, if there be such a term,

on the part of our director. [. . .] If, as an editor, the film is assumed to have my approval after it passes through my hands, then I cannot do it the director's way [. . .] several unique solutions to the problem were suggested. The one adopted goes something like this: live with it.[11]

Disagreements between editors and directors are neither unusual nor unexpected, and frankly, neither is a strong-willed director. But what Timmerman and Fowles hinted at in their production notes would soon be exposed as tensions arising in part from Rothman's position as a woman in power on set.

Duet (1963) was Rothman's thesis film at USC; she conceived the story, wrote the film, and directed it. The story follows two men: Loomis, a salary man at an unnamed company, and Joe, the company's evening janitor. Although they've never met in person, they routinely leave taped recordings for the other to listen to. These recordings form the basis of a friendship across class and collegial lines. The film opens with Joe cleaning Loomis's office and listening to the latest recording that has been left for him. Loomis's voice recounts a story about a former army friend he was never able to say goodbye to, something he always regretted.

Joe's response to the tape indicates the depth of the men's friendship: he narrates the unusually long span of time between tapes from Loomis and his intention to follow up and check in on him if he hadn't received a tape that very evening. Curious and worried about his friend's well-being, Joe wonders to Loomis what has kept him so preoccupied. The audience discovers the answer to Joe's question in the next scene. While Loomis listens to Joe's worried tape his assistant interrupts him, and the conversation between the two of them exposes her duplicitousness: she and his boss conspired to have him fired.

Post-firing, Loomis packs his personal effects and leaves his office. He rushes into the hallway and knocks over a mop bucket as a janitor is cleaning the hallway floor; unbeknownst to him, the janitor is Joe. Loomis continues without acknowledging or apologizing as Joe angrily calls after him, "Hey! Why don't you look where you are going! I should make you clean it up!" The film then cuts to Joe inside Loomis's empty office; he rushes to the tape recorder on the desk and this play. What he hears on the tape is an angry message from Loomis to his boss and no message for himself. Disappointed and hurt at being forgotten like the old army buddy from Loomis's previous story Joe turns and mournfully says to the tape recorder, "You could have said goodbye," before angrily throwing a rag at it.

Duet foregrounds of a consistent theme in Rothman's *oeuvre*: explorations of socioeconomic class. She explains:

> One of the most important things about *Duet* is the class difference between the two men. One is an office worker and the other is a janitor. They never meet because one works during the day and the other at night. The only way they make contact is by speaking to each other on a tape. And they discover they have something to say to each other. [. . .] And the point I was trying to make was very simple: if we met each other, we might have a lot to say to each other. It wouldn't necessarily be conflicting; it might be civil or loving. I've always believed that we all have a lot to learn from one another.[12]

Social class, corresponding economic hierarchies, the conflicts these two things can engender, and the solutions to these issues that interpersonal communication offer are present in all of Rothman's films, although her focus on class is often overlooked:

> Did they notice they were about people from different social classes relating to one another, or that they were not so different from one another? No, that never came up. What always came up was feminism. You know, "Women are more in the foreground here, they are more independent, more aggressive, more free." Feminism has always been the message taken from my films. Which is indeed a prominent message. [Laughs.] But not the only one.[13]

While Rothman was raised in an upper-middle-class home, she was schooled in class-diverse public schools and her professional life offered little of the financial comfort she knew in her childhood. Precarity was a constant during Rothman's filmmaking career and is a repeating theme in her work.

Duet was a critical film for Rothman, as it marked the beginning of Rothman's focus on socioeconomic class issues. Making the film was, however, a difficult creative process, as the tensions simmering between Rothman, Fowles, and Timmerman that began during the production of *We Look and See* reached a boiling point on *Duet*. Fowles and Timmerman, editors for *Duet*, were openly harsh in their assessment of working under Rothman: "Shooting agonizingly slow" (Timmerman) and "A) Never trust the lab B) Ditto a female director C) Sync sound is the curse of the working class" (Fowles).[14] Both men served as unit managers and editors on the film; the final cut of *Duet* had scratches on the negative and incorrectly synched sound. Reflecting on the incident, Rothman says:

> He [Fowles] thought, or wanted to think when he was editing, that he would have complete control over how the film was cut. He wanted the director's job to be over. When I saw his initial rough cut, it was quite crude, and I could see he needed more help than some of the other students. I had to teach him some basic techniques and he had to learn to accept the fact that I was the director and I had designed how the shots were to be assembled. That doesn't mean, however, that I wasn't open to suggestions. I was. [. . .] he and his partner were the ones who scratched the film and misaligned the sound and picture![15] I never had the heart to look at *Duet* again after seeing how it was ruined and, of course, I was unable to use it as a calling card for work.[16]

Despite Rothman's disappointment with the film, her efforts were recognized. She became the first woman to ever be awarded the Directors Guild of America's Student Filmmaking Award, although the decision to grant her the award was significantly debated by the award committee because she was a woman:

> There was a debate in the wardroom as to whether they should give it to me or the other candidates (who were all male) who were there, because they thought that it might be a waste to give it to a woman because she would never become a director. She couldn't. There was no possibility of doing it, and so why waste the money, even though they agreed that I perhaps was the person who should get it.[17]

Rothman's work prevailed, and she was given a $1,500 award to make a film. The project, a documentary on a harpsichordist on faculty at UCLA, was never finished. Rothman was not allowed to supplement the award funds and realized that without additional monies she could not complete the film she envisioned. In 1964 she abandoned the film when she was offered her first professional film production job and went to work for Roger Corman.

ON THE MOVE

Corman had a long history of reaching out to USC to find assistants. On the recommendation of Dr. Bernard Kantor, then head of USC's Department of Cinema, Corman invited Rothman for an interview. She was competing against a woman from UCLA, Julie Halloran, for the position. Rothman won the position, although Corman would eventually hire, and marry, Halloran.

Rothman worked for Corman for two years before her name appeared in a film's title cards, but she would go on to direct four films for Corman at various production companies: *Blood Bath/Track of the Vampire* (1966, AIP), *It's a Bikini World* (1967, AIP), *The Student Nurses* (1971, New World), and *The Velvet Vampire* (1971, New World).

Despite her partnership with Corman, her career was studded with long periods out of the director's chair and an accompanying frustration. After *It's a Bikini World*, Rothman left Corman's employ, hoping to find work in mainstream Hollywood. As she bluntly stated, "Nobody wanted to hire a woman."[18] As she recounted in 1999:

> Everybody felt that because I was a woman there would be tremendous difficulty in getting me to direct a feature that they might produce. And they just didn't think it was worth the effort. Because it's so much effort to make a film. I mean, I heard this. I heard this from people. It was so much effort that they just didn't think it was worth it. Creative Artists Agency [. . .] tried to include me in a package that they might be creating for some of their own clients. But they could not get me included.[19]

The downturn was hard on Rothman. "It tested me. That was a period that really tested me. I very much wanted to make films, but I wasn't going to give up just because I wasn't making them."[20] After spending three years trying to push into the mainstream, she returned to second wave exploitation, working for Corman as production executive on the film *Gas-s-s-s/Gas! -or- How It Became Necessary to Destroy the World in Order to Save It* (Corman, 1970). Working under the title of production executive, she and Swartz location scouted in New Mexico and Texas, arranged accommodations, negotiated shooting permits, storyboarded, and Rothman shot second-unit scenes.[21] Keenly aware of her precarious position in the industry, Rothman understood what Corman provided for her:

> I was not going to get an opportunity to make films anywhere else. Only Roger was giving me that chance, and I really appreciated it because I saw that my chances anywhere else were nonexistent.[22] Roger [. . .] made his career shooting films quickly and efficiently and he taught me how to do that. We would sit and discuss how to do things efficiently and to shoot quickly. We didn't have endless discussions, but we had a number of them. And I found it very useful obviously because I could get the film done on time and close to on

budget. That is about the only thing Roger taught me. But that was very valuable. And he gave me these opportunities for which I will always be profoundly grateful.[23]

After a dispute with AIP over the final edit of *Gas-s-s-s*,[24] Corman ended his partnership with Arkoff and Nicholson. Corman was aware of the talent and drive he had in Rothman. "A couple of weeks after we had all returned to Los Angeles and the film was being edited [Roger] said, 'I'm going to start a new film company, a new film studio in fact, in which I want to produce a regular slate of films, and I would like you to make the first film.'"[25] In 1970, he formed New World; Rothman and Swartz joined him.

New World was comprised of two entities: New World Productions (production) and New World Pictures (distribution and acquisition).[26] Corman originally intended for his brother, Gene, to head production. When Gene declined in order to focus on his own projects, Corman turned to Lawrence "Larry" Woolner.[27] Woolner and his two brothers, Barry and David, started in the film business as the owners of several drive-in theaters across Louisiana. Seeing the potential profits in production, they formed Woolner Brothers Productions. The company was headquartered in Rome, allowing them to benefit from Italian government's film subsidiary program for co-productions.[28] Producing films in Italy and the US, Larry Woolner first worked with Corman on *Swamp Women* (1956), financing the Corman-directed project.[29] Several successful collaborations followed; when Corman needed a partner in New World, Woolner fit the bill.

New World quickly became a hive of activity. In its first four years, the company produced and released twenty-two features, and distributed fifteen foreign and domestic acquisitions.[30] While their in-house features were strictly second wave exploitation fare, their acquisitions, specifically foreign acquisitions, were quite different. In 1972, Corman acquired US/Canadian distribution rights for Ingmar Bergman's *Cries and Whispers*, nominated for Best Picture at the 1973 Academy Awards. New World distributed René Laloux's *Fantastic Planet* (1973), winner of the 1973 Cannes Grand Prix, and Fellini's *Amarcord* (1973), which won the 1974 Oscar for Best Foreign Film.[31] The diversity in product was financially beneficial to the company and established its reputation as an independent player early on.[32]

In 1970 Rothman's *The Student Nurses* was New World's first release; it was a popular and economic success. The film was a particular milestone for Rothman: it wasn't until she read a review of the film in *Variety* that she knew she was directing exploitation films.[33] As she recalls, this realization profoundly affected her:

> It underlined that I was making films of no status that would not get any kind of serious recognition from reviewers, certainly not in the papers or in magazines. And it certainly would not be taken seriously in Hollywood in any way and it would not open up great employment opportunities for me in terms of the tools I would have to work with as a filmmaker. I recognized at that point that I was pretty much at an impasse, and that I was even lucky to have been able to make this kind of film because as a woman, nobody else was making anything else. There was one exception, Elaine May, who made a couple of films. But other than that, nobody was. And I just realized at that point that the best I could expect to go on doing was more of the same.[34]

Cognizant of her precarious professional situation, Rothman continued working with Corman at New World, making *The Velvet Vampire* in 1971. The film generated interest from mainstream studios, although not in the way she wanted:

> I was called in to meet an executive at MGM after I'd made *The Velvet Vampire*, in fact it was perhaps three or four years later. And this person said to me, "Oh, you know, we were talking about you the other day in a meeting, because we've hired the younger brother of Ridley Scott to make a film, and we think we'd like it to be a vampire film, and we were talking about how we would like it to sort of be like *The Velvet Vampire*." And my response was, 'Well, if you want a film like *The Velvet Vampire*, why don't you get Stephanie Rothman to make it?' [. . .] I didn't get the job.[35]

While not as economically successful as *The Student Nurses*, *The Velvet Vampire* did well for New World and secured Rothman's track record as a resourceful, economical, creative, and successful director. Keen to continue their profitable working relationship, Corman proposed Rothman and Swartz stay on through the company's second year. Rothman:

> The first year Charles and I worked for Roger Corman at New World Pictures, which was the first year of New World Pictures, we received a tiny weekly salary and a $2,000 bonus at each film's completion, and we made *The Student Nurses* and *The Velvet Vampire* for him. *The Student Nurses* made him a lot of money. But the second year he proposed that we continue working for him without salaries. Instead, he offered both of us together $2,000 a picture. [Laughs.] Now that New

World Pictures had had a successful first year—thanks in a significant part to Charles's and my work—he had lots of young people crowding in who wanted to make films for him.[36]

The offer was simply impossible for Rothman and Swartz to accept.

Around the same time, Larry Woolner, seeing how much money could be made in production and distribution, decided to strike out on his own. He split amicably from Corman to form Dimension Pictures, asking Rothman and Swartz to join him. As Rothman recalls: "Obviously we couldn't live on Roger's offer, so when Larry Woolner offered us a living wage, we accepted it. It was not a lot of money. But it enabled us to live in an apartment, and buy food, and have a car."[37] With Corman's thanks and appreciation, the pair left New World for the newly formed Dimension. Rothman embarked on a new phase in her career: already one of the very few women filmmakers steadily working, she was about to become something even more rare: a woman executive.

Formed in 1972, Dimension was largely underwritten by Woolner's partnership with Sam Pulitzer, the head of a clothing and accessories company called Wembley Industries.[38] Woolner quickly announced a slate of five productions for the year at average planned budgets of $250,000 each.[39] With Woolner and Wembley as majority stakeholders in the venture, Rothman and Swartz joined as minority partners, with a combined 10 percent ownership of the company staked through their labor rather than financial investment.[40] Despite this commitment, Rothman's time at the company was uneasy and lasted only four years. Rothman was installed in a key creative position. The trades variously listed Rothman's title as creative development chief, head of project development, or vice president for creative development. Rothman clarifies her role in the company:

> Basically, I had the title of vice president, and I was involved in the development of ideas for films. I also watched films for possible acquisition or that were acquired, gave my advice on how to recut them, what additional shooting might be necessary, or whether they were even worth acquiring. But my real, my most primary responsibility, was writing and directing and doing the preproduction on films that I made.[41]

In this role, Rothman was a critical factor in the company's productions and acquisitions. She saw an opportunity to leverage her decision-making capacity to increase the number of women working in film production. She outlined this commitment in a 1972 interview with the *Hollywood Reporter*, pledging to make "a concerted and unprecedented effort [...] to locate and hire qualified women in areas of film-making in which they are rarely if ever found."[42] She added: "There's no area I would not use them. Certainly, being in a position to employ women in a field that has employed them very little in jobs of responsibility, I want to help other women to gain employment in positions of responsibility."[43] Her ambitions, however, did not work out as planned. Rothman: "I found it very hard to find women who had any crew skills at all. It was too early."[44]

Production and acquisition release proceeded quickly at Dimension. Following Corman's strategy from New World, Woolner designed Dimension's films for drive-ins and first-run theaters.[45] Within the first ten months of operations, Dimension had completed five films at a total investment of $1.5 million.[46] At the close of 1972, Woolner announced his plans to form regional distribution exchanges in partnership with the company General Film Group.[47] Bypassing independent sub-distributors and forming their own distribution network allowed the rapidly growing company to reap significant financial benefits. Sub-distributors handled films from multiple companies and exercised total control over where, when, and for how long each film was booked.[48] This control meant that the smaller, independent films Dimension made were often booked into less desirable theaters, decreasing profits. Additionally, sub-distributors were legendarily bad at caring for film prints, often rendering them damaged or unusable, and were equally poor at timely payment of rental fees to the production company.[49] These were critical issues for small, independent Dimension; control over their own exchanges could be an incredible boon for their bottom line as well as their production capabilities—not least of all because rental fees from one film would be used to finance the next.

Rothman's filmic contributions at Dimension—*Group Marriage*, *Terminal Island*, and *The Working Girls*—were key to the company's early success. Her guidance as vice president helped foster success in acquisitions and distribution; during her time with Dimension the company released sixteen films. The partnership between Woolner, Rothman, and Swartz had helped the young company flourish. However, Wembley, Dimension's primarily fiscal sponsor, was unhappy when the company's financial returns were not as fast or as large as what he had expected: Wembley wanted out. Swartz came up with a plan to move the company forward without them. As Rothman narrates:

> Charles told Larry that this was a great opportunity to buy them out and to own and run the company together. Initially Larry doubted

that it could be done. But Charles said "Well, let's go and try." Before they did, Charles and Larry verbally agreed there would be a more equal split of the company ownership if the buyout of Wembley was accomplished. Wembley was located in New Orleans, so the two of them went there. According to Charles, he did most of the negotiating and the breakup was accomplished.[50]

Rothman and Swartz had been working nonstop for years, and after the negotiations in New Orleans they took a rare vacation.[51] When they returned, ready to get back to work in the newly liberated Dimension, they found a much different climate than the one they had left. Rothman:

> When we returned, there was a different attitude toward us at Dimension. On the part of both Larry and his wife, who we suspected heavily influenced him. The papers severing the connection between Dimension and Wembley arrived. The agreement was signed between Wembley and Larry Woolner only, just as the original agreement to found the company had been. This meant that Larry was now the owner of 90 percent of Dimension. And at that point we were told by him that we would continue to own only 10 percent of the new company, not a greater amount as Larry had agreed to verbally with Charles. So, in essence, Charles thought of the idea of the buyout, prodded Larry to ask for it, mostly negotiated it, and then Larry wanted 90 percent of it for himself and his wife. In addition, Charles and I also had a contract to make films with Dimension Pictures that after three years was up for renewal, and Larry suddenly did not want to renew it. So, we left.[52]

The breakup with Dimension was not as easy or convivial as their exit from New World had been:

> Although they didn't want to renew our contracts, they still wanted us to make another film. But we no longer trusted them and wanted to conduct no further business with them. I had already written a script called *The Car Hops*, while still under contract to Dimension, which they wanted to make. But since Charles and I were now unemployed, we asked to take it with us. Ultimately, they agreed to give it to us as severance pay and I was quickly able to sell it, but for not very much. It was above Writers Guild minimum, but not enough to live on—even for half a year.[53]

After splitting from Dimension, Rothman and Swartz still held their 10 percent ownership stake. As Rothman recalls, "We did sue them. And they did make a monetary settlement, and in return we gave up our 10 percent ownership. It too wasn't for very much, but the lawsuit cost them a substantial amount and took several years."[54] After Rothman/Swartz exited, Dimension struggled. As Fred Olen Ray recounts:

> Dimension continued on, presumably unhampered by the absence of two of its founding members and moved into the area of black exploitation and martial arts, but the quality of the product never seemed to rise above mediocre. Their best releases had been their own in-house productions until Rothman and Swartz left.[55]

Dimension continued to announce a growing number of productions and releases, many never coming to fruition. Of the eighty-nine films Dimension announced between 1974 and 1981, only 48 percent of them were ever made and/or released.[56] Looking back on Dimension's troubles after their exit, Rothman contextualizes:

> In those years they were spending like crazy and they were making many terrible . . . they were making, at least in our opinion, many very poor commercial decisions. They were, first of all, choosing a few ambitious films that they didn't know how to market, and secondly they were choosing poorly made exploitation films that were not successful. So, even though they had a few successes along the way, they eventually ran the company into the ground.[57]

In 1981, Dimension filed for bankruptcy and a majority of their films were acquired by 21st Century Distribution Corporation.[58]

Post-Dimension, Rothman made another attempt at breaking into mainstream Hollywood, pitching herself as a writer/director. Rothman wrote a number of story treatments, including *Sweet Sugar* (1972, written with Swartz; both writers listed as R. C. Samuels), and *Beyond Atlantis* (1973). She was given a deal to write and direct three films for a studio.[59] As she recalled in 2008: "The man who hired me also had a slate of other films to produce there. When I finished my first script, the first picture he produced came out and went into release . . . and it bombed. So that was the end of his deal, and that was the end of my deal."[60] After this disappointment, she met regularly with other studio executives, but she was unable to get a job. Ever pragmatic, Rothman evaluated her career:

I could have gone on making exploitation films. This may have been my own fault, for not going on making them. I was *tired* of making them. I felt I had done everything I could in this genre and said everything I could. I was tired of the obligations I had, to sex, nudity, and violence. And so, I was approached by other people who wanted to finance exploitation films. But I just did not wanna go on doing it.[61] I had tried to find work for ten years. After ten years I obviously took stock of my chances of finding work in another ten years [. . .] I looked around at other people who had started at the same time I had, and they had either gone on to great success or they had faded from the scene. And at that time, I was forty-eight, and I said to myself, "I have all these years ahead of me, I might as well enjoy them instead of experiencing the continuing rejection and frustration and depression that this created."[62]

In 1984, after directing seven feature films and serving a three-year term as an independent studio executive, Stephanie Rothman left the film industry forever.

Rothman's professional life after filmmaking was dramatically different from her previous career. Her first non-film job was as a writer for an early union-like organization for professors in the University of California education system; she authored their newsletter. She held the position for several years until she began investing in commercial real estate, a field she worked in until retirement. When Rothman made the decision to leave the film industry, Swartz followed suit. "One day I just said to him, 'I'm finished.' And a few days later he said, 'Well, I guess if you are, I am.'"[63] Although Swartz would leave film production, he continued his association with the industry through his work in academia. Working as a continuing education specialist for UCLA's Extension Department of Entertainment and Performing Arts, he developed "the largest and most comprehensive curriculum of digital media and entertainment management courses offered by any major university."[64] He later ran Charles S. Swartz Consulting, an entertainment strategic consulting firm, and served a term as the Hollywood president of the Society of Motion Picture and Television Engineers.

Returning to USC, his alma mater, he made his lasting mark as the director and CEO of the Entertainment Technology Center, a research unit within the School of Cinema and Television.[65] Under Swartz's guidance, the center's Digital Cinema Lab "became Hollywood's de facto digital cinema forum, hosting and supporting the Digital Cinema Initiatives[66] work toward establishing digital cinema specifications."[67] He also authored the germinal textbook *Understanding Digital Cinema: A Professional Handbook* (2004). Swartz passed away in 2007, following a battle with brain cancer.

THE ROTHMAN GUIDE TO FILMMAKING

Rothman's career, however abbreviated, established her as a versatile filmmaker. She worked in multiple styles, including a documentary-like style achieved with handheld shooting and the inclusion of naturally occurring public events in the diegesis (*The Student Nurses*); fast, kinetic editing (*It's a Bikini World*); surrealistic dreamscapes (*The Velvet Vampire*); and the classical Hollywood style (*The Working Girls*). Rothman maneuvered through styles as a method of control, particularly when required by distributors to film content she would not have normally included in her films. She recalls:

> I was never happy making exploitation films. I did it because it was the only way I could work. While I do not object to violence or nudity in principle, the reason audiences came to see these low-budget films without stars was because they delivered scenes that you could not see in major studio films or more supposedly ambitious independent American films. [. . .] Exploitation films required multiple nude scenes and crude, frequent violence. My struggle was to try to dramatically justify such scenes and to make them transgressive, but not repulsive.[68]

Rothman often turned to comedy as a way to reconcile what she considered the more salacious elements of her films with her own viewpoints. Indeed, she would regularly return to comedic moments in her films as a way to negotiate tension between her personal sensibility and the content requirements of the second wave exploitation style. "Visual style and comic invention were my personal salvation [. . .] to escape what troubled me about the exploitation genre."[69] While *It's a Bikini World* and *Group Marriage* are her only outright comedies, Rothman's repetitive comedic interventions across her filmography are her wink to the audience, saying "we both know this is ridiculous, but we can still have some fun."

Reflecting on her use of multiple styles, she recalls:

> Perhaps the only restrictions I had in terms of executing any particular style that I wanted was being able to afford within the budget to rent film equipment that I might need to execute a certain kind of

stylistic movement or whatever. By that I mean: it was too expensive for example to rent a crane, a camera crane. I could not rent very, very long lenses very often. Charles as the producer would budget *one day* in the shooting when a long lens could be rented—and that would be "long lens day"!⁷⁰

Primary in her filmmaking philosophy was, however, the combination of the image and narrative theme:

I both loved the creation of images [and] making ideas concrete through storytelling. Abstract ideas. That's how I would think of myself as a director. In other words, I was operating on two levels: on the level of the image and the other on the level of the abstract idea, which through storytelling I wanted to demonstrate and make clear.⁷¹

Rothman describes herself as a controlled and yet collaborative filmmaker, especially in her relationships with her editors and directors of photography. This reveals her understanding of her directorial self as an artisan, as opposed to an artist. For Rothman, filmmaking was a process of mobilizing her professional training as a skilled laborer to produce a craft product that both represented the industrial system it was made from as well as the creative artistry that influenced it. Her investment in collaborative creation with other laborers working across technical training and creative imagining, including editors and directors of photography, emphasize a style of filmmaking that acknowledges the formal process of film as professionalized and skilled as well as artistically expressive.

Her focus on collaboration is also a specific strategy that kept her professionalization and training front and center, a critical move when working in an organizational climate (read: Hollywood) whose default assumption was that women were not filmmakers. This is reflected in the undertone of an anecdote she shared about a frequent collaborator:

The greatest compliment I ever got was from the man who shot almost every film I made, Daniel Lacambre. The first time I offered him a job on one of my films, he said, "Well, I think we maybe have one film together." I said, "Really?" and he said, "Yes. I don't think we will have a long-term relationship." And I didn't question him as to why. We went off, we made the film. When it was time to make the next one I contacted him—he lived in France—and I said, "Daniel, would you like to do this?" And he said, "Yes, I would." And he came again. And by the time we were working on *The Working Girls* together he said, "You know, Stephanie, you are no longer my colleague, or my friend, you are my habit."[72]

Her emphasis on craft, and its associations with skilled labor, is underscored when she notes: "Other people can call you an artist if they want to, but you can't call yourself an artist. As far as I am concerned, I was a craftswoman. And I was struggling to perfect my craft and advance it."[73] This concentration on craft would strongly guide her working relationships. On her work with directors of photography:

Well, I was very visually orientated, and I always worked very closely with the directors of photography. I would tell them where I wanted the camera angle to be, and what the action was going to be, and I would tell them what composition I would like to see in the frame and what lens would best suit this. And I would also ask them, if they were good—and I had very good ones, I was very fortunate—"Now, you tell me what you think it should look like. You set it up. I've told you all these things, I've given you lots of elements to work with, now show me what you think needs to be added." And mostly what they showed me was wonderful, and in some way enhanced what I had thought. And if it didn't then we would readjust it. But I almost always took what they had to say, because they knew a lot, and they had a lot to contribute, and anyone would be a fool who didn't take advantage of their skill and knowledge.[74]

Her usage of multiple styles, of comedic interventions to contextualize rather than ignore the more exploitative aspects of her film initiated by others, leveraging the skill and input of the professionals she surrounded herself with, and focusing on the combination of image and abstract idea worked as strategies both for overcoming the limitations she worked under and for proving herself as a skilled professional to the mainstream film industry.

The biggest restriction Rothman worked under was financial. Second wave exploitation film producers expected the films themselves to cost as little as possible in an effort to bolster net earnings. Rothman made films on a budget of $250,000 or (more frequently) less. This affected equipment rentals, shooting time, rehearsal options, locations, set design, etc. Second wave exploitation producers saw no need to hire union crews, so often times the majority of her filmmaking crew were green and untested in their positions. Although a strong supporter of unions, Rothman was never a Directors

Guild of America member; she could not afford to join. "It cost, at that time, $2,000 to join, and $2,000 was a lot of money. I would have had to borrow it, and I wasn't earning enough income to be able to repay it in the foreseeable future."[75] She is, however, a past and current member of the Writers Guild.

Rothman did have a voice in casting, but she was required to cast as many "beautiful" people in her films as possible, regardless of performance abilities.

> It was a requirement from Larry Woolner, from Roger Corman, and it was a requirement from the sub-distributors. Because there were no stars in them, they had to really look good. So, to my frustration, I sometimes could not hire people whom I would have loved to hire.[76]

The emphasis on beauty over talent and the lack of funds for rehearsals required Rothman to improvise basic acting pedagogy on set: "I would have to help them with their line readings and explain their characters' thoughts and motivations to them."[77] For Rothman, accommodations for stylistic, performative, and professional experience were always in service of demonstrating her abilities to the mainstream Hollywood community:

> I hoped that by showing how *much* production value I could extract from so little money, how I could make a film look much *larger* and show by my *technique*—my use of the camera, my choice of lenses, my capacity to use images and color and texture and variation to add emotive force to what I was saying—would somehow communicate to professional filmmakers—not directors, but I'm talking about, now, producers and financers—and that they would be interested in hiring me.[78]

Pushing past external limitations became the overriding motif in Rothman's formal filmmaking as she attempted to prove her abilities to the mainstream industry.

Beyond style, Rothman developed a loose set of directorial principles she applied to her films as a way of rationalizing and transgressing the standard formula of violence, sex, and nudity in second wave exploitation she found hyper-exploitative. While Rothman discussed her filmmaking principles sporadically, working across the historical record I've reconstructed them here as "Rothman's Rules." These rules are guideposts that help to form the roadmap of Rothman's directorial ethos. While successive chapters focus on how these rules manifest in her individual films, they are outlined here to give a more holistic understanding of how she approached filmmaking.

The first two rules concern the primary narrative tropes of second wave exploitation film: nudity and violence. Rothman's first rule was that nudity must be equitable across the sexes. As she noted in 1981, "I think it's highly unfair just to do that to women. It's a reflection of the inequitable distribution of power in our society."[79]

While noting the imbalance, Rothman also acknowledged the desires of women in her audience, constructing nudity on her films as eroticism rather than exhibitionism. She made this connection explicit in 1977:

> There is more nudity in my films than you find in the films of male directors. Eroticism in films has been traditionally conceived with the erotic interests of men while women's interests have usually been ignored. Women have as much interest in men's bodies as men do in women's. As a woman, I naturally take a woman's erotic interests into account.[80]

While Rothman included eroticized nudity, the same was not true for violence; her second rule dictates that violence cannot be eroticized and must be shown with its inevitable consequences. Rothman was blunt in her standpoint on consequential violence: "'I decided there would be no violent action without showing its ugly consequences. When violence occurred, it would not be free of the pain and mess of real violence. Sometimes this made the violence more graphic and upsetting, but that was my intention.'"[81]

Rule three serves as the natural outgrowth of its predecessors: rape cannot be shown, only alluded to. Rothman: "Rape was the only thing I ever refused to do in a film. In *Terminal Island*, I indicated that the women were forced to have sexual relations with the men, but I never showed it . . . I couldn't bring myself to film it—even to show it as a reprehensible act."[82] While these first three filmmaking guideposts dealt with overarching second wave exploitation narrative thematics, the remaining rules highlight Rothman's commitment to social progressivism.

Much like Rothman's own approach to navigating gender roles in her everyday life, rule four, a commitment to gender stereotype reversal, stems from her own ideological construction. In Rothman films, women can be self-determined, and men can be vulnerable. Dannis Peary observes that "men scream often and loudly in the Rothman films."[83] Rothman follows: "When I was a little girl, I was very stoical [. . .] and I could not understand why women in film screamed so much while men rarely did."[84] In committing to show more complicated portrayals of gender roles, Rothman honored rule five: respect for the audience. "In looking at films, I had noticed you could always tell when the filmmakers were patronizing the audience. It just shone through, and that was a lesson to me: don't patronize anybody."[85]

Rothman drew from everyday life often, particularly for characterization and relationship building, as well as in constructing social commentary. Rothman's rule five dictates films should reflect contemporary life. "Once I paid my debt to the requirements of the genre [I could] address what interested me—and continues to interest me today—political and social conflicts and the changes they produce."[86]

This focus on the "now" was filtered through her own perspective. "I write comedy. That is the way I write. I cannot write any other way. I have a rather ironic view of the human condition. I see nothing about us, all of us humans, that doesn't require a great deal of laughter to make life bearable."[87] Rule six follows, then, that humor should be used as commentary. These guidelines are, in part, what help to distinguish Rothman films from her contemporaries.

As a woman with a self-identified social conscience making films in a cycle known for its controversial provocations, Rothman was determined to project her ethical identity in her work. As she explained in 1978:

> A Stephanie Rothman film deals with questions of self-determination. My characters try to forge a humane and rational way of coming to grips with the vicissitudes of existence. [. . .] My films are not always about succeeding, but they are always concerned with fighting the good fight.[88]

Rothman has consistently described herself as a social egalitarian, particularly concerned with fully articulating the potentialities of the human condition. She summarizes:

> Basically, what I am an advocate for is a more fair and egalitarian society. I don't think we have much fairness anywhere in the world. I would like to see a more equitable distribution of power and the possibility of realizing fully what one can be. I know these are noble sentiments and that everybody has them. But I, at least, have the opportunity to do it in a film.[89]

The ethico-political social commentary that formed the intellectual and narrative foundation of Rothman's films caused internal tension for the director as she navigated the demands of working in second wave exploitation.

Undergirding these principles was Rothman's stated commitment to equality and her self-avowed feminist identity. Raised to be independent, she was instilled early on with a deep belief in liberal meritocracy as a pathway to professional advancement. Even so, she articulated the challenges that faced her as one of the only women directors working in the film industry in the 1960s and 1970s. Rothman in 1972:

> I don't know how many women have tried to be directors, but I doubt if they would get much of a sympathetic ear in many places. It may not be true in all places, but from attitudes I've heard expressed I don't think there would be too much sympathy at this point in this industry.[90]

This lived reality influenced Rothman's commitment to modeling success for other women looking to break into the film industry. In the limited press she received while she was working, she spoke about herself as an aspirational model for other women. She claimed particular investment in the idea that as a woman working in a male-dominated field, she could inspire other women to the idea that they too could work in film production, despite the seemingly overwhelming odds.

> What I did encounter when I first started out were dire warnings from men who were film executives, but not filmmakers, that I would never be allowed to direct, and that even if I were, male crews would never work for me. I have always thought this was a veiled way, or what they mistook for a veiled way, of telling me that they didn't want to see me progress. [. . .] I feel that calling attention to the fact that I am a woman might suggest to other women that they too could become directors if they wished. It might make the possibility of accomplishing this seem a little less bleak. When I left film school eight years ago, I found that at least one woman, Shirley Clarke, was actively working in a field otherwise monopolized by men [and that] was a source of reassurance to me that I might be able to do it too.[91]

Her commitment to serving as a model for future women film professionals echoed in her emphasis on professionalism. She credited her discipline in filmmaking to her training as a dancer and took seriously how her behavior on set affected the overall tone and energy of her cast and crew: "I never flagged, I never stopped; the most energetic person on a set has to be the director. The director sets the pace for everyone else."[92] She would emphasize the irrelevancy of gender to the act of directing when speaking to the press with comments like: "No special masculine or feminine qualities are required for this job."[93] Rothman's avowal of film work as gender neutral work has a past and present in Hollywood. J. E. Smyth recounts a story in *Nobody's Girl Friday: The Women Who Ran Hollywood* about screenwriter Lillian Hellman dismissing the idea of women writers as a benefit; for Hellman a good writer is a good writer, gender be damned. As Smyth observes, "Many prominent Hollywood women speaking about gender and work ... believed that qualifying it, even by pointing out their exceptional status, was offensive and derisory to women's equality with men."[94] Decades later, director Kathryn Bigelow echoed Hellman and Rothman when she stated: "I think that this notion that there's a women's aesthetic, a woman's eye, is really debilitating. It ghettoizes women."[95] Rather than regularly advocate for neutrality, Rothman kept a public emphasis on professionalism, her construction of herself as a craftswoman, and her focus on training and merit-based work as strategies to de-gender the idea of "director," working to normalize her role as a method of cultivating acceptance, and thereby, employment.

Although Rothman has regularly stated a personal and professional commitment to feminism, women's labor empowerment, and equality, she had a complicated relationship to political second wave feminism. In part, she attributes this to her age and her upbringing. When Betty Friedan's germinal second wave feminist book *The Feminine Mystique* was published, Rothman was twenty-seven years old, married, and working in a male-dominated profession. In the book, Friedan tackles what she calls "the problem that has no name": women's desire to be more than wives, mothers, and homemakers.[96] Rothman saw herself as having already escaped the trap of forced domesticity and embodied many of the ideal qualities and life choices the book laid bare as aspirational. Rothman notes, "I was already an adult [. . .] it had no influence on me [laughs]. She had nothing to teach me. I was happy that she came along and gained the attention of large numbers of women who, by necessity or choice, accepted this subservient role."[97]

As the movement crested in the late 1960s and early 1970s Rothman remained linked to the movement's ideology, and was supportive of its aims and goals, but did not connect to its more public, collective activities:

> I had always been connected to it, even before it existed! [Laughs.] I mean, I had gone my own way. I had decided I was going to live my life in a way that did not conform to the standards of the 1950s. But did I join consciousness-raising groups? Did I know women who were suddenly making the discovery that they had been herded into or had willingly chosen very narrow possibilities for self-development? No. I really didn't. I was more of an observer, an outsider, but I've been that way all my life. [. . .] I mean, it obviously brought about enormous

positive social change and opened up many opportunities for women that were previously unavailable to them. But did I personally find it liberating or freeing? No. It really had very little to do with me.[98]

Despite this, members of the press simplistically aligned Rothman as a product and symbol of the movement first because she was a woman, and second, because the feminist leanings in her work were easily identifiable. Articles on Rothman throughout the 1970s, such as "Exploitation and Feminism,"[99] "Fully Female,"[100] "R-Rated Feminist,"[101] and "Feminism, Fantasy, and Violence"[102] highlighted either her feminist achievements or feminist failings. As someone invested in narrating her own story, this was frustrating to Rothman, as indeed any simplistic public description of an artist may be for that individual. However, given her unique place in the industry, the type of films she made, and the inability for any creative professional to fully control the public shaping of their image, the one-dimensional focus on Rothman as a feminist is not surprising. It does bear scrutiny, as she became naïvely constructed through unrefined understandings of the political, social, economic, and cultural implications of second wave feminism. In this sense, Rothman's own subjecthood (director Stephanie Rothman) was supplanted by her value as blunt public symbol (women's lib director Stephanie Rothman). Rothman did not fight this label, although she was careful not to add to her own subjective marginalization:

> I was conducting my own life in a style that women's liberationists now advocate long before there was a movement. However, it was good to see that the dissatisfactions that women feel with her social and economic roles are at last being publicly expressed. At least it is a first step toward correcting some of the numerous injustices that exist. I do not belong to any organized women's liberation group. The only reason I can give for this is that I am basically a nonjoiner, a lone wolf. However, I do try to help my fellow women get ahead when it is in my own power to do so.[103]

Initially, I had assumed that Rothman's reluctant connection to the movement was a strategy she employed to remain legible to potential employers. Although her personal ideology was rarely in question, perhaps by supporting the political movement through more abstract statements she was hoping that future (male) employers would not consider her too "radical" (read: difficult) to hire. However, this was never a concern for her:

First of all, I thought that when people saw my films they'd know what my convictions were. So, obviously, if they wanted to hire me they understood that this would probably seep out in one way or another. But beyond that, when I was interviewed for getting a job it wasn't for anything that would *ever* display this kind of thought, never. It was never in anybody's mind that I know of. So, I wasn't afraid that I would have to compromise anything because there was nothing to compromise! There was just . . . it was a completely different realm; the subjects that my films were concerned with were not discussed in films or on television in those days. So, it didn't matter.[104]

Her disconnect from the movement was simply that. Her age, the life choices she made, and her disposition toward solitude set her apart from the political movement she was ideologically connected to. Of course, second wave feminism was not a political movement without faults. Indeed, it left many groups of women—women of color, queer women, trans women, poor and working-class women, women who actively chose the role of homemaker—out. While it is not unique to find women that did not connect with the movement, it is important to consider Rothman's tension with second wave feminism as a political movement in light of the media's uncomplicated alignment of the two.

Rothman desperately wanted her films to be received with her intent intact. She made no secret of her desire to control her own professional narrative, despite that desire's impossible execution. When asked if she resented the media's consistent and blunt construction of her as a feminist symbol, she explained:

Only when critics or reviewers saw my films and would say what a strong vein of feminism was in them, which delighted me but also dismayed me a little bit in the sense that it meant that they couldn't just examine the material for what it was. There are many ideas in my films that have nothing to do with feminism, and everybody always imposed this, well . . . interpreted it as mostly feminist. It is feminist. I am proud of that. I'm happy I was able to convey this message. But that's not all it is. And sometimes I thought then, and I still think, that other things are lost in that one-note interpretation.[105]

Rothman's films certainly are feminist, but to understand them *only* as feminist flattens the understanding of her films by assuming a universal and single definition of the concept of feminism while obscuring how Rothman's films also speak to issues of race, class, and sexuality. By applying the blanket label of "feminism" to her films, what we now consider their intersectional nature—and the critical issues that an intersectional perspective bring—is obscured.

The result of this ideological simplification underscores the need to examine Rothman's films individually, teasing out their lost complications and transitioning Rothman from filmic footnote to object of regular study. Indeed, Rothman's personal and professional history, and the contradictions embedded within, facilitated seven films, hybrids of her directorial ethos, filmmaking craft, and the boundaries of her industry. Just as this chapter inserted Rothman back into her own history through a combination of her voice and critical evaluation of her films, the following section tackles Rothman's body of work, integrating close textual analysis and dissection of her industrial conditions of production as the first step in her undoing Rothman's historical neglect.

Part II

INTERVENINGS

Chapter 5

EVERYONE STARTS SOMEWHERE

> Many people are surprised and don't believe that women can assume positions of leadership and decision-making, that they can come to grips with the various technical aspects of film-making—which of course, is nonsense. If they can be nuclear physicists, they can be film directors.
> —STEPHANIE ROTHMAN [1]

Despite her abbreviated career, Stephanie Rothman traversed the second wave exploitation industry at its zenith. Her films and her relationships with some of the industry's pivotal, and most memorable, figures are, in many ways, indicative of second wave exploitation's diversified output. Her films and their representative industrial connections, however, were heretofore unexplored. As a corrective, the next several chapters are an in-depth analysis of Rothman's films, focusing inwardly on the director and her work. Dissections of her oeuvre requires a multi-nodal analysis of form, style, theme, historical discourse, industrial position, and the filmmaking system she worked under. The function of industrial production systems is particularly salient when parsing Rothman's films as products of second wave exploitation. As an industrialized art form, film has always been subject to the pressures, desires, directions, and opinions of those providing the capital for production. Moreover, second wave exploitation films' meager budgets drove filmmaking decisions. Rothman's films were heavily impacted by their financers, particularly their production company and the sub-distributors who made preproduction agreements to distribute the films. Her films cannot be isolated from the system that produced them, and any approach to her career and films must consider circumstances of production. Subsequently, production and industrial histories germane to each film are interwoven into filmic analysis.

Rothman engaged with a number of filmic styles, but her visual fingerprint is consistent across her career. While her access to the filmmaking apparatus was largely based on her films' economic successes, wherein each film built on the returns of the previous, her visual competency remained consistent. This consistency does not equate to staticity. Rather, it signals Rothman's commitment, beyond rhetoric, to craft and her ability therein. Her thematic corpus, however, reveals a more tumultuous connection to her material, as her films oscillate between being idealistic, fatalistic, chimeric, and dystopic. Her films chronicle social problems and offer social solutions that range from altruistic to deeply pessimistic. This fissure is a reflection of her personal commitment to using film as a common visual language to expose broad inequality and social division while negotiating her deeply fraught and unsatisfying relationship to the industry that never fully embraced her.

Rothman's legacy is as a filmmaker who leverages film as a contemporary chronicle of, and solutional template for, tenacious thematic universals. This reputation is carefully built through films that function as couplets, each providing its own perspective on shared issues or thematic circumstances. Encompassing this segmentation are two critical attributes shared across her comprehensive body of work. First, each are products of their specific place and time, Los Angeles in the 1960s and 1970s, and chronicle their contemporary moment. Second, each film conceptualizes abstract themes as a method for imaginative rejoinders to persistent social issues. To unpack how her filmic dyads function and integrate into her oeuvre's endemic thematic construction, this and successive chapters move past the chronological construction of her personal and professional biography, considering her work by connective substance.

Rothman's filmic duos are all, in some way, concerned with the condition of contemporary womanhood. *The Student Nurses* and *Terminal Island*, arguably her most well-known films, are simultaneously practical and quixotic speculative narratives that offer solutions to the burden of patriarchal control over women's lives. *The Velvet Vampire* and *Group Marriage*, examined in chapter seven, are her statements in women's sexuality and desires, sexual and otherwise. Both are grounded in outcomes of the sexual revolution of the 1960s and 1970s, what was "not only a change in manners and morals; that had already been occurring discreetly in minds and bedrooms across the nation. It was the fact that sex was no longer a private matter that took place behind closed doors."[2] *The Working Girls*, Rothman's most personal film, speaks to the conditions of women's labor; its focus on women's un- and underemployment pairs with the history of her unproduced adaptation of the Philip K. Dick novel *The Man in the High Castle*.

This chapter opens my extended analysis of her extent works with the brace of films that exemplify the industrial ethos of second wave exploitation:

Blood Bath/Track of the Vampire and *It's a Bikini World*. The former is an amalgamation of a repurposed foreign film acquisition and footage from two separate directors shooting for two different narratives. The latter is a potent combination of second wave's exploitation investment in faddism, teenagers, and skin: a beach party film. These films engender a fruitful examination of Rothman's first attempt at ideological filmmaking, her beginnings in the industry, and the dangers of historicizing women in film when their subjectivity is excluded.

Both films were produced by Corman, *Blood Bath/Track of the Vampire* under his FilmGroup banner, and *It's a Bikini World* by AIP; both were distributed by AIP. As noted in chapter three, AIP was founded by James (Jim) Nicholson and Samuel (Sam) Arkoff in 1954. At the time Nicholson, an ex-theater owner, was working at Realart, a rereleasing company that owned the theatrical rights to the entire Universal Pictures library.[3] He met Arkoff, a lawyer, through Realart. Looking to start his own distribution company, Nicholson approached Arkoff and after a courtship of six months the two went into business together, with Arkoff in charge of the business end of AIP and Nicholson handling the creative side.[4] Capitalizing on the teenager demographic as core audience, AIP became one of the most successful producers and distributors of second wave exploitation films, releasing films organized around "fads" like surfing, rock'n' roll, hot rods, etc., and incorporating a growing sense of youth dissatisfaction with the social and cultural norms of previous generations. One of their earliest and most fruitful collaborations was with Roger Corman. As Corman recalls:

> We agreed to do three pictures, the first of which would be *The Fast and the Furious*. But Jim has to sell the pictures to sub-distributors, or franchise holders, who were willing to advance money for the other film. So Jim, Sam, and I then flew to New Orleans, Chicago, and New York to arrange the backing from franchise holders. The West Coast was handled out of Los Angeles. Jim and Sam had a great deal. I was providing the movies as producer/director and the franchise holders advanced the money—about $5,000 to $15,000 per distributor per picture depending on the size of his territory. My deal was that Jim and Sam had to raise all the money from the sub-distributors or it was no deal.[5]

It was during Corman's time with AIP that Rothman began to work for him. Based on her film school reputation and her Directors Guild Award, Rothman was quickly hired as Corman's assistant. Corman: "There was no way I could not hire Stephanie."[6]

SALVAGE JOBS AND HISTORICAL DISSONANCE

The first professional film to bear the title card "Directed by Stephanie Rothman" is one Rothman does not consider a film she, in fact, directed. As part of her work as Corman's assistant, she was responsible for taking films he had purchased internationally and re-shaping them for US release. In this capacity, she worked on projects colloquially termed "Iron Curtain salvage jobs": films purchased from Eastern Europe and the then-USSR that needed to be edited, dubbed, and "Americanized" for US exhibition. In this role, Rothman served as Associate Producer on *Voyage to the Prehistoric Planet* (Curtis Harrington, 1965) and *Queen of Blood* (Curtis Harrington, 1966), two films that were "built around Soviet special effects extracted from, respectively, *Planeta Bur* (1962), *Niebo Zowiet* (1959), and *Mechte Nevstruchi* (1961)."[7] Rothman recalls her partnership with Harrington fondly: "Curtis was very cordial, and I enjoyed watching him work, and you know, I learned something from watching how he functioned on the set, and how the production went along. He was comfortable having me there and I was grateful to learn from him."[8]

The films she worked on with Harrington emanated from FilmGroup, a production and distribution company Corman operated outside of his work with AIP. Before Rothman, FilmGroup's resident salvage jobs expert was Francis Ford Coppola, who left the company after his first Corman-funded feature, *Dementia 13* (1963). After Coppola left, "Rothman had clearly established herself as his [Corman's] resident expert in the field of international patchwork."[9] Her reputation for revising-through-editing international films for the domestic market would eventually lead to her "directorial" credit on *Blood Bath/Track of the Vampire*, a film that took a circuitous route into Rothman's hands.

Video Watchdog's Tim Lucas chronicles *Blood Bath/Track of the Vampire*'s production history in a three-part series in early 1991 that shaped Rothman's historical interaction with the film as a narrative of contestation. The impacts of Lucas's history are emblematic of what stories are told about women when those same women are denied narrative agency and voice. His positioning of Rothman's involvement in the film has contributed to a broader construction of Rothman in second wave exploitation film history as little more than a barrier to the work of fellow director Jack Hill. Spending most of his career in second wave exploitation, Hill is most remembered as the man who "discovered" the iconic exploitation actress Pam Grier. Hill's films *Spider Baby* (1967), *The Big Doll House* (1971), *The Big Bird Cage* (1972), *Coffy* (1973), *Foxy Brown* (1974), and *Switchblade Sisters* (1975) are considered classics of the second wave exploitation cycle. Lucas's historical construction is highly dependent on interviews with the wide variety of people involved with various iterations of the film, from directors to actors to producers. The one notable exception is Rothman: her voice, point of view, or recollections are completely absent. Rather, Lucas recounts Rothman's participation through other players in the process, discursively constructing her outside of her own subjectivity. To counter this, I've taken Lucas's narrative and interwoven Rothman back into the film's history. While, as Erin Hill notes, "there's no such thing as The Truth, especially not in a place like film history," there is value is presenting all narratives of the "truth."[10]

Hill was a friend and classmate of Francis Ford Coppola at USC. Coppola introduced Hill to Corman, which precipitated Hill's first working relationship with the producer in 1962: salvaging a Yugoslavian film called *Operation: Titan/Operacija Ticijan*, which Corman had purchased to recut, supplement, and release.[11] Corman hired Coppola as script supervisor to provide the dialogue,[12] and sent a cast with him to Dubrovnik to complete the film. When Corman saw the film, he declared it unfit for release. Corman hired Hill to recut the film and "shoot some extra footage of the star, William Campbell, as an insane painter who murders his models."[13] Hill shot new characters, story, and locations around Southern California and retitled the film *Blood Bath*.[14] Rothman recounts:

> Roger invited me to a screening Jack was giving of a cut of it, and I went and I watched it with Roger and afterwards Roger asked what I could do with this, and he took it away from Jack.[15] He asked me to come up with a new screenplay which would incorporate the original Yugoslavian footage, as much of it as I could use, and any footage I could use of . . . Jack's, and my own original footage, which I would write and then incorporate into this, so that a whole new film would be created.[16]

Rothman gave her version of the film the working title *Track of the Vampire* and attempted to craft a unified whole out of the disparate footage she was given. The resulting film—a combination of the original *Operation: Titan/Operacija Ticijan*, Coppola's additions, Hill's footage and new storyline, and Rothman's pivot to a vampire film—makes about as much sense as one would assume. The basic plot follows painter Antonio Sordi, who is possessed by his ancient ancestor Erno, a painter who was burned at the stake for stealing the souls of his model by painting them into his canvas. In his possessed state, Sordi is a vampire, killing young women and embalming them in wax in his art studio. Sordi is infatuated with a ballerina named Dorian, whom he believes is the reincarnation of Melizza, Erno's former lover who turned on him to save herself from prosecution as a witch. As Sordi/Erno attempts to kill Dorian as revenge against Melizza, Melizza herself manifests from her portrait in Sordi/Erno's studio, bringing three of his wax covered victims back to life. They kill Sordi/Erno, boiling him alive in a vat of wax and Dorian is saved. Actor Sig Haig, who worked with both Hill and Rothman on the film, recalled: "That was a pretty confusing film wasn't it? Particularly since—I forgot what version it was—but we were running down the street, and turned a corner, and in the next shot I went from clean-shaven to a beard. It was pretty weird."[17]

Rothman's version of the film sat on a shelf for a year until released under the title *Blood Bath* as part of a double bill with *Queen of Blood* in 1966.[18] Both Hill and Rothman were given directing and writing credits, with Hill listed as producer. When the film was sold for screening on television, additional padding scenes were added to lengthen it, and its title switched yet again to Rothman's preferred *Track of the Vampire*.[19] With so many hands crafting the film, it is unsurprising that Rothman disowns the film.[20] She declared: "I don't look at *Blood Bath* as my film—I look at it as something I finished. Someone in Yugoslavia began it, then Hill took over, and then I finished it."[21] Yet the film has played an important role in Rothman's historicization in certain film histories, particularly those concerned with the legacy of Jack Hill, including Hill himself.

Hill's legacy includes chastisement of Rothman for "ruining" *Blood Bath*, a reproach that has come from Hill and Hill scholars alike. Hill has most often taken issue with the narrative changes Rothman made to the film. In Lucas's history, Hill commented: "I think the footage I shot was pretty good, but for whatever reason, Stephanie was fascinated with vampires and she decided to make a vampire movie out of it. To tell you the truth, I felt like throwing up when I heard about it."[22] Hill was no longer working for FilmGroup or Corman when Rothman was given the film and was not involved in conversations about the direction of the film, and yet comments freely. Hill's attribution of sole agency to Rothman in the changes made is presumptive, and that presumption forms his discursive position as ascribing blame to Rothman for mangling his vision. When one balances Rothman's account of her role in the film against the dominant history that excluded her voice altogether, a more complicated picture beings to emerge, as she narrates a more collaborative approach to the film after Hill's departure:

> I had to invent something, and working this way was so restrictive. What could I do with it? It had originally been an action murder

mystery. Or actually, it hadn't been, I think it had been a tale of smugglers and revenge, and then the Jack Hill version had been a story about a mad artist who killed beautiful young women. After suggesting several story lines to Roger he picked one of them, which was, why not turn this shadowy figure who was the mad artist in the second version that was shot into a vampire who stalks people? So that's what I did. It was because it was the only way I could figure out, and Roger agreed, to make all this material comprehensible.[23] I mean, the only way to be able to do something with all this disparate footage was to have a character who looked completely different from the lead, and dressed completely different, and did things that were completely unrelated. And then to take these scenes and try to interweave them with the other scenes from the Yugoslavian film and what could be salvaged from what Jack had shot. Because we had to throw out, I had to throw out, a portion of that.[24]

Adding Rothman's voice to the conversation destabilizes the overreliance on Hill as omniscient historical narrator and forces an expansion of historical thought.

While it is unsurprising for any filmmaker to defend their own work, scholars who research his career echo his aggression towards Rothman as objective history rather than subjective positioning. Calum Waddell, who authored a book on Hill, notes Rothman's involvement in the film in discursive alignment with Hill when he pens comments including: "Certainly, it is not difficult to see which parts of the movie are Rothman's—with her ridiculous, not to mention infantile, vampire interlude largely disrupting the flow of the picture and featuring randomly in the plotline";[25] "Still, if one can accept the preposterous vampire interludes";[26] and "if Rothman's vampire inserts were not bad enough."[27] Criticism of a film by scholars is part of the rigor of cinema studies, and criticism itself isn't inherently problematic in assessing the film's directorial vision. Yet the discursive and tonal construction of Rothman that Hill promotes is echoed uncritically by Waddell, culminating in statements where author and subject are difficult to distinguish.[28] For example, Hill comments on the film by saying: "I had more of a psychological thriller so I thought she just messed it up."[29] Waddell follows with a remarkably similar comment when he says: "Rothman's attempt to turn what might have been a fine psycho-thriller into a vampire flick."[30]

Lucas falls into the same rhetoric. Of Hill's version of the film he pronounces, "[it] appears to have been more than a sum of its parts,"[31] and that "Rothman was responsible for most of the completed film's *worst* footage."[32]

In reference to an individual scene included by Hill and reshot by Rothman, he asserts: "as originally directed and edited by Jack Hill, however, it may have been a *tour de force*."[33] The most puzzling circumstance of the strident defense of Hill's film that Waddell and Lucas give is that *they've never seen it*. Hill's version of the film was never released, and his footage was recut by Rothman; no copy of his version of *Blood Bath* exists. While their lack of access to the film is not something Hill's champions dispute, it is something they easily and willingly overlook, basing their complaints about Rothman's involvement on what they assume the film *would have been*.

Prognostications of what Hill may have created move past film analysis into speculative fiction, a slippage fostered by Rothman's lack of inclusion in the historical accounting. The *Blood Bath/Track of the Vampire* history provides a micro-example of the larger impacts of excluding women's authorial voice from film history. When women's voices are absent from film history, what trace of them that is preserved is often created outside of their own voice and divorced from their lived experience, memorializing a flawed accounting of their participation, labor, and influence. When women are not able to represent themselves, or when their voices are removed entirely from the historical conversation, their trace is either distorted or erased, leading to the re-codification of the idea that women do not direct films because there is no record of it in historical accounts. Rothman's participation in the film has been codified through assumptive discourse: Hill's assumptions about how and why the film's core story was changed, scholars' assumptions about the value of the work Hill produced, and assumptions surrounding Rothman's unrestrained agency in the process. These issues are recurring, as Rothman's future interactions with Hill, chronicled in a subsequent chapter, would continue to shadow her.

THE LAST BEACH BLANKET BINGO

After *Blood Bath/Track of the Vampire*, Rothman served as associate producer on Lennie Weinrib's *Beach Ball* (1965) and directed second unit on the film.[34] Her next film, however, was her own. *It's a Bikini World*, which Rothman considers her first "true" directorial credit, was the last of AIP's beach party movies. Jump-started by the release of *Beach Party* (William Asher, 1963), AIP released numerous beach party films over a four-year span.[35] The beach party films were a result of AIP's philosophy for production and marketing decisions, known as the "Peter Pan Syndrome." This credo defined AIP's filmmaking logic as:

a) a younger child will watch anything an older child will watch;
b) an older child will not watch anything a younger child will watch;
c) a girl will watch anything a boy will watch;
d) a boy will not watch anything a girl will watch; therefore
e) to catch your greatest audience, you zero in on the 19-year-old male.[36]

Concretizing teenage men as the most desirable audience demographic, it's no surprise that the company doubled down on beach party films, which combined beautiful women in bikinis, popular music, and a lack of authoritative adults.

Beach party films showcased Southern California as an endless apolitical party of surf, sand, and fun.[37] Notable entries include *Beach Blanket Bingo* (William Asher, 1965), *How to Stuff a Wild Bikini* (William Asher, 1965), *Dr. Goldfoot and the Bikini Machine* (Norman Taurog, 1965), and *Bikini Beach* (William Asher, 1964), one of the company's highest grossing films.[38] The films were so popular that, Pablo Dominguez Andersen notes, mainstream studios like "Paramount and Columbia began to emulate their smaller competitors' success formula . . . all in all, between 1959 and 1966 Hollywood would produce more than thirty surf and beach films."[39] Rothman and Swartz share writing credits on *It's a Bikini World*; production began in 1965 with Swartz producing, although it would not be released until late 1967 through AIP subsidiary Trans American. The delay in releasing the film saw it debut in theaters as the popularity of the cycle waned significantly. Rothman describes the film as the last—if not one of the last—of the beach movies, and one that killed off the cycle.[40]

The film follows Delilah (Deborah Walley), who is spending the summer with her friend Pebbles (Suzie Kaye) on an anonymous Southern California beach. Delilah soon meets Mike (Tommy Kirk), the beach's resident heartthrob. Mike immediately tries to seduce Delilah, expecting his reputation and charm to quickly win her over. Delilah is unimpressed, spurning Mike's advances and telling him she prefers someone "serious." Mike takes her rejection as a challenge, concocting revenge: he will win Delilah over and then break her heart. Mike trades in his bare chest and bathing suit for a sweater, shorts, knee socks, glasses, and a bowtie, calling himself "Herbert," Mike's serious, scholarly, and imaginary brother.

Herbert begins courting Delilah, while Delilah plans Mike's comeuppance for his arrogance. Her plan is to best Mike, the beach's resident sports star, at several athletic contests. Herbert trains Delilah to beat his "brother" while developing genuine feelings for her. A local dance club and the kids' primary hangout, Daddy's Dungeon, has partnered with a new magazine catering to the teenager crowd to sponsor a series of races to promote the latest teen fad: skate boarding. Daddy (Sig Haig) uses the opportunity to hawk his latest product line: skateboardz, which follows in his line of teen-approved consumables like kuztom kartz, cyclez, surfboardz, and discz.[41] Mike beats Delilah in the first race, but she refuses to give up, challenging him to contest after contest.

The climax of the film comes when Daddy announces a multi-sport race, the winner of which will go on tour across the country promoting his products and the magazine venture. Just before the race, Delilah learns of Mike's deception and exposes his lies. Mike attempts to explain and apologize, to no end. The two enter Daddy's cross-country race and compete in a series of events: car racing, speed swimming, speedboat racing, long-distance furniture moving, motorcycle racing, long-distance swimming, running, camel racing, and skateboarding. During the race the lead oscillates between Mike and Delilah, and at the end Mike feigns a foot injury, conceding defeat to Delilah. Sublimating his ego to his newfound love wins Delilah over, and the film ends with the two beginning their new romantic relationship with mutual respect and playful competition.

It's a Bikini World shares a number of similarities with other entries in AIP's beach party series that position it squarely within the bounds of the cycle, including casting, musical performances as spectacle, and characterization. Deborah Walley and Tommy Kirk appeared in a number of beach party films; Walley became somewhat of a regular AIP "bikini girl," with roles in *Beach Blanket Bingo*, *Dr. Goldfoot and the Bikini Machine*, and *The Ghost in the Invisible Bikini* (Don Weiss, 1966). While Kirk is perhaps most well-known for his work in Disney films like *The Shaggy Dog* (Charles Barton, 1959), *Swiss Family Robinson* (Ken Annakin, 1960) and *The Absent-Minded Professor* (Robert Stevenson, 1961), he reunited with Walley in *The Ghost in the Invisible Bikini* the year after *Bikini World* and starred in the beach party-musical heist mash-up *Catalina Caper* (Lee Sholem, 1967). *Bikini World* also invested in beach party films' moments of spectacle, particularly around rock 'n' roll music. The film uses Daddy's to stage performances from popular bands such as The Animals, The Toys, The Gentrys, The Castaways, and Pat and Lolly Vegas. Rothman had no control over what bands would appear in the film. As she explained: "We got an agent, a music agent, who told us who the hottest groups were at the time, whoever was top on the Billboard charts the week we called. We got them."[42]

Incorporating popular music acts into beach party movies was *de rigueur*, allowing the actors to shimmy, shake, and gyrate in skimpy bathing suits, heightening "the sexuality and sense of freedom associated with teens and rock and roll."[43] The inclusion of popular music also facilitated a key aspect of beach party films: women go-go dancing in miniscule fringed bikinis. *Beach Party* and *Bikini Beach* both feature a character named Miss Perpetual Motion, whose "gyrations accentuated by her fringed bikini top and pants . . . bowl men over with the sexuality of her dancing."[44] *Bikini World* features two go-go dancing scenes that halt the narrative so the diegetic and non-diegetic audiences can watch these women move unobstructed by the cinematic function of the film itself. The second go-go dancing scene literalizes this, as Daddy, Mr. Pulp and his assistant, Mike, and Mike's roommate Woody (Bobby Pickett) sit and watch a dancer in a glittering red fringe bikini audition on an empty dance floor while The Castaways play from the stage.

While scholars like Gary Morris and Thomas Doherty[45] have described beach party films as "middle-class teen normality"[46] that offer "clean" fun, the spectacularization of dance in beach party films hints at a more complicated set of ideological values at work. While sexual activity in beach films is kept to kissing, sex—and bodies—are constantly on display. In *Bikini World*, teenagers are almost always in some state of exposure: women wear bikinis at the beach, at home, at Daddy's, at the ice cream parlor, and men in these spaces rarely have shirts on. The ethos of "the beach" as a space of hedonistic freedom and barely concealed sexual tension spills over into the non-beach world as the teenagers refuse to distinguish between beachwear and other types of clothing. R. L. Rutsky sees this as emblematic of how beach party films foreground "elements of teenage culture, rock-and-roll, bohemian philosophy, and beat culture."[47] Integrating various aspects of these subcultural elements complicates the films' ideological commitments, something Rothman leverages in *Bikini World* to comment both on the cycle and the presentation of women within it. As Winton Wheeler Dixon remarks: "Rothman's film, far from objectifying women, posits a world of cheerful indolence in which men and women are equally engaged in the pursuit of pleasure alone."[48]

More often than not, that pursuit brings the characters to Sid Haig's Daddy and his club Daddy's Dungeon, recognizable tropes pulled from other beach party films. *Beach Party* and *Muscle Beach Party* both feature beat-like coffee houses called Big Daddy's whose owner sports a goatee, black sunglasses, and "beat" inspired clothing. In *Bikini World*, Daddy has a carefully crafted "beat" look: beard, turtlenecks, beret, dark sunglasses, and a leather jacket. Invoking the Beat Generation's rejection of cultural norms, dismissal of materialism, and sexual exploration, Daddy is a visual reminder of dangerous ideological nonconformism simmering just under the surface of middle-class teenage rebellion. Daddy's Dungeon reinforces this threat through its unusual aesthetic. Rothman used the Haunted House Club as the location for the Dungeon. The Haunted House Club was known for its macabre decorations: a spider web made from white lights topped its sign on Hollywood and Vine, skeletons, ghosts, and other supernatural paraphernalia adorned the ceiling and walls, and notoriously, the performance stage was set in the yawing mouth of a monster replete with smoke pouring from its nostrils, horns, glowing eyes, and jagged teeth that surrounded the band playing in the monster's mouth.[49] But Daddy's threat of nonconformity is performative, and Rothman uses his character to satirize the idea of the "teenager market," a comment on AIP's own capitalization of the youth market through the Peter Pan Syndrome and beach films themselves.[50] Daddy's partnership with Harvey Pulp (Jack Bernardi), the magazine founder, is the clearest example of this. Pulp is invested in creating a magazine that appeals to the teenager market but has no knowledge of what that appeal may be. He turns to Daddy for partnership, banking on Daddy's successful history of commercial capitalization on teenage trends to make his new magazine venture work. Daddy, like Pulp, is no teenager. However, his deliberately constructed "outsider" aesthetic and casual but careful usage of "hip" lingo maintains his "cool" and influential status with the teenagers. He is so aware of his performative aesthetic as the key to his sway with the desired market that he refuses to be photographed without his sunglasses on, lest he ruin his credibility. He leverages that cultural capital to brand "Daddy's" on all the products the teenagers buy from him, from skateboards to bathing suits: shameless capitalist gain obscured by his reputation in the community.

Rothman also attacks the "middle-class" fun of beach party movies with a brief but key integration of class politics in the film. At the Dungeon, Daddy introduces English rock band The Animals, who perform what would become their legendary "working man's anthem" of loss, economic precarity, and frustrated ambition, "We Gotta Get Out of This Place." The performance opens with lead singer Eric Burden standing center stage, hands on his hips, glowering at the bikini-clad crowd on the dance floor. As the first bass notes of the song begin, smoke pours from the stage monster's nostrils, swirling around Burden's head, and the camera cuts to a low angle shot of the singer, a monster fang rising from his bottom left as he intones the song's opening lines: "In this dirty part of the city / Where the sun refuse to shine / People tell me there ain't no use in trying."[51] Rothman then cuts to a straight on close-up of Burden as he looks out over the bathing-suited crowd and sings "My girl you're so young and pretty / And one thing I know is true / You'll be dead before your time is due."[52] As the last line of that verse rings out, the camera pulls out into a medium wide shot, juxtaposing the lyric's macabre sentiment with the monster's glowing eyes, wide-stretched and menacing red mouth, and Burden centered between the stage monster's fangs. The song ramps up to the chorus, building speed and volume, and Rothman's camera roves across the stage, quick-cutting between Burden's face, his hand rhythmically tapping against his thigh, and the other band members. Keyboardist Dave Rowberry looks directly into the camera and sings, "We gotta get out of this place."[53]

The intensity of the song and performance, highlighted for the viewer by Rothman's shot choices and editing patterns, goes unnoticed by Daddy's beach party crowd. Burden, in khaki pants, a button-down red shirt, and jean jacket, is a startling contrast to the bathing-suited, barefooted teenagers in the audience. As he sings lines like "Now my girl you're so young and pretty, and one thing I know is true, you'll be dead before your time is due" and "Watch my daddy in bed a-dyin,' watched his hair been turnin' grey, he's been workin' and slavin' his life away,"[54] Rothman cuts to the audience, smiling and dancing happily, oblivious to the song's lyrics and plaintive cry for autonomy and respect.[55] The camera lingers on the dancers from the shoulders up, emphasizing their placid smiles and obtuseness to the anger and despair emanating from the stage. The dissonance between the song and the audience's reaction to it is jarring. In aligning a song about the desperate struggles of the working class against the systemic oppression of capitalism with the blinding obliviousness of the audience to those struggles, Rothman indicates the apolitical nature of the beach party films while highlighting the capitalist exploitation of the demographic at which the films are aimed. She said of the sequence: "I think it speaks for itself."[56]

Taking the standardized beach party formula and combining it with a story that explicitly tackles thorny political issues like economic exploitation and gender equity gives Rothman leverage to complicate the film past the simple adventures of "a group of white middle-class teenagers who rent a beach cabin for a last summer flight before adulthood."[57] Dixon calls the film "arguably the first feminist surf film,"[58] and from the outset, Rothman presents Delilah as a woman who demands respect from, and substance in, any potential paramour, unlike the amenable and interchangeable "bikini girls" that populated most beach party films. Her immediate disdain for Mike's ego and presumptuousness pervades their first conversation:

MIKE: Why don't you join the party?
DELILAH: It's nice to feel wanted.
MIKE: There is a vacancy.
DELILAH: There sure is. Right between your ears.[59]

When Pebbles asks Delilah why she is not interested in Mike, she responds: "He's conceited and he's got no right to be."[60] She elaborates that his reputation and athletic prowess does not make him automatically irresistible, nor does it excuse his intense narcissism and sense of entitlement to women's romantic affections. While there is no definition of a "feminist" film, and feminism manifests as a multiplicity of beliefs and behaviors, Rothman manages to achieve something empowering in *Bikini World* that other beach party films do not: Delilah, the film's leading lady, is unimpressed.

Following Rothman's commitment to comedy as social commentary, the film's gender politics are narrated through humor. After Delilah decides to enter Daddy's first skateboard race, she and Herbert go to Daddy's Dungeon to purchase her a skateboard. Daddy asks her what color board she wants, and she replies, "Fuchsia." Herbert scoffs at her choice, patronizingly telling her skateboards don't come in that color, and implying the ridiculousness of her feminization of the sport. Daddy looks at them both and replies, "Fuchsia #1, fuchsia #2, or fuchsia #3?"[61] Rothman's punch line implicates Mike's regressive gender-based ideas around sport, rather than Delilah's request, as laughable. Rothman uses supporting characters in a similar way. Pebbles, a seemingly stereotypical "blonde" has a series of exchanges with her boyfriend Woody that function as stand-alone comic moments underscoring the film's take on gender politics and gendered expectations in romantic relationships. One such exchange happens as the two are dancing at Daddy's Dungeon:

PEBBLES: Woody, let's go to a movie tonight.
WOODY: Can't, left my discount card at home. How about having dinner instead?
PEBBLES: Great!
WOODY: Ok! What time will you have it ready?[62]
[Pebbles rolls her eyes, exasperatedly pats him on the chest, and dances away, leaving Woody befuddled and alone.]

The comedy in these scenes matches the light-hearted tone of the film while simultaneously foregrounded its "equality of the sexes" message, giving "us a tantalizing peak at what might have been a less sexist and more egalitarian genre, in which men and women at play exist as equals, rather than rivals."[63] While the trend of newly assertive women was popular in mainstream romantic comedies of the time like those of Doris Day and Rock Hudson, it was uncommon in the beach party cycle, providing Rothman with a novel "hook."

Delilah's pursuit of sport as pathway to proving equality reflects real-world efforts. In 1966 Roberta "Bobbi" Gibb became the first woman to run the Boston Marathon, despite the race director pronouncing women "not physiologically able" to do so.[64] Less than ten years later, in 1973, a global audience of 90 million people[65] watched as tennis superstar Billie Jean King beat the game's elder statesman Bobby Riggs in three quick sets. Dubbed the "Battle of the Sexes," the match, like Gibb's run, was women "proving" their equality through sport. But while Rothman is an egalitarian, she's also a cynic, and the women in *Bikini World* don't excise chauvinistic men from their lives entirely. Pebbles briefly leaves Woody after he underappreciates her one too many times, and Woody takes up with several anonymous bikini babes until Pebbles eventually takes him back. While Delilah says she is inclined to a boyfriend who is "serious," her first date with Herbert questions her commitment to that idea. Rothman does so through a set of visual gags and linguistic reversals. Delilah asks Herbert to show her the sites around town that "really swing"; he takes her to a zoo to watch a monkey swing on a bar. Herbert asks if she enjoys records. When Delilah happily answers yes, he takes her to the Los Angeles Hall of Records. He won't dance with her at Daddy's and dismisses the rock 'n' roll music, proclaiming to prefer classical and polka. In getting what she thinks she wants Delilah is forced to interrogate her desires and question her commitment to her stated principles, as Rothman prods the audience to see Delilah as she believes Mike's to be, only in different ways. Additionally, almost everything Delilah does in the film is motivated by a man she professes to disdain and with whom she believes she has only interacted once. Many of the conversations she has with Herbert are about Mike, and the time they spend together is only so Herbert can help her best Mike is the sporting contests. Delilah may be the vessel for Rothman's ideological message of gender equality, but Rothman refuses to simplify that message by allowing Delilah to be uncomplicated in her beliefs. It is precisely complexity like this that reflect Rothman's early filmmaking as exploration into contemporary social issues commentary, infusing nuance and refusing easy answers, even within a rote filmic cycle like beach party movies.

This same commitment to complication is showcased in the film's formal style. As Rothman noted, "Most of these beach movies were made by elderly men who directed them in an antiquated style. They were cronies of Sam Arkoff. I just wanted to make it look like a contemporary film with some excitement."[66] The pace of the film's kinetic energy is set by the opening title sequence. As generic surf-rock plays, Rothman films beachgoers performing aerial stunts using a small trampoline, running playfully around the beach, and using taut blankets to toss one another into the air. The title sequence alternates between these live-action stunts and static animation title cards with Pop Art-inspired comic word bubbles displaying credit information. Rothman recalls: "It was made in '66 and I believe it was the first or among the first to use animated bubbles coming out of people's mouths. I was inspired to do this by the pop art movement. But the film wasn't released until late '67 early '68 so by then this looked tired."[67] The title card animation is reminiscent of Lichtenstein's early 1960s work, and Pop Art references reoccur throughout the film's mise-en-scène, most noticeably the Warholesque "soup can" print in Mike and Woody's apartment.

Rothman peppers the film with varied shot types to maintain audience interest in a familiar setting. Delilah first appears on the beach as a reflection in a pair of sunglasses. A short beach volleyball scene moves from background to foreground when the ball is hit directly into the lens of the camera, and the sports sequences feature sped-up action, showing what Dixon calls "a Monty Python flair for the absurd."[68] Perhaps the most interesting sequences she composed are the musical performance interludes. As noted earlier, the musical performances are the type of spectacular segments that stop narrative. The performances are straightforwardly staged: musicians clustered together in middle ground and center frame, facing the audience; even the one performance that does not take place on a proper stage is organized in the same manner. In part this is because these segments are meant to reflect nightclub performances. Rather than film them in the same straightforward manner in which they are staged, Rothman again employs quick cutting, combined with alternative camera angles and other devices like superimposition, to breathe life and movement into the segments. This is best exemplified in The Toys' performance at Daddy's.

A girl group in the vein of The Supremes or The Shangri-Las, The Toys perform on the Dungeon's monster stage in matching dresses, similar hairstyles, and synchronized dance movements while backed by a house band. Outside of some arm and shoulder gesticulations, the three women move very little while they sing their hit song "Attack" and the segment has the potential to be visually rote. Instead, Rothman opens the performance with a medium shot with a slightly elevated angle of lead singer Barbara Harris singing directly into the camera. As in the sequence with The Animals, Rothman slowly pulls out to show singers Barbara Parritt and June Montiero arranged behind Harris, singing backup; the house band occupies the background. A series of quick cuts follow: a close-up of Montiero, a close-up of Parritt, a wide shot of the entire stage, a close-up of Harris, and two sequences of medium shots that move from Harris to Montiero to Harris to Parritt and back to Harris again. Rothman holds on a wide shot of the stage for three beats and then shoots Harris in a close-up from the right side as a Harris's mirror image is superimposed on the left side of the screen, making it appear as if she is singing to herself. She holds on this shot for a verse, fades the right image to black, holds on the left image for one beat, and then returns to a wide shot. All of these cuts happen in one minute and fifty-three seconds of a two-minute-and-fifteen-second segment. She finishes the performance pushing in on Harris, bringing the sequence full circle, giving the segment a dynamism unusual to staged performances in beach films. Rothman uses similar strategies in the other musical performances, conveying movement and emotion in otherwise static scenes.

Both *Blood Bath/Track of the Vampire* and *It's a Bikini World* contain themes and ideas that would resurface in Rothman's work. The figure of the vampire as equally desirous and deadly forms the foundation for her fourth film, *The Velvet Vampire*. As in *Blood Bath/Track of the Vampire*, *Velvet*'s vampire protagonist would be haunted and defeated by ancient love. The comedy in *It's a Bikini World* templated how Rothman would skewer romantic relationships in all her successive films, particularly in *Group Marriage*. Most importantly, *It's a Bikini World* proved a major milestone for Rothman's career; as she says, "It's main importance to me is that it proved I could direct a feature film."[69]

Chapter 6

IMAGINING A POST-PATRIARCHY

> Rothman's films are not so much a cinema of social
> problems as ones of social solutions.
> —TERRY CURTIS FOX[1]

In 1968, one hundred women on the Atlantic City, New Jersey, boardwalk protested what they saw as the categorical example of US racism, sexism, and capitalism: the Miss America pageant.[2] Holdings signs that read "Welcome to the Miss America Cattle Auction," "All women are beautiful," and "Let's judge ourselves as people," the protesters took aim at misogynistic and racist beauty standards. The following year, Redstockings, a socialist feminist group in New York City, organized an abortion speak out where a crowd of three hundred listened to women tell the stories of their illegal abortions.[3] In 1970, a group of women led by representatives of the National Organization of Women (NOW), New York Radical Feminists, Media Women, and other groups held a five-hour sit-in at the editorial offices of the *Ladies' Home Journal* to demand a "liberation" issue.[4] That same year, Black Panther Party co-founder Huey Newton released an open letter wherein "he pushed the organization to express explicit support for the goals of the women's liberation movement"[5] as more and more women took up leadership roles in the party and spearheaded its community programming. These are but a few examples of the drive for gender equality's evolution in the late 1960s and 1970s, as it moved from the interpersonal conflict of *It's a Bikini World* to a swell of collective action. This transformation is reflected in Rothman's yoked films, *The Student Nurses* and *Terminal Island*.

The Student Nurses and *Terminal Island* are social account chronicles proffering imaginative solutions to ideological, political, and patriarchal control over women's lives. In doing so, Rothman moves past the simple gender equality signposting in *It's a Bikini World* to conceptualizing pathways for the broad implementation of a post-patriarchal world. These solutions come in two forms: everyday resistance to control achieved by working within the patriarchal system to disband it, or utopic social imagining outside of the systemic oppression of hierarchy and patriarchy.

Patriarchy in Rothman's films exists as the normative order of social and gender relations, a generally referenced framework of hegemonic control that is neither natural nor naturally occurring but all-encompassing. While Rothman does not claim a specific feminist identity, *The Student Nurses* and *Terminal Island* are indicative of the milieu of liberal and radical feminisms of the early and mid-1970s. As the student nurses each work toward self-autonomy across discrete stories, the criminal women banished to the San Bruno Maximum Security Detention Center, aka Terminal Island, collectively destroy the oppressive "homegrown" patriarchy on the island in a bid to create an equitable utopia. The films represent an evolution of political thinking that highlights how the ERA-inflected, legislative, mainstream strategies of entities like NOW (read: *The Student Nurses*) won't prevail in a social order where gender is criminalized without a revolutionary reordering of the relation between men and women (read: *Terminal Island*), echoing statements like those from Black Panther Elaine Brown, who said, "We cannot be free in a system that oppressed us in the first place."[6]

To trace this progression, this chapter provides close textual analysis of these two films in order to highlight Rothman's statement on the possibilities of social change and the potentialities of utopias. Importantly, both films are indicative of Rothman as ideologue director: *The Student Nurses* inaugurated Corman's New World reputation for "progressive pictures." and *Terminal Island* serves as a stark reminder of how Rothman was forced to navigate the strictures of sub-distributor production funding while maintaining her ethical sense of self.

"THE STUDENT NURSES . . . THEY COULD BE YOUR KIND OF WOMEN"[7]

Many successful films have multiple voices claiming credit for its achievements. The origin story of *The Student Nurses*, its resulting attributive citation, and Rothman's continued decentering in her own filmography is no different. While the film was critically influential in establishing Rothman's directorial ideology and formal style, it was also New World's first in-house film and grossed one million dollars in rentals on a budget of $150,000. The film, in combination with their critically successful foreign releases, cemented New World's place in the market. Beyond its financial success, the film was significant to New World for two reasons. First, it was the urtext for a highly profitable and much imitated cycle of "nurse" films. Second, the film is widely credited with jump-starting New World's—and Corman's—hematic commitment to films that advanced progressive thematic agenda particularly focused on broadly "feminist" content. By 1974, New World was being touted as "the only company producing films with a decided and committed feminist bent,"[8] thanks in large part to *The Student Nurses*. Given these multiple nodes of accomplishment and influence, the issue of credit is neither lightly taken nor easily adjudicated. As with *Blood Bath/Track of the Vampire*, my goal is not to rule on contentious positions of credit in Rothman's favor; assigning sole credit to a collaboratively constructed project like a film is naïve at best and disingenuous at worst. Rather, I add her voice into the historical conversation to challenge her industrial erasure and broaden the acknowledgment of women's creative contributions to second wave exploitation filmmaking.

Similar to the narrative of agency and recognition on *Blood Bath/Track of the Vampire*, the prevailing history of the inception of *The Student Nurses* exists outside of Rothman. The standard story is as follows: as part of his role in New World, Larry Woolner traveled around the country, speaking with distributors in various circuits about what type of film they would be interested in picking up or, perhaps, for which film they would be contributing financing.[9] From these discussions and on the strong performance of the 1969 film *The Babysitter* (Don Henderson), the story of a district attorney blackmailed to let a murderer go free by proof of his affair with his babysitter, Woolner thought a film about a student nurse would perform well. He pitched the idea to Corman, who agreed, but thought the idea could be even better if the film were about four student nurses rather than one.[10] With a basic idea in hand, Corman approached Rothman about making the film. Rothman relates:

> They wanted a film that was sexy like *The Babysitter*. Their idea of sexy, of course, was to have nudity in it, because only recently American films had started to have nudity in them, and the films that had nudity in them were much more successful than the ones that didn't. So that was required. But aside from that, I could do anything I wanted. Roger said that, you know, "Make it exciting, and I want some action in it, I want some excitement. I want lots of nudity and come up with an interesting story."[11]

Starting from the brief concept of "four nurses + sex and nudity = interesting story," Rothman and Swartz sat down with long-time Corman employee and New World's story editor, Frances Dole, and spent a week hammering out the basics of the plot.[12]

Rothman's contribution to the narrative and ideological construction of the film was significant. Her primary goal was to craft a film that was aware of, influenced by, and responding to the social, political, and cultural upheaval the United States was embroiled in during the late 1960s and early 1970s. As she said: "I wanted to make this something that reflected the major concerns of the time and was rooted in the conflicts of the time."[13] Outside of representing her volatile contemporary moment, and demonstrating creativity under constraint, Rothman decided to use the dictated defining characteristic of the film—a story about student nurses—to upend expectations and explore the progressive themes she was invested in. Eschewing the conventional second wave exploitation impression of "student nurses" as nubile co-eds in revealing uniforms engaged in various hospital-based sexcapades,[14] Rothman used the nursing profession as a way for the women, and the audience, to explore the world outside the hospital. She explains:

> They were going to work in a hospital, they were going to be exposed to the various historical currents washing over all of us at that time, more so perhaps than many people who led more isolated and insular lives. [. . .] They were not frivolous. They were not looking for husbands. They were not obsessed with clothing, or their looks, or all the other disparaging associations that at that time were made with youth in women. They were serious young women about to embark on adult life, and they had placed themselves in a very challenging place, a hospital, where there were a lot of grim realities that they were going to not be able to avoid, and which most of them openly embraced.[15]

The focus on their profession serves as a handy vehicle for each woman to confront and overcome their own challenges while underscoring Rothman's commitment to the professionalization of women's labor. As recounted in chapter four, Rothman had an intense focus on professionalization in her own career, in part as a path to acceptance by the broader film establishment. Similar threads run through *The Student Nurses* where she establishes, as Dannis Peary notes, "professional roadblocks for each woman throughout the film, making it clear that for her women to triumph, they must emerge at the end with the occupational goals fulfilled, with nursing diplomas in hand."[16] Even one of the nurses who plans to live a life on the run makes a point to show up for graduation to finalize her professional status.

Corman assigned Rothman the film in February 1970, and shooting was slated to begin at the end of April. With such a short turnaround, there was no time for Rothman to write the film herself. Rothman and Swartz hired screenwriter Don Spencer, a cinema studies graduate student at UCLA,[17] to put together the script from their story under her supervision. Rothman says of Spencer: "He did, in our opinion, very good work. He contributed some excellent dialogue. The attitudes, the approaches, and what happens in the piece were mostly our ideas. The way it was executed, in terms of dialogue and the tone of the dialogue, were largely his."[18] While Spencer wrote, she and Swartz found locations, hired a crew, cast the film, and attended to all the other work necessary to get the film into production in two short months. What emerged from this fast and furious process was a vibrant, contemporary, opinionated, and political film about the nuanced lives of four women in their twenties living in Los Angeles during the turbulent end of the 1960s.

As Rothman described, incorporating these thematics into her film was something she and Swartz did outside of any requests from Corman:

> I mean, would he have said to us, "I want something like this in my piece"? No. He didn't say that. But we had both known him for a number of years now, and we knew that he was very open-minded about these issues, and so we didn't expect him to not accept them, and in fact that turned out to be true. I mean, he felt this was fine, this was interesting. It added richness to the plot, but it was nothing that he, in any way, would have wanted. That was not his selection. It was our selection.[19]

Corman, perhaps unsurprisingly, recounts his role in crafting the ideological stances in the film differently. He has said that it was important to him that the film "have something to say" and that he "insisted each had to work out her problems without relying on a boyfriend."[20] These statements are contradictory both to how he has narrated the germination of the film's idea[21] as well as how Rothman characterizes his reaction:

> When he first looked at the rough cut of *The Student Nurses*, he was a bit anxious about the freedom he had given me. But when it became a box-office success, he decided it was the right decision and a good time to make more films with themes of social activism in them. When he first saw the rough cut, he told me he didn't think it was "raunchy" enough [. . .] it concerned him that the girls were too intelligent. But he changed his mind when it did well in theaters.[22]

Work, Sex, and Liberation in LA

The Student Nurses follows four nursing students during their last days of training; each woman's story comprises roughly a quarter of the plot with various moments of overlap and transition. Phred (Karen Carlson), Sharon (Elaine Giftos), Priscilla (Barbara Leigh), and Lynn (Brioni Farrell) work, train, and live together in hospital-provided housing. Each woman confronts their own moments of patriarchal control, including restrictions on reproductive healthcare, police brutality, and sex-drive shaming, but these instances and challenges are self-contained to each character. As such, each woman embodies liberal feminism's individualization of equality and choice. While the student nurses may live and work together, they struggle separately. The women are introduced to the viewers during their last internship rotation before graduation; their rotation assignments are the catalyst for their storylines throughout the film. Indeed, the hospital as an institution—an amalgamation of home, school, and employment—enforces Foucauldian methods of control in hierarchal observation, normative and normalizing judgement, and examination.[23] This frames the women's struggles as resulting from the institutionality of patriarchy, metaphorized as the hospital. For clarity's sake, the general trajectory of each woman's story is outlined below.

Phred

Phred is assigned to gynecology and obstetrics. During her first shift, she accidently gives a patient an excessive dosage of medication. OB/GYN Dr. Casper (Lawrence P. Casey) successfully and safely resolves the situation. Phred and Casper begin a romantic relationship that eventually ends as a result of a series of ideological disagreements. The first comes when Casper shares with Phred a story about having lost a mother and baby during delivery. Phred is adamant about excluding any talk of death or dying from her life outside of the hospital, regardless of the fact that it is an inextricable part of both their professional lives. She is committed to confining herself to what she calls "clean" areas of medicine, which she defines as ones where people rarely die. Their critical disagreement comes when Casper agrees to perform an abortion on fellow nurse and housemate Priscilla, which Phred is adamantly against. Phred is hyper-concerned about the procedure taking place in the bedroom she and Priscilla share, thereby making it "unclean." She also opposes the procedure politically and ethically, accusing Casper of "murdering" the fetus. Phred leaves Casper for his roommate, Mark (Paul Camen). After graduation, she leaves nursing altogether to become a secretary in a psychiatrist's office, which she has determined to be "a very clean area of medicine."[24]

Sharon

Sharon's rotation is in pediatrics, where she meets Greg (Darnell Larson), an eighteen-year-old patient with terminal cystic fibrosis. Sharon attempts to befriend Greg only to be rebuffed by his aggressive and prickly manner and his obsession with his own mortality. Working hard to break through to him, Sharon makes headway by mothering him, reading to him, making him comfortable in his bed, and taking him on the rare excursion off the hospital's grounds. As their relationship grows, so does Greg's romantic interest for Sharon, but she does not reciprocate. Greg's hurt over his failed romantic advances drives a wedge between the two, and Sharon is forced to learn how to care for a patient without that care extending into emotional involvement or intimacy. At the end of the film, Greg passes away while Sharon is in a different wing of the hospital; she is overcome by her grief and guilt for not being there in his final moments. To assuage her feelings of failure, she chooses a post-graduate position that will allow her to mother other eighteen-year-old boys facing their own mortality: Sharon joins the US Army Nurse Corps headed to Vietnam.

Priscilla

While Priscilla's rotation is in psychiatry and most of her narrative takes place outside of the hospital setting, her interest in the human mind and the process of experience largely informs her arc. Committed to the counterculture principles of free love, chance encounters, living in the moment, and deeply experiencing life, Priscilla picks up a stranger at a café. Despite her rhetoric, Priscilla's experience with the free love, drug-fueled counterculture is fairly limited, and that stranger turns out to be Les (Richard Rust), a drug dealer. Les rides a motorcycle and extolls the benefits of treating the body like "a temple" by avoiding processed and preserved food. The two spend the day together before he disappears from her life for a number of weeks. They meet again at a love-in at MacArthur Park. Les convinces Priscilla to take LSD with him. She agrees, and the two hallucinate while making love on the beach. She wakes up to find him gone and a few weeks later she discovers she's pregnant. After being denied a therapeutic abortion by the hospital's board of directors, she asks Casper to terminate her pregnancy. He performs a safe and effective, albeit illegal, abortion. Priscilla, confident and happy in her decision to terminate her pregnancy, goes on to a hospital position after graduation.

Lynn

For Lynn's final rotation, she is assigned to work in public health. On her way to a community appointment she runs into a street theater group, Teatro Popular, dramatizing the brutality the Mexican American and Mexican immigrant communities suffer at the hands of the Los Angeles Police Department (LAPD). A fight breaks out at the demonstration, and a man named Luis (Pepe Serna) is seriously injured. Lynn ignores the crowd's call for medical assistance, worried about personal liability if she provides aid outside of the hospital setting. Luis's friend Victor Charlie (Reni Santoni) brings him to the hospital where Lynn is coincidentally assigned to treat him under Victor's reproachful gaze. While following up on Luis after he's been released, Lynn runs into Victor at the headquarters of his community activist group, La Causa de La Raza. Victor identifies Lynn as Mexican American by her surname and challenges her lack of support for their shared community. She responds by providing free health services at La Causa, and she begins to understand the crisis of affordable health services for marginalized communities. She effectively disappears from her "regular" life, dedicating herself to La Causa. During one of her community health clinics, Victor brings in a compatriot who has been shot by the LAPD. The police soon follow. A shootout ensues; another La Causa member is gunned down and Victor shoots an officer while he and Lynn escape. The officer lives, but Victor knows he must go underground to avoid prison and continue his work. Lynn decides to go with him but rejoins the rest of the women long enough to attend graduation and reject a job placement offer. She leaves graduation a credentialed nurse alongside the now-fugitive Victor, dedicated to providing health services to a vulnerable and underserved population.

The film is a mix of comedy, drama, and coming-of-age generic conventions, and despite the distinction posed in this chapter's epigraph, it perhaps sits more comfortable as a version of early cinema's social problem film. Kay Sloan describes that "the social problem film originated in primitive melodramas made by filmmakers who actively sought social reforms during the Progressive era."[25] Films like *Traffic in Souls* (George Loane Tucker, 1913), which dealt with sex work and the mythic fear of white slavery, and *Where Are My Children?* (Lois Weber, 1916), focused on abortion, are illustrative examples. Social problem films combined "a contemporary and purposefully socially conscious cinema evolved in harmony with public debate."[26] Protagonists of these films advocated for justice and equity in housing, economics, and politics as they espoused the values of progressive reform.[27]

While the traditional social problem film fell out of style after World War I,[28] the 1940s and 1950s saw a resurgence of the genre, particularly in films addressing racial issues in the United States.[29] Films like *Lost Boundaries* (Alfred L. Werker, 1949), *Blackboard Jungle* (Richard Brooks, 1955), and *Imitation of Life* (Douglas Sirk, 1959) evolved early cinema's social problem films. The progressive era ideologies that shaped early social problem films downplayed racial differences in favor of economic and labor equity, but the social issues films of the 1940s and 1950s pushed specifically against this whitewashing of inequality, focusing specifically on racial injustice as a determining factor in unequal economic, social, education, and political attainment. Rothman's focus on gender as a core category of inequality follows a similar logic but with a foreground of gender, as her characters engage with issues of bodily integrity and autonomy, politicized death, healthcare, and political engagement as gendered issues. In doing so, *The Student Nurses* approaches an intersectional analysis of social issues through Lynn, whose interactions with La Causa and Victor nurture her once-dormant ethnic identification.

One of the most notable things about the narrative and thematic construction of *The Student Nurses* was the centering of women protagonists outside the women's film genre. While most films, whether they were second wave exploitation or not, use women as pathways to advance the male protagonist's narrative and as vehicles for sex and nudity, the women in *The Student Nurses* are foregrounded as each faces the political, ethical, and social challenges of a rapidly changing contemporary world. Critically, they do so unencumbered by stereotypical goals of gaining and pleasing a man or advancing their place in the world through marriage or reproduction. Michael Amedeo notes:

> Audiences who went to see *The Student Nurses* expecting sexploitation—or, clinical attachments—must have been greatly disappointed. Although Stephanie Rothman's Rrated film has its share of naked bodies going bump in the night, it plays fairly seriously—and fairly brightly—as a comingofage story about four independentminded, sometimes hardheaded student nurses. In the genre world, this was perhaps the first class of women who weren't immediately graduating to marriage and family.[30]

The graphic elements Corman insisted on, and that, as expected, Amedeo notes, are referred to by Rothman as "unholy trinity of exploitation values: violence, sex, and nudity."[31] To strike a balance between the trinity and her own ethical framework, Rothman adhered to her core filmmaking principles:

equal nudity across the sexes; the allusion, not illustration, of rape; and violence with corresponding consequences. The first hospital sequence of the film establishes these three principles hard and fast. Lynn enters the hospital room of a male patient to prep him for treatment. The patient is standing in the corner of the room and begins to circle Lynn. Suddenly, he violently attacks, throwing Lynn onto the hospital bed, ripping at her clothes. As the patient tries to rape her, she vigorously fights him off, but does not scream. While Lynn is struggling on the bed, the camera cuts to an I-POV of the attacker, aligning the audience with him as the camera focuses on Lynn's struggling face. This switch in perspective implicates the audience as attacker and voyeur, forcing the viewer to focus on Lynn's distress and fear. The shot, then, deemphasizes the potential erotics of sexual violence in favor of foregrounding Lynn's desperate struggle against violation.

The frame then cuts to a medium shot of the two bodies, the man on top of Lynn, his hands trying to rip off her white nurses' stockings from around her crotch. Lynn's knee moves swiftly up and into her attacker's genitals. He doubles over in pain as Lynn runs from the room; the attack ends with his violation, not hers. Lynn returns to the room with two male orderlies and a doctor. The orderlies pin the man to the bed, face down, and remove his pants, exposing his bare buttocks. Lynn assists the doctor with injecting a sedative into the exposed skin. The man emits a loud and protracted scream, a stark contrast to Lynn's silence. Lynn escapes a de-eroticized sexual assault under her own agency and subdued her attacker while avoiding heinous violation.

This sequence templates Rothman's balance between the "unholy trinity" and her own ethics: she showcases violence, sex, and nudity while replacing their expected function in the film. The first scene of nudity and violence is presented through a male body via a non-voyeuristic sexual assault.[32] The attacker is depersonalized[33]: the character has no name, lacks a motivation for the attack, and disappears from the film entirely after the scene. He serves less as an instigation for the spectacularization of a woman's body in peril and more as a foil to the presumed modes of conveying sex, violence, and nudity. In opening the film with this scene, Rothman is satisfying Corman and the mythical "exploitation audience" in a novel way and drawing a framework for remaining films. In this sense, "a bargain is struck with the audience: you came for sex and violence, here's sex and violence, now we'll move on to things that are more interesting (including political violence and nonexploitative sex)."[34]

It is important to note that this bargain does not rest on a simplistic gendered reversal; men's nude bodies are not substituted in service of the women's empowerment or narrative trajectories. Rather, Rothman includes several scenes of men's nude bodies lovingly presented and naturally occurring in the narrative, for example Les's nude body while making love to Priscilla and Casper's nude torso in several scenes with Phred. Rothman consciously includes these images in the film to foster a sense of equity: "While it was an ironclad requirement that I include scenes of sex and nudity, I tried to make sure men and women were equally nude equally often and the sex was not brutal but sensually evocative for both sexes."[35] Nudity across sexes is presented as a natural act of daily life rather than as a spectacularized event. For example, Phred is shown nude more often than the other characters, but it is commonplace nudity. She is nude while having sex,[36] changing her clothes, or conversing with her partner post-coitus. Her cinematic nudity mirrors real-life nudity, transforming it from the spectacular to the ordinary in the process.

With a clear path for handling requirements for sex, nudity, and violence, Rothman pushes the film into conversations of reproductive agency, police brutality, inequality and oppression, and mortality. Before *Roe v. Wade* codified the federal legalization of abortion, Rothman engaged the debate around a woman's right to dictate her own reproductive choices via Priscilla's unintended pregnancy. Interestingly, she also weaves into this critique a subtle warning against the gender imbalance inherent in the free love hippie movement of the 1960s and early 1970s. Priscilla radiates the cultural effects of counterculture. She reads *Steppenwolf*, attends love-ins, believes nursing is "all about love,"[37] refuses to wear a bra, and has a laissez-faire attitude toward intimate and sexual relationships. Despite this, a conversation between Priscilla and Phred late in the film signals that Priscilla's embrace of free love may be an affectation rather than an expression of pleasure, as she confesses to Phred, "It's never really been good with any guy."[38]

Even so, Priscilla remains rhetorically dedicated to expanding her consciousness and experience by diving headfirst into the world around her. Yet, she is surprisingly naïve. Despite her countercultural alignment, she is inexperienced in drug culture, and once pregnant, plans to live on the streets, using free clinics for healthcare. Les's responsibility for the pregnancy is absolved, highlighting the deeply gendered nature of the concept of free love as removed from the boundaries of traditional sexual relationships; free love is only free for those who don't run the risk of pregnancy. By creating a character whose social progressiveness is troubled by her worldly inexperience, Rothman crafts Priscilla as a three-dimensional embodiment of the idealism, success, naïveté, and disappointment that characterized the youth culture movement of the late 1960s and early 1970s.

When Priscilla decides to terminate her pregnancy, she is faced with a series of hurdles because, as she states, "If I have an abortion, I want a legal one."[39] The potential dangers of an illegal abortion are reinforced in a later sequence, when the women's head nurse counsels Priscilla, "Get a safe one, or don't get one at all." The specter of an illegal—here, synonymous with unsafe—abortion looms over Priscilla, and for good reason. Historian Karissa Haugeberg notes that pre-*Roe*, approximately 200 women a year died from complications from illegal abortions, including from self-induction.[40] Priscilla turns to Casper, consulting him on her options. He recommends applying for a medical abortion at their respective hospital, which requires her to convince a hospital psychiatrist that carrying the fetus to term will threaten her mental health. Her petition is denied; the hospital's board of directors is worried about running afoul of the district attorney should it appear as if they are granting one of their students a special favor. The institution wards off a potential legal issue at Priscilla's expense. As Lynn says: "What do you expect from a bunch of men? Give them a chance to play inquisitor and it's thumbs down on women every time."[41]

Casper agrees to perform the abortion at the women's home, against Phred's strong objections. Despite Phred's relaxed attitude toward sex and rebuke of Casper's judgment of her own sexual drive, her sex-positive attitude doesn't apply to illegal abortion. When Casper comes to the house to perform the procedure, he and Phred have a heated encounter:

PHRED: The abortionist, I presume?
CASPER: That's me.
PHRED [*blocking him from ascending the stairs*]: You aren't going up there. Nobody is getting their insides scraped in my bedroom.
CASPER: Phred, have a little sense.
PHRED: You could lose your license if they hear about this!
CASPER: Who's going to tell them?
PHRED [*yelling up the stairs*]: Pris, are you gonna let this bastard kill your baby?
CASPER: Get the hell out of my way!
PHRED: Not in my bedroom, not in my bed. You go do your butchering somewhere else![42]

Casper prevails and, in a remarkable move for any film, Rothman shows him performing the abortion while Sharon and Lynn attend. It's crucial here to note that the film uses the term "abortion" rather than the euphemisms so often assigned to the procedure in film: "taken care of," "fixed," etc. Indeed, abortion is presented thoughtfully and humanely throughout. Priscilla's abortion is performed by a licensed physician who disagrees with his employer's decision and makes his own ethical choice to participate, the procedure is shown, and there are no physical or psychological side effects. Indeed, at the end of the film Priscilla announces how happy she is with her decision to abort, which has allowed her to successfully move into the next phase of her life and career. Following through on her commitment to ideological complexity, Rothman uses Phred to provide a counter viewpoint on the issue of abortion, continuing to acknowledge the divisiveness of the topic and steering the film away from simplistic political posturing.

While Rothman's humanistic discussion of abortion is unconventional, perhaps the most radical storyline in the film is Lynn's. Her trajectory from rule-following student trainee to outlaw political activist epitomizes how Rothman leverages the dictate of "student nurses" to showcase the blurred boundaries between the world internal and external to the hospital. Indeed, Lynn's external world bleeds into, shapes, and contradicts the sterility and regimentation of the hospital, her training, and the binary mindset it initially cultivates. Her first encounter with political activism comes when she encounters a Mexican American street theater group, Teatro Popular, while walking to her residence. Teatro Popular, or Popular Theater, was a performance group in Los Angeles at the time of filming. Born of the populist theater movement in Mexico and Latin America in the 1960s and 1970s,[43] the *teatro popular* performance genre, also termed *teatro campesino* (peasant theater), is community-based theater that adapts traditional cultural forms like poetry and song to rapidly respond to social issues.[44] Operating as street theater,[45] *teatro popular* improvised performances as political action and organizing tactics. As Jan Cohen-Cruz notes, *teatro popular* was successful in California's Mexican American and Mexican immigrant comminutes, particularly in relation to Chicano activism and farm workers' rights. She explains: "Chicanos recognized traditional cultural forms, farm workers recognized scenes of exploitation in the field, and progressive people recognized the Chicano farm workers' struggle as part of a very real desire to make the United States fulfill its promise of justice and equality for all."[46]

Lynn stops to watch this guerilla-style performance. The scene begins with members of the group—and some members of the gathered audience—chanting "*Teatro popular de la vida y muerte*"[47] (popular theater of life and death). The performers stage an allegorical story condemning the regularized and unchecked police brutality directed at their community, told through a Spanish-speaking narrator and English translator. The US government is represented as "that tyrant Sam," who wields power through his "vicious police department of dogs," in this case, the LAPD.[48] During the course of the performance, a fight breaks out between bystanders and theater members; Victor is introduced, calling for help for the injured Luis. Lynn is too concerned about legal liability to help and quickly leaves the scene. When she meets Victor again on her first trip to La Causa, he is openly hostile toward her for not providing aid to Luis after he was injured in the fight, demonstrating what he believes to be her lack of empathy for her own community:

> VICTOR: With a name like Verdugo, and you don't speak Spanish? You should be ashamed of yourself.
> LYNN: How do you know my name?
> VICTOR: Because it is spelled out in letters over where your heart is supposed to be.[49]

Unintimidated, she questions his name—a reference to the US military slang used to refer to the Viet Cong during the war in Vietnam—in return:

> LYNN: How did you get a name like Victor Charlie?
> VICTOR: Because I am the enemy.[50]

While Victor and Lynn's relationship remains contentious throughout the majority of the film, it is a productive one where Lynn empowers herself. For example, Victor educates Lynn about the lack of affordable healthcare for Mexican Americans and Mexican immigrants. He assumes her indifference toward, and impotence in, combatting the problem. Lynn doesn't shrink before this hostility: she sets up a free clinic at La Causa and begins spending most of her time there. His knowledge of the needs of the community coupled with her medical training combine to produce a vital community resource.

After Victor wounds a police officer during a shoot-out in the third act, he and Lynn go into hiding and discuss his options. Since the officer did not die from his wounds, she encourages him to turn himself in and plead self-defense. He scoffs at her and responds: "If a man shoots a cop, it doesn't matter what he pleads. Especially . . . especially if he's a dirty Mexican."[51] Lynn agrees to stay and help him. Critically, her acquiescence to living a life on the run with Victor is not motivated by a romantic relationship entanglement. Although the end of the film hints at a growing intimacy between Lynn and Victor, the two are never explicitly romantically linked. Their connection is first and foremost ideological, ethical, and activist; Lynn's evolving, active acknowledgment of her Mexican ancestry and their shared sense of injustice bond the two. Lynn begins to manifest that acknowledgment outside of Victor and La Causa: she swaps her nurses whites for jeans, a tee shirt, and army jacket, and when she checks in for her final nursing exam she pronounces her last name with a noticeable accent. The nurse Lynn checks in with has difficulty understanding the accented pronunciation; rather than repeat it in Anglicized form, Lynn spells it. Lastly, when Victor thanks Lynn for deciding to join him underground, she responds: "Don't thank me. I do it for La Causa."[52]

Rothman's commitment to showcasing her contemporary moment has never included a whitewashing of society, or a denial of the multiplicities of races, ethnicities, and sexualities that comprise it. She explicitly commented on her inclusion of a Mexican American narrative in *The Student Nurses* as part of this process of holistic world creation in her films: "Mexican Americans constitute a sizeable portion of the Southern California population, but are rarely shown in film. I grew up with them, and I don't want to ignore a group of people whom I deeply admire and respect."[53] The foregrounding of Lynn's story, her relationship with Victor and La Causa, and their successful escape at the end of the film are indicative of how Rothman leveraged the "required" elements of her filmmaking to craft nuanced, ideologically based, and reflective stories for her characters.

Experimentation in Form

The Student Nurses is marked by a conglomeration of visual styles, as Rothman uses film form to add nuance and dimension to the film. Each woman's story aligns with a particular visual style. Rothman recalls:

> That was part of my design, to make it a very dynamic film, and to give each of the nurses a very different character by varying the visual style as well as by varying the world into which they went [. . .] it was my first chance to do something at *all* of an exploratory nature, since the first picture had been a beach picture. I wanted to try out every visual style I could. I had so much fun making this film in that respect, because I never was able to be that varied again, and the structure of it just welcomed that kind of exploration. It welcomed that kind of variation in style. It was a very conscious decision.[54]

Phred's concern with safety, control, and cleanliness was reflected in the classical Hollywood style her story is allotted. Her story is temporally linear; her actions follow an evident cause and effect pattern, her scenes are cut along classical continuity editing patterns, and her narrative is afforded closure at the end of the film. Shot both outside and inside the hospital, she is primarily lit artificially in medium shots, and the camera moves very little in her scenes. The classical Hollywood style as a hallmark of Fordist production logics and the stability they afford, signal her quest for stability and safety in her professional and personal life.

Sharon is shot in similar ways, albeit primarily on a set. Sharon's story takes place almost entirely inside the hospital itself. Her containment within the physical and psychological structure of the hospital spatially bounds her struggle in coming to grips with the fundamental nature of her chosen profession: life and death. In containing Sharon's story primarily to the hospital, Rothman is using location and mise-en-scène to highlight Sharon's growing understanding of the reality of the emotional and psychic pain attached to nursing. Sharon's scenes with Greg are shot in soft, warm lighting, reflected in the yellow and orange décor of Greg's hospital room. Both Sharon and Greg are usually centered in the frame together, facing one another, two formal constructions that add dimensions of romance, intimacy, and the eventual tragedy that marks Sharon's storyline. Interestingly, Rothman uses location again—her post-graduation job in Vietnam—to underscore Sharon's likely continued intersection with intimacy and tragedy.

Priscilla's story takes place almost entirely in the environs of Los Angeles, and is marked by "languid long takes in sun-drenched picturesque locations, against an acoustic guitar soundtrack."[55] She is often in public spaces and interacting with strangers, a nod to her exploratory nature. Priscilla's outdoor adventures give Rothman an opportunity to showcase contemporary Los Angeles and its inhabitants, giving the film a vital and realistic feel. The love-in that Priscilla attends at MacArthur Park was planned outside of production. Rothman took advantage of the city's vibrant social culture, giving the film the verisimilitude of 1970 Los Angeles. Shooting outside in natural light, whether it be in the park or during one of Priscilla's walks around the city, cultivates a documentary-style aesthetic to Priscilla's storyline.

Rothman also uses Priscilla's storyline as an opportunity to experiment with her art film influences. Priscilla and Les's LSD-shrouded beach sex scene is a particularly effective example of this. As their trip begins, Priscilla stares out toward the ocean, watching the waves. The water moves in slow motion, undulating waves changing color from blue to red and back to blue again. The camera slowly zooms in on her face, tracking up and into her pupil; the shot dissolves into an image of her nude on the beach, turning her head in slow motion to absorb her newly altered surroundings. Les and Priscilla carefully run their hands over each other's nude bodies, exploring one another in tactile discovery; indeed, their sex scene includes more caressing than intercourse. The image of their bodies double, and the double images dissolve into one another. As they join into one, the camera focuses on Priscilla's face as she hallucinates an audience watching them make love: a policeman, her fellow student nurses, a family she had seen earlier on the beach, and a group of imagined surfers. She feels their eyes on her, watching and judging, and the camera zooms in for a close-up of her eyes as her voice-over intones, "Stop it, stop looking at me."[56] The hallucination ends, and she wakes up on the beach alone.

Once her pregnancy is confirmed, Priscilla is regularly shot from a high angle, emphasizing her feelings of powerlessness. More and more, the formal style of her scenes shows her to be at the mercy of the world. An apt example is found when she visits the hospital's psychiatrist to apply for a medical abortion. The psychiatrist is never shown; he is a disembodied male voice, the faceless and nameless pervasive patriarchy, who slouches in a chair lower than his desk. The camera is positioned over his shoulder and squarely at Priscilla. His questions and her answers are presented in a series of jump cuts, disassociating individual questions from their answers and creating a stream of consciousness from Priscilla that drive home her helplessness and disassociation from herself as she attempts to reconcile with the type of person she is, the type she wants to be, and the world around her.

Priscilla's hallucinatory crowd reappears during her abortion, and through a similar experimental style, reflects her turbulent emotional and physical state. As she lays on the bed during her procedure, her fellow student nurses surround her in the same pattern they did during her earlier hallucination. As the anesthesia takes hold, she flashes back to her beach trip and the crowd returns, providing metaphoric insight into her anesthetized mind: the police officer is a haunting reminder of the procedure's criminality; the family shows the idealized outcome of her coupling with Les through marriage and sanctioned reproduction; and the surfers are symbols of the carefree lifestyle she has so desperately sought.

Like Priscilla, Lynn's visuals bring a *cinema verité* feel to the film, and her stylistic associations are also equally important to her character development and narrative trajectory. Most of Lynn's scenes take place in and around the La Causa building and neighborhood. Their look is something closer to documentary or newsreel footage, with liberal use of natural lighting, quick cuts that create a sense of urgency, and a military-inspired color palate of black, tan, and army green. During the fight at the Teatro Popular performance, Rothman uses a handheld camera, putting the viewer into the middle of the action and creating a frenetic pace through a whirl of action as limbs, bodies, and voices flail together *en masse*.

As with the love-in, the Teatro Popular performance Rothman incorporates into the film was a naturally occurring event outside of the shooting environment. The scene contains several people speaking Spanish, none of which is subtitled. Although the lack of subtitles is easily attributable to insufficient funds to add them to the film, it gives the scene an even greater sense of verisimilitude. The extensive Spanish dialogue also naturalizes the city's multilingual character reinforcing Rothman's investment in a diversified Los Angeles.

Non only was stylistic variation an opportunity for Rothman to stretch her filmmaking wings, but it was also a clever way to create a fully formed film on a meager budget. The reliance on her directorial skills to foster success under constraint would become one of Rothman's hallmarks throughout her career. If Rothman had "killed" the beach party movie with *It's a Bikini World*, she jump-started a new trend with *The Student Nurses*. Its success fostered an extensive cycle of "nurse" films produced by New World, all directed by men, including *Private Duty Nurses* (George Armitage, 1971), *Night Call Nurses* (Jonathan Kaplan, 1972), *The Young Nurses* (Clint Kimbrough as Clinton Kimbro, 1973), and *Candy Stripe Nurses* (Alan Holleb, 1974). Never keen to repeat herself, Rothman moved forward and did not make another student nurse film.

"TERMINAL ISLAND: WHERE LIVING IS WORSE THAN DYING!"[57]

Terminal Island harnesses imaginative re-conceptions of social overhaul outside of hierarchical and patriarchal restrictions. The film emphasizes the role that women's bodies and their desires can play in offering solutions to social problems through subversions of structural inequality. It is her most violent and visceral film, and one she was pressed to make by her boss at Dimension, Larry Woolner:

> Larry Woolner said that he would like to make a women's prison picture, because when he had been at New World Pictures they had a series of successful women's prison pictures. It was considered a very good exploitation film topic, because it was about women without men in a confined environment, who are supposedly horny and violent, and can play active assertive roles because they are in control of their environment. So Charles and I sort of refined that.[58]

Rothman recalls sub-distributor funding spurring Woolner's interest in the film: "prison film with leading Black characters."[59] Rothman was conflicted about the racialized narrative and casting request:

> I was always a little uncomfortable about casting Black men or women in my films, for one reason. There was at that time the rise of Black films, and I didn't feel that I should poach on their territory. In other words, their chance to make any kind of film was so limited—as limited as mine—why should I take away from them the opportunity to make films about their own experiences?[60]

Rothman's hands were tied, and she and Charles crafted a film for an ensemble cast of white and Black actors. Script writing was laborious; Rothman and Swartz wrote a story outline and hired television writer Jim Barnett to generate the script.[61] Barnett's version was not what Rothman expected: "His treatment of women was just unbelievable ... so passive and empty."[62] They hired a writer named Henry Rosenbaum to rewrite it; he declined writing credit.[63] Rothman took Rosenbaum's draft and turned it into the shooting script.

The film's basic story is as follows: California has abolished the death penalty, and anyone found guilty of committing first degree murder is banished to the San Bruno Maximum Security Detention Center, Terminal Island, for life. Once a month, the state drops off minimal supplies, but prisoners primarily live off what the island does or does not provide. Two groups form on the island, an authoritative regime led by a prisoner named Bobby and a band of rebels who refused to live under Bobby's tyranny. The film is a battle between the two groups for establishment of island society and everyday life.

Shooting began in the spring of 1972, with Lake Sherwood in Ventura Country, California, standing in for a prison island.[64] It was a difficult shoot, with cast and crew working through persistent rainstorms, and traversing sand, cliffs, and streams with heavy equipment, carrying things by hand because the production did not have a vehicle that could handle the terrain. The script was written with the character of Carmen, played by Ena Hartman, as the lead. Three days into filming, Hartman severely sprained her ankle,[65] and Rothman had to rework the story on the fly to account for Hartman's physical inability to complete most of the existing script. This gives the film somewhat of a disjointed trajectory. Its opening sequences make it clear that Carmen is the film's lead, but Rothman was not able to reshoot the earlier footage. Consequently, Carmen disappears into the ensemble cast after the injury. Rothman does not remember the film fondly: "What I had to go through to make it ... I just didn't have the resources to make it. I just didn't have enough time; I had nothing that I needed to make it. It was the biggest stretch . . . because it was so difficult to make."⁶⁶ A notice in the April 1973 issue of the *Hollywood Reporter* notes the film's premiere was set for June 1 at the State-Lake Theater in Chicago.⁶⁷ Rothman recalls visiting Chicago on a press tour for the film but contends its premiere was at the International Women's Film Festival in Toronto, where she met filmmaker Shirley Clarke. "We had a pleasant conversation in which she was interested in what I was doing, and I told her how much I admired her work, and that was it. It was a mutual admiration conversation."⁶⁸

A key feature of the film are the two conflicting camps. Rothman's construction of the divergent camps pits hierarchical and patriarchal oppression against the possibility of equality and lateral social order. These demarcations in juridical order and social creation manifest through the bodies of the women who inhabit *Terminal Island*. These bodies of difference are essential to Rothman's construction of alternate visions of social order and her juxtaposition of dystopic pain and utopic social reimagining.

Sado-Patriarchal Dystopia

Terminal Island takes place in an alternate but recognizable present where the United States Supreme Court has deemed the death penalty unconstitutional. As a result, the voters of California have passed an initiative in which individuals convicted of murder in the first degree are confined to Terminal Island, where inmates live out their days or die trying. Once on the island, the convict is considered legally dead and the state washes their hands of the responsibility of caring for the prisoners. The viewer is introduced to the island and its inhabitants through a formal device: a television news crew compiling a story on the prison compound using person-on-the street interviews, voice-over narration, and footage of the island and those sentenced there. Rothman uses non-actor interviews she conducted on the streets of Los Angeles to give the segment a recognizable journalistic feel.⁶⁹ When the interviews end, the news director and reporter cutting the piece together introduce some of the key prisoners on the island by reviewing their crimes for inclusion in the story. This gives a quick exposition of the island and its inhabitants, handing the audience a roadmap to the characters who will later play key roles.

Carmen is introduced during this sequence as the island's newest inhabitant. Carmen, a Black woman in her mid-twenties, stands in for the viewer as the audience discovers the island and its society vicariously. Carmen is immediately established as aggressive by her first three actions. She first appears in frame through the lens of the news team's camera, as the station rolls footage of her leaving her sentencing of a crime that is never stated. Carmen walks down the steps of the courthouse while the press harangue her: flashbulbs pop, questions are shouted, and television cameras are pushed into her face. She says nothing, and despite being handcuffed, grabs one of the cameras and throws it to the ground. Second, when the prison guard asks her to sign a form stating that she is legally dead, she grabs the paper, stating, "I never heard of a corpse signing its name before,"[70] and throws the paper into the ocean. Thirdly, on the beach soon after, she is approached by one of the island's current male occupants. She immediately pulls a hatchet out of her rucksack, raises it at him, stating: "Stay there or I'll kill you."[71]

Carmen plays a liminal role in the film, fitting uneasily on the island. While there are other women on the island, she is the only Black woman. She is the only main character whose crime goes unnamed, and while she is the first of the rebels to signal her comfort with violence and demand retribution, a white woman takes the lead in their revolution. She loudly, and often, signals her unwillingness to be victimized, either by the public (courthouse press), the state (the prison system), or her peers (other convicts). Her associative violence is relational to her characterization, not violence for its own sake. Carmen is a woman unlike the other women, a rebel unlike the other rebels, and a criminal unlike the other criminals. Carmen disrupts heavily guarded gender boundaries, much like Rothman in her role as second wave exploitation director. This liminality is unintentionally buttressed by her slippage from main character to ensemble player after the actor's injury.

Carmen's embodied violence is crucial to her liminality. Sharon Marcus notes that women are historically excluded from active participation in social violence, and this exclusion has left them as perpetual victims.[72] Carmen's status as a violent woman, and her refusal of victimization, marks her as different: she is a woman out of bounds. This is compounded by her criminality. In her study of violent filmic women, Hilary Neroni points out how said women are required to be narratively overdetermined. Their violence must come with a rationale, as part of a job or in the name of self-defense for example, to be accepted and believable to the audience.[73] Neroni notes that the "extraordinary lengths to which the narrative must go to explain or situate the violent woman reveals the trauma caused by her violence. In fact, the very existence of the violent woman as such testifies to ideology's propensity for failure."[74] While the other women on the island—Joy (Phyllis Davis), Lee (Marta Kristen), and Bunny (Barbara Leigh)—are assigned explainable crimes, Carmen's crime is unrationalized, as her violence signals ideology's failure. Carmen's characterization is problematized by her race:

all the other women are white. Carmen's violence and aggression outside of a stated reason (read: crime) depends on racist stereotypes of Black women as, in the words of Mia Mask, "tougher, stronger, more masculine, and/or more controlling."[75] Her explanatory refusal superficially reinforces what Mask notes are discursive constructions on Black womanhood as endemically aggressive, stemming from "the political economy of slavery... disenfranchisement, regional migration, and urban decay."[76] However, precisely because her crime is uncontextualized, her on-screen violence manifests primarily as preservative self-defense, something the white women don't engage in until she motivates them. Carmen's regular self-defensive violence marks her as a dangerous woman precisely because of her active refusal of stereotype and subjugation. Her violence-as-rejection is the fulcrum on which Rothman turns post-patriarchal social creation.

After spending the night on the beach, Carmen ventures into the island's main camp. Descending a hill into the central square, she walks past a line of leering male convicts. This is a mirror of the earlier "perp walk" past the media following her sentencing trial. In both instances, Carmen's otherness as a violent woman is wrought into existence by an oppressive gaze, be it mediated or male. Carmen is soon forced into a harsh realization: the camp is run by the tyrannical Bobby (Sean Kenney) and his henchman Monk (Roger E. Mosley). Bobby established life on the island through fear, violence, forced labor, and fulfillment of his sadistic desires. Bobby, who is white, is hegemony's literalized id. Operating on impulse, he randomly decides who lives or dies, who eats or starves, who works or lounges. On the island, Bobby has created a warped and extremist imitation of civil society. He rules as an erratic dictator, commands a platoon of inmates as a faux military, and requires his enslaved labor to build primitive houses and storeroom, a shower for himself, a plough pulled by human oxen, a town square that is really a mud pit, a hand-crank radio, and a method for generating electricity to keep his nyctophobia at bay.

Bobby's power is enforced by erratic violence, both his own and at his direction. When Carmen enters the camp, she greets Monk, who is also Black, by saying, "Hi, brother."[77] At Bobby's order, he immediately assaults her. Monk pins Carmen's head between the ground and his massive boot, using her skull as a pivot. Her screams for help go unanswered. Carmen retreats into a shanty and that evening meets the other women in the camp. Joy informs Carmen that the women are kept in labor and sexual enslavement; Bobby allows the men in the camp to rape them on a schedule he sets. Joy bluntly states: "We are the property of every man on this island."[78] Carmen, incredulous, refuses to participate, declaring her intent to break out of camp, only to see her plans eroded by days of backbreaking labor and physical abuse that leave her exhausted, bruised, and beaten. One evening while Carmen is getting her work-torn hands bandaged, Monk appears to assign the women the names of the men who will rape them that evening. Each woman is assigned four to six men. Carmen asks, "Don't we ever get any sleep?" and Monk replies "All you gotta do is lie back and take it. Nobody says you have to stay awake."[79] Proprietary objects, the women are receptacles to be used and discarded at the men's convenience. Bobby's colonization of the island and its forced inhabitants is emblematic of the long history of white male patriarchal supremacy, a slash-and-burn world order that produces a mutated and sadistically extremist version of the world they've all left behind. Rothman constructs the sadistic manual and sexual enslavement of the women as so gratuitous—in one scene, a group of men lounge in the shade, snacking and watching the women struggle against injury and futility as they dig a massive hole in a mud pit with logs—it reduces the supremacist patriarchal system it reflects to indefensible grotesquery.

Sadism's interrelation here is crucial when considering the confluence of social creation, jurisprudence, and gender that underpins both the island's sociality and the film's ideological core. In *Coldness and Cruelty*, Gilles Deleuze understands sadism as a form of subject creation that brings the subject into being through imbrications of fantasy and the law. He wields the writing of the Marquis de Sade as a critique of law based on reason to illustrate his concept.[80] For de Sade, law takes the form of an imperative driven by the reason that underpins it. Reason-as-law is a form of violence that bounds and immobilizes actions. It forces subjects under the law to agree with reason's logic even when it led to conclusions affectively felt as incorrect. For example, Terminal Island exists as a humane answer to the death penalty, yet a sentence to the prison is as good a death. The reason-as-law—the state no longer assigns death as a punishment—is juridically true yet practically false. Law, then, contains a compulsion toward violent reason while disallowing opposition. Terminal Island is state-sanctioned sadism.

Deleuze understands de Sade's articulations of sadism as a parodic form of law, a perpetual revolution in fantasy positioned against stability and reason, constructing the subject as a parody of the imperative of the law and reason; the patriarchal control asserted on the island is satirically sadistic. This is the organizing principle for Bobby's patriarchy, as the island mirrors the inhumanness of a nation whose reasoned jurisprudence sentences its citizens to a slow and torturous death while claiming otherwise. Bobby recreates Terminal Island as a magnified, sadistic parody of institutional patriarchy. On the mainland, there is a discrepancy in wages between men and women who perform the same work. On the island, men perform no work and reap all the rewards, while women labor for nothing. Patriarchy maintains wives' dependence on, and subordination to, their husbands; in the camp, women are removed from subjecthood altogether and reduced to men's communal property. On the mainland, there is democracy, and on the island, dictatorship. The movement of women demanding equality on the mainland are muted, literally, through Bunny, who does not speak. Bobby favors her; when brought to him for sex, he prefaces his assault by saying, "If you don't want to, all you have to do is say no." Knowing full well she will not speak, Bobby pretends she is complicit in her own rape. These satirical sadistic extremes skewer, and render absurd, normative patriarchal constructions of society and its stereotypical gender delimitations until the camp's eventual downfall at the hands of radical egalitarianism.

Naturalizing the Post-Patriarchy

In contrast to the dystopic sadism of the main camp are the rebels. Prior to Carmen's arrival, a group of men escaped Bobby's tyrannical rule and disappeared into the island's unoccupied areas. The group, led by A. J. (Don Marshall) and Cornell (Ford Clay), has been living on the run. One day, while the women are washing clothes in the river under guarded supervision, A. J. and his crew attack, killing several guards and freeing the women. Incredulous that the men are too afraid of Bobby to oppose his reign, the newly liberated women begin brainstorming ways to take the offensive. Lee, a highly educated political radical, takes the lead. She accidently killed a bank security guard and several employees after threatening to blow up corporate bank branches if they did not withdraw their funding of oppressive regimes in South America.[81] Lee and the other women's fervor for retribution convince the men to join them in overthrowing Bobby. Recognizing rocks in a nearby riverbed as niter, Lee realizes that with niter, charcoal, and sulfur, the group will be able to make gunpowder. Simultaneously, Carmen finds moonseed vine, sharing how it can be boiled down to make poison tips for arrows and darts. Quickly, the group organizes and begins preparations for war.

During these preparations, Rothman sketches the type of society the rebels are fighting for. Men and women are equally valued among the group. They share in the decision-making, the labor, and the women take the lead in the tactical planning for the assault on the main camp. Pam Cook notes, "In this film [. . .] the new social order is based on a division of labour that gives men and women equal but different roles, arguably questioning the patriarchal system in which women are seen as mirror images of the male."[82]

Sex also plays a key role among the rebels, albeit in a stark contradiction to the rape of the main camp. Among the rebels, the women easily and openly swap sexual partners according to the shifting paths of their desire. In these sexual pairings and re-pairings, there is no language or actions of ownership or monogamy. Peary notes: "When making love or conversing with one man, it could just as easily be with another."[83]

Yet patriarchy is not so easily escaped, as hegemonic enculturation attempts to infiltrate the burgeoning post-patriarchal society the rebels are building. Dylan (Clyde Ventura) forces himself onto Joy, who vocally and physically resists him. The assault is interrupted by another man who says, "This ain't right. You should ask her first if she wants to."[84] Joy vows revenge. Later, she lures Dylan into a secluded spot with the promise of sex. She rubs his exposed crotch and buttocks with royal jelly, and then agitates a nearby swarm of bees that attack him immediately. Dylan runs screaming into a nearby lake while the rest of the group looks on, amused by his comeuppance. The post-patriarchal society of the rebel camp stands in stark opposition to Bobby's sadistic patriarchal control. Critical to the creation of this utopian world is the rebel's connection to their natural environment. Joy's use of the royal jelly and bees, Lee's homemade gunpowder, and Carmen's moonseed poison each manifest the women's ability to harness the violence of the natural world. Weaponizing nature as a pathway to an equitable and just social world helps them topple the island's unnatural patriarchy.

Here, it's useful to understand the women's connection to nature through Georges Bataille's continuity and discontinuity, noting how the rebel's world-making process mirrors his theorization of creation, violence, and natural order. Human beings create themselves, in large part, through and against the natural world that spawned them. The natural world seethes, pulsates, undulates, and ruptures, constituting a circular structure of life and death; it is an "orgy of annihilation."[85] This generates a continuous and undifferentiated flow of energy and movement: a plethora of life and death, the intermingling of the matter of production and the waste of reproduction. The contiguous natural world is hypercharged by a churning mass of continuity. Life, death, energy, and excess are relentlessly colliding, absorbing, and merging, curating a living, breathing, and effervescent natural world. "Life is a swelling tumult continuously on the verge of explosion."[86]

Distance is necessary to negotiate this violence, which humanity creates through an overinvestment in work. Labor is a distinctive human endeavor. I do not mean the labor of basic survival, but rather the labor endemic to the human condition under capitalism as one of manufacture. It is the instrumentalization of a relationship with the natural and social world through the means of production. Bataille expounds: "By work man orders the world of things and brings himself down to the level of a thing among things: work makes a worker a means to an end."[87] The movement from natural subject to manufactured thing distances humanity from the violent natural world. *Terminal Island* argues that work, specifically capitalist work, breeds the inequalities embedded in hierarchical social construction and functions as a panacea to said injustices. Bobby forces his subjects to labor for a mimicry of society, sacrificing the natural world to the capitalist one. The rebels also bow to their capitalist enculturation as they assemble their weapons through Fordist factory logics, emphasizing divisions of labor and assembly-line production, but their success comes through integration with the natural world.

Through their righteous and naturalized violence, the rebels win the war, and the film closes with the reconstruction of the island as a post-patriarchal society at peace, where wealth, power, labor, and sexuality are constructed as shared and equal.[88] As the rebels rebuild the main camp, they again harness the continuous world by working with, rather than against it, like weaving fronds for hut roofs and clearing of the land for crops. Their social progression is embodied in their pardoning of Monk, Bobby's primary henchman, as they care for him after he is blinded in the battle. The rebels have leveraged the procreative forces intrinsic to natural violence to best their enemies and transformed the oppressive violence of the social world into compassion. They are now both world creators and world nurturers, destabilizers of repressive patriarchal society, and producers of an imaginative utopia defined by equanimity and fairness.

Chapter 7

NEW WORLDS

The way that women were being treated in films reinforced the idea that men were all-powerful and that women were powerless. I certainly did not have sympathy for that view, nor did I observe it to be particularly true.[1]
—STEPHANIE ROTHMAN

In 1970, Stephanie Rothman was experiencing a heretofore unknown level of success with *The Student Nurses*. Her ostensible boss, Roger Corman, was planning his extended trip to Ireland to direct *Von Richthofen and Brown* (1971), so he asked her and Swartz to manage production at New World.[2] Eager to have them craft another film as successful as *The Student Nurses*, he also asked them to work on a new woman in prison film. Rothman was excited for the dual experiences of managing production in Corman's stead and the prospect of a new film of her own. That excitement quickly dulled when the writing assignment brought her back into contact with Jack Hill. Corman had purchased a screenplay, *The Big Dollhouse*, which Jack had brought to his attention.[3] Corman was interested in the title, but wanted the script rewritten. Corman, Rothman, and Swartz discussed script improvements and Corman assigned Rothman, Swartz, Frances Doel, and Hill to write a new storyline from which Hill could draft the new screenplay.[4] Corman added a caveat to the proposal: if Hill could not agree with the team on the new story, they were free to hire another writer.[5]

The collaborative process with Hill did not go well. Rothman recalls: "He rejected almost everything that we had to say, and he was really angry that I was part of this."[6] At an impasse with Hill, the three took advantage of Corman's qualification and hired Don Spencer—the screenwriter on *The Student Nurses*—to rewrite the script.[7] When Corman returned from Ireland, he greenlit Spencer's script and approached Rothman to direct the film:

Roger returned and read it [Spencer's script] and asked me if I would like to direct it and I said, "No, I wouldn't, this is not the kind of material

I would ever want to do. We created what you said you wanted. We gave the screenwriter guidance following your instructions: you wanted a women's prison picture, and you wanted it to be violent, and sexy. But no, I would not want to work on something like this." I thought it was very demeaning to women and I had very ambivalent feelings about even having had to work on it. But that was my job, and I wanted to make other films so I couldn't let Roger down.[8]

Although Rothman turned down the directing opportunity, she and Swartz worked on the marketing campaign for the film:

we supervised taking the pictures that were used in the film's advertising for the theater one-sheets and newspapers. It showed them in their brief prison dresses, and we worked with the photographer positioning them in their different poses. Roger asked us to do that because he really liked the picture that we had taken for *The Student Nurses* ads, so we went back to the same photographer and he took the *Doll House* pictures, too.[9]

Corman hired Hill to direct the film. *The Big Dollhouse* was an early entry into Corman's successful women in prison (WIP) films cycle, which also included *Women in Cages* (Gerardo de Leon as Gerry de Leon, 1971), *The Big Bird Cage* (Jack Hill, 1972), and *Caged Heat* (Jonathan Demme, 1974). WIP films have a history that traverses classical and second wave exploitation. First developed in the 1930s as melodramas, they are primarily concerned with the use of the prison as rehabilitation for young women who've strayed from their appropriately gendered life path. WIP films stressed heterosexual romance and marriage as a woman's path to social productivity. The melodramatic aspects of early WIP films highlighted stories of "(re)domestication/redemption stories and, by extension, the recuperation of the threat posed by independent women."[10] For example, *Condemned Women* (Lew Landers, 1938) tells the story of embittered prisoner Linda, who is redeemed by her relationship with the kindly prison psychologist. This relationship helps Linda reform her antisocial attitude and her imprisonment through heterosexual coupling, allowing her to reenter the world, albeit in a normatively subservient gender position. Suzanne Bouclin notes that for WIP films, "The habitual narrative follows a young, attractive, naïve, woman who is transformed from a 'criminal' subject to a love interest ready for marriage upon release."[11] This reinscription of gender roles is a constant in early WIP films.

Postwar WIP films in the 1950s, such as *Caged* (John Cromwell, 1950), *Women's Prison* (Lewis Seiler, 1955), and *Girls in Prison* (Edward L. Cahn, 1956), warned women of the dangers of not returning to domesticity.[12] They also slipped subtle reorganizations of gender regimes and heteronormative social structures into their narratives. Masquerading as social message films, they represented varied identities and themes traditional narrative films were not, including foregrounding women as main characters, alluding to lesbianism and bisexuality, showing single women as economically successful, deriding heteronormative marriage and domesticity, and enunciating women to women solidarity.

In the mid-to-late 1960s, WIP films began to turn away from social message films and toward more sensationalist fare typical of the second wave exploitation phase. As Walters notes "while women-in-prison movies can be fairly categorized as B melodramas in the thirties and forties and even into the fifties, they quickly shift into the exploitation genre as the decades progress."[13] This turn coincided with identity-based sociopolitical movements of the 1960s and 1970s. WIP films took advantage of these causes by incorporating their radical politics into characters and narratives. WIP films exemplify the trend of second wave exploitation films' focus on different sets of radical politics, and Suzanna Danuta Walters explains they

> elaborate fully the creation of the marginal subject. Marginalized by gender, stigmatized by sexual preference, victimized by callous bureaucracies physically isolated and preyed upon—these women are most assuredly marked other. Because the genre itself assumes a certain otherness (criminal women)—differences literally explore and proliferate. Interracial friendships, lesbian sexuality, female rebellion, and violence all come into play.[14]

As with much second wave exploitation, WIP films formed an uneasy partnership of marginality and prescriptive sensationalism. They did, however, manage to offer a transformation of second wave exploitation content that could be more easily read and understood as symptomatic of social, cultural, and political change.

While Rothman would eventually make her own version of a WIP film in *Terminal Island* years later, after their marketing material was completed, Rothman and Swartz ended their association with the film. Regardless, as with *Blood Bath/Track of the Vampire,* Hill scholars readily cast Rothman as the villain who tried to "steal" the movie from Hill. According to Calum

Waddell, the "film's genesis is far from smooth—with the original script being thrown out before shooting began and Hill's old *Blood Bath* colleague Stephanie Rothman reportedly seeking to take over the movie."[15] Rothman is keenly aware of how she's been disparaged over the years:

> There is the tiresome claim Jack has made through the years that I had a dispute with him about who would direct *The Big Doll House*. This too is simply false. According to Jack, I instigated all of this. I contacted Roger Corman in Ireland and told him to take Jack off the picture because I wanted to direct it.[16]

The narrative of Rothman as a would-be thief was so pervasive, she took to the internet in 2010 to counter it. In response to yet another iteration of the story, she posted a history of the film's genesis on a popular exploitation/cult film blog, *Temple of Schlock*. She ended her post with her reasoning for finally responding to this decades-old rumor:

> Why do I even care, since it was so long ago and both Jack and I are such insignificant figures in the long and rich history of film? Because once information is put on the Internet it stays there forever. I don't know in how many interviews he has lied about me, and I may not find them all; but on occasions like this when I do, I will not let him defame me. I am silent when criticisms of my films are made because everyone has a right to their opinion. But I will not be silent when my character is falsely attacked.[17]

While the sum of these multiple exchanges recalls the divergent perspectives of *Track of the Vampire/Blood Bath*, it remains worth noting that the historical narrative that spawned the issue has again excluded Rothman's voice almost entirely. The continued erasure of Rothman's perspective and the hyper-focus on her supposed villainy, which she terms "pathological,"[18] is representative of the same patriarchal industrial and archival patriarchal forces that kept Rothman sidelined for so long.

For his part, Corman has never commented on the issue between the two directors. Whether this is a neutrality tactic toward two former employees, a wish to stay above the fray, or a move to leverage the dispute continuation to generate more interest in the films he is still earning money on, one cannot say.[19] He continued to work with both Hill and Rothman; after *The Big Dollhouse* (1971), Hill directed *The Big Bird Cage* (1972) and wrote the story for Eddie Romero's *The Woman Hunt* (1972), all for New World. Rothman and Corman would work together one more time, as Rothman returned to the topic on which she and Hill first clashed: vampirism.

The Velvet Vampire and its partner film, *Group Marriage* (1972), are Rothman's dyad on women's sexuality and expressions of desire, sexual and otherwise. In *Radical Sex Cinema*, Carol Siegel rightly imbricates representations of sexualities on screen as more than sexual politics, but as a cultural node by which sex and sexuality stand in for the multiplicity of beliefs and anxieties that comprise extemporaneous worldviews.[20] These worldviews shed light on both temporally-specifically and universal social issues; here, the change in sexual norms across genders and behaviors. Siegel notes that in the mid-1960s and 1970s, US women availed themselves of new sexual freedoms while experiencing fewer sanctions on their behavior.[21] Like Priscilla and Phred in *The Student Nurses* and the rebel women of *Terminal Island*, women were publicly centering their desire. Therefore, Seigel concludes, "this greater freedom for both sexes led to a revolution in sexual behavior, with significant numbers of people choosing to have sex outside marriage—often with multiple partners—as a form of self-discovery or as a mode of entertainment."[22] *The Velvet Vampire* and *Group Marriage* bring these phenomena together to examine how women's sexuality and multiplicities of desire can thrust change upon cultural instructions.

MÉNAGE À TROIS SANGLANT

The Velvet Vampire was the second and last film Rothman made for Corman and New World. She moved purposefully back into genre directing, despite the trying experience on *Track of the Vampire/Blood Bath*. She recalls this decision-making process with Swartz:

> In particular I felt it was very important for me as a director to explore all types of films, not to restrict myself to anyone—at least not at the beginning, before I discovered what my strengths and weaknesses were. So, we thought what we would do would be a fresh approach to a traditional film genre, the vampire film, and that's what we did.[23]

The pair brought to Corman *Through the Looking Glass*, a contemporary twist on the classic vampire tale, written by Rothman, Swartz, and Maurice Jules. The film was released as *The Velvet Vampire*,[24] a change driven by Woolner as New World's head of distribution. Rothman: "He did not think that would be a very appealing title to audiences, and they tried to think about—his wife [Betty] actually came up with the title *The Velvet Vampire*, and he liked it, I presume, because it suggested sensuality—velvet—and yet it's a vampire movie."[25] The film was shot in the winter of 1971[26] on a budget of $165,000[27] in the Mojave Desert and the Hollywood Hills in Los Angeles.[28] According to Rothman, the desert location proved extremely challenging: "Equipment would get stuck in the sand and we'd have to push it out; the whole crew, everybody. I think there was a maximum of fourteen people on the crew, including the producer and director. So, it was a hard film to shoot."[29] In addition to the troublesome location, Rothman had to manage varying degrees of acting talent, a difficult prospect in a film that focuses primarily on three characters: Diane (Celeste Yarnell), Lee (Michael Blodgett), and Susan (Sherry E. DeBoer as Sherry Miles). Rothman:

> The performance given by the actress who played the vampire in the movie is more riveting. I was very disappointed in the actress that I cast as the young wife. She was very unpleasant on set—to everybody. She was very young, and I think very insecure . . . her fear made it difficult for me to get her to give her the kind of performance that I think would have made her look a lot better.[30]

The film was polarizing; Rothman declares "people either tend to like it or *hate* it."[31] To be sure, it's a nontraditional vampire film with a small cast, static locations, little bloodletting, and consistently surreal images. After witnessing a test audience's divided reaction, Corman had Rothman insert a new bloody death scene—a mechanic is impaled with a pitchfork—to help pacify the more disgruntled viewers.[32]

While an exercise in genre and a departure from her previous work, Rothman held true to her practice of re-visioning established cinematic expectations: "The only way that I could see to make this kind of film and to make it interesting was to reverse expectations, at this point. The obvious passivity of women in vampire films was both disturbing to me and rather boring."[33] Rothman's path to her intervention was through the vampire herself, a sympathetic seductress named Diane. Diane La Fanu, a centuries-old vampire, meets husband and wife Susan and Lee Ritter through mutual acquaintance, Carl (Gene Shane), at a Los Angeles art gallery show. Susan and Lee are playing a private game; each pretend to not know the other as Lee solicits Susan, and she coyly turns him down. It's during this process that Diane meets the couple. Diane and Lee are immediately attracted to one another, and she invites the Ritters to her desert home for the weekend. Susan, jealous of Lee's attraction to this mysterious new woman, is reluctant to go, but the Ritters travel into the California desert for a weekend getaway.

Once at Diane's, the Ritters experience strange, hallucinatory dreams. Susan dreams that she and Lee are in the middle of a desert, nude in a large bed with an ornate brass headboard, making love. Across from the bed is a large mirror, standing alone in the sand. As the couple makes love, a mysterious figure in red (whom the audience recognizes as Diane but whom Susan later calls "a strange woman") appears in the mirror and walks through the glass toward the bed. Diane takes Lee's hand and pulls him away from Susan and out of the bed, leading him farther into the desert before she embraces him. Susan awakes with a cry of "no," jarring Lee from his slumber. Lee reveals that he had the same dream, except in his version Susan was pushing him away from her, rather than she who pulled away.

The following day, the trio travel into the desert in Diane's dune buggy, touring their surroundings. That evening, Lee, assuming Susan is asleep, sneaks out of their room to Diane downstairs. Susan, who had been feigning sleep, follows Lee and sees him and Diane making love in the living room. Rather than interrupting them, she stands at the top of the stairs, watching. Diane sees her watching and smiles; Susan responds with a small smile of her own. After another shared night of dreaming, Susan confronts an unrepentant Lee and hints at her ability—and growing desire—to also sleep with Diane. That night, the Ritters again share the same dream, but with an important change. When Diane materializes out of the mirror, she moves into the bed with Susan, leaving Lee standing on the sidelines.

The next morning, Lee discovers Diane has sabotaged their return to LA. He confronts her, but Diane seduces and kills him. Later that afternoon, Diane seduces Susan. As they are about to make love, Susan discovers Lee's dead body and runs from the house, making her way back to LA with Diane in pursuit. With the aid of a number of crosses, a group of strangers, and sunlight on Diane's exposed skin, Susan vanquishes Diane. She retreats to the home of her friend Carl, who had originally introduced her and Lee to Diane. As she questions Carl about Diane, she begins to realize that Carl is also a vampire. As Carl advances on Susan, the film closes with Susan's realization that her ordeal has come to its preordained end.

Surreal Stylistics

The Velvet Vampire is Rothman's most surrealistic and avant-garde film. She drew inspiration from Salvador Dalí,[34] Jean Cocteau, and Georges Franju,[35] influences visible in the title credits and opening sequence. The film opens with an ominous piano score, and a blood-red abstract image filling the frame. The amorphous form begins to slowly pulsate, mutating into a shape reminiscent of blood cells. Much like the hallucinations in *The Student Nurses*, Rothman uses undulating images and shifting colors to indicate the haptic sense of the image; red, orange, yellow, black, and white slowly grow and dissolve into one another, giving the image a tactile materiality. The sequence ends on the cell-like shape in shades of black and dark red and the camera zooms out from the image. The dark colors dissolve into the background as a bright white cross, framed in a cloudless, bright blue sky, fills the frame in sharp focus.

The camera pans down the cross, revealing its placement on top of a modernist church in downtown Los Angeles. It is a sunny day in the city, fronds of the palm trees that line the sidewalk sway in the breeze, and a wave of cars travel down a busy street. The camera pans down further, reaching eye level, and holds a long take of a large, anonymous building. The shot remains static as the sunny day fades into a dark night, the only illumination coming from a lone blue light in the middle of the screen. Rothman managed this transition through a thoughtfully crafted lap dissolve. "Rothman chained the camera down on a scaffold, made the first part of the shot—a zoom and tilt down a cathedral spire to Wilshire Boulevard. Then, after sweating out a forty-mile-an-hour wind, returned at night to find the camera still in position and took the second part of the shot."[36] There is a simplicity to the shot that unbalances the viewer with its foreboding mood while simultaneously constructing a particular spatial and temporal framework of everyday LA.

The image dissolves a second time as the camera focuses in on a new location: the exterior of a dark courtyard, lit only by three streetlamps, and with a pool of water illuminated in the center of the frame. The water in the pool shimmers red, but the viewer is unsure how: the lamps casting light on it are fitted with white bulbs. A woman walks into the frame from the right-hand side, dressed in red and white, a mirror of the courtyard's light. She furtively looks around her and sees a motorcycle, sitting alone, in the yard. The owner suddenly attacks the woman from behind. Wielding a knife, he drags her to the ground and opens his shirt, attempting to assault her. He covers her mouth with his hand so she cannot scream, and she bites him. He draws his hand away and forcibly kisses her. She grabs the knife and stabs him in the heart. Rising from the floor she appears nonplussed and calmly walks to the courtyard pool to wash the blood from her hands. This scene is a reworking of Lynn's subverted rape in *The Student Nurses* with a crucial change: the women is Diane, a killer herself. Diane doesn't drink the attacker's blood or kill him with her fangs; her vampiric activities are reserved for those moments of intertwined intimacy, lust, and longing for companionship.

Rothman quickly trades the LA cityscape for Diane's desert home, constructed from wood, bleached sandstone, and rock. The modernist house is, perhaps, most evocative in its unusual layout. Its multiple-floor layout and oddly placed rooms give it a disorienting effect; the viewer is never sure which part of the house connects to others, or where characters are in relation to one another when they are in different rooms of the house. This effect is highlighted as characters move throughout the house, the disorientation of their spatial positioning reflecting the rapidly changing relationships each has to the other. Rothman explains: "I picked the house that we used [. . .] because it was built on three levels in the Hollywood Hills so there were a lot of stairways between rooms. Part of [the suspense is] the unusual shifting of levels that seem to take place as people go from one room to another."[37] As the love triangle complicates the film's central relationships, the house reflects the ever-changing intimacies between the three.

Natural locations also carry significant weight in the development of mood and metaphor. The Mojave Desert is, at first glance, an incongruous location for a vampire movie. Yet the sparse landscape lends an ethereal feeling to the shared dream sequences: the desert's rock formations, colorless landscape, and hazy light are otherworldly, perhaps interplanetary. Unlike the hallucinations in *The Student Nurses*, the dream sequences in *The Velvet Vampire* are free of diegetic sound, and the slowness of Diane, Lee, and Susan's languid movements in the dream space is disorientating. The characters, so clearly in the desert, are moving as if they are under water. Rothman shoots using natural lighting, letting the camera linger on the sun-bleached sand, the dry and brittle flora, and the dark, sand-bitten rocks. Although seemingly out of place for a vampire film, the desert, in its dryness, its constant thirst for water, its bareness, and its isolation, aptly reflects Diane's queer longing. Indeed, it brings to mind Salvador Dalí's painting, *Remorse, or Sphinx Embedded in the Sand*: the image of a lone and timeless woman, trapped in the desert, on her own save for a tower of silent rocks.

RADICAL VAMP, RADICAL DESIRES

Diane is a contradictory vampire who embodies traditional and nontraditional generic traits. Rothman signals a connection to traditional vampirism primarily through literary references. Diane shares the surname of *Carmilla* author Joseph Thomas Sheridan Le Fanu. She meets the Ritters at the *Night Visions* art show held in the Stoker gallery. The mirror foregrounded in the hallucinatory dream sequences references the film's original title (*Through the Looking Glass*) and Lewis Carroll's novel of experiencing the world beyond the world, or a life beyond death. Much like the sympathetic Stokerian vampire, Diane is likable, while Lee is a selfish boor and Susan is babyish and prone to temper tantrums. These characteristics demonstrate Rothman's flitting focus on vampire myth in the film. Unlike her literary precursors, Diane eats food, albeit uncooked meat, and she is diurnal, eschewing the standard coffin for a king-size bed. While she does protect herself from the sun with long sleeves and hats, she races across the desert during the day in her dune buggy, seemingly unconcerned about the sun. While superficially about a vampire, the film is more concerned with the love triangle and queer erotics between the three lead characters than it is with anything else. Rothman chose a vampire film for the subject's links to eroticism and sexuality, specifically women's sexuality. She explains:

> I started out with the intention of making what I thought was at the heart of all vampire films, which is an erotic tale. I always thought a vampire was a very erotic figure, and I wanted to make a highly erotic vampire who was very appealing and very seductive and was a modern woman—seemingly a modern woman.[38]

Rothman's imbrication of vampirism and eroticism is endemic to the genre; "the cinematic vampire is always about sex."[39] Expectantly, the film honeycombs diegetic sex with desire, death, power, and powerlessness, creating a multifaceted and complex understanding of sexuality. As Rothman states:

> Well, depending on the human being that is practicing it, sex can be dangerous, it can be safe, it can be warm and comforting, it can be cold and terrifying, it can be gratifying, and it can be painful and without any gratification. So, there are many ways to approach the subject, and I never had any intention, during the time I was making films, to say only one thing about it.[40]

Diane is a totem of limitless pleasure, both "abject and exalted"[41] by her human lovers as the site of indulgence, lust, pain, and pleasure. Diane is the aggressor in her sexual encounters with Lee. The only sex between Lee and Susan focuses on Susan's pleasure from receiving oral sex, which she declines to reciprocate. Centering women's sexual desire allows Rothman to explore nuanced portrayals of the various incarnations that satisfaction can take, including voyeuristic pleasure. Diane watches Susan and Lee's intimate moments through a hidden two-way mirror just as Susan watches Diane and Lee from their stairs. The women's shared pleasure is a voyeuristic one: Diane watching Susan, Susan watching Diane, Diane knowingly being watched.

Voyeuristic kinship underpins the women's attraction to one another, alongside a mutual understanding of gendered desire and pleasure. Diane makes this implicit understanding explicit when she asks Susan why men envy women, answering her own question by saying they "envy the pleasure we have that only we can have."[42]

Indeed, Susan's feelings towards Diane evolve from jealousy to desire over the course of the weekend. Lee's adultery is met with little reproach from Susan because it provides her allowance to act on her own queer desire for Diane. The queerness that circulates from Diane is central to the idea of the vampire, what Kimberly Lau sees as "linking same-sex desire, blood, contamination, and death."[43] While not specifically addressing queerness, Jeffrey Jerome Cohen's germinal "Monster Culture (Seven Theses)" locates the danger of the monster in its illogical and independent body,[44] similar to the cultural panic mapped onto queer bodies. The queer monster is culturally and hegemonically dangerous because of its ability to generate instability, to erase borders, and upend normative—and patriarchal—meaning. Vampires are preternaturally queered, as Jeffrey Weinstock explains, "by recklessly transgressing gender expectations and sexual mores they foreground social contractedness of gender and sexual codes, as well as the hegemonic devices that attempt to naturalize those constructions."[45]

Diane-as-vampire erases the boundary between life and death, and for Susan and Lee she removes the walls between waking and dreaming, individual and shared consciousness, and monogamy and polyamory. The move to polyamory here is a crucial one; if we consider queer polyamory as the non-hegemonic satiation of varied desires—sexual and otherwise—*The Velvet Vampire* grounds its love triangle in polyamorous desire, exploring what Pam Cook sees as "contemporary sexual mores while reversing many of the expectations of vampire mythology."[46] The love triangle itself is a formula that removes desire from binary choice; a choice constructed through patriarchy. Agata Łuksz notes: "The love triangle presupposes that no man can fulfill all the needs of a woman and this presumption persistently dismantles male possessiveness and demands of exclusivity. At the same time, it undermines the traditional identification of female love with unlimited devotion and submissiveness."[47] The love triangle and its role in redefining sexual and power boundaries is Rothman's true focus; vampirism is merely a vehicle for sexual politics. Much as Priscilla in *The Student Nurses* was, in part, a cipher for criticism of the gendered politics of free love, the love triangle in *The Velvet Vampire* skewers the centering of men's desire in nonnormative sexual couplings. As attraction grows between Diane and Susan, Lee is increasingly frustrated at being marginalized. Indeed, he attempts to return to the city only once it became glaringly apparent that Diane and Susan are more interested in each other than him. For Lee, polyamorous discovery is only acceptable when it centers heterosexuality and male pleasure.

While Susan and Lee may be interested in sexual exploration, Diane's desires stem firstly from her eagerness for companionship; she is profoundly lonely. Outside of life and death, Diane is outside of time, lost to history and yet required to watch it unfold eternally. Marooned in her ahistoricity, Diane longs for the companionship of her husband while oscillating between grief and guilt: soon after she was turned, she killed him in a bloodlust. If she leaves the desert, his preternaturally preserved body will fall to dust. Bound to his grave, she's trapped herself in isolation for more than one hundred years. Her loneliness fosters her twinned desires of fellowship and feeding; intimacy in bloodletting and in camaraderie are no different. In her book *Feeling Backward*, Heather Love locates queerness in longing, specifically longing across time.[48] Love's queer longing pushes into the past and future, searching for community against historical erasure and isolation. In cultivating her relationship with the Ritters, collectively and individually, Diane is reinserting herself into the human record as her longing transforms into polyamorous desire for partnership, blood, and sexual pleasure, all inseparable in their motivation or manifestation.

The Velvet Vampire establishes the interplay of lust, nonsexual intimacy, sexual and nonsexual companionship, and the impossibility of their satiation under patriarchal constructions of partnership. *Group Marriage* conceptualizes utopic solutions to the aforementioned problems by investing in collectivism, a similar strategy to that used in *Terminal Island* but implemented much differently. Critically, both films use queer logics to conceptualize women's sexuality and desire outside of normative structures. In doing so they function as proto-queer texts: films that leverage nonhegemonic constructions of sexuality, desire, and interpersonal connections to undermine repressive strictures. My use of the term "queer" across this chapter is modeled on Alexander Doty's application in *Making Things Perfectly Queer*, as a way to "describe a wide range of impulses and cultural expressions, including a space for describing and expressing bisexual, transsexual, and straight queerness."[49] Doty leverages "queer" to "challenge and confuse our understanding of and uses of sexual and gender categories"[50] while simultaneously signifying a specific and insistent difference around sexual and intimate marginality, radicality, and possibility.[51]

I want to be purposeful here: I am not suggesting either of these films are explicitly concerned with queer sexuality or the queer experience. Rather, these two films fit into what B. Ruby Rich calls "before the beginning."[52] Before the mainstream reemergence of a vital independent film market in the US during the 1980s and 1990s, queer film was understood as underground art. In *New Queer Cinema*, Rich maps its genealogy, uncovering the traces of queer cinematic life in experimental, art, documentary, and other borderland film forms: Kenneth Anger's *Scorpio Rising* (1964), Jean Genet's *Un Chant d'Amour* (1950), Jim Bidgood's *Pink Narcissus* (1971). *The Velvet Vampire* and *Group Marriage* are additions to this family tree, expanding the prehistory of queer cinema and engaging mainstream spaces like drive-ins and small-town theaters within its apparatus. While *The Velvet Vampire* does address same-sex desire, queerness as a filmic descriptor here is the crack in the foundation of normativity, undermining preconceived identity categories like gender and sex, and "revealing them as socially and historically constructed identities that have often worked to establish and police the line between 'normal' and 'abnormal.'"[53] *The Velvet Vampire* constructs queer longing as an affective resonance born from the strictures of normative expectations of relationship composition, and *Group Marriage* attempts to mitigate said longing by creating alternate lifeworlds for the free expression of sexual desire and intimacy structures. As a result, the films challenge gendered and sexual power dynamics, reshape desire and kinship structures, and affront hegemonic social structures.

QUEERED LIVES, QUEERED WORLDS

While *The Velvet Vampire* interrogates queer longing and polyamorous desire through surrealistic aesthetics, *Group Marriage* attempts to mitigate said longing through queer world-making and comedy. Although Rothman regularly integrated comedic moments into her films, *Group Marriage*, made for Dimension, was her first full-fledged comedy. A combination of farce and a comedy of manners, the film takes its inspiration from George Feydau's play *l'Hôtel du Libre échange/Hotel Paradiso*.[54] Certainly, the exaggerated situations, physical humor, and broadly stylized performances of the film channel Feydau's mobilization of farce. Rothman was also inspired by Alvin Toffler's *Future Shock*, which examined the implications of massive and rapid structural social change on the global citizenry.[55] When Woolner requested a "sexy" film, Rothman thought to combine an evaluation of evolving sexual customs, structural social and cultural changes, and the potential and pitfalls of a group marriage.

Despite Woolner's original request, *Group Marriage* is set apart from many second wave exploitation films in that there is no violence and almost a complete lack of sex; there is only one on-screen sex scene in the entire film. While the film contains several scenes with nudity, as in *The Student Nurses*, it is de-spectacularized, as when, for example when a character showers or sleeps. One can imagine this surprised audiences attending a film whose title hints at sexual bacchanalia. The second of the film's surprises was its lead, Hong Kong-born actress Aimee Eccles. Rothman: "I like the idea that it was nontraditional casting at the time. The leading lady was definitely an American girl, I mean, a very American girl, and I liked making the point that a very American girl didn't only have to look like somebody whose ancestors came from a European country."[56] Lastly, the film's comedic structure diffuses the destabilizing social challenges in the film with a lighthearted practicality.

The film, which takes place in Los Angeles, follows Chris (Eccles) as she negotiates contemporary relationships. Chris is a mechanic and customer service agent at a car rental company. She has been with her boyfriend, Sander (Solomon Sturges), for several years, but his all-consuming dedication to his work and his growing sexual disinterest in her is beginning to wear thin. In transit to meet Sander after work, she meets Dennis (Jeffrey Pomerantz). Chris and Dennis become friendly and Dennis joins the couple for dinner, staying the night at their home. That evening Chris propositions him and the two have sex.

When Sander discovers Chris's infidelity in the morning, she reassures Sander that she can love him and like Dennis at the same time. The three eventually come to a mutual understanding. Dennis invites Sander and Chris to dinner that evening to meet Jan (Victoria Vetri), his girlfriend. At dinner, the quartet get along well; Sander and Jan are immediately attracted to one another. They all return home to Sander and Chris's house, where Sander and Jan plan on making love. Chris, not yet comfortable with the idea, forces the four of them to all sleep in one bed as she invents a series of excuses to interrupt Sander and Jan's planned intimacy. The next morning, realizing her mistake, she apologizes to Sander, and by the end of the day, Dennis and Jan have moved in.

The two couples begin to live life as a foursome. During an excursion to a local beach, they meet Phil (Zack Taylor), whom Jan has sex with and brings into the relationship. Aware of the odd number of partners, Phil searches for a woman to bring into the expanding relationship. Phil places an ad in a local underground newspaper, but almost immediately afterward meets Elaine (Claudia Jennings) while out jogging. He brings her to the house to meet the rest of the partners, and she agrees to join them. At that moment, the ad Phil had placed and forgotten to retract begins to bear fruit, as all respondents come to the home looking to join in. Although the respondents represent a plethora of sexual proclivities, the sixsome opts to stick with what they have.

With the partners solidified, the group performs a symbolic bonding ceremony by sharing a single glass of wine to cement their group marriage. The harmony of their new collective life, however, is soon shattered. After seeing Phil's newspaper ad, a local television reporter and camera crew comes to the house to interview the sixsome. Once their unusual relationship arrangement becomes public knowledge, a judgmental public target the group: their house is damaged and vandalized, Molotov cocktails alight their front yard, and Chris's car explodes in a ball of flames. Unwilling to be intimidated into abandoning their chosen lifestyle, the group decides to legalize their relationship through marriage. Knowing this will end in their immediate arrest, they plan to use their situation as a test case to advocate for juridical change to standard marriage laws. Concurrently, Chris realizes that she is pregnant and Jan, feeling constrained in the group setting, leaves her partners. Their plans for marriage continue, and Chris's co-worker Judy (Jayne Kennedy) joins the group as Jan's replacement. The film ends with the just-married group escorted in police cars to the hospital so Chris can have her baby before their inevitable arrest.

Totalizing Lifeworlds

The film's comedic structure diffuses its destabilizing social challenges with a lighthearted practicality. Through this levity, the characters leverage queerly constructed intra- and interpersonal strategies to manage their group marriage internally and present themselves externally to society. Understanding first how the intra-personal relationships for the film are managed through lifeworlds, and second how the group's interpersonal and external integration into society generates a type of queer world-making, *Group Marriage* unfolds as a proto-queer text. It's a showcase for alternative living based on desire and collaboration, a structure reminiscent of Fiona Buckland's lifeworlds: "environments created by their participants that contain many voices, many practices, and not a few tensions."[57] Buckland developed the idea of the lifeworlds in her book *Impossible Dance*, which focuses on the ways that queer communities created queer, expressive spaces in clubs and on their dance floors. Lifeworlds rely on multiplicities constructed from the collective agencies of the individuals producing these sites and how those agencies interact, mesh, and disagree with one another.[58] Within these interactions, lifeworlds open up potential for addressing various identity factors of difference—race, ethnicity, class, and gender—that are routinely silenced under heteronormative constructions. To be clear, the film doesn't address race directly, although it does incorporate interracial relationships vis-à-vis Chris and Judy, who is Black. *Group Marriage*, does, however, use the tensions and potentialities inherent in lifeworlds to discuss women's sexual desire and gendered labor.

Women's sexuality and desire drives the collective relationship arrangement of *Group Marriage*. At the opening of the film, Chris is extremely dissatisfied with her and Sander's sexual relationship. Sander has become increasingly focused on his work—he owns a business that capitalizes on the perceived failure of the counterculture of the 1960s by producing nihilistic bumper stickers[59]—and has been ignoring Chris and her sexual needs. Chris spends a majority of her time with Sander either fighting or fixing his car. As she tells him early in the film: "I am more intimate with your car than I am with you."[60] Sander seemingly feels little remorse for his treatment of Chris. Rather than address her needs, he mocks and judges them, calling her a nymphomaniac and an "oversexed grease monkey."[61] Chris refuses to be shamed for her sexual dissatisfaction, calling Sander a "chauvinist pig" and telling him, sweetly, to "go fuck yourself."[62] Resolute that her desire not be cowed by Sander's judgments, she seduces Dennis.

Chris and Dennis's initial sexual encounter is noteworthy in demonstrating the tensions between desire and hegemonic standards of sexualized coupling. Chris waits until Sander is asleep and sneaks into Dennis's room. She undresses, gets into bed with him, and tells him: "I love Sander, but I still wanted to come in here with you."[63] As she advances on Dennis, he becomes increasingly nervous, trying to quell his desire and hers by incessantly talking about how much he likes Sander, what a great person he thinks he is, and how much he respects him. Dennis' constant referencing of Sander is an attempt to diffuse sexual tension reminding Chris of her normative pairing with Sander, her responsibility to the "rightness" of that construct, and his respect for it. His focus on Sander, and the man in the relationship, foregrounds the inherent patriarchal gender dynamics of the "rightness" of normative intimacy; Dennis respects the relationship because he respects the man, rather than the man and the woman, in it.

Chris's response is to refocus the situation on her and her desire. She tells Dennis: "I don't love Sander any less because I am here with you. Why does everyone think you can only care for one person? Look at parents. They can love ten children at the same time."[64] For Chris, love and sexual desire need not be directly correlative, nor do they need to be restrained to a single individual at a specific time. Chris is referencing here what Lauren Berlant and Michael Warner term "border intimacies," which develop when people gain pleasure, eroticism, and self-fulfillment through relationships with strangers and/or acquaintances outside of the heteronormative couple form.[65] In this moment, Chris's desire is neither about Dennis, Sander, nor love. Rather, it is focused on her sexual pleasure and refusal to forgo the satisfaction of that pleasure simply because of the accepted bounds of heteronormative coupling.

Dennis cannot refuse Chris. The next morning, when Sander finds the two of them together, Chris is resolutely unapologetic for her actions, defiantly telling Sander, "There's nothing wrong with what I've done."[66] Although Sander is initially angry for what he sees as a betrayal, by that afternoon the two have come to an understanding that Chris's actions have the potential to enhance, rather than damage, their relationship. Women's desire will again play a constitutive role in making the group's world when Phil is brought into the relationship via the foursome's beach trip. Jan is the one who meets Phil, swimming nude on his day off,[67] and brings him to the group's beach encampment. He spends the night with them (platonically); in the morning, his car won't start and Chris can't fix it, so they give him a ride back to town. Phil shares that since he is in the middle of a divorce he has been sleeping on friends' couches. Chris and Jan prod Sander and Dennis into agreeing that Phil should stay at their house until he is able to get back on his feet. At Sander and Dennis's agreement, the two women are visibly happy. They smile broadly at one another, giving each other knowing looks, and bounce excitedly on the back seat of the car. Their behavior clearly indicates that their offer of housing was less about Phil's well-being and more about their shared sexual desire for him. Once home, both women cling to Phil while walking into the house—one on his back and one on his side. Phil is quickly absorbed as the fifth partner in the relationship, thanks to the women's desire.

Gendered divisions of labor in *Group Marriage* also speak to the ways in which the group's constructed lifeworld interrogates gender equity. All of the partners, with the exception of Jan, are professionally employed. Chris works at the car rental office and is the group's resident mechanic, Sander owns his own business, Dennis is a parole officer, Phil is a lifeguard, and Elaine is a lawyer. Jan is responsible for maintaining the home. She redecorates the formerly sparse space, tends to the yard and gardening, and cooks the group's meals; her labor is the affective labor of home and family maintenance.

When Chris discovers she is pregnant, Jan is vocally upset. As the only person who works within the home, she believes the care of Chris's child will fall primarily to her, something she is adamantly against. When Elaine assures her that the men will also aid in child rearing, she is extremely skeptical, disavowing Elaine's notion that the entire group will help raise the baby. She says, "Sure, Elaine, that's what you went to law school for, to learn how to change diapers."⁶⁸ Jan's very reasonable skepticism highlights the fissures in the group's lifeworld; for all their attempts at alternative world-making, stereotypical assumptions of gendered responsibility are still firmly moored in traditional heteronormative patriarchy. These gender assumptions were also foregrounded in the conversation that ensues when Chris first announces to the group that she is pregnant:

DENNIS: I would like to have a baby.
JAN: Maybe Chris doesn't want it.
DENNIS: Of course, she wants it.
ELAINE: Look, you can't decide that. It's her body, not yours.
SANDER: Chris, what do you think?
CHRIS: I agree with Dennis. *He* should have a baby.⁶⁹

Initially conflicted, Chris decides to carry the pregnancy. Later, patriarchal constructions of fatherhood arise when the men, playing basketball, wonder who the child's biological father really is. While the conversation is quickly ended with the determination that it does not matter who impregnated Chris, that the question was raised demonstrates the limits of the group's lifeworld outside of established patriarchal gendered labor.

Approaching Queer World-Making

Group Marriage is template continuity filmmaking. It lacks the experimental/avant-garde elements of *The Velvet Vampire*, and, unlike *The Student Nurses*, it retains a single prevailing filmic style. Like Rothman's previous works, *Group Marriage* was filmed in and around Los Angeles, and captures the city and its inhabitants in its contemporary moment. What stands out in the film is its foregrounding of a queer collectivity through the group relationship arrangement, approaching a type of queer world-making meant to satisfy the free expression of sexual desire through the rejection of strict normative monogamous sexual and intimacy pairing. Doty argues that reading queerness into a text as a connotative function continues to invisibilize queer mass culture.⁷⁰ Queer connotation perpetuates the celluloid closet, to crib from Vito Russo, monetizing queerness outside of acknowledgment. *Group Marriage* denotes queerness and acknowledges queer structures in the text as a dominant, rather than alternative, reading. I call the film proto-queer, however, because it is indebted to a straight queerness constituted outside of sexuality but within explicit and political nonconforming, anti-hegemonic structures. While there are queer characters in the film, those in the group marriage itself only engage in opposite gender sexual activity, and then only with one other person at a time. Indeed, they adamantly reject group sex; as Jan emphatically says to a television reporter: "We *don't* do it!"[71] Queerness is rooted in reconceptualization of family, kinship, and intimacy.

Rothman underscores the heft of this repudiation of monogamy through the group's neighbors, Rodney (Bill Striglos) and Randy (John McMurtry). Rodney and Randy are a gay couple who establish a friendship with the group through Jan. Privately, however, they question the group's arrangement. For example, Sander, Dennis, Jan, and Chris bring Phil home, Randy and Rodney spy on the group over a wall between their two properties. Randy says, "Two girls and three guys, what do you call that?" and Rodney replies, "A full house."[72] In using explicitly queer characters to highlight the unusual nature of the group dynamic, Rothman emphasizes its marginality and exceptionalism while implicating Randy and Rodney's passive acceptance of structured monogamy, an indictment that tracks across their characterizations.

Randy and Rodney are not flattering queer characters. Rodney is stereotypically flamboyant and effeminate, concerned with cooking and flowers. His relationship with Jan, who has a semi-homemaker role in the group, emphasizes his feminized domesticity. Randy appears dimwitted and put upon. Both are used for comic relief, as are the queer characters who answer the group's personal ad, of which there are several. A young man in his early twenties tells the group, "I go both ways, AC/DC," a leather-clad dominatrix who smiles seductively at Chris while declaring, "Hey honey, you're cute, like to play rough?" and a man who enters the house, strips naked, and says to all six, "I'm ready for anything," are all met with exasperated looks, confusion, deprecating quips, and, in several cases, the front door slammed in their faces. The absurdity here is not a group marriage, but variations of same sex desire. When the sixsome is married, Randy and Rodney are wed at the same time. The officiant happily pronounces Sander, Phil, Dennis, Chris, Elaine, and Judy "husbands and wives"; he looks at Rodney and Randy confusedly, pronouncing them "married," an earlier smile dropped from his face. Sander, Phil, Dennis, Chris, Elaine, and Judy couple and kiss to celebrate their union; Rodney and Randy hug. The film's investment in queerness is committed to queer world-making, not queer characters.

Queer world-making is a concept originated by Lauren Berlant and Michael Warner in "Sex in Public." Berlant and Warner think through the potentialities for queer sex unmediated by the public, not simply in regard to safe zones for queer sex, but also "the changed possibilities of identity, intelligibility, publics, culture, and sex that appear when the heterosexual couple is no longer the referent or the privileged example of sexual culture."[73] Locating the space of the family as the node through which the public concretizes and understands the privatization of citizenship and sex in the United States,[74] Berlant and Warner theorize familial intimacy—specifically the intimacy of the heterosexual couple—as constantly publicly mediated, resulting in the re-inscription of heterosexual coupling as institutionally and ideologically normative. This process reinforces the privilege of the heterosexual couple while "blocking the building of nonnormative or explicit public sexual cultures."[75]

A queer world-making project challenges the public/private logics of compulsory heteronormativity and its focus on the familial couple while unsettling normatively accepted family and kinship patterns.[76] *Group Marriage* approaches a type of queer world-making. The invocation of approach here is purposeful. The film's investment in how desire and relationship structures can be molded into alternate models that foster a sense of social utopia works along the world-making process Berlant and Warner detail. The group's collective living arrangement, partner sharing, joint professional and affective labor, and the construction of their house as a shared living space disrupts the "rightness"[77] embedded in publicly constructed heteronormativity. The intense and violent reaction to the group's public "outing"—the social mediation of heterosexuality undone—reinforces this disruption. Queer world-making links Rothman's expansive concept of social egalitarianism and progressive social utopianism to a political project of broadly constituted queerness, demonstrating the text's position as an indicator of queer cinema, and adding to the growing archive of proto-queer and queer films.

The fluidity of members moving in and out of the group is also symptomatic of queer world-making. Berlant and Warner see a queer world as "a space of entrances, exits, unsystematized lines of acquaintance, projected horizons, typifying examples, alternate routes, blockages, incommensurate geographies."[78] Group members enter and leave the marriage based on personal desire, coincidence, and occasionally, direct recruitment. Each group member finds his or her own route into the collective situation, but the maintenance of the queer world is primary. For example, when Phil wants to bring Elaine into the relationship, he brings her to the house. She meets the other members of the group, observes dynamics, and is asked to determine if their arrangement would work for her or not. However, the viewer must assume this process takes place; it is dialogically framed but visually absent from the film. Rather, in their first meeting, Phil is shown speaking to Elaine, as the pair jog through a public greenway, but what he says is not audible. That shot dissolves into a medium shot of Elaine sitting in the group's backyard, staring out over the Pacific Ocean in contemplation. The camera pulls back into a high-angle wide shot, as Elaine walks across the expansive yard to the rest of the group, who are sitting on the patio, a table set with food and glasses for entertaining. She soon agrees to join the group. The omitted conversations, questions, and negotiations are indicative of the utopic nature of the film. In *Only Entertainment*, Dyer examines how entertainment produces utopia through affective codes that are specific to, and characteristic of, individual modes of cultural production.[79] These affective codes delineate how filmic utopia would feel, not look. Elaine's contemplative look toward the ocean, her position in the center of the frame, and the camera's pull back to frame her and the yard coming together as she crosses it asks the viewer to feel her decision-making and the processes behind it rather than be dialogically privy to it. Indicative of a utopian sentiment in entertainment, then, filmic affective codes have the capacity "to present either complex or unpleasant feelings (e.g., involvement in personal or political events; jealously, loss of love, and defeat) in a way that makes them seem uncomplicated, direct and vivid, not 'qualified' or 'ambiguous' as day-to-day life makes them, and without imitations of self-deception and pretense."[80]

Emblematic of this uncomplicated cinematic utopia, conversations about the intricate logistics of how the group works—partner pairing, financial obligations, sleeping arrangements, household chores, resolution of disputes, and more—do not take place diegetically. Only the two potentially disruptive events of Jan's infidelity and Chris's pregnancy are deliberated on-screen, both discussions requiring a straightforward, moralistic resolution. These yielding agreements are in direct opposition to the utopic social recreation the rebels of *Terminal Island* diegetically engaged in through debate, planning, preparation, and fighting, as outlined in the previous chapter. Nuance troubles *Group Marriage*, as the film creates its space as felt and accepted, rather than explained and quantified. This underscores the simplistic substitution utopic film uses to identify and solve persistent social tensions. Buckland expounds:

> Instead of exhaustion, it promises energy; it replaces dreariness and monotony with an intensity, excitement, and affectivity of living; substitutes the manipulations of advertising, bourgeois democracy, and sex roles with transparency; that is, open, spontaneous, honest communications and relationships; and replaces the experience of fragmentation.[81]

This substitutive process toward the development of contemporary utopic spaces is explicit in *Group Marriage*. For example, when the television news crew is interviewing the group and the reporter questions the logistics of their arrangement, Dennis replies: "If six people can't live together and get along, what hope does the country have?"[82] The evasion of the question of details with the idealistic counter of "getting along" privileges totality over fragmentation and an emphasis on a broadly constructed happiness over divisiveness.

The film's commitment to its utopic project is threatened by Jan's expansive desire. After Phil catches Jan sleeping with a non-group member, she confesses to her partners that her sexual desire exceeds their arrangement. She wants to be able to have sex with whomever she wants, whenever she wants, without necessarily bringing them into the group itself. As she says, "I got to be free."[83] Unable to reconcile Jan's desire for complete sexual freedom with the maintenance of their shared lifeworld, everyone agrees Jan must leave. While this speaks to the power of women's desire in constructing and deconstructing the group, it critically foregrounds the affective "happiness" of the group as critical to maintaining their utopic vision. Sara Ahmed notes that an individual's happiness is conditional of that of another, in that "happiness becomes what is given by being given as a shared orientation toward what is good."[84] Happiness is thus a co-dependent shared object,[85] and Jan's unhappiness threatens the foundation of the group's shared affect, as the individual is sublimated to the cohort once again. It's important here to note that while relationships, sex, labor, and living in the film are all reconceptualized through queer world-making practices, the group is unable to see how shared happiness can exist through similarly evolved frameworks. Dennis underscores this when expressing his disappointment in Jan's infidelity by saying, "A marriage is a marriage. Even this one."[86]

While tensions clearly arise in the group's queerly constructed lifeworld, it is worth noting their dedication to its establishment and maintenance brings to the film, and the process of queer world-making, a sense of possibility in practice. Lifeworlds are not happenstance; they are purposeful and specific. As Buckland theorizes, "a queer lifeworld is not a superorganic form. It is not a given, but rather, queer world-making in a conscious, active way of fashioning the self and the environment, cognitively and physically, through embodied social practices."[87] The group marriage structure, the boundaries around it, and its centrality to the organization of their lives exemplifies the type of practice Buckland theorizes. It also speaks to utopic potentialities in world-making, which is reflective of Rothman's deep commitment to egalitarianism. If, as Buckland posits, queer lifeworlds embody "utopic imagination and power whereby queerness occupied the center, in which the heterosexual couple was no longer the referent of the privileged example of sexual culture,"[88] Rothman's construction of the group marriage and its egalitarian dynamics approaches utopic queer world-making and helps position it as a proto-queer text. While the film may only approach the all-encompassing queerness that Berlant, Warner, and Buckland envision, it provides yet another link in the historical chain of sustained queer world-making on screen.

Chapter 8

MEMORIES OF UNDEREMPLOYMENT

> To ask why these women were forgotten is also to ask why we forgot them. For they were both overlooked by the first generation of traditional historians and not "recognized" by the second generation of scholars.
> —JANE M. GAINES[1]

It is often the case that the most personal and revealing creative work finds its inception in the mundane. This is indeed true for Stephanie Rothman. By 1973, she had made a series of films indebted to the social, political, cultural, and sexual variations of women's contemporary lives. While all of Rothman's films deal, in some way, with economics and social class, she had yet to make a film organized around these indelible issues. This changed in 1974 with *The Working Girls*, Rothman's intimate and ultimately cynical dramatization of women's un- and underemployment. The film stands as the capstone to Rothman's career and her ideological ruminations. Whereas *The Student Nurses* and *Terminal Island* used their filmic space to envision a world outside of patriarchal oppression, and *The Velvet Vampire* and *Group Marriage* dove headlong into the shifting sexual mores of the 1970s to visualize women's expansive desire, *The Working Girls* does not share its predecessors' penchant for solutional filmmaking. Indeed, it steadfastly avoids resolutions. Valuing persistence and realism over hopeful utopianism, the film offers a harsh reflection of Rothman's professional struggle as a woman filmmaker in Hollywood.

The film had a banal beginning: a Canadian distributor offered to finance a film for Dimension, albeit along the distributor's specifications. Rothman: "He'd [the distributor] had seen *The Student Nurses* and he had liked it, and he wanted me to make another film about a group of attractive young women who lived together and their adventure.[2] So, I did another one like that."[3] Despite this routine start, *The Working Girls* stands out not only as Rothman's most personal film and the one she prefers over others, but ultimately her most melancholic.

Certainly, the film's basic premise is reminiscent of *The Student Nurses*; in both, a group of women living together navigate work, relationships, and shifting personal desires and expectations. However, where the eponymous nurses of the earlier film are completing their training and embarking on their professional lives with a mapped career path and jobs in hand, the women of *The Working Girls*—Honey, Denise, and Jill—ace limited job prospects, stalled careers, and the hard economic realities of subsisting off the work one can get, rather than the work one wants. They are each a stark stand-in for Rothman herself. Honey pursued a graduate degree in the hopes of bettering her chances in her chosen field, yet she is chronically unemployed; see Rothman's graduate film degree and years of struggle for work. Denise, a visual artist by training, is forced to paint commercial billboards to make ends meet; see Rothman's career in second wave exploitation working for companies focused on hyper-commercial productions. Jill, a law student, is grudgingly pulled into a world of sex work and crime, as she labors to put herself through school by working in a strip club; see Rothman's personal struggle with the "unholy trinity" of sex, drugs, and violence of second wave exploitation. But beyond these refractions of identity and experience, the film is a potent mix of regret and hope, of bitterness and faith, and of grief for what could have been.

Rothman made *The Working Girls* for $103,000, the smallest budget of all her films. It is the only film she wrote the story and screenplay for by herself, and it is one of only two films, along with *The Student Nurses*, in which she feels she achieved her goals of harmonious synthesis of ideological abstraction manifest through image creation.[4] The film's focus on labor and work was explicit from the start. As she said in 1977: "I am particularly drawn to the problem that the three main characters face, a problem shared by most young people: how to find work that will support them and provide satisfaction at the same time."[5] *The Working Girls* brings together the impulses embedded in Rothman's previous films as a chronicle of contemporary social issues and the desire for social solutions. Despite encoding these twinned impulses in the film, its overall affect is bleak in that the viability and implantation resolutions she offers are half-hearted and suspect. As noted previously, the film revolves around a group of women: Honey (Sarah Kennedy), who is unemployed, without a home, broke, and who has recently arrived to Los Angeles looking for work; Denise (Laurie Rose), an artist by training who desires to support herself as a commercial painter and apartment building manager; and Jill (Lynne Guthrie), a law student working as a cocktail waitress, and later dancer in and manager of a strip club.

Honey hitchhikes into Los Angeles, where she meets Denise, who offers to let her stay with her and her roommate Jill until Honey can establish herself.

Honey searches for a job but to no avail. During her search, she meets Mike (Ken Del Conte), a street musician; the two have a brief sexual encounter after which Mike begins dating Denise. Meanwhile, Honey begins a career as the paid, platonic companion of a rich and eccentric Howard Hughes-esque entrepreneur, Vernon (Solomon Sturges), who makes millions buying and trading commodities, and who only works from the back of his trash-cluttered limousine in pajamas. At the club, Jill agrees to dance as an on-stage performer to earn more money for her tuition. She's later promoted to club manager while her boss Sidney (Gene Elman) takes an extended vacation. As manager she meets Nick (Mark Thomas), a gangster who charges Sidney protection money; they begin a relationship.

Concurrently, Honey is wasting her time as Vernon's companion, putting in maximum hours for minimum wage. Frustrated, she demands some type of workplace stimulation and Vernon charges her with finding a way to make him more money. Finding what she believes to be a profitable opportunity, Honey brings the opportunity to Vernon, who promptly fires her. Meanwhile, Denise realizes that Mike isn't just a street performer; he is also a fence for stolen property. He is good at his criminal activity, so good that Nick's mob friends take notice and decide to punish him for not paying him a share of his profits and for setting up shop without their approval. Nick relays this information to Jill, who attempts to save Mike from harm. She fails, and Mike receives a savage beating from two mob enforcers. Jill, aghast at witnessing firsthand the brutality of Nick's career, seriously questions their relationship. In response, Nick asks her to marry him and become his family's lawyer to protect their criminal interests. Unwilling to give up her dedication to justice or her dream of becoming a judge, Jill declines the proposal and leaves Nick.

Soon after, the women learn their landlord is selling their building, firing Denise from her job as building manager and evicting them all prior to the sale. The landlord is adamant that their "lifestyle" will bring down the property value during the sale process. Soon to be homeless, the women prepare to vacate the building when Honey receives a package from Vernon containing $60,000. It is her commission from the business idea she brought him; he used her research to make millions. Honey plans to use the money to start her own business as a path to job creation for others. Realizing that she will need more capital than she has, she leaves a share of her profits for Denise and Jill and sets off to find Vernon. She is convinced that a combination of her ideas and his capital will make them both even more money, and with her share she can fund her own business plan. The film ends with Honey in search of Vernon, dedicated to forging her own economic opportunity.

STRUGGLE AND SURVIVAL

The film's intense focus on economic survival emphasizes how Rothman used her films to comment on her own reality. The United States in 1973 was experiencing its most severe recession in the post–World War II period.[6] There was an overall decline in job creation, a rise in unemployment, and double-digit inflation rates.[7] Personal income growth was stagnant, and high inflation increased tax rates, decreasing post-tax disposable income, and the reduction in oil supply as a result of OPEC actions dramatically increased the cost of food, gas, and other consumer goods.[8] Simultaneously, recessions hit the global market, decreasing demand for US exports.[9] The combined factors impacted US society across the board, but they hit women workers particularly hard. Since World War II, the number of women working outside the home had grown exponentially and had become one of the most striking changes in the US economy.[10] The recruitment of women into the labor force during World War II and their continued postwar participation in the workforce resulted in a ballooning of women working outside the home.[11] Simultaneously, the 1970s saw women participating in the politics of labor in massive numbers. "Women joined unions in both public and private sectors at a rapid rate. Close to 2 million new women members signed up during the decade, with the number of women represented by unions rising steadily during the decade to over 7 million by 1983."[12] The rise of what Dorothy Sue Cobble terms *labor feminism*—those women who "looked to the labor movement as the primary vehicle through which to end the multiple inequalities women confronted"[13]—wrenched gender and work into a national spotlight.

The development of women's labor as a critical factor in the US workforce was not without significant issues. Discrimination against women in hiring, promotion, and in day-to-day work life was a persistent issue, yet gains were made when the United States Supreme Court ruling in *Reed v. Reed* in 1971 codified the unconstitutionality of gender discrimination in employment.[14] Passed in 1972, Title IX of the Civil Rights Act disallowed any educational program receiving federal funds to discriminate based on sex, and in 1974, the Equal Credit Opportunity Act outlawed discrimination in credit transactions. These were key legislative actions aimed at solving some of the problematic issues arising from women's increased participation in the labor force.[15] Additionally, activist groups like the Coalition of Labor Union Women (CLUW)[16] and Working Women United and the Alliance Against Sexual Coercion formed in the mid-1960s and 1970s, respectively, to advocate for workplace sexual harassment laws.[17]

The recession of the mid-1970s, with its combination of inflation leading to higher priced consumer goods and increased unemployment, forced women workers into a difficult position. Inflation necessitated that households have two wage earners, increasing the supply of women workers.[18] However, the only sector seeing job growth and creating a demand for women workers was the service sector, an area in which women were historically overrepresented.[19] As a result, more women were looking for jobs and only finding them in an employment sector with the lowest wages and highest instability in continued employment. Simultaneously, the wage discrepancy between men and women was growing exponentially even as women's educational levels—a key factor in compensation standards—expanded, with a growing number of women earning college and graduate degrees.[20] As a result of these intersecting variables, Kodras and Padavic note, "women's traditionally subsidiary position in the labor market left them highly vulnerable in the 1970s period of restructuring, as disadvantaged groups of workers bore the brunt of sudden, and often, wrenching, labor market transitions."[21]

These issues burn bright in the film, concentrated in Honey and her storyline. Armed with a master's degree in mathematics, Honey arrives in LA searching for work, and she keenly feels the crunch of decreased employment opportunities. Reporting on her job search to Denise and Jill she matter-of-factly notes: "Wherever I go, there are too many applications and not enough jobs."[22] Rothman highlights this disparity in a montage sequence of Honey's job search. Traversing the city, Honey enters and exits a series of interchangeable office buildings. Many of the buildings are seemingly empty, their anonymous lobbies containing unoccupied chairs and empty escalators during the middle of a workday. Yet, captured in a long shot across LA's wide boulevards, the streets she travels are crowded with people. There is a stark discrepancy between the number of people the city contains, demonstrated via the busy sidewalks, and the number of those people who are working, as indicated by the empty office buildings. The despondency that accompanies chronic unemployment and continued lack of opportunity is hammered home through the lyrics of the non-diegetic soundtrack, as a morose folk singer intones "nowhere to go, nowhere to turn."[23] Similarly, a scene showing Denise painting a billboard in red, white, and blue that reads "Buy USA" and a lack of customers in Jill's club comments on the country's economic difficulties and people's lack of disposable income in the film's contemporary moment.

The specter of work, or lack thereof, hangs over everything in the film. Kathi Weeks notes that "work is crucial not only to those whose lives are centered in it, but also, in a society that expects people to work for wages, to those who are expelled or excluded from work and marginalized in relation to it."[24] Rothman visualizes this relationship throughout the film vis-à-vis the women's interaction with their material and spatial environment. Though the three women share an apartment, there is only one bedroom and one bed; they either sleep in the bed together or take turns rotating between the bed and the living room couch. Everything Honey owns, including her one "good" dress that she wears and re-wears while job hunting, fits into a single backpack. She is often filmed walking the streets alone, carrying the large backpack, which overwhelms her small frame. The inescapability of the backpack looming over her, shadowing in California's bright sun, is emblematic of her economic precarity; no matter where she goes, it follows her. On a bike ride, she and Vernon stand in front of a huge pile of construction rubble, the building project seemingly abandoned, and the affirmation of development unfinished. Rothman swivels the camera one hundred and eighty degrees to show a pristine beach, framed by palm trees and bathed in afternoon sunlight, directly across from the forsaken construction. The blight of interrupted urban and economic renewal contrasted with the promise of lightness, recreation, and disposable income associated with vacationing and casual beachgoing foregrounds the sharp difference between the myth and reality of economic stability and independence. The beach in *The Working Girls* is rendered as an acutely different space than the carefree, fun-loving beach of *It's a Bikini World* or the home of experimental, drug-fueled sex in *The Student Nurses*. The beach as a space of leisure, prosperity, and freedom is gone. Much like the beach in *Terminal Island*—both the barrier and passageway between the life of the mainland and the death of the island—the beach in *The Working Girls* is a last stop. Before Honey met Denise, she planned to sleep on the beach until she found a job. Halfway through the film she makes the beach her temporary home, sleeping among the dunes after a disagreement with Denise and Mike over their new relationship. While the beach is not a home, it does offer a concrete space, a *plan*, for those like Honey trying desperately not to slip completely under the crushing weight of their economic precarity.

To survive in this harsh economic reality, many of the characters turn to illegal or socially disreputable solutions. For example, when the film opens, Honey is seen walking down a street in LA and stopping at a barbeque restaurant; she eats a full dinner. Once finished, she confesses to the owner that she has no money to pay him. She offers to work off the cost of the meal at the restaurant but the owner refuses, offering an alternative solution:

HONEY: There must be some other way I can pay you back.
OWNER: [*leering at Honey*] Yeah, there is.
HONEY: [*sneering at the owner*] Oh, yeah. There's that.
OWNER: Yeah. *That.* I close at nine, cutie pie.
HONEY: [*exasperated*] Well, I can't hang around that long, so it's now or never.

Honey begins to take her clothes in front of the cash register, first stripping down to her bra and then beginning to remove her pants.

OWNER: [*flustered and embarrassed*] Then it's never!

The restaurant owner tries frantically to redress Honey while she tries to continue undressing.[25]

Honey's willingness to trade sex for food, and her refusal to see the exchange as shameful but rather as one of survival, as witnessed by her stripping in front of the cash register, demonstrates the depth of her financial circumstances and social precariousness. Critically, shame in the situation is transferred to the request of the restaurant owner—who is employed, prosperous, and well fed. Later, Jill asks her what she does to get by without an income. She replies: "Some conniving, a little petty theft, a little blackmail."[26] She tells Jill that she used to feel bad about it, until her hunger got the better of her conscience. Interestingly, Honey won't take offered food from Denise. Indeed, she tries to reject as much of Denise's help as possible: food, rides to interviews, etc. Understanding that Denise only has slightly more than she does and is yet willing to share, Honey is careful to not take advantage of Denise and Jill's communitarianism and contributes when she can.

Honey eventually places an employment ad that reads "I will do anything for money. Young woman, MA in math, Phi Beta Kappa, can solve your problems. Will work cheap."[27] Unsurprisingly, she gets a myriad of disreputable offers as responses. One response she follows up on leads her to a woman, Mrs. Borden (Mary Beth Hughes), who offers Honey $10,000 to kill her husband. Honey accepts, demanding $5,000 upfront. She takes the check from Mrs. Hughes, meeting her a few days later claiming to have finished the job, and takes the second $5,000. On the second meeting, however, she brings along an undercover police officer who arrests Mrs. Hughes. Honey, who has not committed murder, seemingly made the "right" choice by turning Mrs. Hughes in. However, the film offers no indication that she returns the first $5,000 payment; Honey has effectively sold Mrs. Hughes to law enforcement. While Jill does not engage in criminal behavior, she does find employment in a socially disreputable industry: exotic dancing. Taking a job as a cocktail waitress at a strip club, the Tiger's Tail, Jill finds herself hustling hard for meager tips. After her first night waitressing she meets Katya (Cassandra Peterson), the club's headline performer, and they begin to talk about the economics of exotic dancing:

> KATYA: You ever thought about being a stripper?
> JILL: Me?!
> KATYA: You.
> JILL: No!
> KATYA: You'd make a good one, you've got the looks
> JILL: But not the desire.
> KATYA: You could make a lot of money.
> JILL: How much?
> KATYA: Well, I get $400 a week, but of course I'm a headliner. To start you'd only get about $250.
> JILL: That much for going bare-assed a few minutes a night?! There's no justice.
> KATYA: I can teach you a simple routine.
> JILL: Katya, can I ask you something personal?
> KATYA: What do you want to know? The usual, like why am I a stripper instead of a social worker?
> JILL: Well, yes.
> KATYA: The money. Why else?[28]

Jill, desperate to make enough money to support herself and pay her law school tuition, doesn't need much to be convinced; she's soon up on stage performing her first striptease (and, in perhaps a wink to a knowing audience, Rothman has Jill perform the dance in character as a nurse). Although Jill's work isn't illegal, she is happy to pay protection money to Nick to keep the club—her source of income—open and date him, both indications that, like Honey, any condemnation of criminal economies is secondary to her own survival.

For Honey and Jill—women in desperate financial circumstances who survive through their own self-sufficiency—boundaries between legal and illegal activity are necessarily crossed. Indeed, it is specifically because their interaction with illegality and socially disreputable work are understood as survival tactics that they are able to escape them; Honey through gainful employment and Jill by moving up to bar manager and ending her relationship with Nick. This trajectory stands in sharp contrast with Mike and Nick, two characters whose embrace of illegal economies is presented as a choice rather than as a necessity. Mike's willingness to fence stolen property and his seeming unwillingness to find legal employment end with a savage beating, and Nick's dedicated life of crime brings him a broken heart. Honey's foray into gainful employment is unusual. She meets Vernon through the employment advertisement she's placed. He contends his eccentric behaviors are meant to maintain his privacy, his constantly mobile office making it difficult for anyone to find him. Vernon hires Honey essentially to be his friend; she meets him at an appointed time and location, and rides around with him all day, keeping him company and occasionally engaging in conversation or having a meal with him. For Honey, this is a terribly boring job. Vernon rarely speaks and she spends most of her time reading the newspaper. She is paid minimum wage but is expected to appear at Vernon's beck and call, twenty-four hours a day, seven days a week. Vernon is also extraordinarily cheap. When Honey demands that the two actually do something together to break her boredom, Vernon promises to show her the city and take her to dinner; his city tour is a forced slog of a bike ride and his dinner a stop at a grimy hotdog stand on a street corner.

Vernon's defining characteristics are paranoia, an obsession with making and hoarding ever more money, and insulating himself from the real world he profits from. He is, in many ways, the anthropomorphic embodiment of the abstract financial market the women in the film are struggling so hard to survive in. His mobility makes him a constant presence, but one impossible to mark in stable time and space. His isolation allows the world and people he profits from to remain illusory to him, the impact of his financial maneuverings figuring in dollars rather than in tangible human impact. His professional friendship contract with Honey is indicative of how, as Kathi Weeks notes, "the workplace . . . is typically figured as a private space, the production of a series of individual contracts rather than a social structure, the province of human need and sphere of individual choice rather than a site for the exercise of political power."[29] Honey's acquiescence to Vernon's human needs—companionship, conversation, and sociality—is the result of their financial power imbalance; her employment transforms her into another commodity product to be managed via his wealth.[30] Indeed, when Vernon feels that the relationship between the two has become too intimate—Honey develops the ability to predict his actions and thoughts after spending so much time together—he fires her to maintain the impersonal aspects of their so-called personal relationship. While she has a measure of success working in Vernon's style, Honey does not transform into the uber-capitalist Vernon models for her. As someone on the receiving end of the financial market's cutthroat individualism and disregard for the people it profits from, Honey is unwilling to participate in the financial exploitation of herself or others.

Rather, she decides to take her profits to build a business under an alternative framework. As she explains: "I can start a business to give people jobs. And everyone could own equal shares and there would be no bosses!"[31] As someone who has directly borne the tremendous burden of supporting increased wealth for people like Vernon, Honey is unwilling to follow in his footsteps. She is focused on using the profits she made from the system—and perhaps the system itself, if her plan to find and use Vernon to make for money for her endeavor comes to fruition—to challenge its dominance.

Rothman's professional career trajectory and its associated hurdles are clearly reflected in the film. For her part, Rothman describes the film as "my favorite film, and it is the least known and least admired. It is most essentially me; that is the interesting thing about it."[32] While Rothman gives the film a type of attitudinal lightness, it is a lightness that underscores, rather than detracts from, the seriousness of women's unemployment and underemployment. Their practical approach to their precarity reads as the rational acceptance of their inability to beat or escape capitalist financial oppression, a type of fatigued acceptance. There is a palpable undercurrent of futility and defeat in the film; despite the best efforts of the women and their work toward economic change, at the end of the film they are as professionally doomed as when the film started. For example, Honey's idea for the communal ownership of her business scarcely hides the fact that she is, effectively, pitching to start an employment agency to plug people into the same capitalist system she is trying to escape. Despite her revolutionary tendencies, Honey cannot think past the system she rails against, as "waged work has been so naturalized as to seem necessary and inevitable, something that might be tinkered with but never escaped."[33] As a result, the film's ending refuses to position women as better off than they were at the beginning; in fact, many things have gotten worse. Although the women have come into some money, this offers a limited solution. Denise and Jill are soon to be homeless, and Denise has lost one of her jobs. Honey, despite her wealth, is back in the position of having no job and no place to live. As she beings to hitchhike across the city in the hopes of finding Vernon and convincing him to help her make her collective business goal a reality, her prospects of success seem slim. The last lines of the film, spoken by Honey in voice-over as she wanders down the Los Angeles freeway looking for a ride—"Something must be out here waiting for me. It's just a matter of me finding it, or it finding me"—resounds with the desperation of those who have been downtrodden so long that giving up even the idea of hope would end their ability to endure.

The Working Girls was the last film Stephanie Rothman ever made. After an unamicable split with Dimension, a handful of sold scripts, and some unrealized directing deals, in 1976 Rothman began working a project she was very passionate about: an adaption of the Philip K. Dick novel *The Man in the High Castle*. She and Swartz had optioned the book and did a major rewrite of the story while keeping the main narrative and thematic bones intact. Rothman recounted,

> It was a film about an America that was no longer America and was struggling to come back to be the America that we know. It was an interesting exercise in alternate world history. I loved the characters we created; I really did. They were marvelous people, and very touching. It was highly imaginative, visually, that is what I liked about it. It was an effort to do all the things that we couldn't do before. It was our desire to break out.[34]

The script circulated through agents and readers without any takers. Between 1977 and 1980, they tried to get the film made. When it became clear no one would financially back them to make it, Rothman and Swartz tried desperately to get other filmmakers to make it:

> We even sent it to Stanley Kubrick and he read it and he said, "I like it, but I have other projects that I am interested in doing myself." We sent it to Irvin Kershner, and he sent back a letter saying—he knew me—"Well, you are a director, why don't you make it?" [Laughs.] We got really depressing answers. We even applied to government film commissions in Europe to give us some seed money. And we couldn't get that either. [. . .] We got it to Dino De Laurentiis, and he wasn't interested. [Laughs.] We got it a lot of places!

The film was never made; its failure is emblematic of the major themes of Rothman's career: perseverance, creativity, and frustration. In 2014, Amazon Studios announced it began production on a television version of *The Man in the High Castle*, executive produced by director Ridley Scott. It was the most watched Amazon Studio original series and ran for four successful seasons.[35]

EVERYTHING OLD IS NEW AGAIN

In late 2020, Stephanie Rothman, reflecting on our first interview together in 2015, said: "One thing that makes me happy is that some of the barriers to women working as directors have fallen since you first interviewed me."[36] I was struck by the qualification of time. She was not making a comparison between her career and today's gendered directorial landscape, but rather comparing the changes that have occurred in most recent memory. In the more than fifty years since Rothman began making films professionally, it is only in the last five years that she has begun to notice more women directors working. Research presents a more complicated picture: of the top 1,300 films between 2015 and 2019 only 6.8 percent were directed by women.[37] The number decreased to 4.8 percent when the timeframe is expanded from 2007 to 2019.[38] Much like the example of the Criterion Collection discussed in an earlier chapter, of this 4.8 percent is comprised primarily of white women, many who made multiple films each over those thirteen years.[39] While 2019 saw the highest number of these films directed by women at 10.6 percent,[40] these films are, however, still just a fraction of the whole.

These disturbing ways in which women are, and are not, represented in the image and production of the contemporary film landscape has inspired groups like the Representation Project and the Women's Media Center, among others, to call for women's increased participation in media production. This is a laudable effort. Yet, elided from the call for participation is a deeper and broader understanding of the ways in which women *have already* participated in film production since its inception and the systemic discriminatory barriers preventing that participation. It cannot be overstated how important this understanding is in light of the blanket call for participation. Women have been fighting to participate in the film industry since there was a film industry. There are the women who succeeded, who persevered. Yet even when they do, they are often not taken seriously on their own sets. Director Susan Seidelman recalls people on her set for *Desperately Seeking Susan* (1985) not realizing she was the director and instead asking her to bring them coffee.[41] Then there are women who do not succeed, certainly not for lack of talent or desire. They were beaten down by a system designed to exclude them. Take, for example, a brief comparison done between a survey of women film professionals—writers, producers, directors, editors, etc.—in 1970 and a selection of 2015 posts from the webpage Shit People Say to Women Directors & Other Women, where women anonymously share their experiences dealing with Hollywood's everyday misogyny and abuse:

- *Comment to a woman screenwriter from a male director, 1970*: "Do you think all those guys on the crew are going to take orders from a woman? Besides, it's a tough job—you have to concentrate and shut out everything else in your life—no appointments with the hairdresser, no

shopping, no dinner parties. What if you're not feeling exactly terrific a few days a month?"[42]
- *Comment to a woman director from a studio employee, 2015:* "Location scouting today. I'm the only woman on the scout. The security guard stops me and asks, 'What do you do?' I answer, 'I'm the director.' He stops and asks without irony, 'But do they listen to you?'"[43]
- *Comment to a producer and writer from a studio executive, 1970:* "As a well-known Hollywood Movie Executive told me when I put forward certain views about how one of our films should be released: 'you're too pretty to worry your head about that.'"[44]
- *Comment to a woman director and actor from a colleague, 2015:* "You shouldn't act in your own films. You're too good looking and it's distracting. People won't pay attention or take you seriously."[45]

How, then, can the reasoned answer to Hollywood's discrimination against women be left at the feet of women themselves? Why are those victimized by the system held responsible for changing the system itself? Equitable labor is the foundation of economic justice and progressive cultural development. It is imperative that we understand the connections between historical labor and contemporary participation, the archival structures that do and do not maintain these histories, and the industrial system codifying these processes.

What do we do, then, with the career of Stephanie Rothman? Rothman's career demonstrates the value of looking past the usual cinematic spaces to find women film laborers, further revealing the potential for multivariant histories in filmmaking industries like second wave exploitation. Narrating women in filmic styles where they are presumed absent increases the holistic understanding of women's participation in film outside of industrial siloes. Correlatively, Rothman's historiography demonstrates the deficits created by our collective overreliance—academic and public—in the exceptional women paradigm in chronicling women's labor in the industry. The exceptional women paradigm is dangerous on multiple levels. It constructs women directors as exceptions to the rule rather than a viable labor and creative workforce. This spectacularizes the very idea of women directors, placing them outside the bounds of normative film production. It necessarily creates a limited history of women directors—a homogenous group—as the representatives of all the variations of women filmmakers. The members of this group, tokenized as the exceptional few, represent a limited—and stereotypical—scope of styles and genres. This erases the history of women working in alternate styles, cycles, and genres, while reinforcing the tired cliché that women are only interested, or only able, to make certain kinds of film, which leads to ongoing and increased hiring discrimination.

These concerns have ever-present practical implications; limits of the exceptional women paradigm are as pressing today as ever. Typecasting exceptional women directors as primarily invested in "artistic" modes of filmmaking is deeply entrenched in the contemporary industry. One needs only to look at both the career of, and comments made by, director Colin Trevorrow as an example of how the biases embedded in the exceptional women paradigm are naturalized, rather than recognized as historically and prejudicially constructed. In 2012, Trevorrow made a name for himself with the independent film *Safety Not Guaranteed*; Trevorrow directed from a script by his creative partner, Derek Connolly. The "no-budget"[46] film was made for $750,000 and made a splash at the Sundance Film Festival;[47] it would eventually gross $4.4 million worldwide.[48] *Safety Not Guaranteed* was the first movie Trevorrow directed. Then, in March 2013, it was announced that Trevorrow had been tapped to direct the new Jurassic Park movie, executive produced by Steven Spielberg, and with a budget of $150 million. Trevorrow's engagement in the project was a shock; he was, after all, a new director untested with such a large project and budget, and he was essentially unknown outside of independent circles. The question "Why Colin Trevorrow?" was frequently asked, but unsatisfactorily answered. *Deadline* reported that "he [Trevorrow] met with the studio and filmmakers, and they felt he was a good match for the material, having grown up a huge fan of the trilogy and part of a new generation of directors steeped in all things dinosaur.[49] *The Verge* said that "the film [*Safety Not Guaranteed*] caught the attention of Steven Spielberg, who picked Trevorrow."[50] A variety of industry and popular press outlets repeated versions the "plucked from obscurity on merit" rationale.

The actual origin story, however, is more indebted to the well-worn networks on which Hollywood leans and how they benefit male directors than a Cinderella-style journey for Trevorrow. After *Safety Not Guaranteed*, Trevorrow and Connolly began an association with Disney: they were hired by the company to write the script for a remake of the 1986 film *Flight of the Navigator* (Randal Kleiser).[51] This was a second partnership with Disney; the pair reportedly sold the studio an untitled project in 2012, and Connolly was working at Pixar in 2012.[52] At the same time, Disney and Lucasfilm were searching for directors for *Star Wars 7* (released as *Star Wars: Episode VII—The Force Awakens* in 2015, directed by J. J. Abrams), a process led by producer Kathleen Kennedy, and Amblin was hiring for *Jurassic World* under the leadership of producer Frank Marshall. Kennedy and Marshall are married. The connection between these mega-franchises, high-profile producers, and Trevorrow is summarized from a *Slashfilm* interview of Marshall and Trevorrow on the set of *Jurassic World*.⁵³ Kennedy approached Brad Bird to direct *Star Wars 7*; Bird was fully engaged making *Tomorrowland* (Brad Bird, 2015) for Disney, but pitched Kennedy a workaround: hire Colin Trevorrow to prep everything on *Star Wars 7* while he finished *Tomorrowland*, and once done, Bird would come in and pick up *Star Wars*. Bird's rationale for Trevorrow was that "this guy reminds me of me."⁵⁴ Kennedy passed on the scheme but shared it with Marshall one evening. Marshall was interested in knowing more about the director Bird had suggested. He watched *Safety Not Guaranteed* and brought the idea—and Trevorrow—to Spielberg. Spielberg, "who has made a point over the years to mentor budding directors . . . said in an email that he was impressed by Mr. Trevorrow's confidence,"⁵⁵ and Universal—the film's distributor—agreed on Trevorrow "in large part because he would be steered by Mr. Spielberg and Mr. Marshall."⁵⁶ Spielberg, indeed, mentored Trevorrow throughout the process; he "approved the script, watched footage daily and emailed and texted suggestions."⁵⁷ Trevorrow benefited from the interconnected, insular networks of Hollywood players and the power of male privilege.⁵⁸ He was given a franchise worth billions of dollars, mentored by one of the most successful and well-regarded contemporary directors, and allowed to "listen and learn in real time"⁵⁹ on a multimillion-dollar film set because men hire men, particularly men that remind them of themselves.

In August 2015, a Twitter user pushed Trevorrow on this privilege, asking the director: "Do you think that if you were a female director in Hollywood you would have gotten the chance to direct Jurassic World?"⁶⁰ Trevorrow's reply demonstrated the entrenchment of the myth of meritocracy in Hollywood combined with the frame of the exceptional woman:

> I want to believe that a filmmaker with both the desire and ability to make a studio blockbuster will be given an opportunity to make their case. I stress desire because I honestly think that's a part of the issue. Many of the top female directors in our industry are not interested in doing a piece of studio business for its own sake. These filmmakers have clear voices and stories to tell that don't necessarily involve superheroes or spaceships or dinosaurs. [. . .] it involves a component that I think is rarely discussed—very high levels of artistic and creative integrity among female directors.⁶¹

Trevorrow's backhanded positioning of women directors as "above" studio production or blockbuster filmmaking is a result of his enculturation into a system that fosters processes of historical and archival erasure through displacement by exceptionalism. Underpinning the displacement is an emphasis on the stereotyping of women directors as "artistic" (read: noncommercial and non-studio), the reducibility of women directors to women's films, and the unquestioned naturalization of certain genres of filmmaking modes as more suitable, appropriate, or desirable for women directors. Women and Hollywood, an advocacy organization, responded to Trevorrow's comments with an open letter, rejoining, in part, that "anecdotes and one person's experience don't tell the whole story. Not to mention how you're repeating and perpetuating gender stereotypes about Hollywood that women have been fighting for decades."[62] For his part, Trevorrow told the *Los Angeles Times* that "it hurts my feeling when I'm used as an example of white, male privilege."[63] It is difficult for me to think that hundreds of women, those with abbreviated careers like Stephanie Rothman and those who were shut out of the industry entirely, are sympathetic.

In the introduction to this book, I called on Vicki Mayer's formulation that stories of labor—stories of the everyday work of entertainment—illuminate broad regimes of economics, politics, and industry. Stephanie Rothman is one of these stories, but there are hundreds more. Earlier, I posed the question, "What do we do with the career of Stephanie Rothman?" It is critical to slate her history and filmmaking into the expanses of film histories. Rothman's historiography clearly highlights the need for transformative archives that function as active sites of investigation. The archive as a variant site is crucial in linking labor patterns across the past, present, and future, opening up spaces for progressive intervention. Yet, that inducement is not enough. Stephanie Rothman's career and the intervention the analysis of her films seeks to locate the archive as a conduit of the past while simultaneously seizing "the archive as an apparatus to legitimate new forms of knowledge and cultural production in an economically and politically precarious *present*."[64] What we must do with Rothman's career is to *use* it. Use it when teaching film histories and filmmaking alike. Use her films in clip packages at award shows, as answers to trivia questions on game shows, as Sunday afternoon matinees on television stations, and as reparatory programming in movie theaters. Write about Rothman and her films in magazines, blogs, and journals. To be sure, some of this has been happening; there has been an increase in screenings of Rothman's films slowly but steadily since 2015.[65] I hope, in some small way, this book may help with that resurgence, but there is still more work to be done for Rothman and the myriad of other women in the same circumstance. Indeed, all women filmmakers must be loudly and regularly acknowledged as critical to the past, present, and future evolution of film. This is a responsibility we all share. The untold histories and the women who comprise them have not been conspiratorially hidden or nefariously obfuscated by shadowy men. They have simply never been thought of by the industry that benefits from them. We cannot accept that any longer.

APPENDIX

ROTHMAN INTERVIEWS

I conducted two interviews with Stephanie Rothman, the first in February 2014 and the second in October 2014. Both interview transcripts are presented here; they have been edited for clarity, not content. Importantly, both interviews are critically informed by an oral history with Rothman conducted by Jane Collings in 2001 for the University of California Center for Oral History Research. The Collings interview is a key precursor to my own interviews in 2014 and is thankfully made available by UCLA.

February 5, 2014: Interview with Stephanie Rothman

Alicia Kozma (AK): What I would like to do is construct a genealogy of your life as a filmmaker, of your life as a thinker, your life as an artistic professional. I would like to start with the connection that has been made between your films, yourself, your career, and the second wave feminist movement of the 1960s and 1970s. Your films have been taken up as feminist texts. Can you share your thoughts on the idea of feminism, your connection to it, and perhaps how these things were influenced by the fact that you were working in the heart of the second wave feminist movement? Following on that, you've stated before that you were raised in a home that valued social consciousness, the idea of equality, and the notion that a "just and fair world" was something that everyone should expect as natural and normal. Were you aware that your upbringing and this kind of development was a space of exception? Were you aware when you were growing up that your home was different?

Stephanie Rothman (SR): Yes. I was very aware of that. I grew up in the San Fernando Valley, where my parents bought a home during World War II.

Normally, I don't think they would have moved into that neighborhood, but it was the only housing available so I went to school—grammar school, junior high school, and the first year and a half of high school—with people who were from different backgrounds than my own. I was the daughter of an upper-middle-class professional, while they were lower middle class to poor. Their parents were generally people that had clerical jobs or worked in factories or as domestics or laborers, and they were mostly Mexican American or children of Oklahoma migrants from the dustbowl who had come to California in the 1930s. Because of this difference in our backgrounds, I learned about the struggles of people who I otherwise would not have met. My parents, who came from poor immigrant backgrounds themselves, thought this was a good education for me. Once I got into high school, I met some children who came from the same socioeconomic background as mine, but I didn't fit in with most of them. We had different interests and by then, different values. I was odd. [Laughs.] But as an only child, I was used to being alone a lot, so I read, I danced, and I imagined.

AK: You've recounted how, as a young woman, you became aware fairly early on about the limitations that marriage and motherhood presented for women—especially for women who were interested in having careers of their own. It struck me as a very common theme for the time, especially after the publication of Betty Friedan's *The Feminine Mystique* in 1963.

Were you familiar with the book when it came out?

SR: Oh, sure. But I was already an adult. You know, I was born in 1936. It had no influence on me. [Laughs.] She had nothing to teach me. I had never bought into the belief that I was put on this earth to marry and reproduce and keep the home of a man and be socially subservient and financially dependent on him. [Laughs.] I was happy that she came along and gained the attention of large numbers of women who, by necessity or choice, accepted this subservient role.

AK: Did you see it affecting people in your social circle, or were they already of the same mind as you?

SR: Already of the same mind as me.

AK: Do you think the timing of this this type of thinking—happening both quite early in your adolescence and before the popularization of the notion through the second wave feminist movement—contributed to the difficulties you had connecting with your peers when you were in high school?

SR: No. I think I didn't connect because I was a very bookish girl, and I also was a dancer, by the way, and spent a lot of time training. I was good enough—I think I mentioned this in my oral history—to turn professional but my parents interfered with that. [Laughs.] And I think because I was an only child I never learned easily how to socialize with my peers, and my parents didn't believe in dressing me or grooming me in the youth styles that were popular then, and so I was not attractive in the way a girl had to be attractive to be popular. There was nothing unhealthy or deformed about me, but I wasn't socially attractive.

AK: It doesn't sound like you were interested in being that kind of person.

SR: No, I wasn't.

AK: Once the ideas that were central to your adolescence began to coalesce around the second wave feminist movement, did you begin to feel connected to it?

SR: No, I didn't. I mean, I did in theory, obviously, I had always been connected to it, even before it existed! [Laughs.] I mean, I had gone my own way. I had decided I was going to live my life in a way that did not conform to the standards of the 1950s. But did I join consciousness-raising groups? Did I know women who were suddenly making the discovery that they had been herded into or had willingly chosen very narrow possibilities for self-development? No. I really didn't. I was more of an observer, an outsider, but I've been that way all my life.

AK: Did you find it a useful movement?

SR: Well, in general, yes. I mean, it obviously brought about enormous positive social change and opened up many opportunities for women that were previously unavailable to them. But did I personally find it liberating or freeing? No. It really had very little to do with me. The only way it may have is that it made some men I encountered aware of the fact that women were not satisfied with the roles that had been allotted to them. But very rarely did men express that to me.

AK: Did you find that when the movement became this public force people would associate you with it, or assume that you were part of it?

SR: Only when critics or reviewers saw my films and would say what a strong vein of feminism was in them, which delighted me but also dismayed me a little bit in the sense that it meant that they couldn't just examine the material for what it was. There are many ideas in my films that have nothing to do with feminism and everybody always imposed this, well . . . interpreted it as mostly feminist. It is feminist. I am proud of that. I'm happy I was able to convey this message. But that's not all it is. And sometimes I thought then, and I still think, that other things are lost in that one-note interpretation.

AK: Your films have always included really wide breadth of women in them, including women of color in main roles. You've previously expressed your support and concern for the issues that Mexican immigrants, certainly in Southern California, and Mexican Americans, were and are going through.

Was it important for you to include a wide variety of women in your films? Is that something that you thought was missing?

SR: Yes. I'm sorry I can't say anything more complex than that. Yes. All those thoughts went through my mind, and that's why I did cast the people from different ethnic groups that I did, but I never, you'll notice—well, I shouldn't say never, I take that back, in *Terminal Island* [1973] I did. I was always a little uncomfortable about casting Black men or women in my films, for one reason. There was at that time the rise of Black films, and I didn't feel that I should poach on their territory. In other words, their chance to make any kind of film was so limited—as limited as mine—why should I take away from them the opportunity to make films about their own experiences? But I did make *Terminal Island*, which did have Black actors in it in the lead roles, and I did that because I was specifically asked to do that. I didn't initiate that, and I did it with some reluctance because I thought that it was important not to poach on the little bit of hard-won turf that they had.

AK: Who asked you to do that?

SR: I made my films for only two companies, New World and . . . well, earlier than that I made a couple for Roger Corman . . . and Dimension Pictures. The head of Dimension Pictures [Lawrence "Larry" Woolner] and the sub-distributors who financed a number of my films wanted a film with Black actors in it.

AK: So, the sub-distributors would communicate casting preferences to Mr. Woolner and then he would pass that on to you?

SR: Yes. And they wanted one because Black films were doing well, so I did it. I tried to do it in a way that was somewhat different than the Black films that were being made in those days. I hope I succeeded. Because some of them were really offensive, you know, the glorification of pimps and whores. This was sometimes interpreted as outcries by Black filmmakers against Black oppression. But in my opinion, it was exploitation at its worst. And I didn't like it.

AK: You've described your films to me as a particular result of the cultural and political times that they were made in. If you picked up a camera today and made a film, what issues do you think would be important for you to include in it?

SR: [Chuckles.] Well, it wouldn't be a sweet coming-of-age story. That's not me. I think probably it would still be a political conflict.

AK: Any particular type of political conflict?

SR: Well, yes. I think that I would want to deal with the backsliding that is taking place today. This is too complicated for me to describe to you in the form of a specific story idea. I suppose what I am trying to say is that the underlying theme would be the assault on the values of the Enlightenment that I think we are witnessing today: the furious desire to push back and destroy—not just in countries that are in chaos or that are under authoritarian rule, but even in the democratic West—the achievements and liberal values of the Enlightenment, which I fear may soon lead to another world war and genocide. Not only another possible genocide of the Jews, but of other vulnerable minorities too. I think that we are in a terrible politically regressive age, not a progressive one.

AK: That seems to speak to a critical contemporary issue: the championing of faith over reason.

SR: You mean the war on reason! [Laughs.] Versus superstition. I think they are back again—the superstitions bred by both religion and political ideology, both god-based and godless—that fuel hatred, meaningless suffering, and death. And fear, especially by people who are not used to the violence that this breeds.

AK: Returning to the idea of your films as being narrowly understood as singularly feminist, I did find some press from when you were working where you don't negate your own feminism, but you specifically don't align yourself with the movement. Was that simply a result of your own conviction? Was there the thought that you needed to "disavow" feminism the movement as a way to negotiate your commercial position as a director who wanted to work in mainstream Hollywood?

SR: No, that wasn't the case, because the limited number of opportunities I had to even be interviewed in mainstream Hollywood, which never touched upon these subjects. I mean, feminism was never the subject, because the men I talked to, and the few women, were not really interested in that. They were interested in whether I could do something commercial. That's all.

AK: You never felt like your own ideological convictions would hinder you in getting a job, or getting the type of films you would have agreed to make if asked?

SR: No, I can't say that. First of all, I thought that when people saw my films, they'd know what my convictions were. So, obviously, if they wanted to hire me, they understood that this would probably seep out in one way or another. But beyond that, when I was interviewed for getting a job, it wasn't for anything that would *ever* display this kind of thought, never. It was never in anybody's mind that I know of. So, I wasn't afraid that I would have to compromise anything because there was nothing to compromise! There was just . . . it was a completely different realm; the subjects that my films were concerned with were not discussed in films or on television in those days. So, it didn't matter.

AK: It was never on their radar.

SR: No. The only thing on their radar was am I competent to do it. And obviously, whether I was competent or not, nobody wanted to hire a woman.

AK: The idea of collectivity, specifically the power of change that can be found in collectivity, is highlighted in a number of your films. Given that you were one of a very few women making films at the time, did you ever reach out to other women, not specifically directors, but other women professionals who were working in the industry?

SR: Well, there were very few. I mean, very few. So no, I can't say I did, because I didn't know who they were or where they were. But even if I had, it would have been very hard because I made a lot of films in a very short time, and I was over a ten-year period working almost constantly. I really didn't have time to reach out or meet anybody who wasn't going to work with me on a project.

AK: I wanted to broach the partnership between you and your husband [Charles S. Swartz]. You were very much partners in filmmaking, which comes across in the films and is something you've been vocal about for the entirety of your career. How did you negotiate structuring your professional partnership versus your life partnership? Was it something you kept totally separate? Did you think about it?

SR: There was no separation, we were just partners. In work and in life; there was no negotiation. We just met, it was love at first sight, we joined our lives together, and we lived and worked together, that's all. There was no "you have to accept this about me, and I have to accept that about you"; we accepted each other without reservations. It worked. I mean, as far as I was concerned, he was everything I wanted. [Laughs.] And I won't speak for him because he isn't here to speak for himself, but there was no negotiation. We just created a life together. And there wasn't work and there wasn't private life; it was all one, it was one continuous fabric.

AK: This not how your partnership has been referenced in the majority of the historical and contemporary writing on your career and films. In press, you were referred to as "wife of Charles S. Swartz" and in parenthesis it will say "who is also a director." During your active career years, did you recognize this as a prevalent discourse?

SR: Yes, I recognized it and I considered it inevitable. That was the time. As time went on, of course, I emerged as just Stephanie Rothman. And now I am often referred to as his wife again because as you know I established an endowed professorship in his name [Charles S. Swartz Endowed Chair in Entertainment Technology at the University of Southern California, established 2013]. During the endowment ceremony and the press write-ups, I was described as "his wife who endowed the chair." Which is fine, I'm thrilled to be his wife. I am proud to have been his wife; I mean, he was the love of my life. It's OK! And at that time, though, what you are talking about obviously was different, and I just knew that was part of the time in which we lived and that initially I would be looked at that way.

AK: Did that resigned acceptance stop you from feeling like you were being slighted?

SR: Sure, I felt like I was being slighted, but I expected to be slighted. I just refused to let it discourage me.

AK: Along related lines is a public and press discourse particularly related to your appearance—I have three examples with me—which spent more time describing your appearance than your films. Is it something that you noticed?

SR: Yeah, I noticed it. Did it disturb me? It disturbed me if that was all that was mentioned. [Laughs.] If it happened in passing then I would say, "Well, apparently that is of some importance to this person." And, of course, with our appearance, to some extent, we all tell a story. It may not be an accurate story, but we tell one. And if they are going to pay attention to my work and if somehow to them my appearance is an important component of that, well, that's alright. There was another reason I didn't mind it, which is since it was in my experience flattering, I thought this might be good for all women. In other words, you could do this kind of work, which was called a man's work, and for which you had to be tough and driven, and guess what? You don't have to be a man to be that way. You can be a woman, and you can also be conventionally thought of as attractive.

AK: That's fascinating, because I will say when I was thinking about this, it connected to a previous comment you have made, talking about how one of the reasons you believe mainstream studios did not want to hire you was because the director is a position of power, and it was—still is—difficult for men to have women in positions of power. My initial reading of the commentary on your appearance was a way to make sure that the reader understood that although you had a position of power you were still "properly feminine."

SR: I never had the anxiety or desire to have people be convinced that I was properly feminine. I never cared about that. *At all.* No, I *never*—in all my life—I have never been concerned or had any anxiety about appearing feminine. It has just never been—and when I say that it applies also to appearing feminine when I was working as a director. I didn't care about that.

AK: Sorry, I may not have been clear. I was trying to relay that I was reading the insistence of journalists commenting on your appearance as a way for them to reassure themselves and their readers that you were still understandable or readable in your place as "woman."

SR: I think that's true. That is one way of interpreting it and an accurate one, but the way I interpreted it was that it was proof that you could be that way, you could be interpreted that way and be just as effective as a director. I want to hear these compliments! [Laughs.]

AK: [Laughs.] Oh, OK! Quote, "An intense, pretty young woman, thin enough to show off delicate collar bones, long neck and high, prominent cheek bones photographers love [. . .]."

SR: Who wrote that?

AK: Kit Snedacker from the *Los Angeles Evening and Sunday Herald Examiner*, California Living (supplement) in 1970.

Um . . . oh . . . Henry Jenkins, when he is describing a picture of you, the picture of you working behind the scenes on *Terminal Island*: "Rothman, an attractive young woman with flowing black hair [. . .]."

SR: Yes, several times he has made comments about my appearance, yes.

AK: Linda Gross, who was a writer for the *Los Angeles Times*, said you could pass for a model. Those were just the three that I picked out. [Laughs.]

AK: I'd like to move toward talking about the end of your career. I've read quotes that say you decided to end your career because you were not finding work and you were tired of making exploitation films, so you just stopped. This type of practicality kind of seems to be a theme in your professional life. I'll take a jump and say it also seems like a theme in your personal life. For example, when you left the master's program at UC Berkeley, you've stated that you did so in large part because you saw no opportunities for women in academia, no viable career paths, no success stories. Is that how you felt about leaving filmmaking?

SR. Yes. I had tried to find work for ten years. After ten years, I obviously took stock of my chances of finding work in another ten years, and the only person I could think of who made a return after that was Luis Buñuel; nobody else had. I looked around at other people who had started at the same time I had, and they had either gone on to great success or they had faded from the scene. And at that time, I was forty-eight, and I said to myself, "I have all these years ahead of me, I might as well enjoy them instead of experiencing the continuing rejection and frustration and depression that this created."

AK: Did you have a sense of what you were going to do next? Did you leave with a plan?

SR: No, I didn't really leave with a plan. I got a job—on my very first job interview—I got a job working for an organization that was a proto-union for University of California professors, writing a newsletter for them about the planning in Sacramento, which is the state capital, for allocations of monies for the university, future faculty salaries, and other issues that they might be interested in. And I did that for a number of years. I also wrote a few treatments, and I optioned a screenplay of mine. It never went anywhere; that's about it. And after that I began to invest in commercial real estate [laughs], and I did reasonably well.

AK: Did you find writing or directing to be more fulfilling? You've done a great deal of writing.

SR: Yes; they are both fulfilling. The idea of writing something and then being able to make it come to life in a film is wonderful; it's a wonderful experience.

AK: Since you and your husband were professional partners, did he have a voice in your decision to leave to industry?

SR: No, actually the way it happened was I decided first, and once I decided, he also decided.

AK: Is that when he started moving toward education?

SR: Yes. That's when he did it. One day I just said to him, "I'm finished." And a few days later he said, "Well, I guess if you are I am." That's how close we were. It was unselfish on both of our parts. What made him happy made me happy, and what made me happy made him happy.

AK: That's amazing.

SR: Everyone says that and yet I'm mystified. I think that's true more than not true in marriages, to tell you the truth. I think that the bad rap that marriage gets is because people only look at the failures, they don't look at the successes.

AK: There are some theorists and artists that talk about there being a freedom in the act of quitting, particularly when one has spent so much time trying to fit yourself into a system that doesn't want you. Is that something that resonates with you?

SR: No, no. I was very sad. And I continue to be very sad until this day. But I also could see that it was hopeless. I'm going to be brutally frank with you about myself. I attribute it, in part (at the very latter stages when I was still looking there were a few unappealing opportunities that did open up) to my not being a very outgoing socially aggressive person, I am not good at networking, in fact I'm terrible at it, in fact I can't do it! I didn't have the kind of temperament and drive to do that. Now, there are people who managed to succeed without that. But they are few and far between; they are anomalies. I just could not network. I don't think that's the whole explanation, and I don't think that's even the key one, but I think that's the one element that I lacked that makes for successful careers for many people.

AK: You said that you "can't" do it, but did you also not *want* to do it?

SR: Well, that's why I can't do it! [Laughs.] Because I didn't want to do it. I just derived no pleasure from it.

AK: I want to move to talking about the idea of exploitation films. What is your definition of an exploitation film?

SR: Oh, God. Well, the only one, and I've given it in many speeches, is the classic one. It's a film whose . . . a film that is sold to the public based upon things that they can't find in conventional films. In other words, it doesn't have stars in it, but it will have scenes that will go farther than what you could see in a conventional studio film. Now, today, of course, that means nothing, as you know, but in those days that is what exploitation film was. And beyond that, I don't know what it is. It's a film that you make without stars, you make with no money, you have to scramble and struggle to make in ways that people who make films with larger budgets don't have to worry about. It's a film where you have to keep your fingers crossed at all times that nothing goes wrong because if it does go wrong you won't have enough money to complete the film.

AK: You have said in the past that you didn't realize you were making exploitation films until you read a review of *The Student Nurses* [1970] that called it an exploitation film.

SR: Correct.

AK: Did that knowledge affect your filmmaking or your understanding of what you were doing as a creative professional?

SR: Well, it underlined that I was making films of no status that would not get any kind of serious recognition from reviewers, certainly not in the papers or in magazines. And it certainly would not be taken seriously in Hollywood in any way, and it would not open up great employment opportunities for me in terms of the tools I would have to work with as a filmmaker. I recognized at that point that I was pretty much at an impasse, and that I was even lucky to have been able to make this kind of film because as a woman, nobody else was making anything else. There was one exception, Elaine May, who made a couple of films. But other than that, nobody was. And I just realized at that point that the best I could expect to go on doing was more of the same. I had hoped maybe I could get some work in television but that that door was firmly shut to me too.

AK: Your characters feel real. They feel relatable. They feel like real people whom real viewers can look at and see themselves in, even if in a small way. Did you ever think about what type of person was going to see your films?

SR: Thank you for noticing that, by the way, because that was my attitude. That everybody I was making a film for was at least at smart as me, and maybe smarter. I really believed that; I still believe that, regardless of their status in the world. I believe that. I believe there is more intelligence out there [laughs] then can ever be taken advantage of. In looking at films, I had noticed you could always tell when the filmmakers were patronizing the audience. It just shone through, and that was a lesson to me: don't patronize anybody.

AK: I know that you would go and watch your films with audiences in different theaters. Did you ever talk to them after they had seen the films? Or did you just kind of sneak out the back?

SR: No. What I did is I would try to file out with them and hear people make comments. It was very interesting. And also, when watching films with them, I would listen to the audience talking to the film because audiences, at least in those days, not so much now because they are told to shut up, audiences talked back to the film a lot, and especially to exploitation films, and especially in the theaters where they were normally played. It was wonderful to listen to the conversation in the audience. I thought that was better, actually, than asking questions. Because then the truth came out without inhibition.

AK: If someone told you before you started your career that the only films you would be able to make would be exploitation films do you think that would have deterred you?

SR: No. I wanted to make films. I was in love with the process. But once I found out what the limitations of exploitation films were, and once it was really brought home to me how low their status was, I had a very strong feeling of defeat.

AK: There is an idea because exploitation films are considered low status, and since after you've included the requisite sex, nudity, and violence, directors could add to the films "whatever they wanted," that exploitation films offer this blank canvas for tackling ideas and issues that that wouldn't necessarily happen in mainstream Hollywood. Do you think this is a romantic idea?

SR: Yes, I do.

AK: Did you feel like you had freedom once you met those exploitation criteria?

SR: Well, I did. First of all, I did with Roger Corman. When he first looked at the rough cut of *The Student Nurses*, he was a bit anxious about the freedom he had given me. But when it became a box-office success, he decided it was the right decision and a good time to make more films with themes of social activism in them. When he first saw the rough cut, he told me he didn't think it was "raunchy" enough (I think I say this in my oral history). It concerned him that the girls were too intelligent. But he changed his mind when it did well in theaters. But the freedom I had with Roger I think was due to his faith in me, not because exploitation films traditionally offered a blank canvas. And then afterward. when my husband and I made films for Dimension, where we had a small percentage of the company, the way I made films was already known to the sub-distributors that financed them and the man who ran Dimension would say that as long as I put conventional exploitation elements in, I could also put in other interesting stuff, it was OK. They didn't care because they couldn't run the same film with only a different title and different actors every week!

AK: You brought up Roger Corman, and I wanted to talk about him for a moment. Right off the bat when you started to work with him it seems like he gave you a tremendous amount of responsibility.

SR: He did.

AK: And it appears as if he had a lot of faith in you and your abilities.

SR: Yes, he did. And he was very supportive.

AK: Is that something that you think came from his recognition of your talents? Or was it a byproduct of the economic production of exploitation films, in that the lack of funds and time force everyone into multiple roles?

SR: Both.

AK: Do you remember talking to him about the level of responsibility you were taking on for him or was it just, "Hey, I need you to do this," and you just picked up and did it?

SR: Well, when he hired me, he said, "You know, I need an assistant, and you've been trained to make films, so I am going to ask you to do anything." And I said, "Fine, I'll do it."

AK: There is a lot of talk about the "Corman school" of filmmaking and the successes that it wrought. Do you think beside the opportunity to make films that being a part of the "Corman school" of filmmaking offered you any other opportunities or understandings of the industry?

SR: No. The one thing Roger did for me is he made his career shooting films quickly and efficiently, and he taught me how to do that. We would sit and discuss how to do things efficiently and to shoot quickly. We didn't have endless discussions, but we had a number of them. And I found it very useful obviously because I could get the film done on time and close to on budget. That is about the only thing Roger taught me. But that was very valuable. And he gave me these opportunities, for which I will always be profoundly grateful.

AK: One of the things that is so interesting to me about Corman is not only the way that he pioneered this style of filmmaking that has been in many ways incredibly influential on contemporary filmmaking. And I think also incredibly influential on independent filmmaking, but also the way in that he is wonderful at mythologizing himself.

SR: [Laughs.]

AK: One of the things I noticed in the Corman myth that both he talks about and I think other people have picked up on, is that any film that he was involved in, in any way, becomes in his recollections "his film."

SR: Yeah.

AK: Did that kind of proprietary language affect you?

SR: No, he never spoke to me that way, or to Charles. He never did. This is after the fact, long after the fact. I never went to a "Corman school." There was no "Corman school." He hired people to make films on a very low budget because he was risking some of his own money. In this way, he was able to found his own studio, New World Pictures. And he succeeded in doing this, but no one spoke of it as the "Corman school," at least not when I worked for him.

AK: Do you feel an ownership over your own films?

SR: Well, I actually, physically, don't own them! Literally, I don't. In fact, in some cases I am not sure where the ownership is anymore because the negatives have disappeared. Do I feel any ownership over them? Well, yes, I made them—with my husband. I mean, we both felt ownership of them in that sense, of course. They wouldn't exist without us; we made what was just an idea—a vague idea—concrete.

AK: Have you ever been approached to be part of the numerous Corman retrospectives—books, documentaries, etc.—about his career?

SR: I think one person wanted to approach me; no one else ever has. I have not been included, and part of the reason for that, I think, is that the people who have been included have become famous and successful. They are the ones who he wants to talk about him.

AK: Moving on. One of your contemporaries when you were working with Roger was [director] Jack Hill. I have found a lot of . . .

SR: Hateful things.

AK: . . . troubling material, particularly in relation to the two films [*Blood Bath/Track of the Vampire*, 1966 and *The Big Doll House*, 1971] that you and he had interactions around. And it is something that, frankly, befuddles me, as there doesn't seem to be a rationale, which I can see, for the conflict repeated both in comments made by Mr. Hill and by authors who write about his films. I wanted to get your take on the situation. He was originally the person that Roger assigned to work on *Blood Bath*, which was being recut from a Yugoslavian film. But Roger took the project from Jack and gave it to you.

SR: And I met Jack once at that time. Roger invited me to a screening Jack was giving of a cut of it, and I went, and I watched it with Roger and afterwards Roger asked what I could do with this, and he took it away from Jack.

AK: Was it your idea to turn it into a vampire film?

SR: Yes, because I couldn't think of what else to do with it. I mean, the only way to be able to do something with all this disparate footage was to have a character who looked completely different from the lead, and dressed completely different, and did things that were completely unrelated. And then to take these scenes and try to interweave them with the other scenes from the Yugoslavian film and what could be salvaged from what Jack had shot. Because we had to throw out, I had to throw out, a portion of that.

AK: Do you remember having conversations with him about the film?

SR: No.

AK: Do you know which storylines you shot? Was it just the vampire storyline?

SR: Yes.

AK: OK. You shot the underwater scenes?

SR: Yes.

AK: And did you shoot the ballet scenes?

SR: Ballet scenes?

AK: One of the lead characters is a ballet dancer, or really, more of a modern dancer. It's an extended kind of dream dancing sequence on the beach.

SR: Yeah, no. [Laughs.] No. No, no, no! [Laughs.] I remember now.

AK: OK. Did you shoot the scenes of the artists in the café?

SR: No. That's all Jack.

AK: That's Jack, OK. Those café scenes are remarkably similar to a film Roger made in 1959 called *A Bucket of Blood*.

SR: Which I've never seen.

AK: That was going to be my question! Did you watch other movies that were coming out of AIP when Roger was working there?

SR: No, I never had watched . . . I hadn't heard of him at that time.

AK: OK. So, on *The Big Doll House*, Corman was in Ireland and he asked you and Charles to oversee productions?

SR: Yes.

AK: Corman had offered the film to you to direct?

SR: Yes, at the end of the writing of the screenplay he did. Jack brought him a script called *The Big Doll House*. You know, I have written about this on a website in response to all his lies. I wrote the complete history of this.

AK: Yes, I read it. There was one thing that I wanted to confirm that was in remarks that you gave at a film festival that wasn't in there. And that was that you and your husband and Frances Doel met with Hill to work on the script and determined that you guys could not collaborate.

SR: That's correct. He was . . . he rejected almost everything that we had to say, and he was really angry that I was part of this. I suppose because I "ruined" his masterpiece, *Blood Bath*. I don't know what else, since I only spoke to him twice in my entire life. Maybe he thinks I stole it from him. I didn't! Roger fired him and asked me to do what I could with it. But Jack was very hostile to me when we tried to collaborate on *The Big Doll House*, really hostile and rude. And beyond that the three of us [Rothman, Swartz, and Doel] decided it was impossible to work with him, because he didn't agree with almost anything anyone said, and he didn't want to work out a storyline together and he rejected almost anything anyone proposed. So, my husband called Roger in Ireland, Roger had said before he left, "Try to do this with Jack because he brought in the screenplay to me." Roger had bought the screenplay for the title, that's all. He wanted a complete rewrite of it. And he said, "Try to work with Jack, but if you find you can't then go ahead and get a script written on your own." So that's what we did.

We hired a screenwriter named Don Spencer, a very able young guy, and he wrote a first draft, and Roger returned and read it and asked me if I would like to direct it, and I said, "No, I wouldn't, this is not the kind of material I would ever want to do. We created what you said you wanted. We gave the screenwriter guidance following your instructions: you wanted a women's prison picture, and you wanted it to be violent, and sexy. But no, I would not want to work on something like this." I thought it was very demeaning to women, and I had very ambivalent feelings about even having had to work on it. But that was my job, and I wanted to make other films so I couldn't let Roger down. So, then Roger said he was going to give it to Jack. And he did, and Jack wrote the second draft and it was his project after that, and I was perfectly happy about that. And I never have exchanged another word with Jack again. And he continues to have such hostility toward me—a man nearly eighty years of age—still repeating these hateful, stupid lies about me. It's pathetic, it really is. Pathological is the word.

AK: OK. Did you and Mr. Swartz do the marketing campaign for that film?

SR: *The Big Doll House*? Yes. We worked . . . well, not the whole marketing campaign. But what we did is we supervised taking the pictures that were used in the film's advertising for the theater one-sheets and newspapers. It showed them in their brief prison dresses, and we worked with the photographer positioning them in their different poses. Roger asked us to do that because he really liked the picture that we had taken for *The Student Nurses* ads, so we went back to the same photographer and he took the *Doll House* pictures, too.

AK: I want to move on, and actually we had started off talking about this when I arrived, about filmmaking today. You've been quoted as identifying some of your early film influences as Bergman, European art films, French New Wave, surrealist films, and I am wondering if there are filmmakers that impress you now?

SR: Interesting question. Yes, I like Michael Haneke very much, I do. Well, I always go to see Woody Allen's films. I don't always like them, but I do go to see them. I think that's the way I really should think of how to describe filmmakers who impress me now. No, really there's nobody who has done a body of work in recent years that impresses me. There are individual films that people have made that impress me.

AK: What are some of those?

SR: Um, OK. Recent films . . . I really like *Up in the Air* [Jason Reitman, 2009]. I think it is a marvelous film. Underrated. I very much like the film, it's a little older, *Fearless* [Peter Weir, 1993]. I probably would like anything Sydney Pollack would make if he was alive now. But we are talking about more recent things. I always go to see Terrence Malick films. I really do like his films. So, I guess I should say that he is someone who has a body of work that I really like. There really is nobody else. There are, as I say, individual films that I like, again I very much like *Gravity* [Alfonso Cuarón, 2013]. I think it's marvelous film. I very much liked *The Social Network* [David Fincher, 2010]—I think it is a superior film that is going to last. There isn't much else that I've seen in recent years that I really like.

AK: Do you think there is a director that you can think of, contemporary or not, someone that you could look back and say, "I wish I had their career"?

SR: Well, let me tell you a funny story. I worked for Roger, and I made several films for him, a number of films for him. And I was hoping that if anything came along that would give me more resources, because he was always very laudatory about what I made, he's always said good things about me to me and to other people in my presence. I always hoped that if he was going to finance a film that was going to give someone a chance to have more time, better actors, all those things that I hadn't had making those films for him, that he would choose me to do it. But one day I discovered that he was going to make such a film, and he had hired a young guy from New York, who had made I think only one or two features before then, named Martin Scorsese. And he got to make it instead. It's called *Boxcar Bertha* [1972]. And I was truly hurt. I've never envied Martin Scorsese because we are very different kinds of filmmakers. And if I had had this opportunity, it probably wouldn't have opened up the doors that opened up for him because of who I am. And I don't even admire all his films. But would I have liked to have his opportunities? Yes!

AK: Is that something you ever talked to Corman about?

SR: No. What's the point?

AK: I know you have been out of the industry for a while...

SR: A long time. Years. Decades!

AK: Your husband was working in the industry in a different way than he had been when you two had your active partnership working. But I think because of your position I feel like you may have a sense of what the industry is like today.

SR: Well, I do. First of all, I am still a member of the Writers Guild, although not active, and I still know a few people who work in the industry.

AK: What is your sense of the industry for women professionals today?

SR: Well, it's better that it was in my day. Women do work in television. And occasionally they get to direct a feature film. But I don't think it's very good. I mean, people point to Kathryn Bigelow, but beyond that what can they point to except Kathryn Bigelow? Oh, by the way, I did like *The Hurt Locker* [2008], very much. I think she's very good.

AK: Do you see the representation of women, how women are portrayed in film today, as being different then it was when you were making films?

SR: Yeah, it's different, but it's still often distorted, in my opinion. Very distorted. Women can be more than housewives now, or they can be Wonder Women or Super Girl or whatever, which I don't think is any advancement because usually the way these female fantasy characters are portrayed is straight out of exploitation films. There are individual films, especially the very young women characters, like *Juno* [Jason Reitman, 2007], or perhaps the one with the little girl in it, I can't think of it now. Anyway, films like that, where they are given more latitude to be original and self-reliant and interesting. But on the whole I don't think women are that well portrayed. But I don't think that most of the films made today are that interesting. There are some exceptions like the role that Charlize Theron [*Monster*, Patty Jenkins, 2003] played when she was a serial killer, and Annette Benning often gets interesting roles... it depends, a few actresses do. But when you are speaking in more general terms, I don't think women are much better off. The way they are portrayed in Kathryn Bigelow films is different. But in most of the films made by men, not so much so.

AK: Are you familiar with something called the Bedchel test?

SR: No, I am not.

AK: It is a measurement and to pass it, it requires that in a piece of media, so in this case film, the film has to feature at least two female characters who talk to each other about something other than a man.

AK: All of your films pass this test. The large majority of films do not. In fact, 2013 was the first time in film history that movies that passed this test made more money than movies that didn't. You were surpassing these measures forty years ago. It has taken the industry four decades to get to a fraction of where you were when you were making films. What do you think about that?

SR: In what respect? That there is such a test? I think it is great. That people are applying it? Good. But that it is going to make any difference in Hollywood? I doubt it. It has always been a boy's club and it continues to be a boy's club.

AK: Given your husband's position as a pioneer of digital filmmaking, was there a reason that you never picked up a camera and started making films again in digital format?

SR: Well, I am a writer and director. I've never been interested in operating a camera. And I was used to making feature films. And in digital format I probably would have had to have taken many steps backwards in terms of ambition. And I suppose once I was finished, I felt I was finished. I was too old. Not physically; I am still in very good shape physically. I just felt it was too late. My heart was broken. And I just couldn't seem to . . . sometimes I would think about it, why don't I do it, and then I'd think, "Oh, what's the use?"

AK: What would you tell a young woman looking to enter the film industry today? Would you encourage or dissuade her?

SR: I would neither encourage nor dissuade. I would just say be prepared to be disappointed but maybe you'll be lucky, and you'll do something so compelling and so unique that you, unlike all the other women trying to, will get under the wire or climb over the fence. Whatever it is. I would never discourage someone, you can't, and it's a terrible thing to discourage people. It's cruel, it really is. I got a lot of it and I know how cruel it is. I would not want to practice that kind of cruelty.

AK: I think one of the obstacles that your career had was that at the time that your films were being exhibited there was a really narrow range of places where people could go and see them. Do you think that now there are so many different platforms for viewing films that there are more opportunities for work made by different filmmakers to be seen by different audiences?

SR: I think so, yes. Of course. The multiple platforms are a great blessing. I mean, I've seen stuff on cable television that obviously goes straight to cable—some of it very good! So, there is an outlet for it, and it can have a long life. I don't know how long a life, but, you know, a life longer than just a few screenings and then it is gone. Yes, I think that is a wonderful thing. And I do think you are right, that it might have made a difference, but you can't look back, you can't change the past.

AK: I have some miscellaneous questions. What, out of the films that you made, is your favorite?

SR: They are all my children. [Laughs.]

AK: Which means you won't have a least favorite either?

SR: Uh, well, if I have a least favorite it's because I had to do things that. . . . yeah, I would say my least favorite is because of what I had to go through to make it, rather than the film itself. And I just didn't have the resources to make it. I just didn't have enough time; I had nothing that I needed to make it. And that is *Terminal Island*. I would say that one is the least favorite of mine. It was the biggest stretch. Not a big stretch in a way that improved me artistically, but only because it was so difficult to make.

AK: Do you have—or did you have, maybe it is the same thing—a passion project? A film that you absolutely wanted to make?

SR: Yes, my husband and I did, and we did not get a chance to make it. We got an option on a novel by Phillip K. Dick called *The Man in the High Castle*. We did a major, major rewrite on it—the setting is the same and the characters are the same, but everything else is different. The world in which it takes place is the same, but I can't tell you how much is different. And we wrote a screenplay and it went around and many literary agents liked it very much and for a number of years after it first came out, we had agents call us and say: "We'd like to show the script to so-and-so." But none of the gatekeepers liked it. Nobody was interested in making it. And yes, that was a passion project that we really wanted to make.

AK: What spoke to you about the film?

SR: Well, it was a film about an America that was no longer America and was struggling to come back to being the America that we know. It was an interesting exercise in alternate world history. I loved the characters we created; I really did. They were marvelous people, and very touching. It was highly imaginative, visually, that is what I liked about it. It was an effort to do all the things that we couldn't do before. It was our desire to break out. And it was a famous and prestigious book. When we couldn't make it we tried to interest other people in making it. We even sent it to Stanley Kubrick, and he read it and he said, "I like it, but I have other projects that I am interested in doing myself." We sent it to Irvin Kershner and he sent back a letter saying—he knew me—"Well, you are a director, why don't you make it?" [Laughs.] We got really depressing answers. We even applied to government film commissions in Europe to give us some seed money. And we couldn't get that either.

AK: When was this?

SR: We wrote it in 1976. And in 1977 we tried to, 1978 . . . 79–80. For about three or four years, we tried very hard. We got it to Dino De Laurentiis and he wasn't interested. [Laughs.] We got it a lot of places! We even got it to some ignoramus who was reading for Jane Fonda—there would have been a good role in there for her—and she sent back the most illiterate comments. I mean, even the spelling was wrong! And she never showed it to Fonda. That is what happened to it.

AK: Around this time, and certainly after you left Dimension, you were writing and really trying to make your way into the mainstream film industry—television as well. Simultaneously there was a growth in independent filmmaking that was, in part, at least a bit more accepting of women filmmakers. Is that something you ever thought about moving into?

SR: No, because what people were making, mostly, were small, personal tales at that time. Often coming-of-age films. For which I have no interest or patience and never did. We hoped that we might be able to make *The Man in the High Castle* independently, but it required more money. It was not a small personal film; it was a film that required a very large canvas.

AK: What was it about the idea of working in Hollywood, as in the mainstream film industry, that was so important for you?

SR: It was the tools. The tools that were available.

AK: So really, the resources, the access?

SR: Yes.

AK: I have some questions about a film, one of your films, that I haven't heard you talk a lot about, *It's a Bikini World* [1967].

SR: [Laughs.]

AK: I really like that movie!

SR: Many people do.

AK: How do you feel about it?

SR: [Sighs.] When I give public talks, which I rarely do, my comment about it is, "If it was not the last beach picture it was one of the last, and I like to think I killed the genre off." I mean, what can you say about it? It's . . . I don't know what to say about it! In my opinion, it is better than the other beach pictures that were made; in my opinion, it's the best of them. I think with more imagination and a cuter story and certainly filmed in a much less stodgy fashion. It was made in '66, and I believe it was the first or among the first to use animated bubbles coming out of people's mouths. I was inspired to do this by the Pop Art movement. But the film wasn't released until late '67 early '68, so by then this looked tired. I have unpleasant memories making this film because the two lead actors, Deborah Walley and Tommy Kirk, were often purposelessly difficult and slowed things down. Its main importance to me is that it proved I could direct a feature film.

AK: I watched it yesterday for the first time in its original cut; I had a really hard time finding an original cut of it. I had gotten a couple versions that were cut in a few different ways. Very thankfully UCLA was able to provide me with . . .

SR: U-C-L-A?! Whoa!

AK: Yes, UCLA had a cut of *Blood Bath* that I could watch, and which made actual sense, because the ones I had gotten had been obviously edited from the original version. The same was true for *It's a Bikini World*. Actually, there are some fan edits of the *Blood Bath* on the internet. While I was watching *It's a Bikini World*, I was struck with the amount of kineticism in the film. The races that take place in the film are really enhanced by the way the energy and movement has clearly been carefully planned and captured.

SR: Most of these beach movies were made by elderly men who directed them in an antiquated style. They were cronies of Sam Arkoff [co-head of American International Pictures]. I just wanted to make it look like a contemporary film with some excitement. I've always done fast cutting. That is the way I like to make films.

AK: Music is part of the fabric of your films in general. In this film, the musical performances are very deliberate moments of attraction that force the film—and the audience—to stop and watch the performers, almost as a moment outside of the film itself. I was actually struck though by the variety and the types of different artists that you had in the film. Was that something that you had a hand in?

SR: No. It was whomever we could get. [Laughs.] We got an agent, a music agent, who told us who the hottest groups were at the time, whoever was top on the Billboard charts, the week we called. We got them.

AK: It is an amazing thing to me, the scene where Eric Burden and The Animals are performing, and the song they are singing ["We Gotta Get Out of This Place"], which is such a legendary, at this point mythic, "working man's hero" song—

SR: And these kids are dancing around in bikinis! [Laughs.]

AK: *Yes!* [Laughs.] And it is this incredible moment: two parts of what is seemingly constructed as "teenager culture," constructed monolithically in the popular imagination are smashing together in this really incredible and unharmonious way, showing you how different the cultures were at the time, how nuanced they were and how segregated they could be, and at least in this case with the kids dancing how blithely unaware one was of the other.

SR: That is who was in town! They were contracted, they came over and did the scene. I shot all those musical numbers in one day and at a nightclub called the Haunted House on Hollywood Boulevard. I have nothing further to say about it because I think it speaks for itself.

AK: This is my last question about it, and it is only a detail—the movie that they go to see on the unintentional group date was Corman's *Attack of the Crab Monsters* [1957].

SR: Yes!

AK: Was that your little wink to him?

SR: Yes, yes. We put that up on the marquee; it was made years earlier and we thought it was a funny title. And since it was Roger's film, we could use it without getting any permission from anyone else, which may have involved the exchange of money and other requirements. Roger was perfectly happy to have his film named up there.

AK: I'm sorry, I meant to ask you this question when we were talking about *Blood Bath*. There is a scene when Sordi—the man who believes he is a reincarnated vampire—had a dream sequence in the desert, where he is remembering, or rather he is transported into a hallucination. There is a canvas in front of him and some sort of scattered items from his workshop . . .

SR: Oh! Yes, on a dry lakebed. I remember that.

AK: Did you film that?

SR: No that was Jack Hill. It was one of the few really nice images he filmed. Really nice.

AK: Yeah it is! It seemed reminiscent of the dream/hallucination scenes in *The Velvet Vampire* [1971].

SR: I'm sorry about that. They had nothing in common. [Laughs.] I did mine on sand dunes and he did his on a dry lakebed. And my inspiration was Salvador Dalí, not Jack Hill. Credit where credit is due.

AK: I recently watched a documentary made in the 1990s by filmmaker and scholar Alexandra Juhasz, about feminist artists. One of the interesting questions that she asked the older artists was did they think that they were "owed something"—by younger artists, by history, by critics, etc. What do you think about that idea?

SR: Well, I don't think they owe me anything. But I think that I might be worth viewing as a historical artifact to see where women were in the era in which I made films. But they don't owe me that. I think it might be educational for them. It might be encouraging for them. On the other hand [laughs], it might be discouraging for them! Depends on how they read my history. But, no, I am owed nothing. But, if I could serve as some kind of lesson, that would please me very much.

AK: My final question for you is this: if a person, unfamiliar with your work, came up to you and asked you to show them the film you made which you believe defines you as a director, which of your films would you have them watch?

SR: *The Student Nurses*. Although I am much fonder of *The Working Girls* [1974], which you didn't even mention, because it is a much smoother more controlled film. I was much more at ease with the camera, and with actors, and with what I wanted to get. I am very fond of that film; I really am, very. Maybe that is my favorite film, and it is the least known and least admired. But I'd have someone watch *The Student Nurses* first because I deliberately wanted to work in a variety of styles, and I deliberately wanted to introduce a number of provocative ideas, and I wanted to do it in that film because when I made it I thought, "This might be the only film I ever get to make, so I've got to cram as much into it as I can."

AK: That film, and honestly *Working Girls*, are the films that people bring up when I mention your name, or they are the ones that people respond to as recognizable when I list your body of work.

SR: My *Working Girls*, or the one that woman made ten years later using the same title?

AK: The Lizzie Borden film? [*Working Girls*, Lizzie Borden, 1986.]

SR: Yeah.

AK: No, no, your film. Which I think is interesting and I am not sure if it is . . .

SR: It is most essentially me; that is the interesting thing about it.

AK: It is a carefree film, and it certainly has the sense of humor that all of your films have, but it also has sense of lightness to it.

SR: Yes, yes. Because I was far more skilled by that time than I was earlier. Also, because I wrote it myself. This was my only screenplay that was made into a film that I wrote entirely by myself. It's completely me and I think more of the kind of person I am . . . this sounds so egotistical and I don't mean it that way . . . just as with actors what you see on the screen is what they are really like. [Laughs.] That is the truth! They say they are playing a role, but there is much more of them that comes through. Because I wrote it by myself and because I was now a more skilled filmmaker after making so many films, I think that is what gives it its light and somewhat effervescent feeling.

AK: I think that film is also one of the most aggressive films that you made in terms of dealing with issues of class, and in particular the underemployment of women and the dark side of the feminist movement in terms of "women's liberation" from the home. It asks the question: what happens when the rhetoric of "you can be anything you want to be" encounters the reality of "no one is going to hire you." There are class politics that run through all of your films, but it is quite explicit in *The Working Girls*. It has this wonderful ending where Honey, says, "Sure, I have all this money but so what? I am going to do something that matters." She opts out in a way that is in line with maintaining a self-identity and as self-preservation.

SR: Honestly. it is my favorite film, it is. Even though most people like *The Student Nurses* or *Group Marriage* [1973] much more. You've never even mentioned *Group Marriage*.

AK: In the past, you've talked so much about *The Student Nurses*, *Group Marriage*, and *The Working Girls* that I don't want to retread on stated territory. It is the lesser known and earlier films that people don't often talk about that I wanted to touch on.

SR: Well, I don't look at *Blood Bath* as my film—I look at it as something I finished. Someone in Yugoslavia began it, then Hill took over, and then I finished it. And as you say, it probably has been screwed around with many, many times since then. I am glad there is a print in existence somewhere, for as long as it will last. Since I've endowed the Chair in Entertainment Technology at USC, I took all my films out of UCLA and gave them to the USC archive, which is much smaller, but it is run by a man who worked in the UCLA archive. I have arranged for all of them to be recorded digitally. And also, as the technology changes every ten years it will be reviewed into eternity, to update the formats, so they can be watched by any scholars or students who want to watch them.

AK: That's fantastic!

SR: See, there was a reason that I went out and started investing in commercial real estate! [Laughs.] I am probably going to give the film school another endowed chair also, but not immediately—one at a time! Maybe it will happen after I've died, or maybe it will happen sooner, that depends on circumstances.

AK: What an amazing thing, to have those films preserved.

SR: Well, that was the deal. The original negatives have mostly disappeared. There is a fellow in New York that used to work at BAM [Brooklyn Academy of Music]—you may know him, Jake Perlin. He really likes my films, and he is trying to find the negatives of two of them—*Student Nurses* and *Velvet Vampire*—and he wants to make prints of them. He's applied for some grants and already gotten one. The Academy of Motion Pictures Arts and Sciences has said that they will do a free inspection for restoration on any negatives that can be found. And he wants to release them for exhibition at revival houses and on college campuses. That is his plan; he is still in the initial stages of it. It is a big undertaking. He is now part of a production and distribution company, and he has only done it so far for some Truffaut films, and I think one by Samuel Fuller. When he came to me I said: "Why me?!"

AK: The more people that can see them, the better!

SR: I hope so. It is very nice to think so. It would be nice. It is like a dream to me. But all the good things that have happened have been like a dream to me.

October 6, 2014: Interview with Stephanie Rothman

Alicia Kozma (AK): Since we last spoke in February, I've been doing some additional research on your student films and your time at Dimension Pictures. The company seemed to disappear in the mid-1980s.

Stephanie Rothman (SR): Was it that late?

AK: I think so.

SR: Oh, OK. I thought it was a little earlier than that.

AK: Yeah, I think by the time they were fully dissolved it was the mid-1980s. The last time I was here I was able to go to USC [University of Southern California] and see some of your student films *Duet* [1963] and *We Look and See* [1963].

SR: Yes, yes, right, that [*We Look and See*] was the little three-minute one. Done to the music of Lily Marlane.

AK: I enjoyed them both. I also had an opportunity to look at the production books that went along with them. I wanted to ask you a little bit about your time at USC, in film school, and then just some general follow-up questions. I have a lot of questions about details and specifics that you may or may not remember; if you remember, wonderful! I wanted to just start with your time at Dimension and retrace the process of how you and Mr. Swartz became involved. I know that you had both worked with Larry Woolner at New World. Can you give me the context around the chronology and context leading up to that?

SR: After seeing how successful New World Pictures was and how much money the films were making, within a year—he was there a little bit over a year—he decided he would like to start a company of his own. This was not the first time he had one. Earlier, he had been in partnership with his brother in a company called Woolner Brothers Pictures. So, he was not unfamiliar with how to start a new company. When he found someone to invest the capital needed to get started, he invited Charles and me to join him as minority partners. The financier was the head of a men's clothing and accessories manufacturing company called Wembley Industries. Its best-known line was Countess Mara ties. I'm sure you've never heard of them.

With an initial stake of half a million dollars, Larry, his wife, and Charles and I started Dimension Pictures. Larry and Wembley Industries had a much, much larger stake in it than we did—together we two had only 10 percent, while Larry had 40 percent, and Wembley had 50 percent. And we were paid far less than Larry. [Laughs.] But there was no other employment we could find in film or television, so we did this. That's how Dimension Pictures started.

AK: Do you know if he approached anyone else that he, or you, had been working with at New World? Or were you the team that he wanted?

SR: We were the team, yes.

AK: You had a 10 percent financial stake in the company?

SR: We had 10 percent ownership. We didn't put any money into it. We didn't have any. Our stake was our labor.

AK: I found your position listed with a couple different titles: creative development chief, head of project development, vice president for creative development. Do you remember if you had an actual title and what it was?

SR: Basically, I had the title of vice president, and I was involved in the development of ideas for films. I also watched films for possible acquisition or that were acquired, gave my advice on how to recut them, what additional shooting might be necessary, or whether they were even worth acquiring.

AK: Those, outside of filmmaking, were your primary responsibilities?

SR: Yes. But my real, my most primary responsibility, was writing and directing and doing the preproduction on films that I made.

AK: Did you have any input in bringing new talent into the company? Screenwriters, directors, etc. I know a lot of the films Dimension had were already made, you brought them in, did whatever you needed to do with them, and then released them. But in terms of putting out new productions, did you have any input in hiring decisions?

SR: No, I didn't. What would happen is people would come to Larry Woolner and sometimes they would bring fully developed projects, and sometimes they would say, "We'd like to make a film with you." But, in order to do either one, they had to bring money with them. They did not get all their financing from Dimension. While we worked there, as I recall, the only films that were fully financed by the company were the ones made by Charles and me. If other people wanted to make films, they had to bring money and an idea that Larry thought was commercial. He would discuss their proposals with Charles and me and his wife, Betty, who ran the, uh, how shall I put it, the print ordering, shipping, play-date recording, and earnings collection end of it. She had previously worked for Larry at Woolner Brothers. But ultimately the decision was up to Larry.

AK: Were there other employees?

SR: Yes, for bookkeeping and clerical work. There was no full-time editor, there was no full-time anything of a creative nature. Such people were hired for individual jobs.

AK: What was your relationship with Larry Woolner like?

SR: Well, actually, it was pretty good. He liked my films. He was almost my first fan [laughs], and we would discuss, as I think I told you in our earlier interview, what the subject of a film that he wanted me to write and direct would be. But then he would let me take it from there and also let Charles take it from there if he was my writing partner, and as the producer, which he usually was. Officially, Larry was the executive producer, but he didn't interfere after the subject of the film was agreed on. He trusted us.

AK: During our last conversation, in specific reference to *Terminal Island*, you shared that some of the sub-distributors would request certain types of plotlines, actors, whatever, in a film.

SR: Well, basically they would request certain genres of films. So, they would want a Black prison film, or, they'd want women in jeopardy film, or something like that.

AK: Did you find that to be most often the case?

SR: Not always, in my own case, I in conjunction with Charles, proposed . . . let's see, I only made three films while I was at Dimension. And *Group Marriage* was a proposal from Charles and me. *Terminal Island* came in response to a request from the sub-distributors, and *The Working Girls* was Larry's suggestion. He said, "You need to make a very low-budget film, I am getting the money from Canada, and they would like something like *The Student Nurses*. Could you do another one like that?" So, I did another one like that.

AK: Was there anything that was pitched to you through a sub-distributor that you refused to do?

SR: No, there really wasn't, because they really didn't have completely obnoxious or offensive suggestions. They weren't trying to make pornography. They weren't trying to make repulsively violent horror films. They basically liked what I did and wanted me to do more of the same. The only really specific request was for a Black prison film. Or rather, a prison film with leading Black characters. Which is different than a Black prison film, because *Terminal Island* is not all about the Black characters; it was about a mixture of characters and races.

AK: What prompted you to leave the company?

SR: The family that owned Wembley decided that the company wasn't making enough profit, and they didn't want to be invested in it anymore. Charles told Larry that this was a great opportunity to buy them out and to own and run the company together. Initially Larry doubted that it could be done. But Charles said, "Well, let's go and try." Before they did, Charles and Larry verbally agreed there would be a more equal split of the company ownership if the buyout of Wembley was accomplished. Wembley was located in New Orleans, so the two of them went there. According to Charles, he did most of the negotiating and the breakup was accomplished. Then, since Charles and I had just finished making *The Working Girls*, we left on a badly needed vacation. When we returned, there was a different attitude toward us at Dimension, on the part of both Larry and his wife, who we suspected heavily influenced him. The papers severing the connection between Dimension and Wembley arrived. The agreement was signed between Wembley and Larry Woolner only, just as the original agreement to found the company had been. This meant that Larry was now the owner of 90 percent of Dimension. At that point we were told by him that we would continue to own only 10 percent of the new company, not a greater amount as Larry had agreed to verbally with Charles. So, in essence, Charles thought of the idea of the buyout, prodded Larry to ask for it, mostly negotiated it, and then Larry wanted 90 percent of it for himself and his wife. In addition, Charles and I also had a contract to make films with Dimension Pictures that after three years was up for renewal and Larry suddenly did not want to renew it. So, we left.

AK: Do you know what prompted the decision to cut you and Mr. Swartz out of the company?

SR: Well, I've always thought, and my husband always thought, and our attorneys always thought it was greed.

AK: After you left, you kept your 10 percent ownership stake?

SR: Yes. And although they didn't want to renew our contracts, they still wanted us to make another film. But we no longer trusted them and wanted to conduct no further business with them. I had already written a script called *The Car Hops*, while still under contract to Dimension, which they wanted to make. But since Charles and I were now unemployed, we asked to take it with us. Ultimately, they agreed to give it to us as severance pay and I was quickly able to sell it, but for not very much. It was above Writers Guild minimum, but not enough to live on—even for half a year.

AK: When they filed for bankruptcy, as minority owners, were you involved in that process at all?

SR: No.

AK: Did you recover any funds after bankruptcy?

SR: No. Not after bankruptcy. However, we did sue them. And they did make a monetary settlement and in return we gave up our 10 percent ownership. It too wasn't for very much, but the lawsuit cost them a substantial amount and took several years, and in those years, they were spending like crazy and they were making many terrible . . . they were making, at least in our opinion, many very poor commercial decisions. They were, first of all, choosing a few ambitious films that they didn't know how to market, and secondly, they were choosing poorly made exploitation films that were not successful. So, even though they had a few successes along the way, they eventually ran the company into the ground.

AK: After 1975, Dimension seemed to expand rapidly, especially in relation to the number of regional distribution exchanges they were opening up across the country—at least as was reported in the trades. Larger and larger budgets were being given to films with smaller return, and it did appear as if the story being told in the trades was one of a company throwing good money after bad.

SR: Well, the budgets they claimed they were solely financing were probably purely PR. I don't think they had the resources to do that sort of thing. I think all of that, or most of that, was exaggeration. I believe they spent most of their money on prints and advertising and bigger salaries and other perks for themselves.

AK: Let's move on to some detail questions about Dimension films you were associated with in the trades. I want to see what can be verified as factual and what was simply PR. Do you remember the film *Sweet Sugar* [1972]? You were listed as writing it.

SR: Yes, but I didn't write it alone. Charles and I wrote the story, and then we decided to put it under the name of R. C. Samuels. Then we hired Don Spencer, the same fellow who wrote *The Student Nurses*, to write *Sweet Sugar*.

AK: Great. And *Beyond Atlantis*?

SR: *Beyond Atlantis* [1973], as I recall, oh God, I think I wrote that myself.

AK: The screenplay?

SR: No, the story. Somebody else wrote the screenplay. Oh! I know who wrote the screenplay, Charles Johnson. I wrote the story and again I did it under a pseudonym.

AK: Why did you do that?

SR: I did it because I didn't like these ideas at all!

AK: Were they ideas that were given to you?

SR: Yes. Well, no. The ideas weren't given to me. The idea that was given to me was "make another woman in jeopardy story." And so, Charles and I thought, "Why not on a sugar cane plantation in Central America," and everybody liked that idea. The women were going to be cane cutters. What had inspired us was *Bitter Rice*. What a come down from *Bitter Rice* [Giuseppe De Santis, 1949]! [Laughs.] But I think also Larry liked *Bitter Rice*, so we all agreed that it was a good model. We didn't try to remake *Bitter Rice*! We wanted to make something broader, and we hoped funnier, and you know ... *Bitter Rice* was a commercially successful film. But it was serious and had fine actors in it. We wanted audiences to laugh. It was not supposed to be a serious film. It was supposed to be robust, sexy, and comic.

AK: Were you ever engaged to direct it?

SR: I never wanted to. I made that very clear.

AK: OK ... a feature titled *Dr. Black and Mr. White* [1976]. You were listed as directing and writing the original screenplay.

SR: That was just PR, meant to show that Dimension had lots of things on its slate. I think probably that a lot of things you found on Dimension's slate after we left may have also been just invented to keep their names in the trades. Now I can't be certain about that, because I was no longer privy to what they were doing. But if they followed the pattern they had while we were there, they were releasing titles when no screenplay existed and for which there was no immediate intention of making a film. I think probably a lot more were reported than were ever released.

AK: Is there anything else ...

SR: There are a couple of things that I actually did write treatments for that they mentioned, but it never went farther than that. One was called *Mama Sweet Life*. And I can't think of ... there may have been one other, but I can't think of it right now.

AK: I've seen that listed as upcoming, but I can't say that I've seen it as released.

SR: No, it wasn't made. It was an idea that I had, and I wrote the treatment. And I believe that my husband even took it with Larry's blessing to someone at American International Pictures, who liked the idea, but when they started negotiating what kind of a deal could be made on the basis of this treatment, they couldn't get together. It never came to fruition.

AK: Were you happy that you made the decision to go to Dimension?

SR: Happiness was not a consideration for me. Working was a consideration, getting the opportunity to work. The first year Charles and I worked for Roger Corman at New World Pictures, which was the first year of New World Pictures, we received a tiny weekly salary and a $2,000 bonus at each film's completion, and we made *The Student Nurses* and *The Velvet Vampire* for him. *The Student Nurses* made him a lot of money. But the second year he proposed that we continue working for him without salaries. Instead, he offered both of us together $2,000 a picture. [Laughs.] Now that New World Pictures had had a successful first year—thanks in a significant part to Charles's and my work—he had lots of young people crowding in who wanted to make films for him. Obviously, we couldn't live on Roger's offer, so when Larry Woolner offered us a living wage, we accepted it. It was not a lot of money. But it enabled us to live in an apartment, and buy food, and have a car. I know this sounds so . . .

You don't know what it was like in those days making low-budget exploitation films. People who didn't own at least a part of their films didn't make any money. I would say we got, altogether . . . I think we were each paid $15,000 a year. So, we had a joint income of $30,000 per year for those three years.

AK: Was that amount standard for other people you knew who were working in the industry at that time?

SR: That depended on whom you were working for. Yes, if you were working in Poverty Row as we were, without the leverage of bringing in some of the financing and making exploitation films for the few companies that financed them. But if you were working for unionized television companies, or were in the Directors Guild, or worked for a major studio, no, of course it wasn't. It was terrible.

AK: You were part of the Writers Guild but not the Directors Guild, correct?

SR: That's right.

AK: Why was that?

SR: Because I never made enough money to be able to afford to join the Directors Guild. It cost, at that time, $2,000 to join, and $2,000 was a lot of money. I would have had to borrow it, and I wasn't earning enough income to be able to repay it in the foreseeable future. Furthermore, I was making nonunion pictures, and the low budgets made DGA personnel at DGA salaries unaffordable. Although I did work with one member! A friend of ours was an assistant director/production manager and we did pay him DGA wages. But when you signed a DGA contract that allowed you to hire guild members, you were required to hire a minimum of three workers, and we couldn't afford to hire a first assistant director, a second assistant director, and a production manager; it was just too much money.

AK: Are you still a member of the Writers Guild?

SR: Oh yeah.

AK: Do you remember being given an award at the International Film Festival in Ottawa? It was called, improbably, the Stanley Cup.

SR: Was it the first Women's International Film Festival?

AK: It was in 1973, and I found it listed about three or four times just simply as the International Festival of Film in Ottawa.

SR: Not in Ottawa; it was in Toronto.

AK: Did you go to the film festival?

SR: Yeah, I went. It was a women's film festival. *Terminal Island* was screened. It had its premiere there.

AK: Do you remember anything about it?

SR: I remember that is where I met Shirley Clarke. We had a . . . how shall I put it . . . a pleasant conversation in which she was interested in what I was doing, and I told her how much I admired her work, and that was it. It was a mutual admiration conversation—that was all.

AK: The last time we spoke you said you would go and watch your films with regular audiences.

SR: Yes.

AK: There was a notice for what sounded like a big premiere of *Terminal Island* in Chicago. Did your films have typical premieres?

SR: No. I don't know about a premiere, but I was sent there to promote the film. There was a PR man who took me around to meet various press people, but I wasn't present at any premiere.

AK: What was the press tour in Chicago like?

SR: Well, it was . . . it was the second press tour I went on in Chicago. They were always very cordial, respectful. I have no complaints about the way the press in Chicago treated me.

AK: And the *Terminal Island* press tour was the second one that you went on in Chicago?

SR: The first one I went on, let's see . . . did I even meet the press the first time I went? Yes! I did. It wasn't . . . it was combined with my being invited by the documentary film group, a student group at the University of Chicago, to the university's festival of the arts.

AK: Really?

SR: Yes, I was their guest artist. And that was in 1970 . . . the fall of 1970 after *The Student Nurses* came out. Maybe it was early '71, I'm not sure. While I was there, I also did some interviews. I went on a talk show, two talk shows. One at a Black radio station, and I went on a TV talk show that also had on it . . . what was her name . . . a young actress who had just finished or was still appearing in *Fiddler on the Roof* in New York, a young singer/actress named Bette Midler. [Laughs.] She was very sweet.

And they were very nice at the radio station, very welcoming and very pleased that I had come. And it was a call-in show, so I got to talk to listeners. I was really impressed with how intelligent the questions were. It was a Chicago lifestyle show and so there wasn't anybody there with an axe to grind. But they didn't ask silly questions . . . after I explained what the film was about and what its issues were, they asked very intelligent questions.

AK: That's great. Let's move on and talk a little bit about your time at USC. I guess I should say that I have to exempt Mr. Swartz from these discussions, so I want to ask you a little about your classmates, but we won't include him in that group. When you think back on your time at USC what do you remember most about it?

SR: Aside from Charles [laughs] and how helpful he was.

AK: [Laughs.] Yes, aside from him.

SR: I remember that the faculty was very helpful, by encouraging students, from the chairman of the department on down. I had no conflicts at all with them. And they were happy to see me. Aside from me, there were only two other women there. Two graduate students, of which I was one, and one undergraduate. We were very rare indeed and we were treated very well and taken very seriously. I think that they tried, because we were so unique, to make us feel more welcome.

AK: Did you find the same kind of welcoming attitude amongst the students?

SR: With a couple of exceptions, yes. There were a couple of exceptions, and that is why, I think, my student film that you saw—*Duet*—has the picture negative scratched and the sound so badly out of sync. I think you saw that.

AK: Yes.

SR: That was because at the completion of the student film that I wrote and directed, the people who did the film editing and sound recording, and who were responsible for cutting the negatives and synchronizing the picture and sound, did a lousy job of negative cutting and synchronizing. And since neither of them were stupid people, I always thought that they didn't care. They just wanted to get in and get out of the negative cutting room as quickly as they could and didn't care if they were sloppy. But I have no proof. That is just my speculation. And, I did not get along well with one of them.

AK: Was that before you started working on the project with them?

SR: No. In my opinion, they had this work attitude of "let's get it over with the least effort we can," and they either didn't care or didn't understand that this would show up in their work.

AK: Did you work with the same group of students on *Duet* and *We Look and See*?

SR: I don't know, I don't remember.

AK: Do you remember what the production of *We Look and See* was like?

SR: It was a lot of fun and it went very quickly.

AK: What I understood from the production books, after the films were made everyone did a write-up about their experience working on the projects.

SR: Uh-huh . . . the two that had, in my opinion, a sometimes-unenthusiastic attitude were Erik Timmerman and Anthony Fowles.

AK: Yes, Anthony Fowles who also went by "Chick."

SR: He was British.

AK: From what I can ascertain from the production books, yes. In fact, there was one really—well, that was on *Duet*; we will get to *Duet* in a moment. It seemed like there were a lot of discussions and disagreements about the roles that everyone had in terms of production on *We Look and See*. Do you remember if the faculty member teaching the class the production ran under dictated those roles? How did you end up being the director, and how did Erik and Anthony end up being the editor or running the sound?

SR: We were assigned what we did by the courses we were taking. I was taking the directing class and I was a year ahead of Fowles and Timmerman. I think in the case of Fowles, he was taking basic editing and Timmerman was taking basic sound. On camera there was John Koester. And . . . I made a directing mistake, but we can talk about that later. It had nothing to do with interpersonal relations; I made a bad decision. My ambition got too great for what we were capable of doing at the time.

AK: What was the issue?

SR: Well, there was a descent down a stairway with the camera moving in. The camera bobbled, and we only had enough film for two takes. And when it did that the first time . . . I just wanted to do a moving shot that also panned while it was moving. It was not the most complicated shot in the world, believe me! And John [Koester] the cameraman ended up being a camera operator in Hollywood, he . . . I think one of the last films he made was *Someone to Watch Over Me* [Ridley Scott, 1987]. So, you know he was very talented, very hard-working, very good. But he was just learning at that time; we were all learning. And it was a more complicated shot than he could do and that the people who were pushing the dolly could do . . . so it was not his fault by any means. It was my fault for wanting a more complicated shot than we could at the time achieve. I should have broken it up into two angles. But I didn't! And I've always said to myself, "Well, that just shows you were bursting with ambition, and you overreached."

AK: And it seems that was part of the process of these films: figuring out how you do this stuff.

SR: Right. But there was no fight over roles in front of me. I can only speculate that maybe they didn't care for some of the preliminary coursework they had to take. They were impatient to achieve their own ambitions and my project was just something to get through on the way to their own. And this attitude finally defeated them when they had to cut and synchronize the sound and picture negatives.

AK: You don't think it was specifically related to you?

SR: Well, that I can't answer. I don't think it was specifically related to me because I think it was their attitude toward doing a project that they didn't control, their unenthusiastic attitude toward working on someone else's film rather than their own. We never had an outright fight that I can remember.

AK: I want to move on to *Duet*. This was your final student film?

SR: Yes.

AK: Where did the idea for it come from?

SR: Well, I've always enjoyed writing, and I wanted to make something both simple and a bit unusual for two good actors. And I wanted to make it in the limited amount of time available. And so I came up with the idea of two lonely men who never meet in person—they only glimpse each other at the very end and do not recognize each other—but they talk to each other using a tape recorder and, for a short period, look forward to sharing their thoughts.

AK: What were you hoping that the film conveyed to those who saw it about you as a director?

SR: Well, that I could write an unusual and interesting story, that I could do depth-of-focus shots, that I could compose things in an interesting way, that I could direct actors, and that I could create visually, by the very limited prop and set choices I had, a mood.

AK: Do you feel the final version of the film displayed what you could do, what you had learned, what you were capable of doing?

SR: That's a hard question for me. Because I was never satisfied, during my entire career, with my work. I always found flaws, and I always felt that my ambition had not . . . the ambition I had, I had not been able to fulfill. Now, I didn't necessarily blame factors outside of myself, although there were factors outside of me that always contributed, as in the case of *Duet*. But I think my answer would be the same . . . I had the same reaction to the first film I made as I had through the years to my other films. I always wanted to do better, and no, I didn't think that *Duet* fully displayed what I hoped it would, leaving aside the damage that was done to it. And of course, I was very, very sad about what they did to the negatives. Because of that I could never show it for work or amusement. Since that faculty screening, I have never looked at it again.

AK: Did you have an opportunity to read the write-ups that they did after the project was over? They are called "What I've Learned During My 10 Week Project." There was one that was particularly mean-spirited, and I had wondered, first if you had been able to see them and second what you thought of them.

SR: Which one was it, Fowles?

AK: Yes.

SR: I knew it. He was an emotional child.

AK: It was a very short write-up that started with three bullet points. It said, "What I Learned During My 10 Week Project. A) Never trust the lab, B) Ditto a female director, C) Sync sound is the curse of the working class." And then he wrote about three sentences about how the lab was there to serve students and they should know that. And that was the extent of his write-up. That statement, plus some of the production notes from *We Look and See*, where he seemed to be critiquing how you were suggesting the film be edited versus how he thought the film should be edited, struck me as acrimonious and unlike the other relationships seemed to be, between you and your crew. I wasn't sure if that was related specifically to your interpersonal relationship with him, or if it was emblematic of something broader that you experienced being one of the only women film students at USC at the time.

SR: No. It was him. And here is what my interpretation is. He thought, or wanted to think when he was editing, that he would have complete control over how the film was cut. He wanted the director's job to be over. When I saw his initial rough cut, it was quite crude, and I could see he needed more help than some of the other students. I had to teach him some basic techniques, and he had to learn to accept the fact that I was the director and I had designed how the shots were to be assembled. That doesn't mean, however, that I wasn't open to suggestions. I was. I've always been open to suggestions. And maybe he made some good ones. I don't recall. But I've never had an authoritarian way of working. And now I learn from you that he was angry at the lab! But he and his partner were the ones who scratched the film and misaligned the sound and picture! It was not the lab's fault. Isn't that interesting!

AK: Have you always worked closely with your editors?

SR: Always. What I did is ask them to make an initial rough cut, and then I would get in there, and so would Charles when we were making films together. And I/we would see if things worked. If they didn't, then I/we would try other things until they did. But I always had a certain pace and rhythm that I wanted. And that was something that had to be refined over time; you couldn't do it in a rough cut. That wasn't the editor's fault. You had to lay out the scenes and then see where you wanted them to go. And when there were other takes of scenes that the editor had not chosen, that I remembered had good material in them, we would examine them to see if something had been missed. So, I worked very closely with editors. I was a competent editor myself and so was Charles. I guess I shouldn't praise my own work, but I was reminded of this by Woody Omens, a fellow graduate student who I ran into a couple months ago when we were both at USC to honor Bernard Kantor, the long-dead chair of the cinema department, and his wife. Woody is retired now, but he had a long well-respected career as a Hollywood cameraman. While we were reminiscing, he told me that my cutting had saved his graduate film. I had completely forgotten I even cut it.

AK: When you are directing, you have an eye towards editing.

SR: Exactly.

AK: One of the things I thought was interesting, and we've touched on this a bit before, but both *We Look and See* and *Duet*, at least in my mind, have significant class critiques in them. And I think that almost all of your films do, and I think that is something that hasn't been pulled out of them.

SR: Thank you!

AK: [Laughs.] Well, I think it is an important aspect of them. In our previous conversation you had said that you were very happy that your films have been received as feminist films, but through an intense focus on that reception some of the other issues that you were addressing tend to get elided. I happened to think the class critiques in your films are one of the things that get overlooked.

SR: Well, yes, certainly in *Duet*, one of the most important things about *Duet* is the class difference between the two men. One is an office worker and the other is a janitor. They never meet because one works during the day and the other at night. The only way they make contact is by speaking to each other on a tape. And they discover they have something to say to each other. I don't think in *The Velvet Vampire* there are class differences, except perhaps between the vampire's wealth and that of her victims, but in *The Student Nurses*, *Terminal Island*, *The Working Girls*, and *Group Marriage*, in all of those films class differences do exist. And the point I was trying to make was very simple: if we met each other, we might have a lot to say to each other. It wouldn't necessarily be conflicting; it might be civil or loving. I've always believed that we all have a lot to learn from each another. I've always had an egalitarian view. I think that everyone is smart in their own way and has something to teach everyone else. They may not have had the opportunity to acquire certain skills or knowledge, they may even have some intellectual and mental deficiencies, but in general, other people are smarter than we think.

AK: Did you find that people would notice these things, that they stood out in the film, or that they would comment on them?

SR: No. They sometimes described the films as good-natured. But did they notice they were about people from different social classes relating to one another, or that they were not so different from one another? No, that never came up. What always came up was feminism. You know, "Women are more in the foreground here, they are more independent, more aggressive, freer." Feminism has always been the message taken from my films. Which is indeed a prominent message. [Laughs.] But not the only one.

AK: How would you describe yourself as a director? If you had to choose a couple adjectives or phrases that you think best described the way you operated as a director, what would they be?

SR: You mean the physical methods I used, or the theoretical methods I used?

AK: I think that those things are intertwined. I am interested in how you understood yourself to exist in the directorial space that you occupied. What would you describe as your calling card as a director?

SR: Well, it certainly wasn't a calling card, as you describe it, to anybody who financed my films, and certainly to none of the people who worked with me! Well, I actually, and this may be too abstract an answer, but I both loved the creation of images and the creation of . . . I loved making ideas concrete through storytelling. Abstract ideas. That's how I would think of myself as a director. In other words, I was operating on two levels: on the level of the image and the other on the level of the abstract idea, which through storytelling I wanted to demonstrate and make clear.

AK: I know you are always critical of your own work, but is there a part of one of your films, or one of your films as a whole, where you think you really achieved the synthesis of that?

SR: I would say there are two films actually: *The Student Nurses* and *The Working Girls*.

AK: They came together for you in that way?

SR: Yes.

AK: What would you consider to be your strengths as a director?

SR: Well, I was very visually orientated, and I always worked very closely with the directors of photography. I would tell them where I wanted the camera angle to be, and what the action was going to be, and I would tell them what composition I would like to see in the frame and what lens would best suit this. And I would also ask them, if they were good—and I had very good ones, I was very fortunate—"Now, you tell me what you think it should look like. You set it up. I've told you all these things, I've given you lots of elements to work with, now show me what you think needs to be added." And mostly what they showed me was wonderful, and in some way enhanced what I had thought. And if it didn't then we would readjust it. But I almost always took what they had to say, because they knew a lot, and they had a lot to contribute, and anyone would be a fool who didn't take advantage of their skill and knowledge.

AK: You really emphasized collaboration.

SR: Yes, I would say, in most cases. Now with actors it was a little different. With actors . . . because of our budgets we had to get a lot of very green actors, and I didn't have the time or money for rehearsals, only for one read-through of the script . . . and so I had to do some, how shall I put it, teaching on the set while we were shooting the film. Not everybody—there were people who were well trained, experienced, and gifted! But there were those who were not so good, and I would have to help them with their line readings and explain their characters thoughts and motivations to them. It had to be done in a reassuring way that did not tear them down but built them up. Rehearsals before shooting would have made such a difference.

AK: Did you have a voice in casting at all?

SR: Yes. But I had great limitations. First of all, the budgets. And second of all, it was imperative that I have as many beautiful people as possible. Everyone always used to say, "Oh, you have such good-looking people in your movies." But that was a requirement! It was a requirement from Larry Woolner, from Roger Corman, and it was a requirement from the sub-distributors. Because there were no stars in them, they had to really look good. So, to my frustration, I sometimes could not hire people whom I would have loved to hire.

AK: What was your least favorite thing about directing?

SR: The first day of shooting before we made the first shot! [Laughs.] It's so scary [laughs], it really is.

AK: Did you do anything special to overcome that fear?

SR: No, I just did it the way I did every shot after that. Well, first I would meet the crew and introduce myself and shake hands, with every crew member. For the camera crew, I usually brought a present, which was a funny little toy animal they could tape to the camera as our joint mascot, and then I would give each of them a rose and we would get started!

AK: How do you think the crew would describe working with you as a director?

SR: Well, the greatest compliment I ever got was from the man who shot almost every film I made, Daniel Lacambre. The first time I offered him a job on one of my films he said, "Well, I think we maybe have one film together." I said, "Really?" and he said, "Yes. I don't think we will have a long-term relationship." And I didn't question him as to why. We went off, we made the film. When it was time to make the next one, I contacted him—he lived in France—and I said, "Daniel, would you like to do this?" And he said, "Yes, I would." And he came again. And by the time we were working on *The Working Girls* together he said, "You know Stephanie, you are no longer my colleague, or my friend, you are my habit." [Laughs.] He said: "You have become a habit of mine." It was one of the loveliest compliments I've ever gotten.

AK: And he never told you why he initially did not think you two would have an extensive working relationship?

SR: No, and I never asked. He was a person who was quick to form opinions. I didn't think that; I thought we would get along smashingly. And we did!

AK: If you had your druthers that you would want to have your career remembered?

SR: I suppose it would be that I was . . . I never was able to break out of making exploitation films. In other words, there was a lot in me that was unrealized because of obstacles that I did not overcome. That is very arrogant of me to say, I know.

AK: I am not sure about that. I think it's the way that most people who are passionate about the work they do operate. For someone to be very invested in the work they do to say that their work is "good enough," I can't imagine that person was very passionate in the first place.

SR: Good enough. Well, I certainly have always thought that mine was not a fully realized life in film.

AK: Do you think the term "artist" applies to you? Would you call yourself an artist?

SR: No, I wouldn't.

AK: Why not?

SR: I've always felt it was a very pretentious word. Other people can call you an artist if they want to, but you can't call yourself an artist. As far as I am concerned, I was a craftswoman. And I was struggling to perfect my craft and advance it. But the word artist is something that should be left to the judgment of others.

AK: Are there filmmakers that you would deem artists?

SR: Yes. Antonioni, Fellini, Jean Cocteau, Jean Renoir, and, of course, the writer-director whose work launched my interest in making films, Ingmar Bergman.

AK: Any contemporary filmmakers you would deem artists?

SR: Well, I don't . . . perhaps that's unfair, but there have been other people whose work I've liked in the past. Well, Truffaut was a true artist. Ernst Lubitsch was a true artist; D. W. Griffith was a true artist, and Jean Renoir. It is harder for me to speak of today because people are still working, and when they are still working, who knows. They have successes and then failures. Based on *The Social Network*, I would say David Fincher is an artist. Based on *Up in the Air*, I would say Jason Reitman is an artist. I would say based on all of her work together, although there is no individual film that I am crazy about, I would say Kathryn Bigelow is an artist. I would say definitely Michael Haneke is an artist. After that I pretty much run out of names.

AK: Do you think your physical, emotional, and psychological work as a dancer when you were younger fed into your career as a director at all?

SR: Yes, it did. It taught me to be very disciplined. If you are going to direct a film, you need to be very disciplined. You have to stay that way the entire time the film is being made, and when I say "made," I mean all the way through the answer print. Yes, it helped greatly with my discipline, but my visual orientation I think I inherit from my mother's family. My aunt Eva was a very fine artist, full of promise. She studied under Robert Henri, who was a prominent early twentieth-century American painter whose work hangs in many museums. Then she got married and had children, and her husband couldn't make a living and she had to go out and open her own business and couldn't pursue her painting any longer. And so, she became a very good amateur. She continued studying with another famous artist, Reginald Marsh, at the Art Students League in New York. I remember she said he told her, "You're very good. You aren't at a professional level, but you could be." So, she told him the whole story of why she wasn't. [Laughs.] Her son and daughter, my cousins, were also very good. He focused on cartooning, and she did both figurative and abstract painting and sold some of her work.

AK: It is interesting to me the way that the discipline and imagination that is required, and the many ways the physical strength that is required to work in the visual arts really crosses over into filmmaking.

SR: Absolutely. There is no question; I've always been in very good physical condition. Strong—both in terms of energy level and just physically strong.

AK: Was that something that was surprising to your crew and actors when you were working?

SR: That I was physically strong? Well, they didn't know; they didn't see me lifting things since there were crew members to do that. But they certainly were witness to my energy. I never flagged, I never stopped; the most energetic person on a set has to be the director. The director sets the pace for everyone else.

AK: Was there ever a point when a film was over where you just collapsed, cocooned for a couple days to get yourself back together?

SR: Oh, yes. I would be exhausted! But it is not just caused by physical exertion; it's what it does to your nervous system. I mean, you have to be functioning at such a high level, you have to be so alert, there is so much you have to watch, and so much you have to communicate and remember. There is so much emotional energy and physical tension. The mind and the body are both put through a great deal of stress. So, you do need to be in good health for it, and you do need to be strong. But no, I did not go around weightlifting in front of the crew and cast.

AK: [Laughs.] No pulling cameras up muddy hills?

SR: No, none of that. Well . . . sometimes, actually, if we were in a remote location and we had to get out because of a weather change or something, yes, I would pick up stuff, along with everybody else. The only people we wouldn't ask to help would be the actors. And lo and behold, now and then one of them graciously would offer to. But that was rare. [Laughs.]

AK: This is a question that is specifically meant to be polemical: do you think women directors intrinsically make different films than men?

SR: Because they are female?

AK: Yes.

SR: Not entirely. Maybe their experiences as a female will make them have a different approach to different characters or different subjects, but intrinsically, I don't think I can say that.

AK: Why do you think it is important for women filmmakers to be specifically recognized?

SR: Because in all of history so few have been able to make films. It is very important for everyone to recognize that women can make films. It is important for social justice, for the sense of identity of all women, and for the art of filmmaking.

AK: What impact do you think that could have?

SR: Well, I suppose there are two kinds. One is inspirational, for the woman aspiring to become a filmmaker or in the process of becoming one. And the second is to change prejudiced attitudes towards the kinds of work that women can do, until it is universally accepted that women can direct films of any sort. I mean, I would have loved to have been the female David Lean. [Laughs.] I should have mentioned him before when I was listing directors who I believe are artists. The problem is that he made these logistically complicated films, and he had to spend months in the desert and other daunting places with an army of technicians and remembering the history of his physical production challenges made me forget that he was foremost an artist.

AK: Under your designation of artist, would you prefer to look at the entire body of work for a filmmaker, or do you think that they can have moments of artistry?

SR: Oh both. I think people can have those moments. I mean, look at Alexander Mackendrick for example, *Sweet Smell of Success* [1957]. That is a great film, in my opinion, a really great film. *A High Wind in Jamaica* [1965], I read the book, I loved the book . . . that's not a great film. [Laughs.]

AK: Is there something that we haven't talked about that you really want to be out there?

SR: The only thing I can say is that I deeply regret that it couldn't have been longer, and I couldn't have grown more.

AK: For what you did do, are you proud of your work?

SR: Well, let me put it this way: when, on the rare occasion that I look at one my films—which is very rare, maybe once in a decade—when I start to look at it I am anxious, and then I am often relieved and sometimes pleasantly surprised. But sometimes not! [Laughs.] Sometimes I am reminded that—ugh!—that was hard to do and I see that I didn't succeed!

AK: When do you have occasion to go back and look at your work?

SR: Well, if I am going to talk about it in public, I will do that. I don't do it often because it is very anxiety-producing. You might find that odd. I am always afraid I am going to be horrified that this was my life, this was what I did, and, "Oh my God, my life is over and what a futile effort this has been if that's all there is." That is the anxiety I have. That is why I say when I look at them, I am often pleasantly surprised. The effort wasn't so futile after all. [Laughs.] I start with low expectations . . . I can't help it. That's the way I am, that is my nature.

AK: Maybe that brings us back to our earlier conversation about being passionate about something.

SR: Yes, exactly. People who care are their own greatest taskmasters. And they should be; people who don't care don't accomplish much. My great conflict is that I didn't get to accomplish much of what I wanted to do, although I have always cared very much. And if you were to ask me, "What did you want to accomplish?" I'd have to say, "Well, I don't know, because I never got to accomplish it!" [Laughs.] Now, to answer your question more seriously: I wanted to make films that passionately debated in a volatile mixture of comedy and drama the social and political battles of our time.

Am I proud of myself . . . do I take pride in that? I don't think "pride" is the word I would use. I think that I am happy I was stubborn enough to persist and prevail, for even as short a time as I did.

EMAIL SELECTIONS

The below excerpts are from email correspondence between Rothman and me from 2013–2020. All quotes come directly from Stephanie Rothman. They have been edited for clarity.

April 13, 2013: "You are correct, I do want to author my own story, but only because I don't want it distorted. I had some early press interviews that were so inaccurate and sloppy that I learned my lesson and I have never forgotten it. I am glad that my films have given you some pleasure. Making a film is sending a message into the world and it is always gratifying to know that someone has received it."

November 13, 2014: "Thank you for forwarding the notes on *Duet*. I have a vague memory of being at that faculty screening. It was the first time I saw it as an answer print. As you can imagine, I was distressed to see that the two negatives, sound and picture, had been cut and assembled out of sync. As I recall there was also some dirt and scratches from the cutting that should not have been there. The faculty did not reprimand the negative cutters, Chick Fowles and Eric Timmerman, at the time. Neither of them apologized to me for their botched work either. But they must have been reprimanded earlier, judging by Chick Fowles "tantrum in a teacup" production notes. It seems his bitterness was sprayed in three directions: at me, at the lab, and at the faculty-designed curriculum. As I recall, and I haven't thought about it in fifty years, he was angry at me because he had the misconception that the editor was the monarch of the editing room and did not have to work with the director. He resented that he had to work with me, and on top of that he was more inexperienced than most of the other students in his class and, instead of being appreciative, apparently, he resented that he needed more training and help from me. His was a passive-aggressive type of anger and so after an initial display of emotion he kept it concealed until the end. I don't know if he and his partner botched their work on the negative because of his resentment, their laziness, or sheer incompetence, probably it was a mixture, but at this late date I don't care, I'm only filling you in on what I think were the reasons for this mess, since you took the time to read the notes. Judging by his animosity toward the lab, he must have gotten a lot of criticism and no sympathy from them. And finally, his criticism of the curriculum: Well, we all had to work hard and carry the same load as he did when we were taking his courses and I never heard anyone else complain. Film school was physically hard work, but for me at least it was joyous work. Apparently not for him. Anyway, in conclusion, I never had the heart to look at *Duet* again after seeing how it was ruined and, of course, I was unable to use it as calling card for work. So, I stored it in the most distant recesses of my memory and I now intend to replace it there and never visit it again."

February 18, 2015: "Thanks for passing this [*an article on* The Man in The High Castle *television show*] onto me. I noticed it being advertised on the Amazon site too, although I didn't know it had been picked up for a full run. I am more than normally curious to see how it has been adapted. I did see a few moments of a promotional trailer and it was reminiscent of a Ridley Scott dystopia, i.e., *Blade Runner*, which isn't surprising since he executive-produced it.

I have a piece of news for you too. *The Student Nurses* was shown the week before last at the Museum of Modern Art [MoMA] in New York. It made it to the Big Apple at last! Roger Corman gave his negatives to the Academy of Motion Pictures Arts and Sciences, and the *Nurses* negative was in good shape, so a new print was made of it and that is what was shown at MoMA. Next up for possible restoration, *The Velvet Vampire*, which is the other film I made for Roger. I'll keep you posted.

And now, I have a small favor to ask of you if it is still possible to accomplish. Could you add three additional names to the directors whose work I most admire? How I managed to leave them out I don't know. Here they are: Jean Cocteau, Jean Renoir and, of course, the writer-director whose work launched my interest in making films—Ingmar Bergman. I hope it's not too late, but I am resigned if it is."

July 2, 2017: "I went to see *Wonder Woman*, something I would never do if it hadn't been directed by a woman. I thought Patty Jenkins did a very polished job and that the actors were quite engaging. She is a talented woman. I found *Monster* a very gripping film, and I believe it was made about fourteen years ago and that she has not directed another film since then. If a man had made it, I think he would have been offered work immediately. So things have changed for the better, somewhat—she got a chance to prove women can direct films with lots of shooting and explosions—only fourteen years later."

June 20, 2019: "I'm pleased to hear that you are enjoying your students and that they enjoyed *The Student Nurses*. My little film is coming up in the world: Turner Classic Movies also showed it this spring at the film festival they have in LA every year.

The Academy of Motion Picture Arts and Sciences made a new and newly timed archival film print of *The Velvet Vampire*, and it was also screened here at UCLA this spring. AMPAS did a beautiful job. And now the rusty wheels of the Museum of Modern Art are turning at last, and they will be making a new archival print of *Terminal Island* this fall. As for the other two films, the curator in charge at MoMA tried to get the Film Foundation, which is headed by Martin Scorsese, to fund digital restorations of them because the original negatives are lost, but she was turned down without an explanation. She finds it curious since they make a point of saying they want to preserve films by women. So, it goes . . . she'll try elsewhere, she says.

You're right. *The Velvet Vampire* is not a conventional horror film, but that hasn't stopped journalists from writing about it as though it was. The most recent article was in *Fangoria* a couple of years ago, after you asked if I would agree to an interview with them and I refused. Well, they did it on their own without either of us and they were very kind to the film."

October 14, 2020: "In answer to your two questions:

[The following questions was posed to Rothman: In your UCLA Oral History you mentioned that Henry Rosenbaum—whom you and Charles hired to rewrite Terminal Island—*did the rewrite but did not want the credit for it. Do you happen to remember why?]* "Henry Rosenbaum wrote the second draft of *Terminal Island*. Charles and I wrote the third draft. Henry was talented and we enjoyed working with him and we respected his wish to not receive a writing credit. He never explained why, and we guessed it was because he didn't want it on his list of credits because it was an exploitation film and he had written for some major studio films. There was no prestige in being associated with exploitation films. So, I can't give you a definite answer to your question."

[The following question was posed to Rothman: The editor on Blood Bath/Track of the Vampire *is listed as "Candance Kane." I assume this is a pseudonym, but I am not sure if it is your pseudonym or someone else's. Do you happen to remember?]* "'Candace Kane' sounds like a weak joke to me too. I've never heard of such a person. The editor who worked on my version was named Mort Tuber. He was a union editor and for that reason didn't want credit on a nonunion film."

October 17, 2020: "Turner Classic Movies is currently screening a series of films by one hundred women directors through history. None of my films are included. However, they managed to screen *Its a Bikini World* a few months ago during primetime (7:30 p.m.). A friend notified me, and I studiously avoided watching it because, as you know, it is my least favorite film except for *Blood Bath*. I got to hear Ben (?) Mankiewicz mumble . . . about three perfunctory sentences afterward. As best as I can remember, he said that my later work was darker. I know I shouldn't be ungrateful, but it's that 'darker' work that I wish they would show instead."

NOTES

CHAPTER 1. RADICAL ACTS

1. Ava DuVernay quoted in Alice Robb, "Women Speak Out about Pulling Off the 'Radical Act' of Filmmaking in the Male-Dominated Movie Business," *New York Times*, April 22, 2015, http://nytlive.nytimes.com/womenintheworld/2015/04/22/women-speak-out-about-pulling-off-the-radical-act-of-filmmaking-in-the-male-dominated-movie-business/ (accessed March 14, 2016).

2. Vicki Mayer, "Bringing the Social Back In: Studies of Production Cultures and Social Theory," in *Production Studies: Cultural Studies of Media Industries*, eds. Vicki Mayer, Miranda J. Banks, and Jon Thornton Caldwell (Routledge: New York and London, 2009), 15.

3. Safiya Umoja Noble, *Algorithms of Oppression* (New York: New York University Press, 2018), 65.

4. Alexandra Juhasz, "The Future Was Then: Reinvesting in Feminist Media Practice and Politics," *Camera Obscura* 61, no. 21:1 (2006): 54.

5. Juhasz, 54.

6. Hansen quoted in Sabine Haenni, "Intellectual Promiscuity: Cultural History in the Age of the Cinema, Network, and the Database," *New German Critique* 122, no. 41:2 (Summer 2014): 191.

7. John T. Caldwell, "Para-Industry, Shadow Academy," *Cultural Studies* 28, no. 4 (2014): 721.

8. John L. Sullivan, "Leo C. Rosten's Hollywood: Power, Status, and the Primacy of Economic and Social Networks in Cultural Production," in *Production Studies: Cultural Studies of Media Industries*, eds. Vicki Mayer, Miranda J. Banks, and Jon Thornton Caldwell (Routledge: New York and London: 2009), 39.

9. Miranda J. Banks, "Oral History and the Media Industries," *Cultural Studies* 28, no. 4 (2014).

10. Richard Maltby, "New Cinema Histories," in *Explorations in New Cinema History: Approaches and Case Studies*, eds. Richard Maltby, Daniel Biltereyst, and Philippe Meers (Oxford, UK, and Malden, MA: Wiley-Blackwell: 2011), 9.

11. Rick Altman, *Silent Film Sound* (New York: Columbia University Press, 2004), 16; italics in original.

12. Eric Schaefer, *Bold! Daring! Shocking! True! A History of Exploitation Films, 1919–1959*. Durham, NC: Duke University Press, 1999.

13. Altman, *Silent Film Sound*, 19.

14. Altman, 19.

15. Thomas Elsaesser, "The New Film History as Media Archaeology," *Cinémas: revue d'études cinématographiques/Cinémas: Journal of Film Studies* 14, nos. 2–3 (2004).

16. Christine Gledhill and Julia Knight, "Introduction," in *Doing Women's Film History: Reframing Cinemas, Past and Future*, eds. Gledhill and Knight (Urbana: University of Illinois Press, 2015), 2.

17. Gledhill and Knight, 2.

18. Vivian Sobchack, "'Presentifying' Film and Media Feminism," *Camera Obscura* 61, no. 21:1 (2006): 66.

19. Marsha Houston, "The Politics of Difference: Race, Class, and Women's Communications," in *Women Make Meaning: New Feminist Directions in Communication*, ed. Lana F. Rakow (London: Routledge, 1992), 47.

20. Vicki Callahan, "Reclaiming the Archive: Archaeological Explorations toward a Feminism 3.0," in *Reclaiming the Archive: Feminism and Film History*, ed. Vicki Callahan (Detroit: Wayne State University Press, 2010), 5.

21. Kate Eichhorn, *The Archival Turn in Feminism: Outrage in Order* (Philadelphia, PA: Temple University Press, 2013), 29.

22. Angela Martin, "Refocusing Authorship in Women's Filmmaking," in *Auteurs and Authorship*, ed. Barry Keith Grant (Malden, MA: Blackwell Publishing, 2008), 127.

23. Judith Mayne, *The Woman at the Keyhole* (Bloomington and Indianapolis: Indiana University Press, 1990), 93.

24. For examples, see: Judith Mayne, *Directed by Dorothy Arzner* (Bloomington: Indiana University Press, 1995); Karen Ward Maher, *Women Filmmakers in Early Hollywood* (Baltimore, MD: Johns Hopkins University Press, 2006); Joan Simon, *Alice Guy-Blaché: Cinema Pioneer* (New Haven, CT: Yale University Press, 2009); Shelly Stamp, *Lois Weber in Early Hollywood* (Berkeley: University of California Press, 2015); Therese Grishman and Julie Grossman, *Ida Lupino, Director: Her Art and Resilience in Times of Transition* (New Brunswick, NJ: Rutgers University Press, 2017); Erin Hill, *Never Done: A History of Women's Work in Media* (New Brunswick, NJ: Rutgers University Press, 2016); Jane M. Gaines, *Pink-Slipped: What Happened to Women in the Silent Film Industry?* (Urbana: University of Illinois Press, 2018); Tami Williams, *Germaine Dulac: A Cinema of Sensations* (Urbana: University of Illinois Press, 2014).

25. For examples, see: Deborah Jermyn and Sean Redmond, *The Cinema of Kathryn Bigelow: Hollywood Transgressor* (London: Wallflower Press, 2003); Marjorie Vecchio, *Claire Denis: Intimacy on the Border* (London: I. B. Tauris, 2014); Kathleen McHugh, *Jane Campion* (Urbana: University of Illinois Press, 2007); Alistair Fox, *Jane Campion: Authorship and Personal Cinema* (Bloomington: Indiana University Press, 2011); Fiona Handyside, *Sofia Coppola: A Cinema of Girlhood* (London: I. B. Tauris, 2017); Amardeep Singh, *The Films of Mira Nair: Diaspora Vérité* (Jackson: University Press of Mississippi, 2018).

26. Kaja Silverman, "The Female Authorial Voice," in *Film and Authorship*, ed. Virginia Wright Wexman (New Brunswick: Rutgers University Press, 2003), 59.

27. Mayne, *The Woman*, 90.

28. Mayne, 93.

29. Mayne, 97.

30. Martha Lauzen, "The Celluloid Ceiling: Behind-the-Scenes Employment of Women in the Top 100, 250, and 500 films of 2019," Center for the Study of Women in Television and Film San Diego University, 2020, https://womenintvfilm.sdsu.edu/wpcontent/uploads/2020/01/2019_Celluloid_Ceiling_Report.pdf.

31. Lauzen, "The Celluloid Ceiling."

32. Lauzen, "The Celluloid Ceiling."

33. Brent Lang, "Female Directors Behind Record Number of Films in 2019 (Study)," *Variety*, January 2, 2020, https://variety.com/2020/film/news/female-directors-record-films-little-women-hustlers-the-farewell-1203454878/.

34. Linda Ruth Williams, "Exploitation Cinema," in *The Cinema Book, 3rd Edition*, ed. Pam Cook (London: British Film Institute, 2007), 289.

35. Eric Schaefer, "Of Hygiene and Hollywood: Origins of Exploitation Film," *Velvet Light Trap*, no. 30 (Fall 1992): 45.

36. Eric Schaefer, "Exploitation Films: Teaching Sin in the Suburbs," *Cinema Journal* 47, no. 1 (2007): 94.

37. Arguably, there is value in considering neo-exploitation from 1979/80 to 2000 as the heyday of exploitation on VHS and home-video markets, and the period from 2000 to the present as a post-exploitation phase, where contemporarily produced exploitation films exist primarily on niche cable television networks and electronic delivery systems like video on demand (VOD). It should be noted that past the classical exploitation phase, which was developed by Eric Schaefer, the subsequent phases are my own formulations.

38. Schaefer, *Bold!*; Eric Schaefer, "Resisting Refinement: The Exploitation Film and Self-Censorship," *Film History*, no. 6 (1994): 292–313.

39. Elena Gorfinkel, "Wet Dreams: Erotic Film Festivals of the Early 1970s and the Utopian Sexual Public Sphere," *Framework: The Journal of Cinema and Media* 47, no. 2 (Fall 2006): 59–86; Elena Gorfinkel, "Tales of Times Square: Sexploitation's Secret History of Place," in *Taking Place: Location and the Moving Image*, eds. John David Rhodes and Elena Gorfinkel (Minneapolis and London: University of Minnesota Press, 2011), 55–76.

40. Pam Cook, "At the Edges of Hollywood: Stephanie Rothman," in *The Cinema Book, 3rd Edition*, ed. Pam Cook (London: BFI, 2007), 470–71.

CHAPTER 2. THE LIMITS OF EXCEPTIONAL WOMEN

1. Bill Nichols, "Film Theory and the Revolt Against Master Narratives," in *Reinventing Film Studies*, eds. Christine Gledhill and Linda Williams (London: Hodder Arnold, 2000), 34.

2. Kaja Silverman, "The Female Authorial Voice," in *Film and Authorship*, ed. Virginia Wright Wexman (New Brunswick: Rutgers University Press, 2003), 59.

3. Marcia M. Gallo, "Radicalesbians Issues 'The Woman Identified Woman' Manifesto," *Salem Press Encyclopedia*, 2020, http://search.ebscohost.com.washcoll.idm.oclc.org/login.aspx?direct=true&db=ers&AN=96775960&site=eds-live.

4. Jennifer Rich, *An Introduction to Modern Feminist Thought*, Penrith Philosophy Insights: Humanities e-book (2007): 21–22, http://search.ebscohost.com.washcoll.idm.oclc.org/login.aspx?direct=true&db=nlebk&AN=373396&site=eds-live.

5. Shulamith Firestone, *The Dialectic of Sex* (New York: Bantam Books, 1970), 13.

6. Jacqueline Rhodes, *Radical Feminism, Writing, and Critical Agency: From Manifesto to Modem* (Albany: State University of New York Press, 2005). Redstockings and NYRW were offshoot organizations of New York Radical Feminists, co-founded by Firestone. While essentialism was a core principle for radical feminists, the idea that there was unity in essentialism feminism was troubled by other radical feminist groups, who attached the movement's classism and racism. See Rhodes for an intricate mapping of these intra- and inter-group tensions.

7. Alison Stone, "Essentialism and Anti-Essentialism in Feminist Philosophy," *Journal of Moral Philosophy* 1, no. 2 (2004): 135.

8. Charlotte Witt, "Anti-Essentialism in Feminist Theory," *Philosophical Topics* 23, no. 2 (1995): 321–44.

9. Witt, 323.

10. Stone, "Essentialism."

11. Discussion of essentialism and anti-essentialism would renew in the late 1980s and throughout the 1990s.

12. Kathi Weeks, "The Vanishing *Dialectic*: Shulamith Firestone and the Future of the Feminist 1970s," *South Atlantic Quarterly* 114, no. 4 (October 2015): 735.

13. Annette Kuhn, "The State of Film and Media Feminism.," *Signs* 30, no. 1 (Autumn 2004): 1223.

14. Kuhn, 1223.

15. Alison Butler, *Women's Cinema: The Contested Screen* (London and New York: Wallflower, 2002), 1.

16. Annette Kuhn, "Women's Pictures," *Schirmer Encyclopedia of Film*, ed. Barry Keith Grant (New York: Schirmer Reference, 2007), 367.

17. Kuhn, 367.

18. For particularly salient examples of this burden, see Douglas Sirk's *Imitation of Life* (1959) and *All That Heaven Allows* (1955), and Joseph L. Mankiewicz's *All About Eve* (1950).

19. Mary Ann Doane, Patricia Mellencamp, and Linda Williams, "Feminist Film Criticism: An Introduction," in *Re-Vision: Essays in Feminist Film Criticism*, eds. Mary Ann Doane, Patricia Mellencamp, and Linda Williams (California: American Film Institute, 1984), 10.

20. Doane, Mellencamp, and Williams, 9.

21. See, for example, Mulvey's work around *Duel in the Sun* (King Vidor, 1946).

22. Camera Obscura Collective (Janet Bergstrom, Sandy Flitterman, Elisabeth Hary Lyon, Constance Penly), "Feminist and Film: Critical Approaches," in *The Feminist and Visual Culture Reader 2nd Edition*, ed. Amelia Jones (London and New York: Routledge, 2003), 269.

23. The introductory section to Laura Mulvey's germinal "Visual Pleasure and Narrative Cinema" is an apt example of this. See Laura Mulvey, "Visual Pleasure and Narrative Cinema," *Screen* 16, no. 3 (October 1, 1975): 6–18.

24. Peter Wollen, "Goddard and Counter Cinema: Vent d'Est," *Afterimage*, no. 4 (Autumn 1971): 6–17.

25. Claire Johnston, "Women's Cinema as Counter-Cinema (UK, 1973)," in *Film Manifestos and Global Cinema Cultures*, ed. Scott MacKenzie (Berkeley: University of California Press, 2014), 352.

26. Johnston, 355.

27. Johnston, 353.

28. Lucy Fisher, *Shot/Countershot: Film Tradition and Women's Cinema* (Princeton: Princeton University Press, 2014), 7.

29. Mayne, *Keyhole*, 96.

30. Ernest Mathijs and Jamie Sexton, *Cult Cinema: An Introduction* (London: Blackwell, 2011), 67.

31. Robert Stam, *Film Theory*, (Malden, MA: Blackwell Publishing, 2000), 85.

32. W. K. Wimsatt Jr. and M. C. Beardsley, "The Intentional Fallacy," *Sewanee Review* 54, no. 3 (July–September 1946), 468.

33. Kael was specifically responding to Andrew Sarris. Their debate over auteurism has become something of legend in cinema studies. See Andrew Sarris, "Notes on the Auteur Theory in 1962," in *Film Theory and Criticism: Introductory Readings, 5th Edition*, eds. Leo Braudy and Marshall Cohen (New York and Oxford: Oxford University Press, 1999), 515–18, and Pauline Kael, "Circles and Squares," *Film Quarterly* 16, no. 3 (Spring 1963): 12–26.

34. Christine Gledhill, "Afterthoughts: Development in Feminist Film Criticism," in *Re-Vision: Essays in Feminist Film Criticism*, eds. Mary Ann Doane, Patricia Mellencamp, and Linda Williams (California: American Film Institute, 1984), 42.

35. Judith Mayne, *The Woman at the Keyhole* (Bloomington and Indianapolis: Indiana University Press, 1990), 90.

36. Mayne, 93–94.

37. Mayne, 98.

38. Angela Martin, "Refocusing Authorship in Women's Filmmaking," in *Auteurs and Authorship*, ed. Barry Keith Grant (Malden, MA: Blackwell Publishing, 2008), 131.

39. Jane M. Gaines, *Pink-Slipped: What Happened to Women in the Silent Film Industry?* (Urbana: University of Illinois Press, 2018), 165; italics in original.

40. James Kendrick, "What is the Criterion? The Criterion Collection as an Archive of Film as Culture," *Journal of Film and Video* 53, nos. 2–3 (Summer–Fall 2001): 126.

41. As of January 2020, they are: Agnès Varda (10 films), Catherine Breillat (1 film), Chantal Akerman (6 films), Claire Denis (2 films), Andrea Arnold (1 film), Lynne Ramsay (1 film), Sam Taylor-Johnson (1 film), Agnieszka Holland (1 film), Agnieszka Smoczyńska (1 film), Allison Anders (1 film), Barbara Kopple (1 film), Barbara Loden (1 film), Barbra Streisand (1 film), Donna Deitch (1 film), Elaine May (1 film), Jennie Livingston (1 film), Kelly Reichardt (2 films), Kirsten Johnson (1 film), Laurie Anderson (1 film), Lena Dunham (1 film), Lucille Carra (1 film), Miranda July (1 film), Susan Seidelman (1 film), Gillian Armstrong (1 film), Jane Campion (2 films), Larisa Shepitko (1 film), Euzhan Palcy (1 film), Liliana Cavani (1 film), Marie Nyreröd (1 film), Mira Nair (1 film), Olivia Neergaard-Holm (1 film), and Lucrecia Martel (1 film).

42. Twenty-four of the directors are from the US, Australia, or Western Europe; two are from Eastern Europe; two are from Scandinavian countries; and one is from South America. There are no Asian women directors represented in the Criterion Collection.

43. "Our Mission," the Criterion Collection, accessed July 25, 2020, https://www.criterion.com/about.

44. Keijo Rahkonen, "Bourdieu and Nietzsche: Taste of Struggle," in *The Legacy of Pierre Bourdieu: Critical Essays*, eds. Simon Susen and Bryan S. Turner (London: Anthem Press, 2011), 126.

45. Dick Hebdige, "Towards a Cartography of Taste, 1935–1962," in *Popular Culture: Past and Present*, eds. Bernard Waites, Tony Bennett, and Graham Martin (London: Croom Helm, 1982), 194.

46. Gaines, *Pink-Slipped*, 116.

47. Randal Johnson, "Introduction," in *The Field of Cultural Production: Essays on Art and Literature*, written by Pierre Bourdieu, trans. and ed. Randal Johnson (New York: Columbia University Press, 1993), 2.

48. Alexa L. Foreman, *Women in Motion* (Bowling Green, OH: Bowling Green University Popular Press, 1983), 1.

49. For additional examples, see Gwendolyn Audrey Foster's *Women Film Directors: An International Bio-Critical Dictionary* (Connecticut: Greenwood Press, 1995) and Amy L. Unterburger's *Women Filmmakers and Their Films*, (Detroit: St. James Press, 1998).

50. For a contextualization of these issues see Melissa Goodman and Ariela Migdal, "Letter to the EEOC Los Angeles District Office," American Civil Liberties Union, May 12, 2015, http://www.nytimes.com/interactive/2015/05/12/movies/document-13filmwomen.html?_r=1.

51. Alicia Kozma and Finley Freibert, "Introduction: Making Films in Hell," in *ReFocus: The Films of Doris Wishman* (Edinburgh: Edinburgh University Press, 2021), 1–2.

52. To be sure, work by Moya Luckett, Elena Gorfinkel, Rebekah McKendry, Michael Bowen, and Tania Modeliski was critical in developing any kind of awareness of Wishman and her filmography.

53. See Alicia Kozma and Finley Freibert, *ReFocus: The Films of Doris Wishman* (Edinburgh: Edinburgh University Press, 2021).

54. Pierre Bourdieu, *Distinction: A Social Critique of the Judgment of Taste*, trans. Richard Nice (Cambridge: Harvard University Press, 1984), 12.

55. José Esteban Muñoz, *Disidentifications* (Minneapolis: University of Minnesota Press, 1999), 5.

56. Charles Merewether, "Introduction: Art and the Archive," in *The Archive: Documents in Contemporary Art*, ed. Charles Merewether (London and Boston: Whitechapel Gallery and MIT Press, 2006), 13.

57. Paul Ricoeur, "Archives, Documents, Traces," in *The Archive: Documents in Contemporary Art*, ed. Charles Merewether (London and Boston: Whitechapel Gallery and MIT Press, 2006), 67.

58. Diana Taylor, *The Archive and the Repertoire: Performing Cultural Memory in the Americas*, (Durham, NC: Duke University Press, 2003), 19.

59. Jacques Derrida, *Archive Fever: A Freudian Impression*, trans. Eric Prenowitz (Chicago and London: University of Chicago Press, 1995), 4.

60. Marlene Manoff, "Theories of the Archive from Across Disciplines," *Libraries and the Academy* 4, no. 1 (January 2004), 14.

61. Siegfried Zielinksi, *Deep Time of the Media: Toward an Archaeology of Hearing and Seeing by Technical Means*, trans. Gloria Custance (Cambridge, MA: MIT Press, 2006), 5.

62. Vicki Callahan, "Reclaiming the Archive: Archaeological Explorations toward a Feminism 3.0," in *Reclaiming the Archive: Feminism and Film History*, ed. Vicki Callahan (Detroit: Wayne State University Press, 2010), 2.

63. Erin Hill. *Never Done: A History of Women's Work in Media Production* (New Brunswick, NJ: Rutgers University Press, 2016).

64. Lana F. Rakow, "Feminist Approaches to Popular Culture: Giving Patriarchy its Due," in *Cultural Theory and Popular Culture, 2nd Edition*, ed. John Storey (England: Prentice Hall, 1998), 282–84.

65. Gaines, *Pink-Slipped*, 77; italics in original.

66. Gaines, 77.

67. Women Film Pioneer Project, "Homepage," https://wfpp.columbia.edu/ (accessed January 25, 2020).

68. Antoinette Burton, "Forward: 'Small Stories' and the Promise of New Narratives," in *Contesting Archives: Finding Women in the Sources*, eds. Nupur Chaudhuri, Sherry J. Katz, and Mary Elizabeth Perry (Urbana, Chicago, and Springfield: University of Illinois Press, 2010), i.

69. Helen Warner, "Below-the-(Hem)line," *Feminist Media Histories* 4, no. 1 (Winter 2018): 38.

70. Denise McKenna, Labor, *Feminist Media Histories* 4, no. 1 (Winter 2018): 4.

71. Kate Eichhorn, *The Archival Turn in Feminism: Outrage in Order* (Philadelphia, PA: Temple University Press, 2013), 3.

72. Eichhorn, 9.

73. Sara Ahmed, *The Cultural Politics of Emotion* (New York and London: Routledge, 2004), 14.

74. Ann Cvetkovich, *An Archive of Feelings* (Durham: Duke University Press, 2003), 7.

75. Cvetkovich, 286.

76. Cvetkovich, 11.

77. It is worth noting that Muñoz's book offers a volatile and shifting archive of its own, an archive that purposefully rejects coherence as a way of allowing him space for theoretical and analytical thought.

78. Cari Beauchamp, "Forward: Finding Frances Marion," in *When Women Wrote Hollywood*, ed. Rosanne Welch (Jefferson, NC: McFarland & Company, 2018), 2.

79. Gaines, *Pink-Slipped*, 127.

80. Gaines, 140.

81. Leo Enticknap, *Moving Image Technology: From Zoetrope to Digital* (London & New York: Wallflower Press, 2005), 188.

82. Enticknap, 188.

83. Science and Technology Council of the Academy of Motion Picture Arts and Sciences, *The Digital Dilemma: Strategic Issues in Archiving and Accessing Digital Motion Picture Materials*, http://www.oscars.org/science-technology/sci-tech-projects/digital-dilemma (Beverly Hills, CA: Academy of Motion Picture Arts and Sciences, 2007).

84. Science and Technology Council of the Academy of Motion Picture Arts and Sciences.

85. Giovanna Fossati, *The Archival Life of Film in Transition* (Amsterdam: Amsterdam University Press, 2009).

86. Fossati, 65.

87. Fossati, 65.

88. Fossati, 15.

89. Eric Schaefer, "Dirty Little Secrets: Scholars, Archivists, and Dirty Movies," *Moving Image: The Journal of the Association of Moving Image Archivists* 5, no. 2 (Fall 2005).

90. Leo Goldsmith, "Adventures in Preservation: A Report from the 7th Orphan Film Symposium," *Moving Image Source*, http://www.movingimagesource.us/articles/adventures-in-preservation-20100610 posted July 10, 2010 (accessed September 10, 2014).

91. Goldsmith.

92. Heide Solbrig, "Orphans No More: Definitions, Disciplines, and Institutions," *Journal of Popular Film and Television* 37, no. 3 (Fall 2009): 100.

93. Emily Cohen, "The Orphanista Manifesto: Orphan Films and the Politics of Reproduction," *American Anthropologist* 106, no. 4 (December 2004): 722.

94. Prelinger Archives, "About," www.archive.org, https://archive.org/details/prelinger&tab=about (accessed September 30, 2015).

95. Cohen, "The Orphanista," 719.

96. Solbrig, "Orphans," 100–102.

97. Caroline Frick, "Beyond Hollywood: Enhancing Heritage with the 'Orphan' Film," *International Journal of Heritage Studies* 14, no. 4 (July 2008): 323.

98. Stephanie Rothman, interview by Alicia Kozma, February 4, 2014, transcript.

99. For a full accounting of restoration efforts around Rothman's films, see Alicia Kozma, "The Rothman Renaissance, or, The Politics of Archival (Re)Discovery," in *Women and New Hollywood*, eds. Aaron Hunter and Martha Shearer (Rutgers University Press, 2023).

100. Kozma, "The Rothman Renaissance."

101. American Academy of Arts and Sciences Humanities Indicators, "Research and Development Expenditures at Colleges and Universities, accessed July 11, 2020, https://www.amacad.org/humanities-indicators/funding-and-research/research-and-development-expenditures-colleges-and.

102. While I realize $80 may not seem exorbitant, when I was doing the majority of my archival work, I was a graduate student making $17,000 a year before taxes. In that situation, $80 was grocery money for two weeks.

103. Thank you, Martina, Mark, Amber, Luzmilla, and George for your endless kindness.

CHAPTER 3. MARGIN AND CENTER

1. Dudley Andrew, "Hermeneutics and Cinema: The Issue of History," in *The Cinematic Text: Methods and Approaches*, ed. R. Barton Palmer (New York: AMS Press, 1989), 176–77.

2. Vivian Sobchack, "What is Film History?, or, the Riddle of the Sphinxes," in *Reinventing Film Studies*, eds. Christine Gledhill and Linda Williams (London: Hodder Arnold, 2000), 302.

3. Paolo Cherchi Usai, *The Death of Cinema: History, Cultural Memory and the Digital Dark Age* (London: BFI Publishing, 2001), 65.

4. Wolfgang Ernst, "Media Archaeology: Method and Machine versus History and Narrative of Media," in *Media Archaeology: Approached, Applications, and Implications*, eds. Erikki Huhtamo and Jussi Parikka (Berkeley and Los Angeles: University of California Press, 2011), 239.

5. Thomas Elsaesser, "The New Film History as Media Archaeology," *Cinémas: revue d'études cinématographiques/Cinémas: Journal of Film Studies* 14, no. 2–3 (2004): 99.

6. Elsaesser, 99.

7. For example, see Randall Clark, *At a Theater or Drive-In Near You: The History, Culture, and Politics of the American Exploitation Film* (New York: Garland Publishing, 1995), and Richard Meyers, *For One Week Only: The World of Exploitation Film* (New Jersey, New Century Publishers, 1983).

8. For this expansive construction of independence, see Matthew Bernstein, "Hollywood's Semi-Independent Production," *Cinema Journal* 32, no. 3 (Spring 1993): 41.

9. Eric Schaefer, *Bold! Daring! Shocking! True! A History of Exploitation Films, 1919–1959* (Durham, NC: Duke University Press, 1999), 5.

10. Schaefer, 95.

11. Schaefer, 43.

12. Robert G. Weiner, "The Prince of Exploitation: Dwain Esper," in *From the Arthouse to the Grindhouse: Highbrow and Lowbrow Transgression in Cinema's First Century*, eds. John Cline and Robert G. Weiner (Maryland: Scarecrow Press, 2010), 41.

13. Schaefer, *Bold! Daring!*, 42.

14. The 1948 decision was the result of nearly ten years of legal maneuverings between the eight major Hollywood studios and the United States Department of Justice acting on behalf of independent producers, distributors, and exhibitors. In 1948, the US Supreme Court declared that the major film studios were in violation of the antitrust laws as a result of their vertically integrated of the means of production, distribution, and exhibition. The decision found the studios guilty of restricting trade through monopoly. After the decision, studios were forced to divest themselves of many of their holdings, including their theaters, and they were required to give up lucrative block-booking practices. The decision brought about the first dissolution of a major studio, RKO. The others soon sold their holdings off piece by piece. It was the death knell for the classic Hollywood studio system, and from an economic perspective, studios took a serious hit to both their finances and their prestige.

15. Schaefer, *Bold! Daring!*, 326.

16. Thomas Doherty, *Teenagers and Teenpics: The Juvenilization of American Movies in the 1950s* (Philadelphia: Temple University Press, 2002), 32.

17. Paul Monaco *The Sixties, 1960–1969* (Berkeley: University of California Press, 2001), 40.

18. Barbara Jane Brickman, "Riot Girls in Town: Remaking, Revising, and Redressing the Teenpic," *Journal of Film and Video* 59, no. 4. (Winter 2007): 21.

19. The company was originally a releasing company called, appropriately enough, American Releasing Corporation.

20. Assigning creative credit for any film involving Roger Corman is often difficult. Corman himself has an overriding tendency to call any movies he has ever come into contact with, even in the slightest capacity, "his" movie. As actual directors often came and went on Corman-related projects fairly quickly, there are cases where screen credits, filmmaking records, and Corman's own narrative tell radically different stories. Such is the case with the directorial credit on *The Fast and the Furious*.

21. Roger Corman and Jim Jerome, *How I Made a Hundred Movies in Hollywood and Never Lost a Dime* (New York: Random House, 1990), 23.

22. Corman and Jerome, 167.

23. This includes, but is not limited to Robert Towne, Jack Nicholson, Francis Ford Coppola, Peter Bogdanovich, Dennis Hopper, Martin Scorsese, Jonathan Demme, Joe Dante, Jonathan Kaplan, Allan Arkush, John Sayles, James Cameron, and Gale Ann Hurd.

24. Randell Clark, *At a Theater or Drive-In Near You: The History, Culture, and Politics of the American Exploitation Film* (New York: Garland Publishing, 1995), 43.

25. Kerry Seagrave, *Drive-In Theaters: A History from Their Inception in 1933* (Jefferson, NC: McFarland & Company, 1992), 142.

26. Doherty, *Teenagers*, 52–53.

27. Doherty, 91–92.

28. Ernest Mathijs and Jamie Sexton, *Cult Cinema: An Introduction* (London: Blackwell Publishing, 2011), 149.

29. Mathijs and Sexton, 149.

30. The states' rights system divided the country into a number of different territories, and within those territories operated distribution companies or exchanges. Companies bought the distribution rights of a film from the producers, usually for a period of three to five years. The distributor was then responsible for advertising the film, booking it into theaters, generating tickets sales, etc., in whatever manner they deemed necessary and appropriate, or perhaps inappropriate in the case of exploitation films. The system required no upfront investment by the producer and allowed the distributor a percentage of the film's grosses. While the producer would provide the basic outline of advertising materials, campaigns in different markets were primarily at the discretion of the distribution companies. Contractual standards and terms between exchanges and producers would necessarily evolve with the market.

31. Mark Hartley, *Machete Maidens Unleashed!*, DVD, dir. Mark Hartley (Australia: Dark Sky Films, 2010).

32. Monaco, *The Sixties*, 45.

33. Monaco, 45; italics in original.

34. Mia Mask, *Divas on Screen: Black Women in American Film* (Urbana and Chicago: University of Illinois Press, 2009), 59.

35. Stephen Paul Miller, *The Seventies Now: Culture as Surveillance* (Durham, NC: Duke University Press, 1999): 1.

36. Stephane Dunn, *"Bad Bitches" and Sassy Supermamas: Black Power Action Films* (Urbana and Chicago: University of Illinois Press, 2008), 4–5.

37. Dunn, 4–5.

38. Elena Gorfinkel, "'Dated Sexuality': Anna Biller's *Viva* and the Retrospective Life of Sexploitation Cinema," *Camera Obscura* 78, no. 26:3 (2011): 95.

39. Elena Gorfinkel, *Lewd Looks: American Sexploitation Cinema in the 1960s* (Minneapolis: University of Minnesota Press, 217), 153.

40. Gorfinkel, 96–97.

41. Nudist camp films began in the 1950s and are true to name: some thin plot machinations would force the protagonist(s) to seek refuge in a nudist camp environment, and film would spend most of its time lingering over the bodies of nude men and women (primarily women) going through their daily activities in the nude. There was no suggestion of sex in these films, and no frontal nudity was shown below the waist. From the nudist camp film

developed nudie cuties, films that moved nudity into the broader world. The first of these films is widely considered to be Russ Meyer's *The Immoral Mr. Teas* (1959), which follows the eponymous character as he uses his X-ray vision to see under the clothes of women.

42. Although at this time censorship regulations were being actively challenged in the courts, and the challenges were by and large successful, it would not be until later in the decade that these restrictions truly began to fall away.

43. Tania Modleski, "Women's Cinema as Counterphobic Cinema: Doris Wishman as the Last Auteur," in *Sleaze Artists: Cinema at the Margins of Taste, Style, and Politics*, ed. Jeffrey Sconce (Durham: Duke University Press, 2007), 49.

44. Clark, *At a Theater*.

45. Elena Gorfinkel, "Tales of Times Square: Sexploitation's Secret History of Place," in *Taking Place: Location and the Moving Image*, eds. John David Rhodes and Elena Gorfinkel (Minneapolis and London: University of Minnesota Press, 2011), 67.

46. The films of Doris Wishman exemplify this tactic. See Moya Luckett, "Sexploitation as Feminine Territory: The Films of Doris Wishman," in *Defining Cult Movies: The Cultural Politics of Oppositional Taste*, eds. Mark Jancovich, Antonio Lázaro Reboll, Julian Stringer and Andy Willis (Manchester, UK: Manchester University Press, 2003), and Rebekah McKendry, "Fondling Your Eyeballs: Watching Doris Wishman," in *From the Arthouse to the Grindhouse: Highbrow and Lowbrow Transgression in Cinema's First Century*," eds. John Cline and Robert G. Weiner (Maryland: Scarecrow Press, 2010).

47. The "New Hollywood" would overhaul Hollywood with movies like *The Godfather* and *The Godfather Part II* (Francis Ford Coppola, 1972 and 1974), *Taxi Driver* (Martin Scorsese, 1976), *The Last Picture Show* (Bogdanovich, 1971), and *Nashville* (Robert Altman, 1975). Raised on television, educated in film school, and molded in the kill-or-be-killed world of second-wave exploitation films, the New Hollywood generation would serve as the bridge between the two industries, and leave a contradictory legacy for the future, as "partial nudity, coarse language and brutal violence are now commonplace in mainstream movies, but truly dissident themes, thorny characters and ambiguous narratives are not. The exploitation generation stormed the gates of Hollywood's citadel and paved the way for filmmakers with backgrounds in media that didn't even exist in the 1970s." Maitland McDonagh, "The Exploitation Generation or: How Marginal Movies Came in from the Cold," in *The Last Great American Picture Show: New Hollywood Cinema in the 1970s*, eds. Thomas Elsaesser, Alexander Horwath, and Noel King (Amsterdam: Amsterdam University Press, 2004), 109.

48. Second-wave exploitation was an important workspace for this group; although they were trained and pedigreed, Hollywood's "closed shop" unions and cronyism in hiring made it difficult for new talent to break into studio work.

49. McDonagh, "The Exploitation Generation," 109–10.

50. The producer-driven system of classical Hollywood served critical functions. It allowed for stricter economic control over individual films. The producer became the figure to which the studio executives could assign accountability—and correspondingly blame—for a film's performance. The producer also served as the organizing point in the studio system's strictly defined division of labor for all aspects of production, including pre- and postproduction.

51. David Bordwell, Janet Staiger and Kristin Thompson, *The Classical Hollywood Cinema: Film Style & Mode of Production to 1960* (New York: Columbia University Press, 1985).

52. Balio, *The Foreign Film*, 79.

53. Monaco, *The Sixties*, 124.

54. Bordwell, Staiger, and Thompson, *Classical Hollywood*, 6.

55. Eric Schaefer, "Exploitation Films: Teaching Sin in the Suburbs," *Cinema Journal* 47, no. 1 (Fall 2007): 95.

56. For two examples of the ways in which this hybridity works on the screen, see Roger Corman's *The Trip* (1967) and a later entry, John Sayles's *The Brother from Another Planet* (1984).

57. Monaco *The Sixties*, 182.

58. David A. Cook, *Lost Illusions: American Cinema in the Shadow of Watergate and Vietnam, 1970–1979* (Berkeley: University of California Press, 2000), 4.

59. Balio, *Foreign Film*, 42.

60. Andrew Sarris, "Why the Foreign Film Has Lost Its Cachet," *New York Times*, May 2, 1999.

61. Schaefer, *Bold! Daring!*, 331.

62. One of most significant challenges to censorship through foreign film came in what is known as "The Miracle Decision," which referred to a segment titled "The Miracle" in Rossellini's anthology film *L'Amore* (1948). The 1952 decision would find the US Supreme Court authorizing the challenge of state and municipal censorship boards, opening the door for a succession of legal challenges. Several more foreign films would work to challenge legal censorship when finally, "governmental censorship effectively ended in 1965 when the Supreme Court handed down a decision involving the Danish film *A Stranger Knocks*, which declare that the statutes governing the New York Board of Censors were unconstitutional." Balio, *Foreign Film*, 279.

63. Foreign films quickly found viewers in what *Variety* termed the "lost audience"—sophisticated and educated viewers who had abandoned theatergoing when US productions began to focus on niche audiences within younger generations. Interestingly, just as second-wave exploitation was targeting the niche teenager audience as part of their strategies for success, they were creating a "leftover" audience for foreign films to solicit in much the same ways. As the interest in foreign films began to generate a significant audience, the number of theaters showing these films, primarily art house theaters, began to grow exponentially. "In 1946 art houses were rarities outside New York; whereas by 1960 the number had risen to around 450. By comparison, there were approximately eleven thousand four-wall theaters and six thousand drive-ins operating in the United States." Balio, *Foreign*, 79–81.

64. Balio, *Foreign*, 227.

65. Thomas Schatz, "The New Hollywood," in *Film Theory Goes to the Movies*, eds. Jim Collins, Hilary Radner, and Ava Preacher Collins (New York and London: Routledge, 1992), 18.

66. Justin Wyatt, *High Concept: Movies and Marketing in Hollywood* (Austin: University of Texas Press, 1994).

67. Cook, *Lost Illusions*, 19.

CHAPTER 4. STEPHANIE ROTHMAN DOES NOT EXIST

1. Terry Curtis Fox, "Fully Female," *Film Comment* 12, no. 6 (November–December 1976): 50.
2. Stephanie Rothman, interview by Alicia Kozma, February 4, 2014, transcript.
3. Rothman, Kozma, February interview.
4. Rothman, Kozma, February interview.
5. Stephanie Rothman, interviewed by Jane Collings for Center for Oral History Research, University of California, Los Angeles, December 11, 2001, transcript, http://oralhistory.library.ucla.edu/.
6. Girls, Gangs, and Guns Festival, Diskussion im Anschlub an den Virtrag von Stephanie Rothman/Post-Film Discussion with Stephanie Rothman, 11.28.1999.
7. Stephanie Rothman, interview by Alicia Kozma, October 6, 2014, transcript.
8. Knight was a long-time public film critic for publications like the *Saturday Review* and *Playboy*.
9. Production book, *We Look and See*, Hugh M. Heffner Moving Image Archive, University of Southern California, 1963.
10. *We Look and See*.
11. *We Look and See*; underlined in original.
12. Rothman, Kozma, October interview.
13. Rothman, Kozma, October interview.
14. Production Book, *Duet*, The Hugh M. Heffner Moving Image Archive, University of Southern California: 1963.
15. Rothman, Kozma, October interview.
16. Stephanie Rothman, email message to author, November 13, 2014.
17. Girls, Gangs, and Guns, Post-Film Discussion.
18. Girls, Gangs, and Guns, Post-Film Discussion.
19. Girls, Gangs, and Guns, Post-Film Discussion.
20. Rothman, Collings, January interview.
21. Rothman, Collings, January interview.
22. Rothman, Kozma, February interview.
23. Rothman, Kozma, February interview.
24. Fred Olen Ray, *The New Poverty Row: Independent Filmmakers as Distributors* (Jefferson, NC: McFarland & Company, 1991), 149.
25. Rothman, Collings, January interview.
26. Barbara D. Boyle, "Independent Distribution: New World Pictures," in *The Movie Business Book*, ed. Jason E. Squire (New Jersey: Prentice-Hall, 1983), 286.
27. Roger Corman and Jim Jerome, *How I Made a Hundred Movies in Hollywood and Never Lost a Dime* (New York: Random House, 1990), 181.
28. *Variety Weekly*, "Woolner, Louisiana Exhibs, Spread as International Producers," June 29, 1966.
29. David Konow, "The First Dimension." *Fangoria*, no. 273 (May 2008): 71.
30. Gary Morris, "Roger Corman on New World Pictures: An Interview from 1974," *Bright Lights Film Journal*, no. 27 (January 2000), www.brightlightsfilm.com/27/cormaninterview1.html.

31. Boyle, "Independent," 286.

32. Tino Balio, *The Foreign Film Renaissance on American Screens, 1946–1973* (Madison: University of Wisconsin Press, 2010).

33. Rothman, Kozma, February interview.

34. Rothman, Kozma, February interview.

35. Ben Sher. "Q&A with Stephanie Rothman. *CSW Update Newsletter*, UCLA Center for the Study of Women, April 1, 2008, http://escholarship.org/uc/item/4jx713vz.

36. Rothman, Kozma, October interview.

37. Rothman, Kozma, October interview.

38. Rothman, Kozma, October interview.

39. *Variety Daily*, "Woolner Set Up Dimension Pictures," October 28, 1971.

40. According to Rothman, Woolner owned 40 percent of the company. Wembly had the majority stake position at 50 percent, and she and Swartz held the remaining 10 percent (Stephanie Rothman, interview by Alicia Kozma, October 6, 2014, transcript).

41. Rothman, Kozma, October interview.

42. Will Tusher, "Dimension Pictures Open up Opportunities for Women," *Hollywood Reporter*, June 1, 1972, 3.

43. Tusher, 3.

44. Rothman, Collings, February interview. Although she was not able to achieve this goal while at Dimension, Rothman did work with a woman sound mixer on *The Student Nurses* and a woman art director on *The Velvet Vampire*, both made at New World. (see J. Pyros, "Women on Women in Films." *Take One* 3, no. 2 [February 1972]: 14).

45. Rothman, Collings, February interview.

46. Bill Ornstein, "Dimension Increase in Film Production Set for Next Year," *Hollywood Reporter*, August 28, 1972.

47. Allen Rich, "Joint Exchanges to Solve Distribution Woes," *Hollywood Reporter*, December 1, 1972. The regional exchanges were planned for New Orleans, Charlotte, Memphis, Dallas, Minneapolis, and Salt Lake City, and would only handle Dimension and General films.

48. Ed Lowry, "Dimension Pictures: Portrait of a '70s Independent," *Velvet Light Trap*, no. 22 (1986): 69.

49. Lowry, 69.

50. Rothman, Kozma, October interview.

51. Rothman, Kozma, October interview.

52. Rothman, Kozma, October interview.

53. Rothman, Kozma, October interview.

54. Rothman, Kozma, October interview.

55. Ray, *The New Poverty Row*, 155.

56. Temple of Schlock Blog. "Dimension Pictures (1971–1981)," accessed November 29, 2012, http://templeofschlock.blogspot.com.au/2009/04/dimension-pictures-1971-1981.html.

57. Rothman, Kozma, October interview.

58. *Film Journal*, "21st Century Gets Dimension Library," July 20, 1981.

59. Sher, "Q&A."

60. Sher, "Q&A."

61. Sher, "Q&A."

62. Rothman, Kozma, February interview.
63. Rothman, Kozma, February interview.
64. Carolyn Giardina, "Led USC Showbiz Tech Unit," *Hollywood Reporter*, February 14, 2007, 42, 45.
65. Giardina, "Led USC."
66. Digital Cinema Initiatives (DCI) is the consortium of the major Hollywood Studios (Disney, Fox, Paramount, Sony Pictures Entertainment, Universal, and Warner Bros.) that is responsible for establishing the specifications of the electronic and procedural architecture for digital cinema distribution and exhibition.
67. Giardina, "Led USC."
68. Henry Jenkins, "Exploiting Feminism: An Interview with Stephanie Rothman (Part One)," *Confessions of an Aca-Fan: The Official Weblog of Henry Jenkins*, accessed November 29, 2012, http://henryjenkins.org/2007/10/stephanie_rothman.html.
69. Jenkins, "Exploiting Feminism."
70. Girls, Gangs, and Guns, Post-Film Discussion; italics in original.
71. Rothman, Kozma, October interview.
72. Rothman, Kozma, October interview.
73. Girls, Gangs, and Guns, Post-Film Discussion.
74. Girls, Gangs, and Guns, Post-Film Discussion.
75. Rothman, Kozma, October interview.
76. Rothman, Kozma, October interview.
77. Rothman, Kozma, October interview.
78. Girls, Gangs, and Guns, Post-Film Discussion; italics in original.
79. Tony Williams, "Feminism, Fantasy, and Violence: An Interview with Stephanie Rothman," *Journal of Popular Film and Television* 9, no. 2 (Summer 1981): 87.
80. Dannis Peary, "Stephanie Rothman: R-Rated Feminist," in *Women and the Cinema*, eds. Karyn Kay and Gerald Peary (New York: E. P. Dutton, 1977), 180–81.
81. Bev Zalcock, *Renegade Sisters: Girl Gangs on Film, 2nd Edition* (Creation Books, 2001), 193–94.
82. Linda Gross, "A Woman's Place Is In . . . Exploitation Films? A Trendsetter in the Youth Market," *Los Angeles Times*, February 12, 1978, 35.
83. Peary, "R-Rated Feminist," 186.
84. Peary, 186.
85. Peary, 186.
86. Jenkins, "Exploiting Feminism."
87. Girls, Gangs, and Guns, Post-Film Discussion.
88. Girls, Gangs, and Guns, Post-Film Discussion.
89. Williams, "Feminism, Fantasy," 88.
90. Tusher, "Dimension Pictures." 3.
91. J. Pyros, "Women on Women," 11–12.
92. Rothman, Kozma October interview.
93. Kit Snedacker, "Movies," *Los Angeles Evening and Sunday Herald Examiner,* California Living supplement, September 20, 1970, 32.

94. J. E. Smyth, *Nobody's Girl Friday: The Women Who Ran Hollywood* (Oxford University Press, 2018), 18.

95. Bigelow quoted in Ann Powell, "Blood on the Borders—*Near Dark* and *Blue Steel*," *Screen* 35, no, 2 (Summer 1994): 136.

96. Betty Friedan, *The Feminist Mystique* (New York: W. W. Norton & Company, 1963).

97. Rothman, Kozma, February interview.

98. Rothman, Kozma, February interview.

99. Pam Cook, "'Exploitation' Films and Feminism," *Screen* 17, no. 2 (Summer 1976): 122–27.

100. Fox, "Fully Female," 46.

101. Peary, "R-Rated Feminist," 179.

102. Williams, "Feminism, Fantasy."

103. J. Pyros, "Women on Women," 10–15.

104. Rothman, Kozma February interview.

105. Rothman, Kozma, February interview.

CHAPTER 5. EVERYONE STARTS SOMEWHERE

1. Rothman quoted in Will Tusher, "Dimension Pictures Open Up Opportunities for Women," *Hollywood Reporter*, June 1, 1972, 3.

2. Eric Schaefer, "Introduction—Sex Seen: 1968 and Rise of 'Public' Sex," in *Sex Scene*, ed. Eric Schaefer (Durham and London: Duke University Press, 2014), 3.

3. Mark Thomas McGee, *Faster and Furiouser: The Revision and Fattened Fable of American International Pictures* (Jefferson, NC: McFarland & Company, 1996), 7.

4. McGee, 14.

5. Roger Corman and Jim Jerome, *How I Made a Hundred Movies in Hollywood and Never Lost a Dime* (New York: Random House, 1990), 25.

6. Corman and Jerome, 124.

7. Tim Lucas, "The Trouble with Titan: Francis Ford Coppola's List Thriller and How Roger Corman Turned It Into 5 Movies! Part 3," *Video Watchdog*, no. 7 (September–October 1991): 21–22.

8. Rothman, Collings, January interview.

9. Lucas, "The Trouble with Part 3," 22.

10. Erin Hill, *Never Done: A History of Women's Work in Media Production* (New Brunswick, NJ: Rutgers University Press, 2016), 6.

11. Dennis Fisher, *Horror Film Directors, 1931–1990* (Jefferson, NC: McFarland & Company, 1991).

12. Wheeler Winston Dixon, *Film Talk: Directors at Work* (Rutgers, New Jersey: Rutgers University Press, 2007).

13. Fisher, *Horror Film Directors*, 814.

14. Tim Lucas, "The Trouble with Titan: Francis Ford Coppola's List Thriller and How Roger Corman Turned It Into 5 Movies! Part 2," *Video Watchdog*, no. 5 (May–June 1991): 22–27.

15. Stephanie Rothman, interview by Alicia Kozma, February 4, 2014, transcript.

16. Stephanie Rothman, interviewed by Jane Collings for Center for Oral History Research, University of California, Los Angeles, January 29, 2002, transcript, http://oralhistory.library.ucla.edu/.

17. Brian Albright, *Wild Beyond Belief!* (Jefferson, NC: McFarland & Company, 2008), 77.

18. Lucas, "The Trouble with Part 3," 25.

19. Michael Weldon, *The Psychotronic Encyclopedia of Film* (New York: Ballantine Books, 1983).

20. The film ultimately became five separate films: the original Yugoslavian version, Coppola's version, Hill's version, Rothman's version, and the television version.

21. Rothman, Kozma, February interview.

22. Lucas, "The Trouble with Part 3," 22.

23. Rothman, Collings, January interview.

24. Rothman, Kozma, February interview.

25. Calum Waddell, *Jack Hill: The Exploitation and Blaxploitation Master, Film by Film* (Jefferson, NC: McFarland & Company, 2009), 28.

26. Waddell, 28.

27. Waddell, 29.

28. To Waddell's great credit, after the publication of his book he acknowledged that Rothman's position and perspective should have played a larger role in his analysis of the tension around the film and between Rothman and Hill. Waddell, personal commination to author, 2020.

29. Waddell, 31.

30. Waddell, 31.

31. Lucas, "The Trouble with Part 2," 26.

32. Lucas, 23.

33. Lucas, 26.

34. Rothman, Collings, January interview.

35. Gary Morris, "Beyond the Beach," *Journal of Popular Film & Television* 21, no. 1 (Spring 1993): 2–11.

36. Thomas Doherty, *Teenagers and Teenpics: The Juvenilization of American Movies in the 1950s* (Philadelphia: Temple University Press, 2002), 128.

37. Perhaps best remembered from this cycle was the pairing of actors Frankie Avalon and Annette Funicello, who appeared in several beach films together as the reigning "king and queen of the beach."

38. R. L. Rutsky, "Surfing the Other: Ideology on the Beach," *Film Quarterly* 52, no. 4 (Summer 1999): 12–23.

39. Pablo Dominguez Andersen, "The Hollywood Beach Party Genre and the Exotification of Youthful White Masculinity in Early 1960s America," *Men and Masculinities* 15, no. 5 (2014): 512.

40. Rothman, Kozma, February interview.

41. Daddy is very loosely inspired by Ed "Big Daddy" Roth, creator of Rat Fink and key member of California's 1950s and 1960s Kustom Kulture.

42. Rothman, Kozma, February interview.

43. Rutsky, "Surfing the Other," 18.

44. Rutsky, 18.

45. See Morris, "Beyond the Beach" and Thomas Doherty, *Teenagers and Teenpics*.

46. Rutsky, "Surfing the Other," 12.

47. Rutsky, 13.

48. Winston Wheeler Dixon, *Visions of Paradise: Images of Eden in the Cinema* (New Brunswick, NJ: Rutgers University Press, 2006), 52.

49. The Haunted House would later be used as the primary set for Ted V. Mikels's 1968 second-wave exploitation cult classic *The Girl in Gold Boots*.

50. Fisher, *Horror Film Directors*, 814.

51. The Animals, *We Gotta Get Out of This Place*, lyrics by Barry Mann and Cynthia Weil, record, 1965.

52. The Animals.

53. The Animals.

54. The Animals.

55. The Animals guitarist Hilton Valentine seems to recognize the absurdity of the situation; as he looks out to the dance floor, a quick smirk appears on his face.

56. Rothman, Kozma, February interview.

57. Morris, "Beyond," 2.

58. Winston, *Visions*, 50.

59. *It's a Bikini World*, directed by Stephanie Rothman (1967; Southfield, MI: N/A), DVD.

60. *It's a Bikini World*.

61. *It's a Bikini World*.

62. *It's a Bikini World*.

63. Dixon, *Visions*, 53.

64. Roy M. Wallock, "How Bobbi Gibb Changed Women's Running, and Finally Got Credit for It," ESPN.com, January 6, 2016, https://www.espn.com/sports/endurance/story/_/id/15090507/endurance-sports-bobbi-gibb-first-woman-run-boston-marathon.

65. Ryan Bort, "Battle of the Sexes: A Guide to the Legendary Tennis Match between Billie Jean King and Bobby Riggs, *Newsweek*, September 22, 2017, https://www.newsweek.com/battle-sexes-guide-billie-jean-king-bobby-riggs-669300.

66. Rothman, Kozma, February interview.

67. Rothman, Kozma, February interview.

68. Dixon, *Visions*, 52.

69. Rothman, Kozma, February interview.

CHAPTER 6. IMAGINING A POST-PATRIARCHY

1. Terry Curtis Fox, "Fully Female," *Film Comment* 12, no. 6 (November–December 1976): 46.

2. Barbara Kantrowitz, "It's Ms. America to You," *Newsweek* 159, no, 121 (November 19, 2007): 58.

3. Nona Willis Aronowitz, "The First Time Women Shouted Their Abortions," *New York Times*, March 23, 2019, https://www.nytimes.com/2019/03/23/opinion/sunday/abortion-speakout-anniversary.html.

4. Grace Lichtenstein, "Feminists Demand 'Liberation' In *Ladies' Home Journal* Sit-In," *New York Times*, March 19, 1970, 51.

5. Robyn C. Spencer, *The Revolution Has Come* (Durham and London: Duke University Press, 2016), 98–99.

6. *The Black Panthers: Vanguard of the Revolution*, directed by Stanley Nelson (New York: Firelight Films, 2015), streaming.

7. Voice-over line from *The Student Nurses*, original trailer, 1970, https://www.youtube.com/watch?v=ubG521MU3yA.

8. Gary Morris, "Roger Corman on New World Pictures: An Interview from 1974," *Bright Lights Film Journal*, January 27, 2000, www.brightlightsfilm.com/27/cormaninterview1.html.

9. Rothman, Collings, February interview.

10. Roger Corman and Jim Jerome, *How I Made a Hundred Movies in Hollywood and Never Lost a Dime* (New York: Random House, 1990), 181.

11. Rothman, Collings, February interview.

12. Rothman, Collings, February interview.

13. Rothman, Collings, February interview.

14. While Rothman does sidestep the successful stereotype of the nubile student nurse, the trailer for the film uses it as bait for second-wave exploitation audiences. The trailer contains, almost exclusively, the scenes of sex, nudity, and violence in the film, providing a marked contrast between the film and its marketing strategy.

15. Rothman, Collings, February interview.

16. Dannis Peary, "Stephanie Rothman: R-Rated Feminist," in *Women and the Cinema: A Critical Anthology*, eds. Karyn Kay and Gerald Peary (New York: E. P. Dutton, 1977), 183.

17. Rothman, Collings, February interview.

18. Rothman, Collings, February interview.

19. Rothman, Collings, February interview.

20. Corman and Jerome, *How I Made*, 181.

21. As a further testament to Corman's habit of revising the history of his role in the films he produced—particularly the successful ones—in his biography he states that in *The Student Nurses*, "one nurse was black, another was involved with street projects" (Corman and Jerome, 181). There is not one Black nurse in the film (as a main character or otherwise), and his presumable description of Lynn's work in public health and neighborhood activism as "street projects" is tenuous at best. I would advance that his failure to accurately describe the film casts sufficient suspicion on his accurate attribution of agency in creating the film's message.

22. Rothman, Kozma, February interview.

23. Michel Foucault, *Discipline and Punish: The Birth of the Prison*, trans. Alan Sheridan (New York: Vintage Book, 1977).

24. *The Student Nurses*, directed by Stephanie Rothman (1990; Los Angeles, CA: New Concorde Home Video, 2003), DVD.

25. Kay Sloan, "A Cinema in Search of Itself: Ideology of the Social Problem Film During the Silent Era," *Cinéaste* 14, no. 2 (1985): 34.

26. Nancy J. Rosenbloom, "Towards a Middle-Class Cinema: Thomas Ince and the Social Problem Film, 1914–1920, *Journal of the Gilded Age and Progressive Era* 8, no. 4 (October 2009): 545.

27. Nancy J. Rosenbloom, "Towards."

28. Kevin Brownlow, "Hungry Hearts: A Hollywood Social Problem Film of the 1920s," *Film History* 1, no. 2 (1987): 113–25.

29. Karen M. Bowdre, "Passing Films and Illusions of Racial Equality," *Black Camera* 5, no. 2 (Spring 2014): 21–43.

30. Michael Amedeo, "Film Series Presents Women's Perspective," *Chicago Sun Times*, January 13, 1991, 3.

31. Bev Zalcock, *Renegade Sisters: Girl Gangs on Film* (Creation Books, 2001), 182.

32. Fox, "Fully," 47.

33. Fox, 47.

34. Fox, 47.

35. Zalcock, *Renegade*, 183

36. It is worth noting that due to MPAA restrictions, full-frontal nudity and simulated sex from the waist down was prohibited in the film, leaving the remaining sex and nudity showcased akin to what is seen in most contemporary PG-13 films.

37. *The Student Nurses*.

38. *The Student Nurses*.

39. *The Student Nurses*.

40. Karissa Haugeberg interviewed by Mary Louise Kelly, *All Things Considered*, NPR, May 20, 2019, https://www.npr.org/2019/05/20/725139713/what-abortion-was-like-in-the-u-s-before-roe-v-wade.

41. *The Student Nurses*.

42. *The Student Nurses*.

43. Donald Frischman, *El Nuevo Teatro Popular en Mexico* [*The New Popular Theater in Mexico*], (Mexico City: Instituto Nacional de Bellas Artes, 1990).

44. Frischman, *El Nuevo*.

45. Stuart A. Day and S. E. Wilmer, "Performing Mexico," in Re/Writing National Theatre Histories, ed. S. E. Witmer, 153–873 (Iowa City: University of Iowa Press).

46. Jan Cohen-Cruz, *Local Acts: Community-Based Performance in the United States* (Newark: Rutgers University Press, 2005), 48.

47. *The Student Nurses*.

48. *The Student Nurses*.

49. *The Student Nurses*.

50. *The Student Nurses*.

51. *The Student Nurses*.

52. *The Student Nurses*.

53. Peary, "Stephanie Rothman," 184.

54. Rothman, Collings, February interview.

55. Zalcock, *Renegade*, 186.

56. *The Student Nurses*.

57. Text from the *Terminal Island* commercial one-sheet poster.

58. Rothman, Collings, February interview.

59. Rothman, Kozma, October interview.

60. Rothman, Kozma, February interview.

61. Rothman, Collings, February interview.
62. Rothman, Collings, February interview.
63. Rothman, Collings, February interview.
64. Rothman, Collings, February interview.
65. Rothman, Collings, February interview.
66. Rothman, Kozma, February interview.
67. "Terminal Island Premiere Charter by Dimension," *Hollywood Reporter* 102, no. 26 (April 1973), 19.
68. Rothman, Kozma, October interview.
69. Rothman, Collings, February interview.
70. *Terminal Island*, directed by Stephanie Rothman (1973; Glendale, CA: Code Red DVD, 2010), DVD.
71. *Terminal Island*.
72. Sharon Marcus, "Fighting Bodies, Fighting Words: A Theory and Politics of Rape Prevention," in *Feminists Theorize the Political*, eds. Judith Butler and Joan W. Scott (New York and London: Routledge, 1993), 385–403.
73. Hilary Neroni, *The Violent Woman: Femininity, Narrative, and Violence in Contemporary American Cinema* (New York: State University of New York Press, 2005), 11.
74. Neroni, 11.
75. Mia Mask, *Divas on Screen: Black Women in American Film* (Urbana and Chicago: University of Illinois Press, 2009), 69.
76. Mask, 69.
77. *Terminal Island*, directed by Stephanie Rothman (1973; Glendale, CA: Code Red DVD, 2010), DVD.
78. *Terminal Island*.
79. *Terminal Island*.
80. Gilles Deleuze, *Coldness and Cruelty* (New York: Zone Books, 1991).
81. Rothman has said Lee's character was inspired by the Weather Underground and their actions.
82. Pam Cook, "At the Edges of Hollywood: Stephanie Rothman," in *The Cinema Book, 3rd Edition*, ed. Pam Cook (London: British Film Institute, 2007), 471.
83. Peary, "Stephanie Rothman," 190.
84. *Terminal Island*.
85. Georges Bataille, *Erotism: Death & Sensuality*, trans. Mary Dalwood, (San Francisco, CA: City Lights Books, 1986), 61.
86. Bataille, *Erotism*, 59.
87. Bataille, 157.
88. Peary, "Stephanie Rothman," 190.

CHAPTER 7. NEW WORLDS

1. Stephanie Rothman quoted in Lizzie Francke, *Script Girls: Women Screenwriters in Hollywood*. London: BFI Publishing, 1994: 92.

2. "Stephanie Rothman Sets the Record Straight," Temple of Schlock blog, accessed November 29, 2012, http://templeofschlock.blogspot.com.au/2010/07/stephanie-rothman-sets-record-straight.html.

3. "Stephanie Rothman Sets the Record Straight."

4. "Stephanie Rothman Sets the Record Straight."

5. "Stephanie Rothman Sets the Record Straight."

6. Rothman, Kozma, February interview.

7. Rothman, Kozma, February interview.

8. Rothman, Kozma, February interview.

9. Rothman, Kozma, February interview.

10. Suzanne Bouclin, "Women in Prison Movies as Feminist Jurisprudence," *Canadian Journal of Women and the Law* 21, no. 1 (2009): 23.

11. Bouclin, "Women," 23.

12. Anne Morey, "'The Judge Called Me an Accessory,'" *Journal of Popular Film and Television* 23, no. 2 (Summer 1995): 80.

13. Suzanna Dannuta Walters, "Caged Heat: The (R)evolution of Women-in-Prison Films," in *Reel Knockouts: Violent Women in the Movies*, eds. Martha McCaughey and Neal King (Austin: University of Texas Press, 2001), 107.

14. Walters, "Caged," 106.

15. Calum Waddell, *Jack Hill: The Exploitation and Blaxploitation Master, Film by Film* (Jefferson, NC: McFarland & Company, 2009), 88.

16. "Stephanie Rothman Sets the Record Straight."

17. "Stephanie Rothman Sets the Record Straight."

18. Rothman, Kozma, February interview.

19. But one could certainly hazard a guess.

20. Carol Siegel, *Sex Radical Cinema* (Bloomington and Indianapolis: Indiana University Press, 2015), 2.

21. It's critical to note there that these freedoms—enabled in part by the birth control pill, increased numbers of women pursuing higher education, legalized abortion, and increased economic independence—were highly inequitable across class and race.

22. Siegel, *Sex*, 8.

23. Rothman, Collings February interview.

24. Throughout the years, the film has been distributed under the titles *Cemetery Girls* and *The Waking Hour*.

25. Rothman, Collings, February interview.

26. Rothman, Collings, February interview.

27. Ben Sher, "Q & A with Stephanie Rothman," *CSW Update Newsletter* (UCLA Center for the Study of Women, 2008), 13.

28. Rothman, Collings, February interview.

29. Sher, "Q & A," 13.

30. Rothman, Collings, February interview.

31. Rothman, Collings, February interview.

32. Rothman, Collings, February interview.

33. Sher, "Q & A," 12.

34. Rothman, Kozma, February interview.
35. Rothman, Kozma, February interview.
36. Fox, "Fully Female," 48.
37. Rothman, Collings, February interview.
38. Rothman, Collings, February interview.
39. Jeffery Weinstock, *The Vampire Film* (London and New York: Wallflower, 2012), 7.
40. Rothman, Collings, February interview.
41. Heather Love, *Feeling Backward* (Cambridge: Harvard University Press, 2007), 4.
42. *The Velvet Vampire*, directed by Stephanie Rothman (1971; Portland, OR: Cheezy Flicks Entertainment, 2007), DVD.
43. Kimberly J. Lau, "The Vampire, the Queer, and the Girl: Reflections on the Politics and Ethics of Immortality's Gendering," *Signs: Journal of Women in Culture and Society* 44, no. 1 (2018): 4.
44. Jeffery Jerome Cohen, "Monster Culture (Seven Theses)," in *Monster Theory: Reading Culture*, ed. Jeffery Jerome Cohen (Minneapolis: University of Minnesota Press, 1996), 3–25.
45. Weinstock, *The Vampire*, 31.
46. Pam Cook, *Screening the Past: Memory and Nostalgia in Cinema* (London and New York: Routledge, 2005), 59.
47. Agata Łuksza, "Sleeping with a Vampire," *Feminist Media Studies* 15, no. 3 (2015): 436.
48. Love, *Feeling Backward*.
49. Alexander Doty, *Making Things Perfectly Queer: Interpreting Mass Culture* (Minneapolis: University of Minnesota Press, 1993), 2.
50. Doty, *Making*, xvii.
51. Doty, 3.
52. B. Ruby Rich, *New Queer Cinema* (Durham and London: Duke University Press, 2013), 3.
53. Siobhan B. Somerville, "Queer," in *Keywords for American Cultural Studies, 2nd Edition*, edited by Bruce Burgett and Glenn Hendler (New York: New York University Press, 2014), accessed May 30, 2019, http://proxy2.1ibrary.illinois.edu/login?url=https://search.credoreference.com/content/entry/nyupacs/queer/0?institutionId=386.
54. "Stefanie Rothman Directs 4th Film for Dimension," *Box Office*, July 24, 1972. A film version of the story, directed by Peter Glenville, was released in 1966. Paul Mazursky's 1969 film *Bob & Carol & Ted & Alice* also serves as likely template for *Group Marriage*.
55. Rothman, Collings, February interview.
56. Rothman, Collings, February interview.
57. Fiona Buckland, *Impossible Dance: Club Culture and Queer World-Making* (Middletown: Wesleyan University Press, 2002), 4.
58. Buckland, *Impossible*, 5.
59. Sander's bumper stickers contain nihilistically ironic phrases that poke at the utopic idealism of the social and cultural reformative ideas of the 1960s counterculture, including: "Have a Rotten Day"; "The CIA is Full of Spies"; "Support Mental Health or I'll Kill You"; "Santa Claus is a Faggot"; "Support Your Local Police—Bribe 'Em"; "Howard Hughes is on Welfare"; and "Stop Overpopulation—Cut Down on Sex."
60. *Group Marriage*, directed by Stephanie Rothman (1972; Glendale, CA: Code Red: 2011), DVD.

61. *Group Marriage.*
62. *Group Marriage.*
63. *Group Marriage.*
64. *Group Marriage.*
65. Lauren Berlant and Michael Warner, "Sex in Public," *Critical Inquiry* 24, no. 2 (Winter 1998): 554–60.
66. *Group Marriage.*
67. Jan, Phil, and Chris are the only actors in the film shown nude on screen. Rothman manages to sneak in her only male frontal nudity of her career in this film; Phil's penis is briefly visible in his introductory scene.
68. *Group Marriage.*
69. *Group Marriage.*
70. Doty, *Making.*
71. *Group Marriage.*
72. *Group Marriage.*
73. Berlant and Warner, "Sex," 548.
74. Berlant and Warner, 549–50.
75. Berlant and Warner, 553.
76. Isaac West, Michaela Frischherz, Allison Panther, and Richard Brophy, "Queer Worldmaking in the 'It Gets Better' Campaign," *QED: A Journal in GLBTQ Worldmaking* (Fall 2013): 56–57.
77. Berlant and Warner, "Sex," 554.
78. Berlant and Warner, 558.
79. Richard Dyer, *Only Entertainment* (New York and London: Routledge, 1992), 18.
80. Berlant and Warner, 23.
81. Buckland, *Impossible*, 88.
82. *Group Marriage.*
83. *Group Marriage.*
84. Sara Ahmed, *The Promise of Happiness* (Durham and London: Duke University Press, 2010), 56.
85. Ahmed, 56.
86. *Group Marriage.*
87. Buckland, *Impossible*, 19.
88. Buckland, 6.

CHAPTER 8. MEMORIES OF UNDEREMPLOYMENT

1. Jane M. Gaines, "Film History and the Two Presents of Feminist Film Theory," *Cinema Journal* 44, no. 1 (Fall 2004): 113.
2. Stephanie Rothman, interviewed by Jane Collings for Center for Oral History Research, University of California, Los Angeles, December 11, 2001, transcript, http://oralhistory.library.ucla.edu/.
3. Stephanie Rothman, interview by Alicia Kozma, October 6, 2014, transcript.

4. Rothman, Kozma, October interview.

5. Dannis Peary, "Stephanie Rothman: R-Rated Feminist," in *Women and the Cinema*, eds. Karyn Kay and Gerald Peary (New York: E. P. Dutton, 1977), 191.

6. Victor Zarnowitz and Geoffrey H. Moore, "The Recession and Recovery of 1973–1976," *Explorations in Economic Research 4(4)*, eds. Victor Zarnowitz and Geoffrey H. Moore (National Bureau of Economic Research, October 1977), 473.

7. Zarnowitz and Moore, 473.

8. Zarnowitz and Moore, 483, 489.

9. Zarnowitz and Moore, 489.

10. Rachel A. Rosenfeld, "Women's Work Histories," *Population and Development Review* 22 (1996): 199.

11. Janet E. Kodras and Irene Padavic, "Economic Restructuring and Women's Sectoral Employment in the 1970s: A Spatial Investigation Across 380 U.S. Labor Markets," *Social Science Quarterly* 74, no. 1 (March 1993): 3.

12. Dorothy Sue Cobble, "A 'Tiger by the Toenail': The 1970s Origin of the New Working-Class Majority," *Labor: Studies in Working-Class History of the Americas* 2, no. 3 (2005): 107.

13. Dorothy Sue Cobble, "Labor Feminists and President Kennedy's Commission on Women," in *No Permanent Waves: Recasting Histories of U.S. Feminism*, ed. Nancy H. Hewitt (New Brunswick: Rutgers University Press, 2010), 145.

14. Vicki Lens, "Reading Between the Lines: Analyzing the Supreme Court's View on Gender Discrimination in Employment, 1971–1982," *Social Service Review* (March 2003): 25.

15. Lens, 27–28.

16. Dorothy Sue Cobble, "The Forgotten American Feminists," *Bulletin of the Society for the Study of Working Women*, no. 48 (August 2005): 1–16.

17. Carrie N. Baker, "The Emergence of Organized Feminist Resistance to Sexual Harassment in the United States in the 1970s," *Journal of Women's History* 19, no. 3 (2007): 161. Governmental policies and laws declaring sexual harassment to be sex discrimination, and therefore illegal, would not go into effect until the 1980s.

18. Kodras and Padavic, "Economic Restructuring," 3.

19. Kodras and Padavic, 4.

20. Maria Sironi and Frank F. Furstenberg "Trends in Economic Independence of Young Adults in the United States, 1973–2007," *Populations and Development Review* 38, no. 4 (December 2012): 610–11.

21. Kodras and Padavic, "Economic Restructuring," 2.

22. *The Working Girls*, directed by Stephanie Rothman (1974; Unknown: Obsession Entertainment, 2002), DVD.

23. *The Working Girls*.

24. Kathi Weeks, *The Problem with Work: Feminism, Marxism, Antiwork Politics, and Postwork Imaginaries* (Durham and London: Duke University Press, 2011), 2.

25. *The Working Girls*, directed by Stephanie Rothman (1974; Unknown: Obsession Entertainment, 2002), DVD.

26. *The Working Girls*.

27. *The Working Girls*.

28. *The Working Girls*.

29. Weeks, *The Problem with Work*, 4.

30. There is an interesting comparison to be made between Vernon and the character of Eric Packer in David Cronenberg's *Cosmopolis* (2012), another multimillionaire who rides around the back of a limousine all day, manipulating the world outside without engaging in it, and who seems to be the living embodiment of capitalism.

31. *The Working Girls*.

32. Stephanie Rothman, interview by Alicia Kozma, February 4, 2014, transcript.

33. Weeks, *The Problem with Work*, 7.

34. Rothman, Kozma February interview.

35. Nancy Tartaglione and Nellie Andreeva, "Amazon Orders 5 Original Series Including 'Man In the High Castle,' 'Mad Dogs,'" *Deadline*, February 18, 2015, https://deadline.com/2015/02/amazon-orders-original-series-man-in-the-high-castle-mad-dogs-video-1201375797/.

36. Stephanie Rothman, email to author, December 27, 2020.

37. Stacy L. Smith, Marc Choueiti, Kevin Yao, Hannah Clark, and Katherine Pieper, "Inclusion in the Director's Chair: Analysis of Director Gender & Race/Ethnicity Across 1,300 Top Films from 2007 to 2019," Annenberg Inclusion Initiative, January 2020, http://assets.uscannenberg.org/docs/aii-inclusion-directors-chair-20200102.pdf

38. Smith, Choueiti, Yao, Clark, and Pieper.

39. Examples include Greta Gerwig, Nancy Meyers, Sam Taylor-Johnson, Angelina Jolie, Lana and Lily Wachowski, Marielle Heller, and Catherine Hardwicke. Of the fifty-seven women, only eleven are women of color. See Stacy et al., "Inclusion in the Director's Chair."

40. Smith et al., "Inclusion in the Director's Chair."

41. Kelly Hankin, "And Introducing . . . The Female Director: Documentaries About Women Filmmakers as Feminist Activism," *NWSA Journal* 19, no. 1 (Spring 2007): 59–88.

42. J. Pyros, "Women on Women in Films," *Take One* 3, no. 2 (November–December 1970): 12.

43. Shit People Say to Women Directors & Other Women in Film, accessed March 20, 2016, http://shitpeoplesaytowomendirectors.tumblr.com/.

44. Pyros, "Women on Women," 11.

45. Shit People Say.

46. Mike Fleming Jr., "Colin Trevorrow to Helm 'Jurassic Park 4' for Universal and Steven Spielberg," Deadline.com, March 14, 2013, https://deadline.com/2013/03/colin-trevorrow-to-helm-jurassic-park-4-for-universal-and-steven-spielberg-453829/.

47. Brooks Barnes, "'Jurassic World' Puts Colin Trevorrow in the Driver's Seat," *New York Times*, June 3, 2015, https://www.nytimes.com/2015/06/07/movies/in-the-shadows-of-a-giant-and-dinosaurs.html

48. Safety Not Guaranteed (2012), the-numbers.com, accessed December 29, 2020, December 29. https://www.the-numbers.com/movie/Safety-Not-Guaranteed#tab=summary.

49. Fleming Jr., "Colin Trevorrow."

50. Bryan Bishop, "How the director of 'Jurassic World' jumped from Sundance to Steven Spielberg," *The Verge*, June 12, 2015, https://www.theverge.com/2015/6/12/8741981/jurassic-world-director-colin-trevorrow-interview.

51. Jesse David Fox, "*Safety Not Guaranteed* Duo Working on *Flight of the Navigator* Remake," *Vulture*, November 28, 2012, https://www.vulture.com/2012/11/flight-of-the-navigator-remake-gets-new-writers.html,

52. Jeff Sneider, "Connolly: College partnership leans to 'Guaranteed' success," *Variety*, November 29, 2012, https://variety.com/2012/film/news/connolly-college-partnership-leads-to-guaranteed-success-1118062700/.

53. Peter Sciretta, "How Brad Bird Almost Helming 'Star Wars' Resulted in Colin Trevorrow Directing 'Jurassic World,'" *Slashfilm*, April 28, 2015, https://www.slashfilm.com/jurassic-world-star-wars/.

54. Sciretta, "How Brad Bird."

55. Barnes, "'Jurassic World.'" That confidence, or what many have called a difficult ego, would eventually get Trevorrow fired from directing *Star Wars: Episode IX—The Rise of Skywalker* (J. J. Abrams, 2019). See Chris Lee, "Colin Trevorrow's Firing from *Star Wars* Is Another Reminder That No Director Will Ever Be Bigger Than the Franchise," *Vulture*, September 8, 2017, https://www.vulture.com/2017/09/star-wars-episode-8-colin-trevorrow-firing-explanation.html.

56. Barnes, "'Jurassic World.'"

57. Barnes, "'Jurassic World.'"

58. Trevorrow is, of course, not the only make director who has benefited in these ways. Others include Josh Trank, Gareth Edwards, Marc Webb, and Joe and Anthony Russo. Directors Carl Rinsch and Rupert Sanders had directed only commercials, never film, before being handed their tentpole films *47 Ronin* (2013, $175 million budget) and *Snow White and the Huntsman* (2012, $170 million budget), respectively.

59. National Film and Television School, "'Jurassic World' Director Reveals his Journey from Indie Features to Blockbuster Franchises," NFTS Blog, accessed December 29, 2020, https://nfts.co.uk/blog/%E2%80%98jurassic-world%E2%80%99-director-reveals-his-journey-indie-features-blockbuster-franchises.

60. @AutisticWeirdo, Twitter, August 21, 2015.

61. @colintrevorrow, Twitter, August 21, 2015.

62. "An Open Letter to Colin Trevorrow," Women and Hollywood, August 25, 2015, https://womenandhollywood.com/an-open-letter-to-colin-trevorrow-c58236e82797/.

63. Josh Rottenberg, "Studios Gamble on Untested Directors for Big Movies with Mixed Results," *Los Angeles Times* August 19, 2015, https://www.latimes.com/entertainment/movies/la-et-first-time-tentpole-directors-20150818-htmlstory.html.

64. Kate Eichhorn, *The Archival Turn in Feminism: Outrage in Order* (Philadelphia: Temple University Press, 2013), 4.

65. For a full accounting of this resurgence, see my chapter, "The Rothman Renaissance," in *Women and New Hollywood*, eds. Aaron Hunter and Martha Shearer (Rutgers University Press, 2023).

BIBLIOGRAPHY

Ahmed, Sara. *The Cultural Politics of Emotion.* New York and London: Routledge, 2004.

Albright, Brian. *Wild Beyond Belief!* Jefferson, NC: McFarland & Company, 2008.

Altman, Rick. *Silent Film Sound.* New York: Columbia University Press, 2004.

Amedeo, Michael. "Film Series Presents Women's Perspective." *Chicago Sun Times*, January 13, 1999: 3.

American Academy of Arts and Sciences Humanities Indicators. "Research and Development Expenditures at Colleges and Universities." Accessed July 11, 2020. https://www.amacad.org/humanities-indicators/funding-and-research/research-and-development-expenditures-colleges-and.

Andersen, Pablo Dominguez. "The Hollywood Beach Party Genre and the Exotification of Youthful White Masculinity in Early 1960s America." *Men and Masculinities* 15, no. 5 (2014): 511–35.

Andrew, Dudley. "Hermeneutics and Cinema: The Issue of History." In *The Cinematic Text: Methods and Approaches*, edited by R. Barton Palmer, 175–94. New York: AMS Press, 1989.

The Animals. *We Gotta Get Out of This Place.* By Barry Mann and Cynthia Weil. Recorded June 15, 1965. Single Side A. Columbia Gramophone-MGM, vinyl.

Aronowitz, Nona Willis. "The First Time Women Shouted Their Abortions." *New York Times*, March 23, 2019. https://www.nytimes.com/2019/03/23/opinion/sunday/abortion-speakout-anniversary.html.

Baker, Carrie N. "The Emergence of Organized Feminist Resistance to Sexual Harassment in the United States in the 1970s." *Journal of Women's History* 19, no. 3 (2007): 161–84.

Balio, Tino. *The Foreign Film Renaissance on American Screens, 1946–1973.* Madison: University of Wisconsin Press, 2010.

Banks, Miranda J. "Oral History and the Media Industries." *Cultural Studies* 28, no. 4 (2014): 545–60.

Barnes, Brooks. "'Jurassic World' Puts Colin Trevorrow in the Driver's Seat." *New York Times*, June 3, 2015. https://www.nytimes.com/2015/06/07/movies/in-the-shadows-of-a-giant-and-dinosaurs.html.

Bataille, Georges. *Erotism: Death & Sensuality.* Translated by Mary Dalwood. San Francisco: City Lights Books, 1986.

Beauchamp, Cari. "Forward: Finding Frances Marion." In *When Women Wrote Hollywood*, edited by Rosanne Welch, 1–4. Jefferson, NC: McFarland & Company, 2018.

Berlant, Lauren, and Michael Warner. "Sex in Public." *Critical Inquiry* 24, no. 2 (Winter 1998): 547–66.

Bishop, Bryan. "How the Director of Jurassic World Jumped from Sundance to Steven Spielberg." *The Verge*, June 12, 2015. https://www.theverge.com/2015/6/12/8741981/jurassic-world-director-colin-trevorrow-interview.

Bordwell, David, Janet Staiger, and Kristin Thompson. *The Classical Hollywood Cinema: Film Style & Mode of Production to 1960, 3rd Edition*. New York: Columbia University Press, 1998.

Bort, Ryan. "Battle of the Sexes: A Guide to the Legendary Tennis Match between Billie Jean King and Bobby Riggs." *Newsweek*, September 22, 2017. https://www.newsweek.com/battle-sexes-guide-billie-jean-king-bobby-riggs-669300.

Bouclin, Suzanne. "Women in Prison Movies as Feminist Jurisprudence." *Canadian Journal of Women and the Law* 21, no. 1 (2009): 19–34.

Bourdieu, Pierre. *Distinction: A Social Critique of the Judgment of Taste*. Translated by Richard Nice. Cambridge: Harvard University Press, 1984.

Bowdre, Karen M. "Passing Films and Illusions of Racial Equality." *Black Camera* 5, no. 2 (Spring 2014): 21–43.

Boyle, Barbara D. "Independent Distribution: New World Pictures." In *The Movie Business Book*, edited by Jason E. Squire, 285–92. New Jersey: Prentice-Hall: 1983.

Brickman, Barbara Jane. "Riot Girls in Town: Remaking, Revising, and Redressing the Teenpic." *Journal of Film and Video* 59, no. 4 (Winter 2007): 20–26.

Buckland, Fiona. *Impossible Dance: Club Culture and Queer World-Making*. Middletown: Wesleyan University Press, 2002.

Burton, Antoinette. "Forward: 'Small Stories' and the Promise of New Narratives." In *Contesting Archives: Finding Women in the Sources*, edited by Nupur Chaudhuri, Sherry J. Katz, and Mary Elizabeth Perry, i–x. Urbana: University of Illinois Press, 2010.

Butler, Alison. *Women's Cinema: The Contested Screen*. London and New York: Wallflower, 2002.

Caldwell, John T. "Para-Industry, Shadow Academy." *Cultural Studies* 28, no. 4 (2014): 720–40. https://doi.org/10.1080/09502386.2014.888922.

Callahan, Vicki. "Reclaiming the Archive: Archaeological Explorations toward a Feminism 3.0." In *Reclaiming the Archive: Feminism and Film History*, edited by Vicki Callahan, 1–8. Detroit: Wayne State University Press, 2010.

Camera Obscura Collective (Janet Bergstrom, Sandy Flitterman, Elisabeth Hary Lyon, Constance Penly). "Feminist and Film: Critical Approaches." In *The Feminist and Visual Culture Reader, 2nd Edition*, edited by Amelia Jones, 268–73. London and New York: Routledge, 2003.

Clark, Randell. *At a Theater or Drive-In Near You: The History, Culture, and Politics of the American Exploitation Film*. New York: Garland Publishing, 1995.

Cobble, Dorothy Sue. "The Forgotten American Feminists." *Bulletin of the Society for the Study of Working Women*, no. 48 (August 2005): 1–16.

Cobble, Dorothy Sue. "Labor Feminists and President Kennedy's Commission on Women." In *No Permanent Waves: Recasting Histories of U.S. Feminism*, edited by Nancy H. Hewitt, 144–67. New Brunswick: Rutgers University Press, 2010).

Cobble, Dorothy Sue. "A 'Tiger by the Toenail': The 1970s Origin of the New Working-Class Majority. *Labor: Studies in Working-Class History of the Americas* 2, no. 3 (2005): 103–14.

Cohen, Emily. "The Orphanista Manifesto: Orphan Films and the Politics of Reproduction." *American Anthropologist* 106, no. 4 (December 2004): 719–31.

Cohen, Jeffery Jerome. "Monster Culture (Seven Theses)." In *Monster Theory: Reading Culture*, edited by Jeffery Jerome Cohen, 3–25. Minneapolis: University of Minnesota Press, 1996.

Cohen-Cruz, Jan. *Local Acts: Community-Based Performance in the United States*. Newark: Rutgers University Press, 2005.

Cook, David A. *Lost Illusions: American Cinema in the Shadow of Watergate and Vietnam, 1970–1979*. Berkeley: University of California Press, 2000.

Cook, Pam. "At the Edges of Hollywood: Stephanie Rothman." In *The Cinema Book, 3rd Edition*, edited by Pam Cook, 470–71. London: BFI, 2007.

Cook, Pam. "'Exploitation' Films and Feminism." *Screen* 17, no. 2 (Summer 1976): 122–27.

Corman, Roger, and Jim Jerome. *How I Made a Hundred Movies in Hollywood and Never Lost a Dime*. New York: Random House, 1990.

Criterion Collection. "Our Mission." Accessed July 25, 2020. https://www.criterion.com/about.

Cvetkovich, Ann. *An Archive of Feelings*. Durham and London: Duke University Press, 2003.

Day, Stuart A., and S. E. Wilmer. "Performing Mexico." In *Re/Writing National Theatre Histories*, edited by S. E. Witmer, 153–73. Iowa City: University of Iowa Press, 2004.

Derrida, Jacques. *Archive Fever: A Freudian Impression*. Translated by Eric Prenowitz. Chicago and London: University of Chicago Press, 1995.

Deleuze, Gilles. *Coldness and Cruelty*. New York: Zone Books, 1991.

"Diskussion im Anschlub an den Virtrag von Stephanie Rothman/Post-Film Discussion." Girls, Gangs, and Guns Festival, Germany, November 28, 1999.

Dixon, Wheeler Winston. *Film Talk: Directors at Work*. Rutgers, NJ: Rutgers University Press, 2007.

Dixon, Winston Wheeler. *Visions of Paradise: Images of Eden in the Cinema*. New Brunswick, NJ: Rutgers University Press, 2006.

Doane, Mary Ann, Patricia Mellencamp, and Linda Williams. "Feminist Film Criticism: An Introduction." In *Re-Vision: Essays in Feminist Film Criticism*, edited by Mary Ann Doane, Patricia Mellencamp, and Linda Williams, 1–17. California: American Film Institute, 1984.

Doherty, Thomas. *Teenagers and Teenpics: The Juvenilization of American Movies in the 1950s*. Philadelphia: Temple University Press, 2002.

Doty, Alexander. *Making Things Perfectly Queer: Interpreting Mass Culture*. Minneapolis: University of Minnesota Press, 1993.

Duet production book. The Hugh M. Heffner Moving Image Archive. University of Southern California: 1963.

Dunn, Stephane. *"Bad Bitches" and Sassy Supermamas: Black Power Action Films*. Urbana: University of Illinois Press, 2008.

Dyer, Richard. *Only Entertainment*. New York and London: Routledge, 1992.

Eichhorn, Kate. *The Archival Turn in Feminism: Outrage in Order*. Philadelphia: Temple University Press, 2013.

Elsaesser, Thomas. "The New Film History as Media Archaeology." *Cinémas: revue d'études cinématographiques / Cinémas: Journal of Film Studies* 14, nos. 2–3 (2004): 75–117.

Enticknap, Leo. *Moving Image Technology: From Zoetrope to Digital*. London & New York: Wallflower Press, 2005.

Ernst, Wolfgang. "Media Archaeology: Method and Machine versus History and Narrative of Media." In *Media Archaeology: Approached, Applications, and Implications*, edited by Erikki Huhtamo and Jussi Parikka, 239–55. Berkeley and Los Angeles: University of California Press, 2011.

Firestone, Shulamith. *The Dialectic of Sex*. New York: Bantam Books, 1970.

Fisher, Dennis. *Horror Film Directors, 1931–1990*. Jefferson, NC: McFarland & Company, 1991.

Fisher, Lucy. *Shot/Countershot: Film Tradition and Women's Cinema*. Princeton: Princeton University Press, 2014.

Fleming, Mike, Jr. "Colin Trevorrow to Helm 'Jurassic Park 4' for Universal and Steven Spielberg." *Deadline*, March 14, 2013. https://deadline.com/2013/03/colin-trevorrow-to-helm-jurassic-park-4-for-universal-and-steven-spielberg-453829/.

Fox, Jesse David. "*Safety Not Guaranteed* Duo Working on *Flight of the Navigator* Remake." *Vulture*, November 28, 2012. https://www.vulture.com/2012/11/flight-of-the-navigator-remake-gets-new-writers.html.

Francke, Lizzie. *Script Girls: Women Screenwriters in Hollywood*. London: BFI Publishing, 1994.

Friedan, Betty. *The Feminist Mystique*. New York: W. W. Norton & Company, 1963.

Frick, Caroline. "Beyond Hollywood: Enhancing Heritage with the 'Orphan' Film." *International Journal of Heritage Studies* 14, no. 4 (July 2008): 319–31.

Frischman, Donald. *El Nuevo Teatro Popular en Mexico [The New Popular Theater in Mexico]*. Mexico City: Instituto Nacional de Bellas Artes, 1990.

Foreman, Alexa L. *Women in Motion*. Bowling Green, OH: Bowling Green University Popular Press, 1983.

Fossati, Giovanna. *The Archival Life of Film in Transition*. Amsterdam: Amsterdam University Press, 2009.

Foucault, Michel. *Discipline and Punish: The Birth of the Prison*. Translated by Alan Sheridan. New York: Vintage Book, 1977.

Fox, Terry Curtis. "Fully Female." *Film Comment* 12, no. 6 (November–December 1976): 46–50.

Gaines, Jane M. "Film History and the Two Presents of Feminist Film Theory." *Cinema Journal* 44, no. 1 (Fall 2004): 113–19.

Gaines, Jane M. *Pink-Slipped: What Happened to Women in the Silent Film Industry?* Urbana: University of Illinois Press, 2018.

Gallo, Marcia M. "Radicalesbians Issues 'The Woman Identified Woman' Manifesto." *Salem Press Encyclopedia*, 2020. http://search.ebscohost.com.washcoll.idm.oclc.org/login.aspx?direct=true&db=ers&AN=96775960&site=eds-live.

Giardina, Carolyn. "Led USC Showbiz Tech Unit." *Hollywood Reporter*, no. 398, February 14, 2007: 42, 45.

Gledhill, Christine. "Afterthoughts: Development in Feminist Film Criticism." In *Re-Vision: Essays in Feminist Film Criticism*, edited by Mary Ann Doane, Patricia Mellencamp, and Linda Williams, 18–48. California: American Film Institute, 1984.

Gledhill, Christine, and Julia Knight. "Introduction." In *Doing Women's Film History: Reframing Cinemas, Past and Future*, edited by Christine Gledhill and Julia Knight, 1–12. Urbana: University of Illinois Press, 2015.

Goldsmith, Leo. "Adventures in Preservation: A Report from the 7th Orphan Film Symposium." *Moving Image Source*, July 10, 2010. http://www.movingimagesource.us/articles/adventures-in-preservation-20100610.

Gorfinkel, Elena. "'Dated Sexuality': Anna Biller's *Viva* and the Retrospective Life of Sexploitation Cinema." *Camera Obscura* 78, no. 26:3 (2011): 95–135.

Gorfinkel, Elena. "Wet Dreams: Erotic Film Festivals of the Early 1970s and the Utopian Sexual Public Sphere." *Framework: The Journal of Cinema and Media* 47, no. 2 (Fall 2006): 59–86.

Gorfinkel, Elena. *Lewd Looks: American Sexploitation Cinema in the 1960s*. Minneapolis: University of Minnesota Press, 2017.

Gorfinkel, Elena. "Tales of Times Square: Sexploitation's Secret History of Place." In *Taking Place: Location and the Moving Image*, edited by John David Rhodes and Elena Gorfinkel, 55–76. Minneapolis and London: University of Minnesota Press, 2011.

Gross, Linda. "A Woman's Place Is In. . . . Exploitation Films?: A Trendsetter in the Youth Market." *Los Angeles Times*, February 12, 1978: 35.

Hankin, Kelly. "And Introducing . . . The Female Director: Documentaries About Women Filmmakers as Feminist Activism." *NWSA Journal* 19, no. 1 (Spring 2007): 59–88.

Haugeberg, Karissa. *All Things Considered*. By Mary Louise Kelly. NPR, May 20, 2019. https://www.npr.org/2019/05/20/725139713/what-abortion-was-like-in-the-u-s-before-roe-v-wade.

Hartley, Mark, dir. *Machete Maidens Unleashed!* 2010. Australia: Dark Sky Films. DVD.

Hebdige, Dick. "Towards a Cartography of Taste, 1935–1962." In *Popular Culture: Past and Present*, edited by Bernard Waites, Tony Bennett and Graham Martin, 194–219. London: Croom Helm, 1982.

Hill, Erin. *Never Done: A History of Women's Work in Media Production*. New Brunswick, NJ: Rutgers University Press, 2016.

Houston, Marsha. "The Politics of Difference: Race, Class, and Women's Communications." In *Women Make Meaning: New Feminist Directions in Communication*, edited by Lana F. Rakow, 45–59. London: Routledge: 1992.

Jenkins, Henry. "Exploiting Feminism: An Interview with Stephanie Rothman (Part One)." *Confessions of an Aca-Fan: The Official Weblog of Henry Jenkins*. Accessed November 29, 2012. http://henryjenkins.org/2007/10/stephanie_rothman.html.

Johnson, Randal. "Introduction." In *The Field of Cultural Production: Essays on Art and Literature*. By Pierre Bourdieu. Translated and edited by Randal Johnson. New York: Columbia University Press, 1993: 1–28.

Johnston, Claire. "Women's Cinema as Counter-Cinema (UK, 1973)." In *Film Manifestos and Global Cinema Cultures*, edited by Scott MacKenzie, 347–55. Berkeley: University of California Press, 2014.

Juhasz, Alexandra. "The Future Was Then: Reinvesting in Feminist Media Practice and Politics." *Camera Obscura* 61, no. 21:1 (2006): 52–57.

Kantrowitz, Barbara. "It's Ms. America to You." *Newsweek* 159, no. 121 (November 19, 2007): 58.

Kendrick, James. "What is the Criterion? The Criterion Collection as an Archive of Film as Culture." *Journal of Film and Video* 53, no. 2–3 (Summer–Fall 2001): 124–39.

Kodras, Janet E., and Irene Padavic. "Economic Restructuring and Women's Sectoral Employment in the 1970s: A Spatial Investigation Across 380 U.S. Labor Markets." *Social Science Quarterly* 74, no. 1 (March 1993): 1–27.

Konow, David. "The First Dimension." *Fangoria*, no. 273 (May 2008): 70–81.
Kuhn, Annette. "The State of Film and Media Feminism." *Signs* 30, no. 1 (Autumn 2004): 1221–28.
Kuhn, Annette. "Women's Pictures." In *Schirmer Encyclopedia of Film*, edited by Barry Keith Grant, 367–73. New York: Schirmer Reference, 2007.
Lang, Brent. "Female Directors Behind Record Number of Films in 2019 (Study)." *Variety*, January 2, 2020. https://variety.com/2020/film/news/female-directors-record-films-little-women-hustlers-the-farewell-1203454878/.
Lau, Kimberly J. "The Vampire, the Queer, and the Girl: Reflections on the Politics and Ethics of Immortality's Gendering." *Signs: Journal of Women in Culture and Society* 44, no. 1 (2018): 3–24.
Lauzen, Martha. "The Celluloid Ceiling: Behind-the-Scenes Employment of Women in the Top 100, 250, and 500 films of 2019." Center for the Study of Women in Television and Film San Diego University, 2020. https://womenintvfilm.sdsu.edu/wpcontent/uploads/2020/01/2019_Celluloid_Ceiling_Report.pdf.
Lens, Vicki. "Reading Between the Lines: Analyzing the Supreme Court's View on Gender Discrimination in Employment, 1971–1982." *Social Service Review* (March 2003): 25–50.
Lichtenstein, Grace. "Feminists Demand 'Liberation' In *Ladies' Home Journal* Sit-In." *New York Times*, March 19, 1970: 51.
Lowry, Ed. "Dimension Pictures: Portrait of a '70s Independent." *Velvet Light Trap*, no. 22 (1986): 65–74.
Love, Heather. *Feeling Backward*. Cambridge: Harvard University Press, 2007.
Łuksza, Agata. "Sleeping with a Vampire," *Feminist Media Studies* 15, no. 3 (2015): 429–43.
Lucas, Tim. "The Trouble with Titan: Francis Ford Coppola's Lost Thriller, Part 1." *Video Watchdog*, no. 4 (March/April 1991): 46–56.
Lucas, Tim. "The Trouble with Titan: Francis Ford Coppola's List Thriller and How Roger Corman Turned It into 5 Movies! Part 2." *Video Watchdog*, no. 5 (May–June 1991): 22–31.
Lucas, Tim. "The Trouble with Titan: Francis Ford Coppola's List Thriller and How Roger Corman Turned it Into 5 Movies! Part 3." *Video Watchdog* 7 (September–October 1991): 18–31.
Maltby, Richard. "New Cinema Histories." In *Explorations in New Cinema History: Approaches and Case Studies*, edited by Richard Maltby, Daniel Biltereyst, and Philippe Meers, 3–39). Oxford, UK, and Malden, MA: Wiley-Blackwell, 2011.
Manoff, Marlene. "Theories of the Archive from Across Disciplines." *Libraries and the Academy* 4, no. 1 (January 2004): 9–25.
Marcus, Sharon. "Fighting Bodies, Fighting Words: A Theory and Politics of Rape Prevention." In *Feminists Theorize the Political*, edited by Judith Butler and Joan W. Scott, 385–403. New York and London: Routledge, 1993.
Martin, Angela. "Refocusing Authorship in Women's Filmmaking." In *Auteurs and Authorship*, edited by Barry Keith Grant, 127–33. Malden, MA: Blackwell Publishing, 2008.
Mask, Mia. *Divas on Screen: Black Women in American Film*. Urbana and Chicago: University of Illinois Press, 2009.
Mathijs, Ernest, and Jamie Sexton. *Cult Cinema: An Introduction*. London, Blackwell Publishing, 2011.

Mayer, Vicki. "Bringing the Social Back In: Studies of Production Cultures and Social Theory." In *Production Studies: Cultural Studies of Media Industries*, edited by Vicki Mayer, Miranda J. Banks, and Jon Thornton Caldwell, 15–24. Routledge: New York and London: 2009.

Mayne, Judith. *The Woman at the Keyhole*. Bloomington and Indianapolis: Indiana University Press, 1990.

McDonagh, Maitland. "The Exploitation Generation or: How Marginal Movies Came in from the Cold." In *The Last Great American Picture Show: New Hollywood Cinema in the 1970s*, edited by Thomas Elsaesser, Alexander Horwath, and Noel King, 107–30. Amsterdam: Amsterdam University Press, 2004.

McGee, Mark Thomas. *Faster and Furiouser: The Revised and Fattened Fable of American International Pictures*. Jefferson, NC: McFarland Publishers. 1996.

McKenna, Denise. Labor, *Feminist Media Histories* 4, no. 1 (Winter 2018): 1–10. https://doi.org/10.1525/fmh.2018.4.1.1.

Merewether, Charles. "Introduction: Art and the Archive." In *The Archive: Documents in Contemporary Art*, edited by Charles Merewether, 10–17. London and Boston: Whitechapel Gallery and MIT Press: 2006.

Miller, Stephen Paul. *The Seventies Now: Culture as Surveillance*. Durham, NC: Duke University Press, 1999.

Modleski, Tania. "Women's Cinema as Counterphobic Cinema: Doris Wishman as the Last Auteur." In *Sleaze Artists: Cinema at the Margins of Taste, Style, and Politics*, edited by Jeffrey Sconce, 47–70. Durham: Duke University Press, 2007.

Monaco, Paul. *The Sixties, 1960–1969*. Berkeley: University of California Press, 2001.

Morey, Anne. "'The judge called me an accessory.'" *Journal of Popular Film and Television* 23, no. 2 (Summer 1995): 80–87. https://doi.org/10.1080/01956051.1995.9943692.

Morris, Gary. "Beyond the Beach." *Journal of Popular Film & Television* vol. 21, no.1 (Spring 1993): 2–11.

Morris, Gary. "Roger Corman on New World Pictures: An Interview from 1974." *Bright Lights Film Journal*, January 27, 2000. www.brightlightsfilm.com/27/cormaninterview1.html.

Muñoz, José Esteban. *Disidentifications*. Minneapolis: University of Minnesota Press, 1999.

National Film and Television School. "'Jurassic World' Director Reveals his Journey from Indie Features to Blockbuster Franchises." NFTS Blog, December 29, 2020. https://nfts.co.uk/blog/%E2%80%98jurassic-world%E2%80%99-director-reveals-his-journey-indie-features-blockbuster-franchises.

Nelson, Stanley, dir. *Black Panthers: Vanguard of the Revolution*. 2015. New York, NY: Firelight Films, 2015: streaming.

Neroni, Hilary. *The Violent Woman: Femininity, Narrative, and Violence in Contemporary American Cinema*. Albany: State University of New York Press, 2005.

Nichols, Bill. "Film Theory and the Revolt Against Master Narratives." In *Reinventing Film Studies*, edited by Christine Gledhill and Linda Williams, 34–52. London: Hodder Arnold, 2000.

Noble, Safiya Umoja. *Algorithms of Oppression*. New York: New York University Press, 2018.

Ornstein, Bill. "Dimension Increase in Film Production Set for Next Year." *Hollywood Reporter*, August 28, 1972.

Peary, Dannis. "Stephanie Rothman: R-Rated Feminist." In *Women and the Cinema*, edited by Karyn Kay and Gerald Peary, 179–92. New York: E. P. Dutton, 1977.

Powell, Ann "Blood on the Borders—*Near Dark* and *Blue Steel*." Screen 35, no. 2 (Summer 1994): 136–53. https://doi.org/10.1093/screen/35.2.136.

Prelinger Archives. "About." Accessed September 30, 2015. https://archive.org/details/prelinger&tab=about.

Pyros, J. "Women on Women in Films." *Take One* 3, no. 2 (November–December 1970): 10–15.

Rahkonen, Keijo. "Bourdieu and Nietzsche: Taste of Struggle." In *The Legacy of Pierre Bourdieu: Critical Essays*, edited by Simon Susen and Bryan S. Turner, 125–44. London: Anthem Press, 2011.

Rakow, Lana F. "Feminist Approaches to Popular Culture: Giving Patriarchy its Due." In *Cultural Theory and Popular Culture, 2nd Edition*, edited by John Storey, 275–91. England: Prentice Hall, 1998.

Ray, Fred Olen. *The New Poverty Row: Independent Filmmakers as Distributors*. North Carolina: MacFarland & Company, 1991.

Rhodes, Jacqueline. *Radical Feminism, Writing, and Critical Agency: From Manifesto to Modem*. Albany: State University of New York Press, 2005.

Rich, Allen. "Joint Exchanges to Solve Distribution Woes." *Hollywood Reporter*, December 1, 1972.

Rich, B. Ruby. *New Queer Cinema*. Durham and London: Duke University Press, 2013.

Rich, Jennifer. *An Introduction to Modern Feminist Thought*. Penrith Philosophy Insights: Humanities E-Book, 2007. http://search.ebscohost.com.washcoll.idm.oclc.org/login.aspx?direct=true&db=nlebk&AN=373396&site=eds-live.

Ricoeur, Paul. "Archives, Documents, Traces." In *The Archive: Documents in Contemporary Art*, edited by Charles Merewether, 66–69. London and Boston: Whitechapel Gallery and MIT Press, 2006.

Robb, Alice. "Women Speak Out about Pulling Off the 'Radical Act' of Filmmaking in the Male-Dominated Movie Business." *New York Times*, April 22, 2015. http://nytlive.nytimes.com/womenintheworld/2015/04/22/women-speak-out-about-pulling-off-the-radical-act-of-filmmaking-in-the-male-dominated-movie-business/.

Rosenbloom, Nancy J. "Towards a Middle-Class Cinema: Thomas Ince and the Social Problem Film, 1914–1920. *Journal of the Gilded Age and Progressive Era* 8, no. 4 (October 2009): 545–72.

Rosenfeld, Rachel A. "Women's Work Histories," *Population and Development Review* 22 (1996): 199–222.

Rothman, Stephanie. Interview by Jane Collings. Center for Oral History Research, University of California, Los Angeles, December 11, 2001. Transcript, http://oralhistory.library.ucla.edu/.

Rothman, Stephanie. Interview by Alicia Kozma. Transcript. February 4, 2014.

Rothman, Stephanie. Interview by Alicia Kozma. Transcript. October 6, 2014.

Rothman, Stephanie, dir. *Group Marriage*. 1972. Glendale, CA: Code Red, 2011. DVD.

Rothman, Stephanie, dir. *It's a Bikini World*. 1967. Southfield, MI: N/A. DVD.

Rothman, Stephanie, dir. *The Student Nurses*. 1970. Los Angeles, CA: New Concorde Home Video, 2003. DVD.

Rothman, Stephanie, dir. *Terminal Island*. 1973. Glendale, CA: Code Red, 2010. DVD.

Rothman, Stephanie, dir. *The Velvet Vampire*. 1971. Portland, OR: Cheezy Flicks Entertainment, 2007. DVD.

Rothman, Stephanie, dir. *The Working Girls*. 1974. Unknown: Obsession Entertainment, 2002. DVD.

Rottenberg, Josh. "Studios Gamble on Untested Directors for Big Movies with Mixed Results." *Los Angeles Times*, August 19, 2015. https://www.latimes.com/entertainment/movies/la-et-first-time-tentpole-directors-20150818-htmlstory.html.

Rutsky, R. L. "Surfing the Other: Ideology on the Beach." *Film Quarterly*, vol. 52, no. 4 (Summer 1999): 12–23.

Safety Not Guaranteed (2012). the-numbers.com. Accessed December 29, 2020. https://www.the-numbers.com/movie/Safety-Not-Guaranteed#tab=summary.

Schaefer, Eric. *Bold! Daring! Shocking! True! A History of Exploitation Films, 1919–1959*. Durham, NC: Duke University Press, 1999.

Schaefer, Eric. "Dirty Little Secrets: Scholars, Archivists, and Dirty Movies." *Moving Image: The Journal of the Association of Moving Image Archivists* 5, no. 2 (Fall 2005): 79–105.

Schaefer, Eric. "Exploitation Films: Teaching Sin in the Suburbs." *Cinema Journal* 47, no. 1 (Fall 2007): 94–97.

Schaefer, Eric. "Of Hygiene and Hollywood: Origins of Exploitation Film." *Velvet Light Trap*, no. 30 (Fall 1992): 34–47.

Schatz, Thomas. "The New Hollywood." In *Film Theory Goes to the Movies*, edited by Jim Collins, Hilary Radner, and Ava Preacher Collins, 8–36. New York and London: Routledge, 1992.

Science and Technology Council of the Academy of Motion Picture Arts and Sciences. *The Digital Dilemma: Strategic Issues in Archiving and Accessing Digital Motion Picture Materials*. Beverly Hills, CA: Academy of Motion Picture Arts and Sciences, 2007. http://www.oscars.org/science-technology/sci-tech-projects/digital-dilemma.

Sciretta, Peter. "How Brad Bird Almost Helming 'Star Wars' Resulted in Colin Trevorrow Directing 'Jurassic World.'" *Slashfilm*, April 28, 2015. https://www.slashfilm.com/jurassic-world-star-wars/.

Seagrave, Kerry. *Drive-In Theaters: A History from Their Inception in 1933*. Jefferson, NC: McFarland & Company, 1992.

Sher, Ben. "Q & A with Stephanie Rothman." *CSW Update Newsletter*, UCLA Center for the Study of Women, 2008: 11–14.

"Shit People Say to Women Directors & Other Women in Film." Accessed March 20, 2016. http://shitpeoplesaytowomendirectors.tumblr.com/.

Siegel, Carol. *Sex Radical Cinema*. Bloomington and Indianapolis: Indiana University Press, 2015.

Silverman, Kaja. "The Female Authorial Voice." In *Film and Authorship*, edited by Virginia Wright Wexman, 50–75. New Brunswick: Rutgers University Press, 2003.

Sneider, Jeff. "Connolly: College Partnership Leans to 'Guaranteed' Success." *Variety*, November 29, 2012, https://variety.com/2012/film/news/connolly-college-partnership-leads-to-guaranteed-success-1118062700/.

Sironi, Maria, and Frank F. Furstenberg. "Trends in Economic Independence of Young Adults in the United States, 1973–2007." *Populations and Development Review* 38, no. 4 (December 2012): 609–30.

Sloan, Kay. "A Cinema in Search of Itself: Ideology of the Social Problem Film During the Silent Era." *Cineaste* 14, no. 2 (1985): 34–37.

Smith, Stacy L., Marc Choueiti, Kevin Yao, Hannah Clark, and Katherine Pieper. "Inclusion in the Director's Chair: Analysis of Director Gender & Race/Ethnicity Across 1,300 Top Films from 2007 to 2019." Annenberg Inclusion Initiative, January 2020. http://assets.uscannenberg.org/docs/aii-inclusion-directors-chair-20200102.pdf.

Smyth, J. E. *Nobody's Girl Friday: The Women Who Ran Hollywood*. Oxford University Press, 2018.

Snedacker, Kit. "Movies." *Los Angeles Evening and Sunday Herald Examiner*, California Living supplement, September 20, 1970: 32.

Sobchack, Vivian. "'Presentifying' Film and Media Feminism." *Camera Obscura* 61, no. 21 (2006): 65–68.

Sobchack, Vivian. "What is Film History?, or, the Riddle of the Sphinxes." In *Reinventing Film Studies*, edited by Christine Gledhill and Linda Williams, 300–315. London: Hodder Arnold, 2000.

Solbrig, Heide. "Orphans No More: Definitions, Disciplines, and Institutions." *Journal of Popular Film and Television* 37, no. 3 (Fall 2009): 98–105.

Somerville, Siobhan B. "Queer." In *Keywords for American Cultural Studies, 2nd Edition*, edited by Bruce Burgett and Glenn Hendler. New York: New York University Press, 2014. http://proxy2.library.illinois.edu/login?url=https://search.credoreference.com/content/entry/nyupacs/queer/0?institutionId=386.

Spencer, Robyn C. *The Revolution Has Come*. Durham and London: Duke University Press, 2016.

"Stefanie Rothman Directs 4th Film for Dimension." *Box Office*, July 24, 1972.

Stone, Alison. "Essentialism and Anti-Essentialism in Feminist Philosophy." *Journal of Moral Philosophy* 1, no. 2 (2004): 135–53. https://doi.org/10.1177/174046810400100202.

The Student Nurses. "Original Theatrical Trailer." Accessed May 17, 2015. https://www.youtube.com/watch?v=ubG521MU3yA.

Sullivan, John L. "Leo C. Rosten's Hollywood: Power, Status, and the Primacy of Economic and Social Networks in Cultural Production." In *Production Studies: Cultural Studies of Media Industries*, edited by Vicki Mayer, Miranda J. Banks, and Jon Thornton Caldwell, 39–53. Routledge: New York and London: 2009.

Tartaglione, Nancy, and Nellie Andreeva. "Amazon Orders 5 Original Series Including 'Man in the High Castle,' 'Mad Dogs.'" *Deadline*, February 18, 2015. https://deadline.com/2015/02/amazon-orders-original-series-man-in-the-high-castle-mad-dogs-video-1201375797/.

Taylor, Diana. *The Archive and the Repertoire: Performing Cultural Memory in the Americas*. Durham, NC: Duke University Press, 2003.

Temple of Schlock Blog. "Stephanie Rothman Sets the Record Straight." Accessed November 29, 2012. http://templeofschlock.blogspot.com.au/2010/07/stephanie-rothman-sets-record-straight.html.

"Terminal Island Premiere Charter by Dimension." *Hollywood Reporter* 102, no. 26 (April 1973): 19.

Tusher, Will. "Dimension Pictures open up opportunities for women." *Hollywood Reporter*, June 1, 1972: 3.

"21st Century Gets Dimension Library." *Film Journal*, July 20, 1981.

Usai, Paolo Cherchi. *The Death of Cinema: History, Cultural Memory and the Digital Dark Age*. London: BFI Publishing, 2001.

Waddell, Calum. *Jack Hill: The Exploitation and Blaxploitation Master, Film by Film*. Jefferson, NC: McFarland & Company, 2009.

Wallock, Roy M. "How Bobbi Gibb Changed Women's Running, and Finally Got Credit for It." ESPN.com, January 6, 2016. https://www.espn.com/sports/endurance/story/_/id/15090507/endurance-sports-bobbi-gibb-first-woman-run-boston-marathon.

Walters, Suzanna Danuta. "Caged Heat: The (R)evolution of Women-in-Prison Films." In *Reel Knockouts: Violent Women in the Movies*, edited by Martha McCaughey and Neal King, 106–23. Austin, TX: University of Texas Press, 2001.

Warner, Helen. "Below-the-(Hem)line." *Feminist Media Histories* 4, no. 1 (Winter 2018): 37–57. https://doi.org/10.1525/fmh.2018.4.1.37.

We Look and See production book. The Hugh M. Heffner Moving Image Archive, University of Southern California: 1963.

Weeks, Kathi. *The Problem with Work: Feminism, Marxism, Antiwork Politics, and Postwork Imaginaries*. Durham and London: Duke University Press, 2011.

Weeks, Kathi. "The Vanishing *Dialectic*: Shulamith Firestone and the Future of the Feminist 1970s." *South Atlantic Quarterly* 114, no. 4 (October 2015): 735–54.

Weiner, Robert G. "The Prince of Exploitation: Dwain Esper." In *From the Arthouse to the Grindhouse: Highbrow and Lowbrow Transgression in Cinema's First Century*, edited by John Cline and Robert G. Weiner, 41–54. Maryland: Scarecrow Press, 2010.

Weinstock, Jeffery. *The Vampire Film*. London and New York: Wallflower, 2012.

Weldon, Michael. *The Psychotronic Encyclopedia of Film*. New York: Ballantine Books, 1983.

West, Isaac, Michaela Frischherz, Allison Panther, and Richard Brophy. "Queer Worldmaking in the 'It Gets Better' Campaign." *QED: A Journal in GLBTQ Worldmaking* (Fall 2013): 49–85.

Williams, Linda Ruth. "Exploitation Cinema." In *The Cinema Book, 3rd Edition*, edited by Pam Cook, 298–301. London: British Film Institute: 2007.

Williams, Tony. "Feminism, Fantasy, and Violence: An Interview with Stephanie Rothman." *Journal of Popular Film and Television* 9, no. 2 (Summer 1981): 84–90.

Wimsatt, W. K., Jr., and M. C. Beardsley. "The Intentional Fallacy." *Sewanee Review* 54, no. 3 (July–September 1946): 468–88.

Witt, Charlotte. "Anti-Essentialism in Feminist Theory." *Philosophical Topics* 23, no. 2 (1995): 321–44.

Wollen, Peter. "Godard and Counter Cinema: Vent d'Est." *Afterimage*, no. 4 (Autumn 1972): 6–17.

Women and Hollywood. "An Open Letter to Colin Trevorrow." *Women and Hollywood*, August 25, 2015. https://womenandhollywood.com/an-open-letter-to-colin-trevorrow-c58236e82797/.

Women Film Pioneer Project. "Homepage." Accessed January 25, 2020. https://wfpp.columbia.edu/.
"Woolner Set Up Dimension Pictures." *Variety Daily*, October 28, 1971.
"Woolner, Louisiana Exhibs, Spread as International Producers." *Variety Weekly*, June 29, 1966.
Zalcock, Bev. *Renegade Sisters: Girl Gangs on Film, 2nd Edition*. Creation Books: 2001.
Zarnowitz, Victor, and Geoffrey H. Moore. "The Recession and Recovery of 1973–1976." *Explorations in Economic Research* 4, no. 4. National Bureau of Economic Research (October 1977): 1–87.
Zielinksi, Siegfried. *Deep Time of the Media: Toward an Archaeology of Hearing and Seeing by Technical Means*. Translated by Gloria Custance. Cambridge, MA: MIT Press, 2006.

INDEX

abortion, 113–15, 118–20, 124
Absent-Minded Professor, The (1961), 100
Academy Awards, 4, 71
Academy of Motion Picture Arts and Sciences, 35–36, 39, 197, 218–19
Ahmed, Sara, 33, 39, 155
Akerman, Chantal, 27
Allen, Woody, 189
Alliance Against Sexual Coercion, 160
Altman, Rick, 7–8
Amadeo, Michael, 116
Amarcord (1973), 72
Amazon Studios, 167, 218
American Academy of Arts and Sciences, 40
American Film Institute, 3–4
American International Pictures, 41, 48–49, 52, 71, 93–94, 98–102, 187, 203
Andersen, Pablo Dominguez, 99
Andrew, Dudley, 42–43
Anger, Kenneth, 146
Animals, The (band), 100, 102–3, 106, 194
Antonioni, Michelangelo, 213
archives: of feelings, 33–34; practices of, 4–9, 12–13, 16, 18, 27–41, 169–73
Arkoff, Samuel, 48–49, 57, 71, 93, 105, 194
Arnheim, Rudolph, 24
Art Students League, 214
Arzner, Dorothy, 23, 27
Asher, William, 51
"Attack" (The Toys song), 106–7
Attack of the Crab Monsters (1957), 195
auteur theory, 10–12, 19, 23–25

Babysitter, The (1969), 110
Balio, Tino, 57
Banks, Miranda J., 7
Bardot, Brigitte, 61
Barnett, Jim, 126
Barthes, Roland, 24
Bataille, Georges, 132–33
Bazin, André, 23
Beach Ball (1965), 98
Beach Blanket Bingo (1965), 51, 99–100
Beach Party (1963), 98, 101
Beat Generation, 101
Beauchamp, Cari, 35
Bechdel test, 190–91
Bergman, Ingmar, 61, 65, 71, 213, 218
Berlant, Lauren, 152–53, 156
Bernardi, Jack, 102
Beyond Atlantis (1973), 76, 202
Bidgood, Jim, 146
Big Bird Cage, The (1972), 94, 135, 137–38
Big Dollhouse, The (1971), 94, 134–38, 186–88
Bigelow, Kathryn, 85, 190, 214
Bikini Beach (1964), 99, 101
Billboard charts, 100
Bird, Brad, 171
birth control, 52, 55
Bitter Rice (1949), 202–3
Black Mama, White Mama (1973), 53
Black Panther Party, 108–9
Blackboard Jungle (1955), 116
Blade Runner (1982), 218
blaxploitation films. *See* exploitation films

INDEX   261

Blodgett, Michael, 139
Blood Bath/Track of the Vampire (1966), 17, 35, 39, 41, 70, 93–98, 107, 110, 136–37, 186–88, 194–95, 197, 219–20
Bogdanovich, Peter, 56
Bonnie and Clyde (1967), 59
Borden, Lizzie, 196
Born Losers, The (1967), 51
Boston Marathon, 105
Bouclin, Suzanne, 135
Bourdieu, Pierre, 27
Boxcar Bertha (1972), 189
Brickman, Barbara, 48
British Film Institute, 36
Brooklyn Academy of Music, 197
Brown, Elaine, 109
Brown, Helen Gurley, 55
Bucket of Blood, A (1959), 187
Buckland, Fiona, 148–49, 154–56
Buñuel, Luis, 181
Burden, Eric, 102–3, 194
Burton, Antoinette, 32
Butler, Alison, 21

Caged (1950), 136
Caged Heat (1974), 135
Cahiers du Cinéma, 23
Caldwell, John T., 7
Callahan, Vicki, 9, 31
Camen, Paul, 113
Cameron, Ian, 23
Campbell, William, 95
Candy Stripe Nurses (1974), 125
Cannes Film Festival, 71
Car Hops, The. See *Starhops*
Carlson, Karen, 113
Carmilla (Le Fanu novella), 142–43
Carroll, Lewis, 143
Casey, Lawrence P., 113
Castaways, The (band), 100–101
Catalina Caper (1967), 100
censorship regulations, 46, 54, 59–61
Chant d'amour, Un (1950), 146
cinema: of attractions, 46; classical Hollywood, 44–45, 57–59, 122–23

Clarke, Shirley, 23, 84, 127, 205
Clay, Ford, 131
Cleopatra Jones (1973), 60
Coalition of Labor Union Women, 160
Cobble, Dorothy Sue, 160
Cocteau, Jean, 140, 213, 218
Coffy (1974), 60, 94
Cohen, Jeffrey Jerome, 144
Cohen-Cruz, Jan, 120
Collings, Jane, 174
Columbia Pictures, 51–52, 99
Condemned Women (1938), 135
Connolly, Derek, 170
Cook, David, 60
Cook, Pam, 15, 131, 144
Cool Hand Luke (1967), 59
Coppola, Francis Ford, 56, 94–95
Corman, Gene, 71
Corman, Roger, 39, 49, 52, 56–57, 63, 69–74, 81, 93–97, 109–12, 116–17, 134–39, 177, 184–90, 195, 203–4, 212, 218; school, 49, 56, 185–86
Costume Designer, 32
Costume Designers Guild, 32
Crawford, Joan, 56
Creative Artists Agency, 70
Cries and Whispers (1972), 61, 71
crisis historiography, 7–8
Criterion Collection, 26–27, 168
Cvetkovich, Ann, 33–34, 36, 39

Dalí, Salvador, 140, 142, 195
Davis, Phyllis, 128
Day, Doris, 104
De Laurentiis, Dino, 167, 193
Deadline website, 170
DeBoer, Sherry E., 139
Del Conte, Ken, 159
Deleuze, Gilles, 130
Dementia 13 (1963), 94
Deren, Maya, 27
Derrida, Jacques, 30
Desperately Seeking Susan (1985), 168
Diary of a High School Bride, The (1959), 50
Dick, Philip K., 17, 92, 167, 192

digital filmmaking, 191
Dimension Pictures, 73–76, 125, 157, 166–67, 177, 185, 193, 198–204
Directors Guild of America, 4, 32, 69, 80–81, 93, 204
disidentification, 29
Disney, 170
Dixon, Winton Wheeler, 101, 103, 106
Doane, Mary Ann, 21
documentaries, 45, 78, 123–24, 205
Doel, Frances, 111, 134, 187–88
Doherty, Thomas, 101
Dolce Vita, La (1960), 61
Doty, Alexander, 145–46, 151
double features, 50, 57
Dr. Goldfoot and the Bikini Machine (1965), 99–100
Duet (1963), 67–69, 198, 206–10, 217–18
Dunn, Stephanie, 53
DuVernay, Ava, 3
Dyer, Richard, 154

Easy Rider (1969), 51–52, 56
Eccles, Aimee, 147
Eichhorn, Kate, 10, 32
Elman, Gene, 159
Elsaesser, Thomas, 7–8, 44
Epstein, Jean, 24
Equal Credit Opportunity Act, 160
Ernst, Wolfgang, 43
Evans, Robert, 57
Everett, Anna, 21
exploitation films: beach party, 51, 93, 98–103, 107, 125, 193; blaxploitation, 52–55, 59–61; classic, 42, 45–46, 135; classifications and definitions, 13–16; nichesploitation, 52; nurse, 110–11, 125; preservation of, 37–41; second wave, 4–5, 8, 13–17, 29, 37, 39, 42, 44–45, 47–62, 63, 82, 91–94, 135–36, 147, 158; sexploitation, 28, 52–55; women's prison, 125–26, 134–38

Fangoria, 219
Fantastic Planet (1973), 71

Farrell, Brioni, 113
Fast and the Furious, The (1954), 48–49, 93
Fearless (1993), 189
Fellini, Federico, 61, 71, 213
Feminine Mystique, The (Friedan), 85, 175
feminism: and film scholarship, 6, 11–13, 18–26, 29; interventionist methodology of, 9–10, 16, 29; movements, 52, 85–88, 105, 108–9, 113, 196–97
Feydeau, George, 146
Fiddler on the Roof (musical), 205
Film Foundation, 219
FilmGroup, 93–94, 96
films: adult, 37; avant-garde, 59, 140–42; B-, 50, 57; and feminist scholarship, 6, 11–13, 18–26, 29; foreign distribution, 5, 60–61; independent, 58, 146; noir, 14–15; orphan, 37–38; preservation of, 36–38; social messages in, 136; social problem in, 115–16; and women, 18, 20–23, 116. *See also* exploitation films
Fincher, David, 214
Firestone, Shulamith, 19
Fisher, Lucy, 23
Flight of the Navigator (1986), 170
Fonda, Jane, 193
Fossanti, Giovanna, 37
Foucault, Michel, 113
Fowles, Anthony, 66–69, 206–9, 217
Fox, Terry Curtis, 63
Foxy Brown (1974), 60, 94
Franju, Georges, 140
Friedan, Betty, 85, 175
Fuller, Samuel, 197–98
Future Shock (Toffler), 146

Gaines, Jane, 21, 25, 27, 31, 157
Gas-s-s-s (1970), 70–71
General Film Group, 74
Genet, Jean, 146
Gentrys, The (band), 100
Ghost in the Invisible Bikini, The (1966), 100
Giant (1956), 56
Gibb, Roberta, 105
Giftos, Elaine, 113

Girls in Prison (1956), 136
Gledhill, Christine, 8–9, 24
Goffman, Erving, 65
Gorfinkel, Elena, 15, 53–55
Graduate, The (1967), 59
Gravity (2013), 189
Grier, Pam, 60, 94
Griffith, D. W., 213
Gross, Linda, 181
Group Marriage (1972), 17, 74, 78, 92, 107, 138, 145–56, 157, 197, 200, 210
Guthrie, Lynne, 158

Haig, Sid, 96, 100–101
Halloran, Julie, 69
Haneke, Michael, 189, 214
Hansen, Miriam, 7
Harrington, Curtis, 94
Harris, Barbara, 106–7
Hartman, Ena, 126
Haskell, Molly, 20
Haugeberg, Karissa, 119
Haunted House Club, 102, 195
Hebdige, Dick, 27
Hellman, Lillian, 85
Henri, Robert, 214
High Wind in Jamaica, A (1965), 216
Hill, Erin, 31, 95
Hill, Jack, 35, 94–98, 134–37, 186–88, 195
hippies, 51–52, 114, 118
Hollingshead, Richard, 50
Hollywood Reporter, 73–74, 127
hooks, bell, 21
Hopper, Dennis, 56
Hotel Paradiso (Feydeau), 146
How to Stuff a Wild Bikini (1965), 51, 99
Hudson, Rock, 104
Hughes, Mary Beth, 163
Hurt Locker, The (2008), 190

I Was a Teenage Werewolf (1957), 50
Imitation of Life (1959), 116
inflation, 160–61
International Women's Film Festival, 127, 204–5

It's a Bikini World (1967), 17, 39–41, 51, 70, 78, 92–93, 98–107, 108, 125, 162, 193–95, 220

Jaws (1975), 61–62
Jenkins, Henry, 181
Jenkins, Patty, 218
Jennings, Claudia, 147–48
Johnson, Charles, 202
Johnson, Randall, 27–28
Johnston, Claire, 22–23
Juhasz, Alexandra, 6, 195
Jules, Maurice, 138
Juno (2007), 190
Juno, Andrea, 15
Jurassic World (2015), 170–71

Kael, Pauline, 24
Kantor, Bernard, 69, 210
Karloff, Boris, 56
Kaye, Suzie, 99
Kennedy, Jayne, 148
Kennedy, Kathleen, 170–71
Kennedy, Sarah, 158
Kenney, Sean, 129
Kershner, Irvin, 167, 192
King, Billie Jean, 105
Kirk, Tommy, 99–100, 193–94
Knight, Arthur, 66
Knight, Julia, 8–9
Kodras, Janet E., 161
Koester, John, 207
Kristen, Marta, 128
Kubrick, Stanley, 65, 167, 192
Kuhn, Annette, 20–21

Lacambre, Daniel, 79–80, 212–13
Ladies' Home Journal (magazine), 108
Laloux, René, 71
Larson, Darnell, 114
Lau, Kimberly, 144
Le Fanu, Sheridan, 143
Lean, David, 215
Legend of Nigger Charley, The (1972), 60
Leigh, Barbara, 113, 128

Library of Congress, 38
Liechtenstein, Roy, 106
lifeworlds, 148–56
Loren, Sophia, 61
Lorna (1964), 54
Los Angeles Evening and Sunday Herald Examiner, 181
Los Angeles Police Department, 115, 120–21
Los Angeles Times, 181
Lost Boundaries (1949), 116
Love, Heather, 145
Lucas, Tim, 94, 97–98
Lucasfilm, 170
Lukasz, Agata, 144
Lupino, Ida, 23

Mackendrick, Alexander, 216
male gaze, 54, 117–18, 129, 147
Malick, Terrence, 189
Man in the High Castle, The (Dick), 17, 92, 167, 192–93
Man in the High Castle, The (television series), 167, 218
Mankiewicz, Ben, 220
Marcus, Sharon, 128
Margaret Herrick Library, 35
Marion, Frances, 35
Marsh, Reginald, 214
Marshall, Don, 131
Marshall, Frank, 170–71
martial arts movies, 53
Martin, Angela, 25
Mask, Mia, 129
May, Elaine, 72
Mayer, Vicki, 5, 32, 172
Mayne, Judith, 11–12, 25
McDonagh, Maitland, 56
McMurtry, John, 152
Mechte Nevstruchi (1961), 94
media archaeology, 8, 43–44
Media Woman, 108
Mellencamp, Patricia, 21
melodrama, 21, 135
Meyer, Russ, 54
MGM, 41, 60, 72

Midler, Bette, 205
Miller-Young, Mireille, 32
Miss America, 108
Monaco, Paul, 48, 52
Montiero, June, 106–7
Monster (2003), 190, 218
Monty Python, 106
Morris, Gary, 101
Mosley, Roger E., 129
Motorcycle Gang (1957), 50
motorcycle gang movies, 51
Movie (journal), 23
Mulvey, Laura, 20
Muñoz, José Esteban, 29
Muscle Beach Party (1964), 101
Museum of Modern Art, 36, 39, 218–19

Nair, Mira, 27
National Organization of Women, 108
Neroni, Hilary, 128
new cinema history, 7–8
new criticism, 24
New Hollywood, 56, 59, 61
new queer cinema, 146
New World Pictures, 49, 56, 71–75, 109–12, 125, 137–38, 177, 186, 198–99, 203–4
New York Radical Feminists, 108
Newton, Huey, 108
Nichols, Bill, 18
Nicholson, Jim, 48–49, 57, 71, 93
Niebo Zowiet (1959), 94
Night Call Nurses (1972), 125
1973–75 recession, 160–61
Noble, Safiya Umoja, 6

Omens, Woody, 210
OPEC, 160
Operation: Titan/Operacija Ticijan. See *Blood Bath/Track of the Vampire*
Orphan Film Symposium, 38

Padavic, Irene, 161
Palcy, Euzhan, 27
Paramount Decision, 46, 57
Paramount Pictures, 57, 60, 99

Parritt, Barbara, 106–7
Pat and Lolly Vegas (band), 100
Paths of Glory (1957), 65
Peary, Dannis, 82, 111, 132
Penley, Constance, 32
Perkins, V. F., 23
Perlin, Jake, 197
Peter Pan Syndrome, 98–99, 102
Pickett, Bobby, 101
Pink Narcissus (1971), 146
Pixar, 170
Planeta Bur (1962), 94
Pollack, Sydney, 189
Pomerantz, Jeffrey, 147
Pop Art, 106, 193
Prelinger, Rick, 38
Price, Vincent, 56
Private Duty Nurses (1971), 125
Production Code Administration, 59–61
promiscuous methodology, 7
psychedelic movies, 51
psychoanalytic theory, 20
Pulitzer, Sam, 73

Queen of Blood (1966), 94, 96
queer world-making, 152–56
queerness, 136, 142–56

Radicalesbians, "The Woman-Identified Woman," 19
Rainer, Yvonne, 23
Rakow, Lana, 31
rape, 54, 82, 116–17, 129–33, 141–42
Ray, Fred Olen, 76
Raynal, Jackie, 23
Realart, 93
Rebel Without a Cause (1955), 56
recovery and reappraisal, 31–32
Redstockings, 108
Reed v. Reed, 160
Reitman, Jason, 214
Remorse, or Sphinx Embedded in the Sand (Dalí), 142
Renoir, Jean, 213, 218
Representation Project, 168

Rich, B. Ruby, 146
Riggs, Bobby, 105
Riot on Sunset Strip (1967), 51
roadshowing, 51
Roe v. Wade, 52, 118–19
Rome, Open City (1945), 60
Rony, Fatima Tobing, 21
Rose, Laurie, 158
Rosenbaum, Henry, 126, 219
Rossellini, Roberto, 60
Rothman, Stephanie: archive, 29, 34–41; biography, 63–78; career beginnings, 93–107; career overview, 91–93; as case study, 4–7, 10–13, 15–17, 167–73; depiction of sexuality, 134–56; depiction of socioeconomic class, 67–68, 102–3, 157–67, 210–11; and exploitation films, 56, 71–72, 76–77, 157–58, 183–88; and feminism, 25, 83–88, 103–5, 108–9, 174–81, 211, 215; filmmaking style and practice, 78–88, 206–13; as ideological filmmaker, 108–33; interviews and emails, 174–220; Rothman Rules, 16, 81–88
Rowberry, Dave, 103
Russo, Vito, 151
Rust, Richard, 114
Rutsky, R. L., 101

Sade, Marquis de, 130–31
sadism, 130–31
Safety Not Guaranteed (2012), 170
Santoni, Reni, 115
Sarris, Andrew, 23–24, 60–61
saturation booking, 51, 62
Schaefer, Eric, 13, 15, 37, 45–47, 58–59
Schatz, Thomas, 61–62
Schneemann, Carolee, 23
Scorpio Rising (1964), 146
Scorsese, Martin, 56, 189, 219
Scott, Ridley, 167, 218
second wave exploitation films. *See* exploitation films
second wave feminism, 19
Seidelman, Susan, 168

Serna, Pepe, 115
Selznick, David O., 57
Seventh Seal, The (1957), 65
sex work, 54, 115, 158, 162–64
sexploitation films. *See* exploitation films
sexual revolution, 92
Shaft (1971), 13, 59–60
Shaggy Dog, The (1959), 100
Shane, Gene, 139
Shangri-Las, 106
Shaw Brothers, 53
Shimizu, Celine Parreñas, 21, 32
Shit People Say to Women Directors & Other Women webpage, 168
Siegel, Carol, 138
Sight and Sound, 4
Silverman, Kaja, 11, 18
Slashfilm blog, 170–71
Sloan, Kay, 115
Smuckler, Maya Montañez, 32
Smyth, J. E., 85
Snedacker, Kit, 181
Sobchak, Vivian, 9, 43
Social Network, The (2010), 189, 214
Society of Motion Picture and Television Engineers, 77
Solbrig, Heidi, 38
Someone to Watch Over Me (1987), 207
Sorority Girl (1957), 50
spectacle, 45–46, 49–50, 58
Spelman, Elizabeth, 20
Spencer, Don, 112, 134–35, 202
Spider Baby (1967), 94
Spielberg, Steven, 61–62, 170–71
Spook Who Sat by the Door, The (1973), 53
Star Wars: Episode VII—The Force Awakens (2015), 170–71
Starhops (1978), 75, 201
states' rights system, 51
Steppenwolf (Hesse), 118
Stonewall riots, 52
Striglos, Bill, 152
Student Nurses, The (1970), 17, 39–41, 52, 70–71, 92, 108–25, 134–35, 138, 141–42, 145, 147, 151, 157–58, 162, 183–84, 196–97, 200, 203, 210–11, 218
Sturges, Solomon, 147, 159
suburbs, 47–48, 52
Sundance Film Festival, 170
Superfly (1972), 60
Supremes, The, 106
Swamp Women (1956), 71
Swartz, Charles, 66, 70–78, 99, 112, 125–26, 134–36, 167, 179–80, 182, 185–86, 188, 190, 198–204, 206, 209–16, 219
Sweet Smell of Success (1957), 216
Sweet Sugar (1972), 76, 202
Sweet Sweetback's Badasssss Song (1971), 53
Swiss Family Robinson (1960), 100
Switchblade Sisters (1975), 94
Systems Development Corporation, 65

Taormino, Tristan, 32
Taylor, Diana, 30
Taylor, Zack, 147
Teatro Popular, 115, 120–21, 124–25
teenagers, 47–48, 50–51, 93, 99, 100–103
teenpics, 48, 50, 52
television, 46, 127, 148, 152, 190
Temple of Schlock blog, 137
Terminal Island (1973), 17, 52, 74, 82, 92, 108–9, 125–33, 136, 138, 145, 154, 157, 162, 177, 181, 192, 200, 205, 210, 219
Thalberg, Irving, 57
theaters: drive-ins, 50, 54, 74; grindhouse, 54
Theron, Charlize, 190
Thomas, Mark, 159
Times Square, 54–55
Timmerman, Eric, 66–69, 206–9, 217
Title IX of the Civil Rights Act, 160
Toffler, Alvin, 146
Tomorrowland (2015), 71
Toys, The, 100, 106–7
Track of the Vampire. See Blood Bath/Track of the Vampire
Traffic in Souls (1913), 115
Trans American, 99
Trevorrow, Colin, 170–72

Trip, The (1967), 51
Truffaut, François, 23, 197–98, 213
Tuber, Mort, 219
Turner Classic Movies, 40, 218, 220
21st Century Distribution Corporation, 76

United States Supreme Court, 127, 160
Universal Pictures, 93, 171
University of California: Berkeley, 65, 181; Los Angeles, 65, 69, 77, 112, 174, 194, 197, 219; Southern California, 65–69, 77, 95, 179–80, 197–98, 206–9, 217–18; UCLA Film and Television Archive, 40–41, 197
University of Chicago, 205
Up in the Air (2009), 189, 214
Usai, Paolo Cherchi, 43

Vale, V., 15
vampires, 95–98, 107, 138–46, 186–87, 195
Varda, Agnès, 27
Variety, 71
Velvet Vampire, The (1971), 17, 70, 72, 92, 107, 138–46, 151, 157, 195, 197, 203, 210, 218–19
Ventura, Clyde, 132
Verge, The website, 170
vertical integration, 45
Vetri, Victoria, 147
Video Watchdog, 94
Vietnam War, 52, 114, 121, 123
Von Richthofen and Brown (1971), 134
Voyage to the Prehistoric Planet (1966), 94

Waddell, Calum, 97–98, 136–37
Walley, Deborah, 99–100, 193–94
Walters, Suzanna Danuta, 136
Warhol, Andy, 106
Warner, Helen, 32
Warner, Michael, 152–53, 156
Warner Bros., 60
Watergate scandal, 52
"We Gotta Get Out of This Place," 102–3, 194–95
We Look and See (1963), 66–67, 198, 206–10

Weber, Lois, 27
Weeks, Kathi, 20, 161–62, 165
Weinrib, Lennie, 98
Weinstock, Jeffrey, 144
Wembley Industries, 73–74, 199–201
Where Are My Children? (1916), 115
wide release, 62
Wild Angels, The (1966), 51
Williams, Linda, 13, 21–22
Wishman, Doris, 28
Witt, Charlotte, 20
Wollen, Peter, 22
Woman Hunt, The (1972), 137–38
women: and films, 18, 20–23, 116; and labor, 4–9, 11–13, 15–16, 18, 26, 28–29, 31–32, 42, 79–80, 84–85, 92, 111, 129–33, 150–51, 157–73; paradigm of exceptional, 5, 16, 18–19, 26–29, 169–73; and prison exploitation films, 125–26, 134–38
Women and Hollywood, 172
Women Film Pioneers Project, 31–32
Women in Cages (1971), 135
Women in Motion, 28
Women's Media Center, 168
Women's Prison (1955), 136
Wonder Woman (2017), 218
Wood, Robin, 23
Woolner, Larry, 71, 73–75, 81, 110, 125–26, 138–39, 146–47, 177, 198–204, 212
Woolner Brothers, 71, 198–99
Working Girls (1986), 196
Working Girls, The (1974), 17, 52, 74, 79–80, 92, 157–66, 196–97, 200, 210–11, 213
Working Women United, 160
World War I, 116
World War II, 65, 160
Writers Guild of America, 75, 81, 190, 201, 204

Yarnell, Celeste, 139
Young Nurses, The (1973), 125

Zielinski, Siegfried, 30–31

ABOUT THE AUTHOR

Dr. **Alicia Kozma** combines a practical focus on media labor with critical inquiry to understand how media industries work, who works in them, and how the labor of media workers is constructed. Dr. Kozma is intimately concerned with the role of women laborers, their hiring and employment conditions, and the industrial structures that have led to historically inequality, specifically in film and television workspaces. She has a secondary interest in gender bodies, and horror.

She is the co-editor of *ReFocus: The Films of Doris Wishman* (Edinburgh University Press, 2021), the first book-length examination of the pioneering director, as well as a co-editor of *Mobilized Identities: Mediated Subjectivity and Cultural Crisis in the Neoliberal Era* (Common Ground, 2014). Her work has appeared in the journals *Media Industries*, *Film Comment*, *The Projector*, *Camera Obscura*, *Television and New Media*, the *Journal of Japanese and Korean Cinema*, *Bright Lights Film Journal*, and *In Media Res*. She has also published in a wide variety of anthologies and edited collections.

Dr. Kozma is Director of Indiana University Cinema. She holds a PhD in communication and media studies from the Institute of Communication Research at the University of Illinois, Urbana-Champaign. You can learn more about her and her work at www.aliciakozma.com.